Ferruccio Busoni:
Selected Letters

By the same author
Busoni the Composer

Ferruccio
BUSONI

Selected
Letters

Translated, edited and
with an introduction by

Antony
Beaumont

New York   Columbia University Press   1987

Library of Congress Cataloging-in-Publication Data

Busoni, Ferruccio, 1866–1924.
Selected letters.
Includes index.
1. Busoni, Ferruccio, 1866–1924—Correspondence.
2. Composers—Correspondence. I. Beaumont, Antony.
ML410.B98 A4 1986   780'.92'4   86-12951
ISBN 0-231-06460-8

for Alfred Brendel

Contents

Illustrations

All photographs by kind permission of the Deutsche Staatsbibliothek, Berlin GDR, Musikabteilung

Facsimiles 2 and 3: Newberry Library, Chicago; facsimile 4: Rowe Music Library, Cambridge.

Introduction

Ferruccio Busoni was one of the finest and most copious letter writers of his time. As much a virtuoso of the pen as of the pianoforte, he commanded a literary style capable of the same dazzling variety of attack and nuance, of the subtlety and flexibility of form for which he is remembered as pianist and composer.

The range of subject matter in these letters is exceptionally wide. Many of them are miniature essays, consciously conceived as travelogue or self-portrait, feuilleton, reportage, political statement and – particularly in later years – protest and lament. One form of communication is, however, conspicuously absent: the love-letter. A volume entitled *Letters to his Wife*, the considerably abridged and expurgated edition of about half the surviving thousand letters from Busoni to Gerda Sjöstrand, appeared in 1935 (Rosamond Ley's English translation was published in 1938). This correspondence breathes affection and devotion in every page. Yet, just as Busoni had no taste for love scenes on the operatic stage, so do his private communications remain within the bounds of discretion and good taste. This did not prevent him, however, from cultivating a flourishing and sometimes intimate correspondence with several lady friends. In the following pages there are fine and interesting letters to some of these confidantes: Melanie Mayer, Jella Oppenheimer, Irma Bekh, Harriet Lanier, Alicja Simon and Edith Andreae.

Discretion is otherwise not written large in Busoni's letters. Their elegant outspokenness affords many an insight into contemporary figures and events, and is notable for regular diatribes on certain *bêtes noires* such as Wagner, Schumann, the Americans and the critics. The polarity of North and South in Busoni's personality also prompts him to revealing and not often flattering comments on Italy, the land of his birth, and Germany, his chosen country of residence. The situation of this cosmopolitan, whose home was 'everywhere and nowhere', then culminates in the catastrophe of the First World War.

From a Germany which had become unpalatable Busoni flees to the New World. His letters tell the whole sad story of his last American sojourn. Prolonged through the uncertainties of the political situation, this concert tour of the United States becomes a moral and artistic incarceration from which a return to the European inferno offers the only possible release. Thus we follow Busoni to Zurich, where he settles to await the peace and begins to compose his masterwork, *Doktor Faust*, then back to Berlin, where protracted illness on the one hand and the prevailing political upheaval on the other serve to tinge much of his later writing with bitterness.

In the earlier letters, the vitality of the child, the adolescent and the young virtuoso is scarcely dampened by mention of personal setbacks and bereavements. The death of Busoni's childhood friend Luigi Cimoso, repeated failure to obtain a performance of his first major orchestral work, the *Symphonic Suite*, the dissolution of the piano master-class in Vienna, the disappointing end to his directorship of the Liceo Musicale in Bologna – these storms are all weathered. Significantly, however, the profoundest crisis of all – the death of Busoni's mother in 1909 – is not mentioned at all. On the other hand, considerable space is devoted to two failed operatic projects, *Sigune*, which was never finished, and *Die Brautwahl*, a work whose epic proportions and odd jumble of musical styles prevented its success at the world première in 1912 and have confounded all subsequent attempts at reassessment. *Die Brautwahl* represents nevertheless one of the most important stages in Busoni's development. Its composition, publication, performance and reception are recorded in countless letters (from 1906 to 1913) which tell us more about this work than we can later glean about *Doktor Faust*.

Altogether, Busoni was a prolific correspondent. In August 1920 he wrote to the Marchese di Casanova that during five years in Zurich he had 'evidently written about 5,000 letters' (and 1918 had been a particularly lean year for letter writing, largely devoted as it had been to work on the score of *Doktor Faust*). This implies an average output of over one thousand letters a year or between two and three every day. There seems no reason to suppose that, in fifty years of letter writing, Busoni ever greatly diverged from this quota.

From an early age he was almost constantly separated from one parent or the other and, as soon as he was capable of putting pen to paper, he was encouraged to write 'home', if possible every week, with detailed reports of his achievements (on which his parents set the highest expectations). Thus there survives a large collection of letters to Anna and Ferdinando Busoni, several specimens of which are published here for the first time. They reveal a strikingly perceptive youngster and, later, a son suffering under the strain of exaggerated demands on his filial piety. The young Busoni led an isolated existence, constantly on the move, harassed by his father's financial ineptitude and extravagance, dedicated to music for the highest aesthetic reasons and yet also reliant on his art for the slender lucrative possibilities it then afforded him. His isolation, accentuated by his early maturity, soon led to correspondence with other partners, such as Luigi Cimoso, Antonio Zampieri or Melanie Mayer, as a means of closer communication, of free expression and hence liberation.

This selection presents 352 letters chronologically ordered between the years 1872 and 1924. Most – 293 – were written in German, forty-four in Italian, ten in French and five in English. Of these, 274 are published here for the first time in any language, while fifty-seven have appeared in diverse books, journals or newspapers. Excerpts from several unpublished letters appear in Edward J. Dent's *Ferruccio Busoni: a Biography* (Oxford, 1933). The complete correspondence with Arnold Schoenberg, published in German in 1977, forms a self-contained unit whose integration into the main body of the selection seemed inappropriate. It is therefore published as an Appendix.

My concern has been primarily to select those documents which present an autobiographical outline of Busoni's entire career. Having established this framework as a point of reference, I have then sought out letters on the most diverse of non-autobiographical topics, avoiding those principally concerned with concert schedules or other such ephemeral matters. The maintenance of chronological continuity has led to the inclusion of a few pages of diary jottings (Busoni never kept a regular diary). Passages from several letters in this selection are quoted in my study, *Busoni the Composer* (London, 1985), which however also includes substantial extracts from some important letters not published here (notably to Frida Kwast-Hodapp, Albert Biolley and Franz Ludwig Hörth).

The backbone of the present selection is provided by 122 of the 361 extant letters to Henri, Kathi and (in particular) Egon Petri, which reflect a friendship with the Petri family of thirty-nine years' duration. In 1885, when Henri Petri was *Konzertmeister* of the Leipzig Gewandhaus Orchestra, he and his wife Kathi took the young Busoni under their wing. Their son Egon was then four years old. Later we can follow the various stages in the master-pupil relationship between Busoni and Egon Petri in great detail. Despite the moments of hilarity and solemnity typical of such a close friendship, there is an element of tyranny which the young Petri does his best to escape by taking a teaching post in Manchester, and later by settling in the South Polish town of Zakopane. During the spring of 1915 the atmosphere cools noticeably, due, it would appear, to hurtful comments in a letter from Petri to Busoni in America. Contact subsequently becomes more sporadic and the role of confidant is allotted to others – Philipp Jarnach, Hans Huber, Volkmar Andreae and Isidor Philipp. Finally there is a reconciliation: Petri returns to Berlin, submits once again to the assistant's yoke and begins to prepare the vocal score of *Doktor Faust*. Correspondence becomes more frequent and cordial again.

Discontent with the world at large is a frequent topic of Busoni's letters, whether concerned with the American way of life, the Germans' insistence on 'musicality', the Italians' inability to move with the times or the Parisians' over-indulgence in doing just that. The First World War brought matters to a head. Despite his abhorrence of all warfare, Busoni nevertheless refused to be categorized as a pacifist, for that connotation would have implied identification with a specific group or movement whose 'anti-war orisons' he had been quick to hear and reject. Busoni, for all his penetrating comment on world affairs, remained an apolitical person and, as such, an isolationist.

In the last four years of his life, solitariness was further exacerbated by illness. Time after time Busoni alludes to Balzac's *La peau de chagrin*, the horrifying vision of a finite span of time palpably shrinking away. The completion of *Doktor Faust* became a race against the clock – which he lost. In those final years, Busoni seems to have moved on a spiritual plane already far removed from the world of the living. Something of this abstractedness can be detected in Man Ray's photographic portrait (Plate 17), taken in November 1923, and something of it can, of course, be detected in the later letters. But here, too, the dominating mood is often anger or outrage.

A clearer idea of Busoni's final spiritual phase can be found, perhaps, in a hitherto forgotten essay on John Field,★ dated Christmas 1923:

> Musical works of art could also be categorized as follows: as 'chaste' or as 'sensual'. Amongst those of the former variety there are some (not many) that intimate more than they reveal at first hearing . . . In the case of the latter variety . . . the content is exhausted when heard: nothing remains to be elucidated, there is no surrounding aureole: around [such music] there hovers no spiritual radiance [Sternenhof]; over it nothing elevated (astral): nothing undisclosed, nothing to awaken our yearning.

Such expectations of his art as Busoni here implies may bear the stamp of a 'spiritual mountain-climbing' which he himself would decry, but we are afforded a glimpse of an aspect of his personality which is otherwise only to be detected in a few passages of his last compositions (most strikingly, perhaps, in Faust's monologue, 'Traum der Jugend' in the Second Tableau of *Doktor Faust*). It is no surprise that an artist prepared to 'leave Earth to find such music' (*New Aesthetic*) so frequently had cause to express his discontent with and distaste for the real world.

It may strike the reader as a disappointment that there are so few letters to the truly famous in this selection. There is no particular lack of such material from Busoni, but none of those letters available for publication is of particular significance. Busoni voices his sometimes alarming criticisms of accepted values and respected persons only when writing to friends whose belief in him was unquestionable. Written contact with such men as Richard Strauss, Gerhard Hauptmann, Jean Sibelius or Max Reinhardt was rarely more than polite or formal, while Busoni's letter to Verdi, which was never sent (here printed as No. 32), is humility itself. The exception to this rule is with Arnold Schoenberg. Indeed the correspondence between these two musical 'demi-gods' is a document of the greatest historical importance.

For Busoni the *form* of a letter was as essential to its success as that of a composition or concert programme. In this sense, many of his letters are seemingly directed at a wider public and hence lend themselves uncommonly well to publication. Certain passages were indeed already published during the composer's lifetime and at his behest. Writing to Egon Petri of his appointment as Director of the Liceo Musicale in Bologna (letter No. 142), Busoni closes with the paradoxical statement: 'Consider this letter as a page of a diary . . . (You can show it to anybody you wish.)'

The editor of the *Letters to his Wife*, the late Dr Friedrich Schnapp, was

★'Franz Liszts Vorrede zur ersten Kollektivausgabe von Fields Nocturnes' in *Die Musik* Vol. 16, 1923–4, pp. 309–16.

obliged to expurgate the text and suppress names. I have avoided any such editorial constraints but have sometimes abbreviated in the interests of space. Where a passage has been omitted it is indicated by [. . .]; but this has been done only in the case of ephemera ('Thank you for your letter', 'Don't forget next Thursday' etc.) or where material already included in an adjacent letter would have been repeated. A few letters have survived only in expurgated copies, where there was no choice but to publish the remaining torso – provided, of course, that this was still of interest. Opening and closing formulae have generally been omitted, as modern English is inadequately equipped for the florid greetings customary in Italian and German epistolary style. Exceptions occur wherever a greeting is an inextricable part of the letter's content or when it is intended as witticism or pointed comment.

While Busoni's Italian develops from childish beginnings to a complex and antiquated mature style, his treatment of the German language is often whimsical or eccentric. This presents the translator with many a tough nut to crack. I have attempted to equate colloquialism with colloquialism, pun with pun wherever possible, resorting to footnotes only where a more laborious explanation seemed necessary.

I am extremely grateful to Patrick Carnegy and the directors of Faber and Faber for their staunch support of my work on this project. With this book we hope to have erected a modest monument to an artist who is only now beginning to receive the detailed attention that he most certainly deserves.

My warmest thanks go to the following owners or administrators of source material (a detailed list is to be found on p. 430): the Provost and Fellows of King's College, Cambridge; Dietrich Fischer-Dieskau; Library of Congress, Washington DC; Stiftung Rychenberg, Winterthur; Universal Edition AG, Vienna; Bibliothèque Nationale, Paris; Newberry Library, Chicago; Museo del Teatro Verdi, Trieste; Öffentliche Bibliothek der Universität, Basle.

I am also indebted to Margaret Cranmer (Rowe Music Library, Cambridge), Sig. Dott. Laura Loseri Ruaro (Civici Musei di Storia ed Arte, Trieste), Frau Dr Jutta Theurich (Deutsche Staatsbibliothek, Berlin GDR, Musikabteilung), Dr Rudolf Elvers (Staatsbibliothek Preussischer Kulturbesitz, West Berlin, Musikabteilung), Prof. Dr Werner Zimmermann (Stadtarchiv, Zurich), Dr Otto Biba (Gesellschaft der Musikfreunde, Vienna), Dr Felix Ganz (Roosevelt University, Chicago), Walter Labhart (Dokumentations-bibliothek Walter Labhart, Endingen, Switzerland), Prof. Pierluigi Petrobelli (Istituto di Studi Verdiani, Parma), Dr Sergio Sablich (Centro Studi Musicali Ferruccio Busoni, Empoli), Mrs Laura Dallapiccola, Dr Bernd Kortländer (Heinrich-Heine-Institut, Dusseldorf), Jacques and Nelly Lasserre (Zurich), Prof. Eero Tarasti and Mr Tomi Mäkelä (University of Helsinki), Mr Maurice Hinson (The American Liszt Society) and Mr Claus H. Henneberg (Cologne Opera), all of whom have been of immense assist-ance in the preparation and researching of this book.

ANTONY BEAUMONT
Cologne 1986

Chronology

1913 Appointed Director of the Liceo Musicale, Bologna.
1914 Returns to Berlin; conducts four concerts of his own works. Writes the libretto of *Arlecchino* and, at Christmas, completes the text of *Doktor Faust*.
1915 Settles in New York, but eventually returns to Europe and finds refuge in Zurich.
1916 Completes *Arlecchino*; begins work on the music for *Doktor Faust*.
1917 First performances of the operas *Turandot* and *Arlecchino*. Completion of Bach–Busoni complete edition.
1919 Elected Doctor h.c. at the University of Zurich. A lengthy English visit terminates his refuge in Switzerland.
1920 Returns to Berlin.
1921 Conducts three retrospective concerts. Busoni-number of the *Musikblätter des Anbruch*. Opens a composition class under the auspices of the Prussian Academy of Arts. First signs of serious illness.
1922 Last public appearance as pianist.
1923 Journeys to Weimar and Paris. Further periods of illness.
1924 Dies in Berlin on 27 July.
1925 First performance of *Doktor Faust*.

Editor's Note

In the interests of consistency, the various styles and forms of dating used by Busoni have been unified and placed at the head of each letter. (Dating is in European style, i.e. day, month, year.) His original punctuation has been retained as far as possible, particularly his use of colons, semi-colons and dashes. German words, when they occur, have been spelt in modern style. Where isolated words, phrases or longer passages were originally written in English, these are underlined. In editing the five letters originally written in English, orthographical errors have been corrected but otherwise (unless specifically indicated) no attempt has been made to 'improve' on Busoni's occasional linguistic idiosyncrasies. Translations of poetry and prose quotations have been made by the editor unless otherwise indicated; as a general rule the original text is retained in the main body of the letter, the translation is to be found in a footnote.

Busoni made frequent use of underlining, often double and occasionally even triple. In the interests of clarity – and also of economy – all forms of underlining have been indicated by *italics*. The typographical style conforms as closely as possible to that of Busoni's manuscript: titles of musical compositions, etc, have only been standardized in footnotes and other editorial material.

Biographical notes on recipients are to be found on pp. 424–9.

The continental convention of indicating modality by upper and lower case letters has been used in editorial comments, thus Quartet in c is in C Minor, and Sonata in F is in F Major.

I

1872 – 1886
Childhood and Adolescence

I   TO FERDINANDO BUSONI[1]
in Italian

Trieste 21.10.1872

Since Mamma told me you had bought me a lovely dog, I haven't stopped wanting to have it by me! I hope it will also be as faithful and intelligent as poor Fede. I want you to write to me soon, not only to hear about the dog but also about you, my dear Babbo, whom I love.

Best wishes from all the family and 1000 kisses from

your
loving
Ferruccio

[1]Several earlier letters to Ferdinando Busoni have been preserved, but it was not until 2 August 1872 that the six-year-old Ferruccio wrote one down himself: 'Questa lettera ho scritto solo'. Thus this correspondence opens with Nanni the poodle, who will later be succeeded by Lesko the Newfoundland bitch and Giotto the St Bernard. Evidently Ferdinando Busoni was at Empoli, Ferruccio Busoni's birthplace.

2   TO FERDINANDO BUSONI [fragment]
in Italian

Trieste [undated][1]

I forgot to mention another thing. In geography I have finished cosmography and gone on to the forms of the earth and the seas. In German 4 tenses of the verb to have and have finished the verb to be. In natural history we have finished human anatomy and gone on to the domestic animals. I have written out the cat in fair copy.

When I see you again I shall recite from memory a beautiful poem by Zaiotti,[2] the president of the Tribunale, who is dead now. The poem is entitled 'Il ritorno del crociato'. And then tell me a little more about Nanni and I beg you not to lie to me because I want her very much and if you have given her away tell me openly which will please me more than if you say nothing.

[1]Dent estimates that this letter was written in 1874.
[2]Paride Zajotti, 1793–1843, was born and studied at Trento. He was president of the Trieste department Tribunal from 1838, and a friend of Manzoni.

3   TO ANNA BUSONI
        in Italian

Vienna [undated][1]

A few days ago I received your letter in which you told me to correct the fugue.[2] I find this an excellent correction, here it is:

The Conservatoire is 3 times a week and I am only tested once or twice at the most (every week). So you can see that if it weren't for Papa it would be fairly fruitless and I would get worse rather than better.

The études of Cramer are fairly easy for me and now they are making me do the sonatas of Clementi, but we are going no further.

This year my studies are easy enough and I should have moved up to the third [class] especially as Epstein[3] said that if I had a little more physical strength I could have joined the final class.

So I shall have to remain at the Conservatoire for five (5) years.

Here in Vienna there have already been two performances of Faust (since I arrived) and both times I missed the opportunity of going (which disappointed me), but the other evening I went to Dinorah; I didn't like the performance very much but the production was done very realistically.

In the second act when the bridge breaks, a whole cataract of real water fell onto the stage, giving the genuine impression that it had been ruined.

The other day I acquired some other operas for voice and piano. Together with the 4 which I had when I left Trieste I now have 12 (a dozen). [. . .]

I have started a symphony[4] for piano 4 hands of which I have already finished the first movement.

[1]Of the operas referred to in this letter, Gounod's *Faust* was performed at the Vienna Hofoper on 1 and 20 October 1875, Meyerbeer's *Dinorah* on 15 October. Thus this letter can be dated *c.* 25 October 1875.
[2]The work in question is an unpublished *Studio contrappuntato*, the manuscript of which is preserved in the Staatsbibliothek Preussischer Kulturbesitz, West Berlin, and is dated '14 October 1875 at the age of 9½ years in Vienna'.
[3]Julius Epstein, 1832–1926, was director of the Vienna Conservatoire's piano class from 1867 until 1901.
[4]*Ouverture per Grande Orchestra* which remains unfinished (see letter No. 4).

4   TO ANNA BUSONI
    in Italian

                                                    Vienna 20.11.1875

Papa received your letter this morning with the note that you will be
sending 34 fl. for the rent, and I thank you in advance.

He is in the best of health; but he is also in a good mood and not without
reason. This evening, Saturday 20 November, he had to play at the Künstler-
Abend where he earned 50 fl.

Tomorrow evening, Sunday 21 November, he and I are both to play at the
'Nobles' Club' and this and the other, both fees in one go! With these two
takings, Papa has been calculating how to pay everything we owe this month.
We should already have received the stipendium; but here too, the devil only
knows how long we shall have to wait for it. As for the signora Contessa,[1] she
is in the country; she will be coming to live in Vienna for two months.

Meanwhile Papa knows very well that the Contessa has no music teacher;
and the stipendium of at least 130 or 150 fl. per month is not exaggerated,
because even the most beggardly music teacher doesn't give lessons in Vienna
for less than 2 or three fl. the hour; so Papa is astonished that you always said
that lessons in Vienna are poorly paid.

You are so afraid of Vienna, but I tell you that music is played by the yard
here, just like the merchants sell cloth, counting out loud, ein, zwei, drei,
vier, and that's all. If you were to come to Vienna and play a piece by Litolff
with orchestra, or by some other composer, you would have a great success;
because the most idiotic people have the greatest success (the other evening
I saw a violinist who played with his sister at the piano, what simpletons)
and are applauded to the skies! But you want to remain in Trieste.

The other day I heard Brahms;[2] but he didn't please me entirely, except
for his composition; I very much liked the quartet, but it had the opposite
effect on Papa, who said that it is much inferior to the Quartetto fiorentino. I
have nothing more to tell you today, except that the other day I showed my
score to the professor of harmony, who said that it was very well written.[3]

Goodbye for today.

[1]Busoni's Viennese patron was Baroness Sophie von Todesco.
[2]This was a concert on 18 November 1875 at the Vienna Musikverein, given by
Brahms and the Hellmesberger Quartet. The programme:

Mozart	Quartet in Eb, K.428
Brahms	Piano Quartet in c, op. 60 (world première)
Beethoven	Quartet in a, op. 132

[3]Busoni's overture (see letter No. 3) is a fragment of 158 bars composed in a curious
variant of rondo form. The musical language is considerably cruder than that of his
piano works written during the same period, while the orchestration betrays little of
Busoni's later brilliance. There are prominent parts for harp and, later, campanello
(glockenspiel); although the key of the work is E, the timpani are tuned to D, A and
C. The manuscript, preserved in the Preussische Staatsbibliothek, West Berlin, is
dated '1876, Vienna'.

5 FRAGMENT OF A DIARY[1]
in Italian

Today, Wednesday 8 March 1876
in spite of superstitious people
I am opening my diary and
'Daily Review'.

I am still half asleep. I become aware of confused noises and, now almost entirely awake, I hear these words spoken in German.

'. . . . . noch etwas zu warten'.[2] They are uttered by my mother who is receiving someone, to whom she has addressed them. For answer the words 'Jo, scho guat',[3] also in German.

'Mamma', I begin to shout. And she, 'Yes dear', but she doesn't stir. I wait a moment and then, impatiently, I repeat 'Mamma'. 'What do you want?' – Has my tea been made? Yes, straight away, do you want to put your jacket on? – Yes?

And then my long-awaited mother at last arrives and helps me on with my jacket. A little later she returns with the tea, accompanied by my dog Nanni who always was and still is faithful and obedient. Meanwhile she puts her paws on my bed to wish me good morning, expecting caresses from me, with which I am not sparing.

Having finished the tea, I ask Mamma for manuscript paper and a pencil so as to compose.

I try to write a fugue with my left hand; it is successful and well inspired; but, after a page, inspiration leaves me. So I set aside paper and pencil and begin to get dressed. Meanwhile 3 hours have passed and now the cathedral clock strikes eleven. I have finished getting dressed and prepare to try out what I have composed at the piano.

It's not bad, eh! eh! But it could go better, this fugue. Meanwhile the serving girl comes in to do the room; accustomed as she is to the light and carefree music of Strauss, she stops her ears and, aping my music, dutifully takes flight.[4]

---

[1]Written in Trieste. Busoni returned there, having fallen ill after a concert in Vienna on 8 February.
[2]. . . to wait a little longer.
[3]Ja, schon gut = Yes, all right (Austrian dialect).
[4]Orig. prende la fuga.

6 TO OTTO VON KAPFF[1]
in German

Klagenfurt 29.3.1879

Please don't imagine that I had been forgetting you all this time, I had been planning to write at least a few lines all along. Everything has conspired against it, concerts, the weather, everything possible has prevented me getting down to it, finally, to crown it all, I fell ill as well and only today, as I feel a little better, have I found time to answer your second letter, which I also received today.

Let me assure you above all that this illness did not arise from over-exertion or excitement (I have never suffered from such things in concerts), but that it was entirely due to the following: what happened was: everybody thought that I was sickly etc. and advised Papa to strengthen me up somehow, and as he had heard so much about indoor gymnastics and also as many people had spoken to him about it, he had the idea of giving it a try. For the first few days it seemed to be helping a little but unfortunately the gym teacher was careless enough to make me lie on the ground after having got hot with the exercises, and I inhaled the colder air; this brought on a catarrh, from which I am still recovering, so that I have to write to you from in bed and with a very high temperature, which also did me no particular good and has resulted in my having to look forward to a really miserable birthday (1 April). [. . .]

Although I have been ill and still am, I have worked fairly hard as far as composition is concerned. In Tyrol I wrote amongst other things a whole 4-part mass (6 long movements) in the old style of the 16th century.[2] Then two long pieces for 2 pianos,[3] a solo for clarinet[4] and other shorter piano pieces.[5] Now I am busy making a setting of Uhland's Des Sängers Fluch for solo voice and *orchestra*, but I haven't finished it yet.[6]

---

[1]Not one of the numerous letters from Busoni to Otto von Kapff is in the composer's handwriting. This correspondence was evidently the work of Anna Busoni (even the signatures) and she proves herself to be fond of exaggeration, particularly in the question of her son's compositions (see also letter no. 7).

[2]Missa I Quatuor vocibus cantanda, op. 34, (unpublished).

[3]Capriccio for two pianos, op. 36 (unpublished). The work is 320 bars long. There is no trace of a second piece for two pianos unless the untitled composition for four hands, op. 43, is meant.

[4]*Solo dramatique*, op. 13 (unpublished). Two further works for clarinet and piano date from this period, an Andantino, op. 18, and a Serenade no. 2, op. 19, but these were not composed until May 1879. Their manuscripts were mislaid during the Second World War.

[5]The only remaining work from this period is the Scherzo for piano, op. 17, whose manuscript is likewise mislaid.

[6]*Des Sängers Fluch*, ballad for alto voice and piano, op. 39, was published by Cranz, Leipzig, probably in 1879. The (unpublished) orchestral version mentioned here was completed on 13 April 1879.

7   TO OTTO VON KAPFF
         in German

Klagenfurt 11.4.1879

[. . . I would] ask you to thank Frl. Polko[1] warmly for her proposed sketch; be so good as to hurry her along if possible, as the matter could be of the greatest value to me. [. . .]

The leading Italian critic (approximately like Hanslik [sic] here) has also written a lengthy feuilleton [about me], which I shall send you as soon as it arrives here. Please tell Frl. Polko not to omit certain details as for example: that I have written something like 150 pieces[2] (good and bad) including 4 string quartets,[3] 4 piano sonatas,[4] a concerto,[5] a mass,[6] a fairly large (70–80 page) score,[7] also larger and smaller sacred works, choruses and songs, pieces for clarinet, violin and several works for piano. Of all these, about 50–60 can be regarded as of good quality and free of error, hence these are ready for publication.[8]

I was born on 1 April 1866 and am hence 13 years old, have already played for important personages, as for example at the court of Austria, for the Emperor of Brasil, the Queen of Hanover, the Archduchess Elisabeth, and also passed examinations (tests) with several leading artistic and musical figures, for example with Liszt, Rubinstein, Brahms, Goldmark etc. and have always met with the greatest approbation; altogether I have played about 50–60 concerts, my first at the age of 7, so few because I have mostly devoted my time to studies, also that I have learned and practised the greater part of the rules of harmony and counterpoint on my own and without a teacher. Please do not imagine that I am telling you all this for vanity's sake, but only in the desire that the sketch should be a complete biography![9] [. . .]

---

[1]Elise Polko, a writer and journalist. Busoni's *Lied der Klage* (text by Otto von Kapff) is dedicated to her.
[2]Two days after this letter was written, Busoni finished orchestrating *Des Sängers Fluch*; this was only – approximately – his hundredth composition.
[3]There were two full-scale quartets, in c (1876) and in f (1876), then a Minuet in F (1877), an Andante and Allegro Vivace, op. 13 (1878) and a Menuetto, op. 15 (February 1879).
[4]There were only three piano sonatas: in C, op. 7 (1877), in D, op. 8 (1877) and in E, op. 9 (two movements, also 1877).
[5]Concerto in d for piano and string quartet, op. 17 (1878).
[6]The mass, mentioned in the previous letter, which was completed on 12 February 1879.
[7]This is presumably the orchestral version of *Des Sängers Fluch*, but the manuscript is only 46 pages long.
[8]By this time Busoni had published five or six works.
[9]Around this time, the composer Wilhelm Kienzl also published an article on Busoni, in the *Grazer Tagespost*. An extract from his reminiscences (Wilhelm Kienzl *Meine*

Lebenswanderung – Erlebtes und Erschautes in Hans Sittner *Kienzl – Rosegger*, Zurich-Leipzig-Vienna, 1953) will help complete the picture of the thirteen-year old Busoni: The young lad had at that time already composed 130 pieces [!], most of them in polyphonic style, including a string quartet, although he had not enjoyed the privilege of systematic tuition. He also improvised in an astonishing manner on themes I gave him. Sitting at the piano he was inspired to the deepest seriousness and entirely absorbed in his task. Then, a child once more, he leaped around the room and played ball games. Moreover Ferruccio was then already fully conversant in three languages and had an almost adult, entirely 'developed' handwriting.

8   TO FERDINANDO BUSONI
in Italian

Trieste 29.5.1881

[. . .] I have begun my sketch of the Tuba mirum,[1] which I believe I shall not use. But I think that a better idea will come to me in a few days. I have looked over the Dies irae, which seems very good to me and also well scored. I have also resumed my piano studies on an instrument which I don't like (it doesn't sound) and I am impatiently awaiting our Schnabel, which is much better. [. . .] I am getting up early and profiting from the coolness of the morning to go out and sketch some 'views' of Trieste. Today I began to copy the church of the Schiavoni, which is a beautiful building in Moorish style and also perhaps one of the most beautiful pieces of architecture in Trieste. [. . .]

[1]This and the following letter are representative of several concerned with the composition of the *Requiem* for soli, chorus and orchestra, which occupied Busoni from 3 May to 10 July 1881. The work is incomplete.

9   TO FERDINANDO BUSONI
in Italian

Trieste 7.6.1881

I shall open my letter with a piece of good news: the 'Tuba mirum' was finished 3 days ago, and since then I have also set to work on the score, of which I have written a few pages.

– This composition (No. 3 in the Requiem) consists of 5 verses: this is the sequence:

cresc	Tuba mirum spargens sonum
Trumpets	Per sepulcra regionum
dim	Coget omnes ante thronum

mysterious theme	Mors stupebit et natura Cum resurget creatura Judicanti responsura	4 solo voices
agitato	Liber scriptus proferetur In quo totum continetur Unde mundus judicetur	bass and tenor *soloists* later chorus
reprise of verse I	Judex ergo cum sedebit Quidquid latet apparebit Nil inultum remanebit.	then dim
pp theme of the trombones which had not yet been given to the voices.	Quid sum miser tunc dicturus Quem patronem rogaturus Cum vix justus sit securus.	

Here then is a brief analysis of this movement, which seems to me to have been as successful as the other two.

Yesterday I had lunch with Cimoso.[1] We ate well. After the meal Bianchini[2] arrived. I played him the new published fugue[3] which he liked so much that he wanted to hear it again. He considered it *masterful*. Then he wanted me to hear one of his sonatas for piano and violin and, as Luigi said that he had not yet learnt it, I offered to play it at sight myself, which surprised them greatly, even more so after I had read it very well. Bianchini was beside himself with joy and kissed me several times, saying he would dedicate his next work to me. Then I played them *my* sonata,[4] which they liked very much on the whole. Bianchini assured Luigi that today only the likes of a Rubinstein could write such a work. And Luigi turned to me and said: you see, you are already beginning to be counted amongst such people. I am writing you all these things because I know that they will give you pleasure, not as an act of pride or arrogance. You know my character better than I do.

Bianchini has also recently written a *Requiem*, from which he played me various sections. The Tuba mirum is the best of all the movements and I like it far more than Verdi's, because it does not indulge in the grandiose manner or the charlatanry which one finds in the latter. Verdi's always seems to me like a battle-field on which the soldiers' trumpet calls are heard as a warning of the enemy's attack. I shall be happy if you find *my* idea 'persuasive'.

[1]Luigi Cimoso, ?–1884, one of a family of Trieste musicians and a close friend of Busoni.

[2]Pietro Bianchini, 1828–1905, violinist, composer and conductor. Resident in Trieste from 1878 to 1887 as orchestral violinist, teacher of counterpoint and composition. His works include a *Marcia trionfale*, two masses, several violin sonatas, etc.

[3]*Praeludium (Basso ostinato) und Fuge (Doppelfuge zum Choral)*, for organ, op. 76. Published as op. 7 by Cranz, Hamburg in 1881.

[4]Piano sonata in f, completed in Graz in September 1880.

10 TO GIOVANNINA LUCCA
in Italian

Trieste 4.5.1883

I do not know why you are *displeased* to hear that I intend to change the 2nd piece in the 'Festa di Villaggio'.[1] Correction of one's compositions has always seemed to me the proof of progress and, for me, *progress* would not be a cause for *displeasure*.

As far as I can see, you would not be making any serious loss. When you have sold out the first edition you could sell the old *Marcia* as a separate piece, with another title. Please consent to this alteration, bearing in mind the truth of the old adage: *to err is human, but to persist in one's error is unreasonable*.

We should let *more competent people* decide whether or not it is artistically viable to leave everything *as it is*.

[1]In 1882, Lucca, who published many of Busoni's early works, brought out *Una Festa di Villaggio*, six character pieces for piano, op. 9. Busoni wished to write an improved second movement to replace the original 'Marcia trionfale'; in August 1883 he then composed a 'Marcia di Paesani e Contadine', op. 32, which was, however, not published by Lucca but by the Trieste firm, Schmidl-Vicentini.

11 TO ANTONIO ZAMPIERI
in Italian

Lubljana 5.9.1883

[. . .] I shall not send you any detailed notes about the Suite,[1] as you will already have received these from Luigi [Cimoso], but rather summarize them in a few words. The idea of the *Preludio* is just as you wanted it. It came to me spontaneously and clearly. I don't think it would be excessively proud of me to say that the result is a most significant piece, in the desired character, that is purely classical. You know the 2nd movement. The Allegro fugato has an energetic manner which has also been applied to the orchestration. I wrote a more extensive description of the Adagio in a letter to Luigi. The first part is reminiscent of Handel. The second is a kind of recitative in a style which would be Bach-Mendelssohn, if it didn't also contain a little Busoni (there's pride for you). The restlessness produced by the movement of the recitative is interrupted by a reminiscence of the *Allegro* (celestial chords), which sounds very well. In a coda, elaborated versions of both themes are inter-laced. Despite the imitations of Handel and Bach, this *movement* has more modern a character than the others and perhaps even that mixture of classical and modern for which I am striving.

The Minuetto on the other hand, in which the brass is reduced to just two horns and two trumpets, is truly classical. You know the *Gigue* and therefore I shall say nothing further about it.

While recently thumbing through a catalogue of the works of Saint-Saëns, I found a *Suite for orchestra*[2] which consists of: Prelude (!), *Gavotte*, *Sarabande* (so far so good, but now:) Romance (!!), Finale (!!!). I would be interested to see the mould of this *Finale*, which is so out of keeping with the names Gavotte and Sarabande. Massenet and Bizet have composed suites in the hateful romantic manner, although they are attractive in their way. Then *Lachner*,[3] but he is a pedant, Zopf, Philistine. Strange coincidence: the *first symphony* of Haydn was divided into five sections: 1. Larghetto (Introduzione). 2. Allegro, which begins with an *energetic unison* passage for the strings (!). 3. Recitativo e Adagio (!). 4. Menuetto. 5. Finale (!).[4] This is because Haydn had followed the example of the old *suites* which (as the history book tells us) all finished with a *Gigue* (!). When I read this (Nohl, Musikgeschichte, Universalbibliothek, 36 soldi[5]), I was greatly delighted because it convinced me that I had had fine intuition, also in the choice of movements for the Suite. Any day now I am expecting the publication of the Macchiette medioevali.[6] Here too I had the strange coincidence of finding in an old catalogue a composition by Hiller[7] entitled *Mittelalterliche Gestalten*, which includes amongst others *Ritter*, *Edelfrau*, *Mönch*, *Nonne* etc.[8] I would be interested to see it. At the Vienna opera this season they are performing for the first time *La Gioconda*, Massenet's *Hérodiade* and another piece which I do not remember.[9] They are also performing a one-act opera (!) by Grisar[10] and this reminds me of the sad business of *La Figlia del Re Renato*. I have written *3 letters* to *Buono*,[11] the last one *registered*, but have received no reply. Thus I have missed the chance of taking part in this competition and, even if I had had no success with it, the opera would have been of use to me later, for instance for a performance in Vienna in German. But! . . . But! . . . Here is a case where one could lose one's respect for an older man, which is not my nature but which would have been apt under the circumstances.

[. . .] Have you received the complimentary copy of the Marcia?[12] I asked Carlotto[13] to have it sent.

---

[1]*Symphonic Suite* for orchestra, op. 25.
[2]Saint-Saëns, Suite, op. 49, composed in 1877.

[3]Franz Paul Lachner, 1803–1890, Bavarian composer. He wrote seven orchestral suites between 1861 and 1881.

[4]Busoni refers here to Haydn's Symphony no. 7, 'Le Midi' (1761), which is divided as follows: Adagio–Allegro; Recitativo; Adagio; Menuetto; Finale: Allegro.

[5]Ludwig Nohl *Allgemeine Musikgeschichte. Populär dargestellt*, Leipzig, 1881, 2nd edn.

[6]*Macchiette medioevali* (Medieval characters), op. 33, for piano, which Busoni composed between 1882 and 1883. There are six movements: Dama, Cavaliere, Paggio, Guerriero, Astrologo, Trovatore (Lady, Knight, Page, Soldier, Astrologer, Minstrel).

[7]Ferdinand Hiller, 1811–1885. His *'Gestalten aus dem Mittelalter'* (sic), op. 158, were published *c*. 1875 by Senff, Leipzig.

[8]Medieval figures: Knight, Gentlewoman, Monk, Nun.

[9]The first Viennese performance of Ponchielli's *La Gioconda* was given on 29 April 1884. There is no record of Massenet's *Hérodiade* ever having been staged in Vienna.

[10]Albert Grisar, 1808–1869, Belgian composer, mostly of light comic operas. His one-act opera *Der Hund des Gärtners* was performed in Vienna on 18 February 1884.

[11]Michele Buono, 1826–1892, poet and editor of a Trieste literary journal, *L'Arte*. Busoni had asked him to adapt *Kong René's Datter* (King René's daughter) by the Danish playwright Henrik Hertz into a one-act opera, which he intended to enter for a competition in Vienna. The play, based on a medieval saga, later served as the source for Tchaikovsky's opera *Iolanta* (1892).

[12]'Marcia di Paesani e Contadine' (see previous letter).

[13]Carlo Schmidl, the Trieste music publisher.

12 TO ANNA BUSONI
in Italian

Vienna 14.10.1883

Yesterday I was at Richter's,[1] who received me after I had 6 times vainly sought to see him. He lives near Döbling, which is to say miles away. He gave me a somewhat cool reception to begin with, but agreed to listen to the Suite[2] (which – I am told – is in itself extraordinary) but he had scarcely heard the Preludio when he exclaimed: 'Bravo! If all the movements are like this, I shall perform it at once.'

He was most surprised – as he himself said – by the *Allegro fugato*, but on the other hand he found the *Menuetto* weak (that is to say, weak compared with the magnificence of the other movements) and with regard to this he advised me – either to alter it in such a manner that it should become less prolix or to leave it out *altogether*. I must admit that, on hearing the whole Suite in one sitting, he has convinced me.

So the outcome is as follows: the parts must be ready for 13 November (because he is absent from Vienna until then) and the Suite will be given a *trial* performance before the *committee*, without whom Richter cannot make a final decision. But he promised to speak favourably of me to the committee and he expects that the Suite will make such an impression on *them* that it will be accepted immediately. [. . .]

Richter also said this: 'If the *Suite* is successful here, he would accept it for his London concerts.' And then he added that the Italians and the English are much more active than the young Germans nowadays, who have been ruined by imitating Wagner, and he spoke well of Sgambati.[3] Richter had heard of my name because *Dr Terč* of *Marburg* had written him a letter about me.

Yesterday I was at the *Flamm's*[4] again, where I played some of my Preludes,[5] about which they were enthusiastic. [. . .]

The first time I went to Hanslick he was extremely courteous, encouraged me greatly and gave me a letter of introduction to Richter. Hanslick remembered me and my concerts and advised me to further myself as a pianist.

[1]Hans Richter, 1843–1916, celebrated conductor.
[2]*Symphonic Suite* (see previous letter).
[3]Giovanni Sgambati, 1841–1914, Italian pianist and composer. A pupil of Liszt, he was a leading figure in the concert life of Rome.
[4]Viennese friends of Busoni. Paula Flamm was the dedicatee of a Minuetto, op. 14, and Gavotta, op. 25, for piano, written and published in 1878.
[5]24 Preludes for piano, op. 37, composed in 1881 and published by Lucca *c.* 1882.

13   TO ANNA BUSONI
        in Italian

                                      Vienna 17.11.1883 [postmark]

[. . .] Hellmesberger[1] received me with his celebrated flashing smile, ever chic, ever elegant, well-dressed, with friendly words on his lips and a je ne sais quoi which arouses little confidence. He told me to return some other morning, and I shall abide by what he says. Door[2] was with him and, when he saw me, he pulled a really *awful* face. While they were talking, a girl was playing and from time to time they would look round and beat time with their feet to make her play *in tempo*. On the stairs I met my old teacher Scheuner, who greeted me with great kindness. And then I met . . . guess who? The daughter of the café proprietor in Trieste who called on us to ask for complimentary tickets, and who studied with *Fumagalli*.[3] – She is going to study at the Conservatoire for a year. Babbo has written to you about Bösendorfer.[4] I have taken advantage of my free tickets at the Theatre to hear *Don Giovanni* and *Die Entführung aus dem Serail*. Both operas astounded me: the first with its strength, the second with its inimitable gracefulness: and with their powers of expression through harmony and the simplest of instrumentation. – How different from Richard Wagner! – The parts of the Suite have already been sent to be copied. –

Yesterday I was a guest of the Flamms, to whom I played various pieces; (they have a good Streicher piano), amongst others my *Studio-Fuga*[5] and the *Schumann Toccata* which bowled them over. The Toccata came off very well.

The Flamms are very fond of me and treat me with the greatest courtesy, taking a lively interest in my development. [. . .]

[1]Joseph Hellmesberger jnr, 1855–1907, violinist and composer, at this time second violin in his father's celebrated string quartet, also professor of violin at the Vienna Conservatoire.
[2]Anton Door, 1833–1919, pianist. A pupil of Czerny and Simon Sechter, he was appointed professor at the Vienna Conservatoire in 1869.
[3]Luca Fumagalli, 1837–1903, Italian pianist and composer, the most distinguished of a family of pianists.
[4]Ludwig von Bösendorfer, 1835–1919, the son of Ignaz Bösendorfer, who founded the famous firm of piano manufacturers.
[5]No. 5 of the 6 Etudes, op. 16, dedicated to Brahms and published by Gutmann, Vienna, 1884.

14 TO ANNA BUSONI
in Italian

Vienna 31.3.1884

I didn't write to you immediately after the concert as I was invited to take part in a charity evening the following day, where I appeared without fee. My concert went *very* well and I played perhaps better than ever before. Before the Beethoven sonata I played – to warm up – a prelude of Bach and the fugue of the Chromatic Fantasy, at the end [Liszt's] Venezia e Napoli *complete*. Thus the programme was respectably long without being too tiring, indeed I was able to conserve my full strength for the end. The success was excellent, my compositions were extremely well received (especially the Preludes and the Etude) and at the close I was presented with a beautiful laurel wreath with a red ribbon, from a florist who always provides the wreaths and flowers for gala occasions. The Baroness (with whom I have recently had something of an argument and who gave me a good dressing down) was present at the concert for the first time and departed satisfied and appeased. Today I called on her – and she was so good and kind, gave me 100 fl. for the month and a further 10 for theatre tickets, – she asked me what clothes I required, as she would give them to me for my birthday, and she invited me to call again soon to inform her of my activities.

'Wenn ich nur eine *Ahnung* hätte[,] was wir jetzt machen sollten!'.[1] To which I replied: as you have been so kind as to take an interest in the matter, please permit me to come and speak to you about it some time. She invited me to dine with her on Wednesday.

I have composed *3 Lieder* to be sung by Miss Bettelheim,[2] one of which is the revision of 'Es ist bestimmt in Gottes Rat'.[3] The other two are settings of *Byron* in German translation, entitled 'Hebräische Melodien', but actually derived from the psalm '*An den Wässern zu Babel sassen wir und weinten*'. Today I played them to Miss Bettelheim: she was most pleased with them and has accepted the dedication. She said she would also like to sing *Il Nonno dorme*, which I wrote for her.[4]

Signor Richter has behaved none too well and finally declared that it would now be too late to rehearse and perform the Suite, but that he would try to make amends, giving me his *word* to consider *me before all else* in the coming season, also to play with the Philharmonic.

I shall approach the committee for a *definite* answer and, in case I should not be in Vienna in September, I shall send my Suite to Richter, as they usually try out *the novelties* only in that month.

I have had my doubts for some time as to the success of this venture and I, for my part, have left no stone unturned to achieve my aim but have told you nothing of all this so as to spare you any unnecessary anxiety. There is no need at present to take it too much to heart; something at least has been achieved, I have made the acquaintance of Vienna, of Richter and of the committee, there has been as much talk of me in the papers as amongst the public. The principal object of my coming to Vienna has not been achieved; but it is not entirely unattainable, it will simply take a little *longer*. [. . .][5]

[1]If only I had the *slightest* notion what we should do now.
[2]Karoline (or Caroline) Gomperz-Bettelheim, 1843–1891, Hungarian-born pianist, later singer at the Carltheater in Vienna, from 1872 contralto at the Vienna Hofoper and a noted concert singer.
[3]Busoni set this poem by Feuchtersleben in Cilli on 8 October 1879 as op. 32. It was published as op. 24 no. 2 by Kahnt, Leipzig, in 1886.
[4]Presumably 'Die Abendglocke schallet', composed on 3 March 1876.
[5]The letter continues with an extensive imaginary drama, to celebrate Busoni's 18th birthday (1 April 1884).

15   TO ANNA BUSONI
         in Italian

                                              Frohnleiten 14.12.1885

With such a dearth of events in my present way of life, it is difficult to persuade oneself to fill a whole sheet of writing paper and even more difficult to do so four times a month. – Life in the outside world, on the other hand, seems to be highly eventful, particularly in the world of politics, where one deed follows the next day by day. If only I could say the same of artistic events! [. . .]

At Weimar, however, the sanctuary of the Lisztians, there was a performance of a new opera, '*Ramiro*',[1] of which one reads that it was the first work of a young man from Leipzig, a certain Eugen Lindner,[2] and that it had a moderate success. –

Rest assured that I, too, am working and, so far as I can tell – with great success. I hope for a good outcome. The ideas also seem to be less unforthcoming. I have already composed the entire first *scene*[3] (i.e. up to the first change of characters) and have sketched out various fine ideas for the remainder, including one of the principal ideas: the motif of the '*stille Dorf*', which will occur frequently during the course of the opera. – The work is not to be divided into arias, choruses, ensembles etc., but into '*scenes*', following the structure of the drama. –

Incidentally, I note that this will be the *third village* I shall have composed;[4] and as the two previous works (*Festa* and *Sabato*) can be counted amongst my better compositions, let us hope (taking our cue from the old adage 'trinum est perfectum') that this third one (*Fantasma*, in the poor Italian translation) will also turn out to my satisfaction.

Stille Dorf is almost untranslatable. *Das stille Haus*, for example, would mean a house of mystery, one which is *presumed* to be uninhabited because it is always shuttered and silent, but behind whose silence some secret is concealed.

Das stille Reich is a delicate expression for the *kingdom of the dead*, not that of ghosts and skeletons but the region in which everything is still. 'The silent kingdom'. It is used in this sense too in Baumbach's novella, 'Das stille Dorf'. 'The silent village, the spectral village'. Taking this difficulty of translation into account, I have preferred to name the opera after its chief protagonist, '*Sigune*', which is not only original but also justified by the action. –

I enclose a vignette for you, which I found in a catalogue and will give you some idea of the costumes which will be required for my opera. The young man right of centre could be a figurine for my tenor.

Then one of my own little drawings[5] which is intended to show you how I dress here, with beret, short trousers and gaiters.[6]

Well, contrary to my expectations, I have filled two pages. [. . .]

[1]*Ramiro*, libretto by Th. A Herrmann, music by Eugen Lindner, op. 4. First performed at the Weimar Hoftheater on 6 December 1885.
[2]Eugen Lindner, 1858–1915, German composer.
[3]Busoni was working on his opera *Sigune oder das stille Dorf*, adapted from a novella by Rudolf Baumbach. The libretto was constructed by Frida Schanz, a popular poetess of the time, together with her husband Ludwig Soyaux. Although Busoni worked at the opera until 1889, he never finished it.
[4]Reference to the piano suite, *Una Festa di Villaggio* (1881) and the cantata, *Il Sabato del Villaggio* (1882).
[5]Unfortunately this drawing has not been preserved.
[6]Melanie Mayer, who often saw Busoni at Frohnleiten, recalls: 'He was dressed in a boyish fashion – his parents loved to accentuate his youthfulness – wore short trousers, a short jacket with a broad, white linen collar, and a black silk tie.'

16 TO MELANIE MAYER
in German

Frohnleiten 21.1.1886

The enclosed press-cutting[1] should be of interest to you; I myself was truly delighted, as it proved to me that merit really is appreciated in the long run. In Leipzig I saw a lithographed (!) edition of the vocal score lying forgotten on a shelf, and derived the best impression from a brief inspection of it. I am writing to tell you about this and also because I felt the urge to gossip awhile after so long an abstinence.

No matter how much I may pretend to be a pessimist or a sceptic, I am in fact a communicative soul who needs the company of his fellow men.

Yesterday I read of the death of the composer Ponchielli,[2] which has made me very sad. Despite his poor music he was a good man, straightforward and unselfish. In Milan I had the pleasure of making his personal acquaintance.

The days here are as alike as two drops of water (the drops are generally frozen). Therefore there is little to report. I hope to come to Graz within the next few days, to see you and your dear parents, and I can already smell the apples.

In the last few days I have been re-reading 'Fathers and Sons',[3] which has made an undiminished impression: this fellow Basarov is and remains a terrific fellow. I should imagine that such a man – in the flesh, I mean – would have been of the greatest interest to you.[4]

========

At present I am enjoying and profiting from the exquisite, exemplary style of Boccaccio, a work whose appeal is most certainly lost in translation, as its content – from a literary standpoint – is innocuous and insignificant to the point of childishness, while the style is unreproduceable, hence in a foreign language the book acquires a veneer of frivolity and raciness, but nothing more. The same could be said to a large extent of Manzoni's 'Promessi sposi', which I have never heard a German single out but which, in Italy, is considered – and rightly so – to be one of the most perfect works of art.

I have often wondered why it is that Italian literature never has that serenity and sparkle which the Italians bring to every other art-form, and which is altogether a characteristic of our nation. The Germans, who are otherwise serious and heavy-handed, write far more readily about trifling matters than we do. In comparison, Dante, Alfieri, Leopardi or Guerazzi afford more of an academic than an artistic pleasure. Also in the question of imaginative powers, the Germans are closer to the French – who remain unsurpassed on this score – than we are. But enough of this pointless chatter. [. . .]

Of course, the opera! It is making good progress and, should the style of the opening be carried through, it will contrast quite strongly with more modern trends. I hope more than ever that I can heroically renounce the trombones!

---

[1]Concerning Heuberger's *Die Abenteuer einer Neujahrsnacht*, comic opera in three acts, op. 30, first performed in Leipzig on 30 January 1886. It was published by Schott, Mainz. Heuberger, like Busoni, had studied composition with Wilhelm Mayer-Rémy, the father of the recipient of this letter.
[2]Amilcare Ponchielli died on 17 January 1886.
[3]Turgenev's novel, which appeared in 1862, had been available in German translation since 1869.
[4]cf. letter no. 24, section dated 7 October 1888.

II

1886 – 1893
Years of Travel

in German

Leipzig 15.12.1886

The fact is that dreams are something out of the ordinary. Last night I dreamed – for the first time since leaving Graz – of you, and the following morning I received your letter, one of the few forms [of communication] with which it seems worthwhile and desirable to persevere. In my dream I saw you and your mother quite distinctly. I don't remember what foodstuff it was that you had piled up in every room of your apartment. But I do remember that I made some witty comment and it pleased you so much that I expressed the desire to write it down in my commonplace book, to which you consented. Dreams are something out of the ordinary. Last night it happened, already for the second if not the third time, that I was of the impression my friend Cimoso was not dead,[1] while knowing very well that the rumour of his death was in circulation. The asylum doctor had hushed up the fact that he was still alive so as to be able to surprise his friends and relatives with the news of his complete recovery, a thing which he had initially declared to be impossible. I found all this perfectly normal and understandable and was overjoyed at the restoration of my friend. My dream was so graphic and vivid that, on awakening, I had to take a firm grasp of my senses in order to readjust to the sad reality. One has no idea what to make of such logically well-organized thinking, based as it is on entirely false foundations, and neither 'dream organism'[2] nor 'second sight' are sufficiently enlightening concepts. But that Schopenhauer was absolutely on the right track with his theories, although intuitive rather than explanatory, was proved to me once again in a story about something which my housekeeper's daughter herself experienced. But more of this some other time, or better not at all.

My housekeeper herself is a very intelligent, educated woman with whom one can make polite conversation about this and that. Incidentally I only see her at mealtimes and then but briefly, as the food leaves much to be desired not only in quality but also quantity. However the cost is so reasonable that, when it is in fact insufficient, I do not hesitate to remove to an inn and add a 'supplementary volume' to my meal. – I am living almost in the centre of town but, however, in a quiet and secluded yet bright and wide street;[3] before me the Thomaskirche, a perpetual exhortation to diligence and application. On these counts I am not lacking. I am active in every way. The following little story should give you some idea:

A few days ago, at 8 in the evening, I was turning into the Grimmaische Strasse.[4] My piano arrived only the following day and the next morning I had to give the removal men my last remaining Thaler. Small wonder, for I had paid for my travel, hotel and monthly rent in advance. Such was my luck that I bumped into Kahnt the publisher, whom I promptly buttonholed. 'Take on some of my compositions, I need money.' (Oskar Schwalm[5] is a very good-natured young man.) 'I can't do anything now, but if you would like to write me a little easy fantasy on the opera "The barber of Baghdad", come and see me tomorrow morning, I can offer you 50 Marks in advance and 100 Marks upon completion.' – 'It's a deal.' And we parted. – The following morning I came to collect my 50 Marks. 'Do we abide by our agreement, Herr Schwalm? 100 Marks upon completion?' 'But of course! Here are the first 50 Marks.' 'And here is the finished work', whereupon I pulled the manuscript out of my briefcase. I had been working from nine in the evening until half past three at night, without a piano and with no previous knowledge of the opera.

More about my activities very soon. – On Sunday I played my cello suite[6] with great success at the 'Lisztverein'. I enclose the reviews. [. . .]

---

[1] Luigi Cimoso died in a mental hospital in Milan on 15 or 16 June 1884.
[2] Orig. Traumorgan. Busoni refers to Schopenhauer's essay *Versuch über das Geistersehen und was damit zusammenhängt*, Frankfurt, 1850.
[3] Busoni's Leipzig address was Centralstrasse (today Zentralstrasse) 14, 3rd floor. His housekeeper was a Frau Hauptmann Spann.
[4] One of Leipzig's chief shopping thoroughfares.
[5] Manager of Kahnt Verlag.
[6] *Kleine Suite*, for cello and piano, op. 23. Published by Kahnt, Leipzig, in 1886.

18   TO MELANIE MAYER
in German

Leipzig 8.2.1887
12 o'clock midnight

'The witching hour draws near' and I am thinking of you so intensely that, according to Schopenhauer's hypothesis, I should be appearing to you in person, indeed tangibly, were it not that we unbelieving, unimaginative children of the New Era are condemned to the fate of never experiencing anything of the sort. After my long silence, my letter itself must appear like a ghost to you, or you might indeed look upon the postman who delivers it to you as one; in which case I would feel obliged to instruct you as to the error of this supposition so as to prevent you from offending the honest man – in the case of so outrageous an assumption – by expecting him to dispense with the modest payment he generally receives. [. . .]

Things are going well for me here, I have achieved a good deal in a short time. My orchestral Suite should be performed here this month and, in the summer, even at the Rheinische Musikfest in Cologne. But don't breathe a word of this to anyone. At the end of February I am playing for the Tonkünstlerverein in Dresden.[1] For this engagement I have to thank Prof. Scholtz[2] (editor of the splendid Chopin Edition), who heard me here and recommended me in Dresden.

My opera is going in leaps and bounds! Hurrah! In 10 days I wrote all of four numbers for it, then came the – past! – In order to earn some money I had to take on a wretched job (the vocal score of Merlin)[3] which is, however, well paid. Altogether my finances are taken care of as I am on the best of terms with two publishers here, although I shall take pains not to sink to the level of an artisan!

A few days ago I met a book-seller who claimed that he already knew me. 'Where from?' I asked. 'I am reading a novel by Frau Kapff-Essenther,' he replied, 'the hero of which is your spitting image.'[4] This is how I am being introduced here. [. . .]

[1]The concert took place on 28 February 1887. Busoni shared the programme with a cellist and a string quartet. His own contributions were the 'Harmonious Blacksmith' variations of Handel, a Scarlatti Sonata in A, Tausig's transcription of Bach's Toccata and Fugue in d and a group of Chopin pieces, including the Polonaise in Ab.

[2]Hermann Scholtz, 1845–1918, who edited the 1879 Peters Edition of Chopin's piano works.

[3]*Merlin*, opera in three acts by Carl Goldmark. Busoni not only made the vocal score but also composed a concert fantasy on themes from the opera (completed in May 1887).

[4]Franziska von Kapff-Essenther, 1849–1891, a now totally forgotten novelist, who was married to Otto von Kapff (see p. 426) from 1880 until 1888. The joke implied by Busoni's comment is that she was a leading feminist! The novel referred to here was probably *Moderne Helden*, published in 1885.

19 TO MELANIE MAYER
in German

Leipzig 8.6.1887

[. . .] Despite certain things which seem to indicate the opposite, I am a communicative soul. (Our only sporadic exchange of letters is no real proof of the contrary.) Hence: I feel the need to communicate. When I work and create something new, I must always have someone who I know will be pleased to hear of it. This stimulates me. This 'someone' must however have sympathy for my 'products', for my feelings and ideas and must value me, have trust in me and hence stimulate me to renewed activity. If this person has true understanding for my creativity and my character, he will not close his eyes to my deficiencies but rather – conscious of the perfection that I could perhaps achieve – draw my attention to them and hence be of value to me. But then the approbation of such a person is also more influential than the abuse of ten celebrated critics. But, for this 'someone' always to be in a position of objectivity in their judgement, he must be so disposed as to feel that he could never in any way become my rival. Particularly if this feeling were to instil itself in him, a sense of competitiveness would soon get the better of him and hence mar the sincerity of his relationship to me. I had such a 'someone' in my deceased and truly unforgettable friend Cimoso, whom you should actually now replace, whom you have indeed in certain respects so far replaced. My relationship to you is, I believe, decidedly ennobling, as was always the case with the relationship of an artist to an intelligent, educated woman (in the sense of her being female rather than of being married).

=====

I have nobody with whom I can communicate as my true self. My Mamma understands me very well in my attitude to life, but we differ seriously on matters of higher philosophy, to a certain extent on social considerations but chiefly on religious matters. Since my childhood, my father has always been able to comprehend my significance for art and is also gradually coming to understand my character, but there was a time when he didn't understand me at all and from this state it is a lengthy path to perfect knowledge. Here I have been unable to win a single friend for myself who is on my level, but have found two others, on the other hand, who can learn from me, hence from whom I benefit only in the joy I experience at seeing them progress under my supervision. – The misfortune of having matured young is that one is unable to associate with people of the same age, while older people have no wish to associate with oneself, hence: total isolation. Were it not for my ability to adapt myself temporarily to others (which is also not at all harmful from time to time, as one exists above all to be together with one's fellow men), I could indeed exist for myself alone for ever.——

I have been working very hard all along, have done all manner of things which it would take too long to enumerate. Happily, my quartet[1] is finished and is indeed my most significant work so far; greater indeed than the orchestral Suite. The first movement is laid out on a grand scale; in its ideas actually a symphony, in its textures entirely a quartet. You have heard the Adagio; although it did not appeal to you, and I too would admit that it could be more melodic, it is at any rate deeply felt and extremely carefully worked out. To the wild and demonic Scherzo I have added a Trio, a new arrangement of the penultimate movement of my Chopin variations,[2] which has an exceptionally pleasing effect. The Finale is preceded by an Andantino sostenuto; the Finale itself (on a humorous theme) pauses contemplatively in the middle section before returning to the boisterousness of the preceding music, then finally combines the theme with that of the first movement, after which a spirited coda makes for a great and effective climax.

The opera is ¾ finished and shall, I hope, be completed this summer. [. . .]

Please forgive me for not having asked your specific permission for the dedication,[3] but I could not have imagined it any other way, and you?——

[1]String quartet no. 2 in d, op. 26.
[2]Variations and Fugue in Free Form on Chopin's C minor Prelude (op. 28 no. 20) for piano, op. 22. Busoni revised the work (which he had written in 1884) much later in his life.
[3]The *Zwei Gesänge* for low voice and piano, op. 24, had just been published by Kahnt, Leipzig, bearing a dedication to Melanie Mayer.

20   TO MELANIE MAYER
in German

Leipzig 22.7.1887

——I could counter your statement that external impressions should influence my artistic creativity with the fact that the greater ease and freedom of movement which I find in forms of absolute music (chamber-music, symphony) speaks against it. Words do indeed instil an atmosphere in me, but their metre inhibits my musical concept and I always have a greater or lesser amount to say, musically speaking, than the text allows for. This is also a drawback of vocal music. In particular, the significance and duration of a theme determine the length of an instrumental piece; but how difficult it is to hit upon a theme which calls for the duration demanded by the poem! In the case of song-form, this is not only acceptable but also interrelated; but what of larger-scale works, of operas? The most extendable and developable idea has to break off abruptly, simply because the baritone bursts in with furrowed brow and shouts 'Revenge'! This alone would be proof of the unwarrantability of opera. And while we are on the subject of opera, let me tell you how delighted I am to hear of a composer like Reznicek,[1] who promises excellent things. – Will he achieve them? How many conditions have to be fulfilled for a talent to reach its fullest development! Wealth and talent are desirable possessions, but both are equally difficult to maintain, let alone increase. And together with the gift of both of these, one must also accept the responsibility for them. Bungled education (by which I also mean the path along which one guides oneself), neglect (so-called loafing around) and discouragement are perils to which every talent is exposed, which it has to suffer, if only to a certain degree. My talent, for instance, has overcome quite a number of perils, but has it won through all of them? There are far more than I have enumerated here. –

The Dresden performance of the opera[2] is still uncertain, hence my silence. Some time ago I wrote to you, however, that I had found a permanent publisher, indeed one who will accept all my works, hence also the opera.[3] The new string quartet has been accepted for the Gewandhaus,[4] the Symphonic Suite for the Philharmonic Concerts in Berlin. When I have finished the opera (still about ¼) I shall write a symphony, for which I have had a good inspiration.

[1]Emil von Reznicek, 1860–1945, was also a pupil of Wilhelm Mayer-Rémy.
[2]*Sigune.*
[3]Busoni had signed an exclusive contract with Breitkopf und Härtel.
[4]The first performance of Busoni's String quartet no. 2 in d was given by the Petri Quartet at the Leipzig Gewandhaus on 28 January 1888.

21   TO FERDINANDO BUSONI
in Italian

Leipzig June 1888

I have lately had so many matters on my mind, so many anxieties and uncertainties, also so very much to do, that I have been unable to find – not just the time, for one can always find a spare half-hour, and I hope I have not wasted any such – but I have not found the concentration to write to you and, more to the point, I wanted to wait until I could tell you of definite news and accomplished deeds. [. . .]

Above all, you should know that *yesterday* I *completed* my *opera*, the score of which I shall sketch out in the summer.[1] It is a most extensive work, very rich and profound, and it undoubtedly signifies the summit of my artistic development so far. It grew, as one could say, under my hands, grew beyond all expectations and, as an essay with which I wished to make an auspicious beginning, it is, let us say, a major work which – more significantly – has a certain wellnigh reformatory importance in matters of style and also of form. – You will certainly be delighted at this news. But there is more. –

The man who gave me the pleasure of his friendship and helped me so munificently is no less than the American [piano] manufacturer *Steinway*;[2] a man with a warm heart and generous nature; whose attitude towards me is more that of a father than of a businessman. He is (hence) proposing to send me to America for a winter season, and the first time he would pay me 25,000 Francs for 4 months. But the offer is not binding, nor has he demanded any kind of contract, as I already told you. I ventured the journey to Hamburg to ask him for a large sum of money, and as he was at his Brunswick address, he cabled me from there, whereupon I called on him at once. Thus I was able to spend 3 beautiful days in his splendid villa. –

The third piece of good news is the following. I have been offered a post as piano professor at the Conservatoire in *Helsinki*[3] (Russia, Finland) for which (*only 9 months* of the year, 3 months holiday) they have proposed *four thousand Francs*, from 15 September until the following June.

Helsinki is a university town, a sea-port, in direct and close contact with St Petersburg.

The four thousand Francs (I have the *contract* in my hand) do not include casual earnings. Prof. *Riemann*[4] surprised me one day with a letter on this subject.

Until 15 September I must remain here and devote my time to writing the score of the opera. Needless to say, I have *accepted*.

Now we must discuss the following. I have never forgotten the promise I made to Mamma to take her with me the moment I was able to offer her a secure existence, and on this occasion I would not like to fail to keep my word. Therefore I suggest that she should join me in September and you can well imagine how much I would value her company, particularly in a city where I am unacquainted with the people, the language and the customs. –

On the other hand, I would point out that this is a case of a complete change of life-style and climate, of a lengthy journey which includes a brief sea-passage. Will she then be happy? I consider the post to be *provisional*, finding it expedient to accept it, as the *title* which I thereby gain will afford me the right to a more splendid position. Young and unknown as I still am, I would not be accepted by any major institution in Germany (be it a conservatoire, a theatre or a philharmonic concert society); matters take on a new light when one has already occupied a post as professor at a conservatoire.

With this I shall finish for today, anxiously awaiting your reply. – [. . .]

=====

PS   I have sent you a fine clarinet sonata by Draeseke,[5] which has just been published. – [. . .]

---

[1]The vocal score sketch of *Sigune* was evidently completed in May 1888, which would suggest that this letter was written early in June. Further sheets of *Sigune* sketches are dated 'Helsinki, 7 Nov. 1888' and 'Weimar, June 1889'. The Prelude to Act I, the only music which Busoni orchestrated, is marked 'Completed 11 March 1889'.
[2]Theodore Steinway (formerly Theodor Steinweg), 1825–1883, the perfector of the Steinway grand piano. He had opened a factory at Hamburg in 1880, while still maintaining the Grotrian-Steinweg works at Brunswick.
[3]Busoni consistently uses the Swedish form, Helsingfors.
[4]Hugo Riemann, 1849–1919, celebrated German musicologist and lexicographer.
[5]Felix Draeseke, 1835–1913, German composer. The young Egon Petri studied with him at the Dresden Conservatoire.

22　TO HENRI AND KATHI PETRI
in German

Helsinki 12.9.1888

Perhaps you are not aware how difficult it was for me to bid you farewell! For the first time I felt that I was leaving home; and just as I had never felt so at home as with you, I have also, methinks, never before so really set out for the unknown. Already in Lübeck I had a feeling of remoteness and strangeness, and when I boarded the ship and it sailed for days on end into the big wide world, I thought that I would finally disembark only to return home again at once.

This not insignificant journey left me with several impressions which I should like to record, but not for myself. It is to you both, my dearest friends, that I would like to address the notes I here set down; you, whose memory constantly animated my journey, shall now share it with me.

The journey to Lübeck was quite distressing. Drawing out of Leipzig, tiredness triumphed over excitement and I sank down in the coupé. I was forcibly woken in Wittenberg, where I and my dog had to change trains, this time with considerable resistance on the part of Lesko. After a brief ride, during which I had resumed my slumbers, I was once again rudely awoken, this time by our arrival at Büchen, where I had to wait two hours for my connection, long hours which seemed never-ending. A roll and butter and a bottle of cognac were the best company I could find. At last we reached Lübeck. Having cleared up the problems of my sea passage, I took a look at the town. A wonderfully characteristic little place, Lübeck, a genuine Hanseatic town from a better age, with its beautiful architectural tokens of a forgotten style and its industrious mercantile community; in the harbour hustle and bustle, picturesque maritime scenes.

I had expected rather more of the boat, the 'Storfursten', which plies regularly to and fro between Lübeck and Helsinki. It is a small, graceful ship which looks more like a pleasure steamer than a vessel suited to a long crossing. – Rather like the ones which sail between Trieste and Venice or Hamburg and Cuxhaven. There is little comfort and the quarters are cramped, but the passengers are few in number and ill-assorted. – In the middle of September one only travels to Finland if one has to! –

One hour after weighing anchor, a young man, whom I had not seen embarking, approached me and asked if he had the pleasure of speaking to Mr Busoni. He introduced himself as a colleague of mine at the school of music in Helsinki, the assistant piano teacher.

Our conversation restricted itself to the most trivial phrases; my every attempt at raising the level rebounded as if against a stone. The following is typical of my 'colleague'. I later found him avidly immersed in the 'Gartenlaube'.[1] I interrupted him and said: 'I do believe you are reading the serials in the Gartenlaube', this in a pretty unambiguous tone of voice. He replied, somewhat offended, 'Do you find anything wrong in that?' I considered this reply not to provide the foundation upon which to develop a literary conversation. – This is one of my colleagues. – The evening was quite pleasant and I went early to bed. My company also included a captain from the Silent Sea, who spoke a mishmash of English and Swedish, which I nevertheless succeeded in construing. He had travelled, as he assured me, in China,[2] India, South America etc., spoke of the climate[3] of these lands, drank a good deal of schnapps, smoked filthy cigarettes, was dressed all in grey (including a hat made of grey checked wool) and, constantly hopping about on bandy legs, he cut a droll figure with his diminutive stature and livid face, creased into a perpetual smile.

My third acquaintance was a young lecturer in Art History at the University of Helsinki,[4] who was returning from 3 years' sabbatical leave in Italy. He seems to be a truly splendid fellow and I spent a pleasant hour in conversation with him. He was travelling with his wife and their only child, who was born in Rome. I met him in Helsinki today and he very kindly invited me to visit him. – In the evening we all repaired to our cabins.

The following morning I was woken by an ominous rocking of the steamer. To observe the after-effects of getting overwhelmingly 'plastered' is a truly dramatic experience. The thin cabin walls may well have ears, but they are also most certainly perfect dancers. In bed it was impossible for me to tolerate the animation of my abode; I leaped out and courageously strode towards my fate. Having reached the foredeck, I was horrified to observe that the ship was the victim of a mental disorder. But what is the point of describing the well-known symptoms of this disease? I commended my stomach into the hands of the Almighty, who was at that moment amusing Himself by alternately raising and lowering the stem and stern of the boat on wires – a counterpart to [Uhland's] 'Riesenspielzeug'. God let nothing disturb His amusement but played all the more wildly; – I swallowed my pride and fed the fishes. Having thus lost my entire fortune, I was obliged – in order to make the tribute a worthy one – to offer up a portion of those generally immobile assets – gall and blood. For the following two days and nights I lay prone like a mummy, in utter gloom, on a sofa, just like a penitent in the wilderness, refusing all food and drink.

On the third day – that the words of the prophet might come to pass – the weather was wonderful and I felt better than ever.

People came up on deck again, looking happy, and greeted each other cordially. The 'silent seaman', with his grey woollen hat, was the only one who had not ceased hopping about during the two days and he laughed ostentatiously into his beard as we – landlubbers – crept out into the sun and air again. The day was a complete compensation for me, our passage and the weather were excellent and nicely varied by the re-sighting of land and our putting in at various ports. In the morning we docked at Hanko, where I and my 'colleague' disembarked. The place had an unique appearance. Passing a row of newly erected, half-finished wooden huts, we came to a more substantial pavilion on which one read the inscription: 'Grand Hôtel'.

Various huts had signs such as: drug store, Boeckhandel, Irish consulate etc. The roads were merely sand-tracks, not all of which had been fully pressed down. In the Hôtel we found a buffet with cold delicatessen, improvised as if at a folk festival on the green. There was no sign of any inhabitants; only after we had knocked several times and consumed half the buffet did a girl appear, who served us ale and beefsteak. – A seaside town in the process of being built. –

After a five-hour journey we arrived at Reval, a part German, part Russian town in Estonia. Our passage into Reval was superb and unforgettable. In the light of the setting sun we saw the town appear on a hilltop to our right, at its centre a palatial building with towers and around it the town houses, whose smoking chimneys made a bustling impression; on our left the thickly wooded coastline with villas and country houses concealed in shadowy groves, rising to a gentle incline; between the two the harbour, the landing-place, where we were greeted by a motley crowd dressed in Russian style, customs officials, soldiers, porters, cab drivers, bystanders and travellers. It was the Tsar's nameday; all the ships were decked with flags; not far from the harbour two mighty Russian frigates lay at anchor, impressive looking ironclad giants. But the sun went down behind the town in the shape of a gigantic dark red sphere and, as it disappeared, it left the whole scene bathed in an indescribable magic twilight which I had otherwise seen only in pictures. I wished you could have been with me. –

We did not reach Helsinki until late at night and thus I was denied the pleasure of what would doubtless have been just as beautiful a sight as the previous one.

Director Wegelius[5] was waiting for us: after we had dined, there was an exchange of friendly, conventional greetings; then I crept into bed and went to sleep only after having given way to the most melancholy thoughts. Far from you and my parents, for the first time amongst complete strangers who – to judge by first impressions – would never come up to my expectations, I felt abandoned and helpless for the first time in my life, at the very moment when I was about to take on an independent and secure position. I do believe – and am not ashamed of it – that I wept. Here I shall come to command the same respect which you accord me; but I shall never be loved here as you love me, and could I ever even partially be so well understood as you, Henri, and you, Kathi, have understood me? I think that as soon as I have satisfied myself that I shall have to remain misunderstood, I shall avoid any such attempt and restrict myself to the level of these people. – How stupid the world is, how insensitive to beauty and goodness! – I loathe stupidity, I can be unmercifully hard on stupid people.

As we were departing from Hanko, there stood a gypsy on the lonely, picturesque, rocky shore: a tall figure with fine features and the characteristically wild, sad expression of his race; his typical Southerner's quaint clothing contrasted strongly with the Nordic character of the landscape. Behind and all around him was the sea, his figure etched against its unending line; to one side, at some distance from him, was a group of holidaymakers in grotesque modern dress, laughing and shouting repulsively, the hollowness of society put on show in contrast to the poetry of an ancient race. I turned to one of my fellow travellers and drew his attention to the figure of the gypsy. 'If only the fellow was more decently clad,' he said. 'What,' I replied sarcastically, 'would he please you better if he wore narrow, checked trousers and an immaculate top-hat?' – 'Of course.' – There you are. –

Today I took a trip around Helsinki. The city is delightful, clean, with many a fine building, while the coast, with its many islands, cliffs and little coves, counts amongst the *most beautiful* I have ever seen. Wouldn't you like to spend your next summer holiday in Helsinki? The crossing from Lübeck only costs 56 Marks, my baggage and my dog travelled free of charge. – I am already making plans for Christmas. [. . .]

(It has grown quite dark.)

[1] 'A popular family periodical in respectable German circles', as Edward Dent describes it.
[2] Orig. Tschaina.
[3] Orig. Klaimäd.
[4] This was Johann Jakob Tikkanen, 1857–1930, who had been a lecturer in Fine Arts at the university of Helsinki since 1884.
[5] Martin Wegelius, 1846–1906, composer and teacher. Founded the Helsinki Musikinstitut in 1882.

23　TO HENRI AND KATHI PETRI
in German

Helsinki mid-September 1888

My lack of knowledge of the 'local' languages is giving rise to considerable difficulties. I can scarcely make myself understood to a waiter or a cab driver. Swedish, Russian, Finnish (a Magyar language) are spoken here but, in society, also German and French – proof of the country's lack of spiritual independence.

– As far as music is concerned, I can *give* but not *take*; one can teach but not learn, one *might* possibly introduce *new* things gradually and with great difficulty, but one could experience nothing new. In the musical centres (where the finest things of our time have already been achieved) one has the rewarding task of striving still *higher*, bringing one's own empathy, creativity and intellect into play. *Here* one has to content oneself with reproducing or imitating *a fragment* of that which has been achieved elsewhere.

There is no opera company here!

Kathi should read *Fathers and Sons* attentively and devotedly. This novel possesses the greatest narrative powers of more recent times. – Kathi should try to read as much as she can, because she has the right mentality for it.

However, as a woman she should aim to develop not so much her critical faculty as her sensitivity. Therefore she should not bother herself with academic books, because she would only come to look at things in an amateurish way and become half-educated. –

In this country one drinks very heavily. Schnapps is called for all day, before and after lunch, for breakfast and to fill in any idle moments.

I spoke with my 'superior', Director Wegelius, about methods of tuition. I asked if I should adhere to a *programme*, a specific method or any particular educational materials. – 'Actually we have no such things but, well – (after reflecting at some length) – one could perhaps take the Inventions of Bach as a starting point.[1] Plenty of Bach, plenty of Bach, also Mozart, Beethoven, Liszt . . . . . . ??!!!!!'

My 'colleague', the assistant piano teacher, is a blockhead and an artisan to boot; he gives lesson after lesson so as to be able to amuse himself pleasantly with the money he has earned. To work on his own initiative or strive for better things is thus out of the question. How could he, a man so very young, otherwise have sat it out here for four years!

The attitude towards women here is said to resemble that of *Gomorrah*. Living is very loose but – read about hereditary disease in Ibsen's 'Ghosts'!!

The *Jews* are restricted by law to a very small, fixed population, may only live in their own quarter, and as soon as the permitted number increases due to a childbirth, a family is transported over the border. A wretched, medieval outlook!

In return, the place is overrun with dogs, who run around quite freely. This actually makes life quite dangerous for Lesko, as all sorts of uncontrolled, vicious curs are nosing about.

I am going to have to live chiefly for my own work, only in *myself* am I likely to find any incentive to progress. I am hoping to rent a really comfortable apartment, so that I shall be strongly drawn to staying at home.

Tell Kathi that I have satisfactorily sorted out the matter with my librettist. I made a down payment of 200 Marks; he shall be paid the remaining 200 Marks as soon as I myself receive a royalty for the opera, also, in consideration of the three years' wait, which are contrary to the terms of the contract, an additional 100 Marks. –

Soon I shall be back in Germany.

---

[1]It was indeed with an instructive edition of Bach's Two- and Three-part Inventions, completed in Moscow in 1891 and dedicated to the Helsinki Musikinstitut, that Busoni inaugurated his lifelong dedication to the editing and performing of Bach's keyboard works.

24 TO HENRI AND KATHI PETRI
in German

Helsinki 25.9.1888
11 p.m.

[. . .] On average I give four hours' tuition daily: – do you know the picture of the circus clown with the trained geese? If you had a mind to see this very picture in the flesh, you would dress your dear friend Ferruccio in a pair of baggy trousers and paint his face white – but would have to change nothing as far as the young lady pupils are concerned! I have command of fifteen such waterfowl: Lesko has been promoted to the rank of sheep-dog and it's her job, if not to watch over the herd, then at least to give them a good sniff. –

My friend Stolz[1] became tired and debilitated when I played him classical masterworks, in good form, for a couple of hours – but just imagine four hours of Cramer études and Clementi sonatinas! Quite wretched! And yet I think I could in due course derive a certain amount of pleasure from the pedagogical aspect of my art; I could find interest in gradually developing my own system, in the gift of communication and in acquiring a general view of the technical organization of the subject etc.

But I am afraid that, with such continuous exposure to low standards, my own will fall, or I shall lose my yardstick for assessing the quality of a performance. From the standpoint of our most commendable institution, nothing appears that is not *good* or *talented* – while my vastly superior knowledge and ability in the higher echelons of the art world – compared with that of my pupils – is looked upon as a necessity, a foregone conclusion. If I were to get into the habit of assessing my ability in relation to my surroundings, what kind of a figure would I *actually* cut? I find this disturbing. – Perhaps the very dread of lagging behind will bring forth fruit and thus result in the opposite effect to what I fear.

Our 'Musikinstitut' (for this is its official name) scarcely even boasts a string quartet: the middle parts are played by students[2] (what sort of wonders Bolland[3] would work here) and the cello professor, until three years ago a travelling salesman, having given up his life in business, having been married for ten years and sired several children, is more or less at the beginning of his new career.[4] – The violinist is a man called Csillag,[5] who claims to have been a fellow student of Henri's for a short time at the Hochschule in Berlin. He was a professor at Rotterdam and lives on memories of early successes, triumphantly producing old programmes and reviews as evidence thereof. A sad existence! He is Jewish and has a talent for treading on everyone's toes; he has not yet succeeded in doing so with me, because I in turn have no talent for reacting to 'having my toes trodden on'. – As in all small towns, there is rivalry and the pettiest enviousness everywhere. To wit, we are at arms against an entire institution, the so-called orchestra. The leader of this band is a brother of Hans Sitt;[6] I have not yet made his acquaintance. A young man, a Finnish 'talent', conducts orchestral concerts with them, in which I shall probably soon be appearing as piano soloist. My intention is to waive my fee and, in return, demand a performance of my orchestral Suite in a further concert. I have also scheduled a *Beethoven* recital in the Conservatoire, in which I shall play solely and exclusively the music of this master. If this concert is successful, I shall follow it with three or four further recitals dedicated to the other masters of the piano literature. I shall scarcely be able to do more than that here. From what I have heard, the 'orchestra' seems to be the more ambitious, powerful and promising of the two institutions and it is therefore my intention not to demonstrate any hostile feeling towards it. And the orchestra itself will make it its business to maintain friendly relations with the '*best player*' in town. –

All in all I must still look upon this stay as a stepping stone and at present I do not *wish* to think more of it than that. –

I shall interrupt my writing to go to bed. I am tired and not very well. It is 12.30 in the morning. – I can picture your bedroom. Egon, at least, is in bed. You two not yet, perhaps, for in Leipzig there is still half an hour before midnight. But soon all three of you will be gently breathing side by side. I can also picture the Kurprinzstrasse, dark and deserted, just as it was when I used to close your front door behind me. Your dear silhouettes appear once again at the window and wave to me, Henri whistles and I answer – I wave my hat for the last time and turn the corner . . . Sometimes I view the panoramic lights of the town and then pass your house again. Of course I peer up at the window – every time I am almost hurt that everything has gone dark up there, and sadly I hurry on towards the Albertkirche. I can see everything, but everything so clearly – I could count the paces I imagine I have taken. What a wonderful time we had together! And I came to be very fond of Leipzig as well. At the end I was on good terms with everyone. I found the business dealings of the publishers and my involvement with them so very interesting. Breitkopfs were already treating me as if I were their oldest, most trustworthy fellow-worker. I always heard of the latest developments at once – well! You can tell that it is late at night, for I am beginning to dream! Farewell for now, good night, my friends; how I would like to embrace you all!——

1 o'clock in the morning
25–26 Sept

One meets one's compatriots everywhere. Where in Leipzig it was the dance-prodigy Golinelli and the Mandelbäcker brothers, in Hamburg the grey-haired heldentenor Paneani[7] and the Siamese twins, here too the honourable representatives of my country, whose company I have to consider my duty to the fatherland, are a circus troupe. The same types the world over. Thus, for instance, there is one specimen that can be found just as readily in Cairo as in Berlin, the so-called 'professeur de langue française'. We had such a fellow on board ship. So striking was his similarity to those colleagues of his I had met

in Vienna and other places that he seemed almost like an old friend. I heard
an amusing story about one of these fellows. He wanted to translate a Finnish
folksong which begins:

'Oh Finland, land of a thousand lakes'.

No, said the professeur, that is an exaggeration, c'est exagéré. I shall write:

'Finland, oh land of a hundred lakes'.

The Finn who was helping him with the translation presented the professeur
with a survey map of the country, with the aid of which, after taking a precise
count, it was established that the Finnish lakes go well into the *hundreds*. So
Monsieur made up his mind to write:

'Salut Finnlande,
beau pays des milles lacs'.

=====

Lest I forget, I shall ask Henri now if he knows Rubinstein's violin concerto
and what he thinks of it. I find it very fine and considerably better than
most of Rubinstein's works. Henri should play it. The Adagio is superbly
beautiful. – [. . .]

Sunday 7 October 1888

I was certain you would be pleased, indeed impressed by the figure of
Basarov. At the age of nineteen I made the great but forgivable mistake of
artificially assuming the air of a Turgenev hero, whereby I succeeded in
provoking the desired feeling of astonishment and stupefaction in certain so-
called 'highbrow' women. But my 'character pose' collapsed due to the
inconsistency that I as an artist, like Basarov, could *not* renounce my art. So I
modified this point by defining art as technical accomplishment in imitating
life – whether in colours, words or forms. Indeed, I even tried to explain the
sensation inspired and aroused by art in terms of purely physical or scientific
causes and effects. This period was also one of virtual sterility for me as a
composer; at that time I started my [second] string quartet and was able to
carry on from the two opening pages only after an interval of two years!
Fortunately I had in the meantime learnt an individual and sincere mode of
behaviour.[8]

I only wanted to imply thereby how seductive Basarov's personality is and,
above all, how flexible and tangible Turgenev makes him and how directly
he can impinge upon susceptible souls. The author's art in this book is also
truly unparalleled; look at the way he depicts, for example, Basarov's
parents! It must have been this passage where I scribbled remarks about my
father in the margin. [. . .]

The beginning of this letter was written several days ago. In the meantime
I have performed in the Institut's first 'Musikabend' with exceptional success. After this triumph it has now been decided that I am to give a series of
piano recitals, which I shall wish to have counted as extra hours of tuition.

The programme: I. Beethoven; II. Bach (Mozart, Scarlatti, Handel); III. Chopin; IV. Schumann, Mendelssohn, Weber; V. Modern composers (Brahms, Rubinstein, Grieg, Sgambati etc.) which may be followed by a 6th recital with my own works. I also already have many private pupils. I must admit that my life as piano teacher *privatim* seems to be extremely pitiable. At the appointed hour I arrive at some young lady's house. I can vividly imagine how, 5 minutes before, in expectation of me, she has just put away her French homework. A ring at the door. Mamma exclaims (interestedly to her daughter but quite indifferent towards me), 'Ah, the piano teacher.' – Whereupon I enter to encounter mother and daughter 'in the oncoming direction' already in the salon. A brief, conventional exchange of handshakes and phrases, after which Mamma retires. At the end of the lesson she reappears and goes through the same procedure as before, but in the reverse order. On my *first* visit Papa, councillor of commerce, attorney general or wholesaler, also makes an appearance in order to settle the price, treating me like some better prospective manservant. In a word, the outward appearance is the contrary of what I feel; a doleful part I have to play, even if I might occupy the most prominent and respected post here as ivory tickler! –

In the first Musikabend I played Grieg's new violin sonata[9] (which – incidentally – is already coming out of my ears) with Herr Csillag, Henri's former and my present colleague. It took a great effort of persuasion on my part, because he had insisted on playing Goldmark or Rubinstein.

14 October

To return to Csillag, he subscribes to an outmoded, mannered (Viennese) school. He scoops all the time and is unable to play so much as a third without slithering through it in microtones. He also plays in such a way that, when a triplet crops up, he has to drag it out really slowly.

Da-da-da-doo – that's how it sounds. – [. . .]

The day before yesterday I played my Beethoven recital. (Sonatas: op. 2 [no. 1?], op. 31 Appassionata and the last (op. 111), also: Variations and fugue in E major (Eroica) and the posthumous Ecossaises).[10] – It was said that nothing like it had been heard here since Bülow and Rubinstein. I was also in superb form and played as I only rarely can. The success was enormous, the Ecossaises had to be encored, the critics have praised me to the skies. It was perhaps my most *significant* achievement as a pianist so far, a Beethoven concert which lasted 2¼ hours! – At least the *compulsion* here can do the *pianist* Ferruccio some good. –

Unfortunately I have very, very little time to myself. And even if I have kept every morning free until 1 o'clock, the five lessons in the afternoons (as many as that now) are so tiring that I am happiest to spend the mornings going for walks. In the evenings I am idle too. Nothing doing. There is a miserable theatre where every night for the last two weeks *La Traviata* has been performed in Swedish. You can imagine it! – Director Faltin,[11] a good musician (perhaps the only really serious one here) has showed me a good deal of sympathy and understanding; but he is so busy that I am able to call on him only infrequently.

I am gladder than ever of Lesko's company. I have come to see that there is actually *no* danger for her. The first impression was like that recounted of the prisoner who, having served a long term, on finally being released, steps with initial regret out of the building of which he has become so fond. Indeed Lesko has made some good *personal* friends and I almost fear that one of these has come too close . . . . . . !

The quality of life is also as yet still imperfect here. Although one can eat very well (but expensively), the water, for example, is undrinkable and, with its muddy yellow colour, is disgusting even for washing. A decent cigar is not to be had for less than 50 Pfennigs (= 50 Centimes), while a closed droshky is like something out of Wonderland; a land whose realization is to be found in the words 'St Petersburg'. –

Our droshkys are small, *scarcely* big enough for two people, all are unlit and have no brakes: they drive uphill at the gallop and downhill like the wind. All the drivers wear caftans and indescribable hats, something between a topper and a cap, broader at the top than at the brim, with a buckle in front. The cabbies all look like brothers, with snub noses, cleanshaven white faces and stringy blond hair. Finnish women of all stations could be said to offer them a fair counterpart; something like Artner's face rendered into yellow or ash-blond, while their figures tend to be angular, their curves flattened! Only the wives of the officers are pretty, and they are all Russian.

The word 'Petersburg' reminded me of Edition *Peters*, who have sent me my '*Bagatelles*'[12] which, to my surprise and delight, they have published. This is no slight satisfaction to me. As I only received 5 free copies, I assume that the sixth has been sent to you.

=====

I am still unable to concentrate on my own work and yesterday, when I came to realize this, felt horrendously down in the dumps – on top of which my nerves were so on edge that I felt like 'exploding'! However, the previous day I had taught for 4 hours, practised just as long and, in the evening, given my Beethoven recital! – I would give anything for a theatre here like the one in Leipzig, which we never stopped running down! And the much despised *Gewandhaus* [orchestra] appears from this distance as the ideal of all musical aspirations! [. . .]

=====

It's about time that I finished this letter.

The orchestral concerts under the direction of Kajanus[13] (with Sitt as leader) have begun and are at any rate the best things to be had here. The popular concerts are given *twice* (!) a week (I enclose the first programme, which should raise an eyebrow) and cost one Mark for admission with a place at a table (after the manner of Bilse);[14] which is certainly laudable. The orchestra is young but also small (6 1st violins, 2 double-basses), while the conductor has absolutely no understanding of the classics (Mozart's Adagio was rushed, slovenly and dull, lacking in patience and care), but despite this and that it is *something*; something which may reconcile me a little to the conditions in Helsinki but which shows up the appalling state of *our* Institut, on the other hand, only too clearly. – Just imagine, after my much admired, stunningly reviewed, in a word quite mind-boggling Beethoven recital, an entirely *inept student* is supposed to perform – hard on its heels – for the same concert series, Beethoven's great (or at least intellectually gigantic) Trio in D major! – The cheek of it! I shall oppose this (the lady is a pupil of mine).[15] – [. . .]

======

I got to know Paderewski's Variations[16] (a pleasant, well-written piece) nearly 4 years ago. P. himself lived in Vienna and was a protégé of Leschetitzky.

How can one open the wonderful series of Gewandhaus concerts with Eyr![17] And Beethoven's *wretched* 'Ritterballett' music![18] (As is generally known, Beethoven permitted a *Count* who had devised the ballet to *attribute* the work to him; – you can read about it in one of the Almanacs from Gotha from the last century.)[19] On the other hand I played (my own arrangement of) Beethoven's *Ecossaises* here (which were also previously unknown) with great success. I wrote about them earlier. *Svendsen*[20] should be encouraged, I have heard some very attractive, fine, tasteful and original things of his. [. . .]

======

Give Egon a fond kiss from me for his good behaviour at school. I am pleased and delighted at his liveliness too, even if it verges on indiscipline.

Later on in life, especially in the hazardous years of puberty, I hope he will retain his healthy disposition, which nowadays tends to disappear after childhood, even though it can be a useful asset in the seriousness of professional life.

But my advice to open the boy's eyes to the facts of life at the right time is premature and superfluous (you know this better than I). Reticence or embarrassment on the part of a father, strict supervision without any explanation to justify it, these things are harmful to a growing young *man*, because nothing that is natural can forcibly be subdued and when an outlet has to be found, it could otherwise be sought in wrong and detrimental directions. Please forgive this outburst of sermonizing: of course it has less bearing on you and Egon than on *myself* and my own recollections. [. . .]

Finally one more thing.

I ask you once again to take up the matter in question with Nikisch, and to take Reinecke[21] on one side as soon as the opportunity occurs, to ask him to intervene with the former in the matter of my orchestral Suite, which he had *once again* half promised to perform. I really don't want to waste time on an official letter, so would beg you to consider carrying out this small, unpleasant errand (perhaps unpleasant) as a good turn (shall we say, a half-turn).

My fondest greetings to you all.

[1]Leopold Stolz, 1866–1957, Austrian conductor and composer, brother of the operetta composer Robert Stolz. For many years he was a conductor at the theatre in Wiesbaden.

[2]The second violinist was Jean Sibelius.

[3]Bolland was second violinist in the Petri Quartet during the 1880s.

[4]This was Wilhelm Renck, ?–?, a German musician who had come to Helsinki in 1887 but remained there only for two years.

[5]Hermann Csillag, ?–?, remembered chiefly for having taught Sibelius the violin.

[6]Anton Sitt, 1847–1929, Bohemian violinist. He came to Helsinki in 1882 and became leader of the Philharmonic Orchestra in 1885, a post he retained until his retirement in 1923. His brother, Hans Sitt, 1850–1922, was one of the most celebrated violinists of his time.

[7]Busoni met Paneani at Hamburg in October 1887. He described him, in an undated letter to Ferdinando Busoni, as 'a highly distinguished person who has befriended the leading Hamburg families. What a character!!'

[8]Melanie Mayer recalls: 'When he was still very young, he was characterized by a strange coolness and reserve. He knew this and regretfully sensed it to be an inhibition. He doubted whether he could open his heart to anyone and did not know that the ability to show deep feeling was nevertheless given to him and was merely still latent.' (Melanie Prelinger, 'Erinnerungen und Briefe aus Ferruccio Busonis Jugendzeit', in *Neue Musik-Zeitung*, 1927, 6–10, 37–40, 57–61.)

[9]Sonata no. 3 in c, op. 45 (composed 1885–7). The performance with Hermann Csillag took place at the Musikinstitut on 4 October 1888.

[10]Busoni's transcription of the *Ecossaises*, dedicated to his fiancée, Gerda Sjöstrand, was published in 1889.

[11]Richard Faltin, 1835–1918, German virtuoso organist and conductor. He came to Helsinki in 1869 as conductor and director of music at the university.

[12]Bagatelles, op. 28, for violin and piano. These are four easy pieces, composed in April 1888 for the six-year-old Egon Petri (who studied the violin before becoming a pianist).

[13]Robert Kajanus, 1856–1933, the distinguished Finnish conductor. So great was the enmity between Orchestra and Musikinstitut in Helsinki that Sibelius did not meet him personally until 1890, while studying in Berlin.

[14]Benjamin Bilse, 1816–1902, conducted daily concerts in Berlin from 1868 to 1884. In 1882 members of his orchestra formed the Berlin Philharmonic on democratic principles, in protest against the poor working conditions in Bilse's orchestra.

[15]Busoni himself played two other Beethoven trios in Helsinki, op. 1 no. 2 in c on 21 November 1888 and op. 70 no. 2 in E flat on 16 March 1889, both with Csillag and Renck, at the Musikinstitut.

[16]*Variations et fugue sur un thème original* (composed *c.* 1883, published 1885).
[17]Eyr = Weber's overture to *Euryanthe*. The Gewandhaus season 1888–9 opened with
this work on 29 September 1888.
[18]*Musik zu einem Ritterballett*, WoO 1, composed 1790–1 in Bonn.
[19]Busoni is wrong. Although H. Reichard attributes the work to Count Ferdinand
von Waldstein in his *Theater-Kalender auf das Jahr 1792*, Gotha, it was in fact
composed by Beethoven.
[20]Johan Svendsen, 1840–1911, Norwegian composer, today best remembered for his
Romance for violin and orchestra.
[21]Carl Reinecke, 1824–1910, German pianist, composer and conductor. From 1860 he
was professor of composition at the Leipzig Conservatoire.

25   TO HENRI PETRI
in German

Weimar 18.8.1889

The quartet,[1] Bach fugue[2] and libretto[3] are to be published in September or
October.

In the next few days I shall have completed all the revisions.

NB. I have heard that the [Ring of the] Nibelung is being given in Dresden
on 24, 26, 28 and 31 August.[4] This would be a good opportunity of
'educating' Mamma (and also *Paul*),[5] and simultaneously making them
acquainted with the splendours of Dresden and above all with you, my
dearest ones.

So, my friend, tell me if it is altogether unfeasible, some mere composer's
whim, to obtain complimentary tickets for the three of us at the performances.

(I realize, all too late, that I am again trying to scrounge something from
you; but then, I come from Italy where, as everybody knows, crowds of
beggars lie on the steps of the holy places.)

But it is the method and also the fate of the creative artist to *give* so as to
take. I am not taking (am thus taking no advantage of my fair rights) but am
merely *asking* and will if necessary condescend to supplicate.

Kindest greetings to you and Kathi.

No. 2 Mother sends 'respectful' greetings.

No. 3 We are both agreed that Egon should be given a big kiss.

No. 4 Paul reiterates Nos. 2 and 3.

[1]Quartet No. 2 in d, op. 26.
[2]Prelude and Fugue in D, BWV 532, transcribed for piano. Busoni's first Bach
transcription, made in May 1888.
[3]*Sigune*, which was published privately under the auspices of Breitkopf und Härtel.
[4]In August 1888 Busoni had visited the Bayreuth festival.
[5]Adolf Paul, 1863–1943, real name Georg Wiedersheim, Swedish pupil of Busoni's at
Helsinki. Later became a writer and close friend of Strindberg.

26 TO HENRI PETRI
in German

Helsinki 11.12.1889

Recently I seem to have read in the 'Signale for the world of music and muttonheads'[1] that Concertmaster Petri, instead of behaving with due reserve during his first season in Dresden and only appearing on a few worthy occasions, played Schubert with a certain Mr Johannes (who was 'moreover' not well) and was actually the success of the evening.

From afar I can already see how my esteemed friend will be getting all excited about the 'young talents' whose qualities 'one did not detect at all from first, fleeting impressions', how he will be inviting 'just Johannes' round and playing works through with him etc. etc. – [. . .]

=====

I'm afraid I cannot spend Christmas with you. My work demands that I make full use of the final days before having to travel to Leipzig, where on 8 and 9 January I am playing [Beethoven's] E♭ major concerto and a new concerto of my own, and then, on the 11th, Tchaikovsky's A minor Trio with Brodsky.[2]

What news is there of your trip to Russia?

What are you up to altogether?

As for my own concerto or Konzertstück or symphonic piano concerto,[3] I consider it to have come off well, as it is characterized less by 'counterpoint, rhythmic energy and harmonic agitation' than by power of imagination, original structure and effective orchestration.

I very much hope you can be in Leipzig for the event and also hope to see you.

A fond kiss to the dearest of children (also from Lesko, who has now become a most worthy mother of 10) and kindest greetings to Kathi. –

[1] i.e. *Signale für die musikalische Welt.*

[2] Adolf Brodsky, 1851–1929, Russian violinist. At that time professor at the Leipzig Conservatoire.

[3] Concert-Fantasie for orchestra with piano obbligato, op. 29, composed in Helsinki 1888–9, unpublished. Busoni later re-wrote the work for orchestra alone as *Symphonisches Tongedicht*, op. 32a.

27 TO HENRI PETRI
in German

Helsinki 3.4.1890

Your letter and the greetings from your dear ones came as an almost unexpected and most welcome birthday gift, all the more desirable in that it affords me the opportunity of making up my mind: in particular to unburden my heart to you fully once again.

Truly, this is something of a necessity, especially since I have had to do without the familiar company of your hospitable household and the attendant pleasures of *communication*: the comforting feeling of always having an ear prepared to hear, a heart prepared to sympathize. – If ever I was (or was *considered*) taciturn towards you, I am now in certain respects more silent than the pillars of Memnon, which at least make a sound at sunrise. My mother differs from me so widely in her views that I dare not express an opinion for fear of hearing some reply of the kind that I have at last, with the greatest struggle, eliminated from my beliefs and superstitions!

I believe I am speaking very obscurely; and that anyone but yourselves would fail to understand me: – but it would be ungrateful if I were to fail to mention that I have in my fiancée a great compensation for your remoteness, a companion who is ready to sacrifice and risk everything to enable me to reach my goal, – who understands me completely, even if not musically then at least spiritually, without being blind: so that her high opinion of me and her criticisms unite to become a beneficial influence.——

Herewith I shall terminate this report on my fiancée, to avoid any suspicion of becoming sentimental or lovesick. I consider that I have also said the last word about my mother for the time being.

As for that other individual indispensable for the act of procreation, I would say, with Heine: 'Es ist eine alte Geschichte'——He is the embodiment of the great cycle of Nature with its periodically recurring phenomena, as for instance: spring storms, autumn winds, ebb and flow, lunar eclipse and other such eternal truths. In the case of Nature, the blessing emanates from the Creator; in this case, it is to the Creator that it finds its way back.

My situation here has remained so unpropitious for the furtherance of my artistic aims that – despite my tripartite responsibility – I shall *shelve* the matter or, to put it plainly: let it go to Hell.

My vacation, which does not begin until *1 June*, shall find me as deposed piano professor and fortunate non-owner of everything imaginable. Therefore the news about Breslau was highly relevant. Such a post would be the only kind of '*dependence*' I would really happily shoulder and my thanks for your kind actions could not be warmer. So I would ask you to take steps to guarantee me a trial period there. I shall take this opportunity to tell you that my orchestral Suite has been performed here *under my own direction*[1] and that it was generally felt: the local orchestra's performance was the *best* it had ever given; the orchestral players themselves also said that they played with greater confidence and inspiration under me. This only so as to indicate my aptitude for conducting, in which I nevertheless still require experience and practice.

But I have something else to tell you. I have played in St Petersburg. First for the Kammermusikverein, later with Auer[2] in the presence of Rubinstein.[3] I had an uncommon success. It does not often happen that two encores of solo pieces are demanded after a Beethoven trio, but this was the case. The result was that I had to play for a third time, in the orchestral series (exceptionally, under *R.*'s own direction), with equal success.[4]

Strangely enough, it has since become an accepted fact that I shall be settling in St Petersburg: but I myself (despite much encouragement from influential persons) would not dream of burying myself as a piano teacher in this city of tainted artistic taste and social prejudice.

On the other hand I intend to take part in the major competition for pianists and composers which Rubinstein is promoting at the end of the summer and in which 10,000 Francs are to be won. What do *you* think of that? I was also strongly urged to this. In which case I would consider spending the summer here. Participation in the competition calls for hard work. – From which I have not shirked all winter, incidentally, so that I now feel fairly exhausted. Amongst other things I should mention the arrangement of a further organ fugue of Bach,[5] which has turned out even greater and more powerful than the first; I hope dear Kathi has already received a copy of the latter. So, now I have nothing more to say of myself! –

As for dear Egon, I must admit to having no particular scruples at present. Consider yourself fortunate in having so talented a boy. –

What I can say from my own memories of being an infant prodigy is that it was very useful to me to have been impressed from the outset by the possibility and necessity of becoming a great man; whereby dissatisfaction was always expressed at my achievements so far. My attention was successfully drawn to young men who had just attained some distinction and were mentioned in the papers; I remember that such reports always gave me a jolt. The system was one of spurring on my highly developed sense of ambition. But apparent dissatisfaction, head-shaking and lecturing should not be exaggerated; for it can easily lead to discouragement or defiance.

Later too, in my student days, competitiveness towards my fellow students was more of an incentive than the actual thing. True seriousness did not appear until the onset of adulthood and independent character. Until a few years ago I hated and neglected my piano playing. I used to prefer reading to making music.

While appearing to speak only of myself, I am actually directing my words chiefly towards Egon, about whom (I repeat) you can at present rest assured.

As there are no suitable teachers in the world of music nowadays for such as he (particularly those who make it clear that everything theoretical is easy and straightforward and quickly learnt; instead of the opposite), it would be my special wish to become Egon's master myself later on. For it seems inevitable to me that he is to be a musician. Send him my fondest greetings. [. . .]

Lesko is well and has become a mother for the second time. Her romance (which happened at Christmas time) was almost human.[6] More another time. [. . .]

[1]Busoni conducted his *Symphonic Suite*, op. 25, for the Orkesterföreningen, Helsinki, on 27 February 1890.

[2]Leopold Auer, 1845–1930, distinguished Hungarian violinist. Professor at the St Petersburg Conservatoire from 1868.

[3]The first concert, on 17 (29) January 1890, for the Kammermusikverein (Chamber Music Society) included Sinding's Piano quartet in e, op. 5, a Bach organ fugue transcribed by Liszt, Beethoven's Ecossaises and Paganini–Liszt *La Campanella*. The second concert, on 20 January (1 February), for the Russian Musical Society, included Beethoven's 'Geister' Trio, Busoni's transcription of a Bach organ fugue (not specified on the programme) and, again, Beethoven's Ecossaises.

[4]There is no traceable record of this concert.

[5]Prelude and Fugue in Eb, BWV 552 ('St Anne'), published by Rahter, Hamburg, in 1890.

[6]Lesko moved to Moscow with her master later in 1890 and died there in January 1895.

28 TO FERDINANDO BUSONI
in Italian

Moscow 6(18).5.1891

I am recovering from a bout of *influenza* which started with a temperature and sore throat and has dragged itself out now for eight days, apart from which I am *so* busy that I feel truly exhausted and prostrate. Hence, for example, the day before yesterday I had to be present at *7 hours of examinations* and give a further *3 hours' tuition* at the Conservatoire, making altogether *ten* hours of the pianoforte for my poor head! This month will be hard because of the examinations; moreover I myself have my hands full with work (e.g. the Bach *Inventions* and other smaller works, which are being published), I may not neglect the piano and, to crown it all, I am learning English. Add to this a fairly lively correspondence and you will not be surprised, at least I hope you will forgive me for having had to delay so long in writing to you. –

This is why I am studying English:

Already some months ago, I told you how dissatisfied I was with my position in Moscow. *Deceitful colleagues*, a *disinclination towards foreigners* (because of *nationalism*), the *decline in musical taste* and finally the constrained *financial situation* due to the conditions in the country (in case you do not always believe in my financial difficulties), in which I find myself.

It so happened (already in Berlin in January) that I had a *splendid* offer for *America*, and negotiations have continued until today. I therefore wanted to wait until the matter was concluded; I had anyway ascertained that I would be able to opt out, should I change my mind.

I have had an offer (in the same capacity as here) from the Conservatoire in Boston (which is the leading city in musical life) with 18 thousand Francs for ten months, not including various additional emoluments. Apart from this, *Steinway*[1] (the brother of my deceased protector) has assured me of his support and thirdly my old acquaintance *Nikisch* is there (in Gericke's[2] position), where he has earned a great reputation, and he will certainly give me the opportunity for publicity and financial gain.

My plan is: to occupy a permanent post for the first year and then, in the second, (having made my name) to embark on a major *tour*, thus gaining peace of mind for two or three years in which I can improve myself. –

Many of my friends are over there; the cellist *Schröder*[3] is also leaving this autumn to become principal cellist in Nikisch's orchestra.

Tell me, my dear ones, I beg you – what do you think of this plan? I shall be occupying the *leading position in the country*; while here in Russia I shall never manage to oust the Russian celebrities, who have been established here for a long time. –

And if I should not be happy, well – after a year I shall return with a little money in my pocket and the pleasure of having made a fine journey free of charge!

The confusion brought about by this plan prevents me sending you the money you need until June. I myself have no more than 50 Rubles for the whole month (note that here it is only the *6th*, and in June I shall be paid a larger amount). –

At all events, should the plan be confirmed, I hope to make a rendezvous with you and Mamma in Vienna, to embrace you before my departure.

Meanwhile I greet you with all my heart, together with Gerda.[4]

---

[1]William Steinway, 1836–1896. Theodore Steinway had died on 20 March 1889.
[2]Wilhelm Gericke, 1845–1925, distinguished Austrian conductor and dedicatee of Busoni's *Comedy Overture*. He later worked in Boston again from 1898 until 1908.
[3]Alwin Schröder, 1855–1928, cellist of the Petri Quartet and dedicatee of Busoni's *Kleine Suite*, op. 23. In Boston he also played in the Kneisel Quartet.
[4]Busoni had married Gerda Sjöstrand on 27 September 1890.

29 TO THEODORE THOMAS
in German

Boston Mass. 25.6.1892

Through Mr Trelbar[1] you have come to hear – as I believe – of my great desire to come into artistic contact with you. –

My participation in one of your world-famous symphony concerts in the coming season would be of decisive value for my reputation, and therefore I would ask you to be so kind as to grant me such an opportunity. –

Unfortunately my personal commitments do not permit me to meet you during the summer, which I would otherwise not have failed to do.

---

[1]Evidently Busoni's agent in Boston.

30   TO THEODORE THOMAS
in German

Boston Mass. 29.7.1892

[. . .] I would prefer to come to Chicago in the period *before Christmas,* should this somehow be possible.

As for my repertoire, I was very happy in Boston with the *G major concerto of Beethoven* (my own cadenzas);[1] naturally I also play the concerto in Eb major, both Liszt concertos also Schumann, amongst others, and one of my own (in one movement).[2] Would it be advisable to appear for the first time as a *pianist* with this work? It was awarded the Rubinstein prize.

Should you have any particular wish concerning the choice of work, I would ask you to suggest it in good time. –

It would be best if you settled the question of the fee on your own or with Mr Trelbar. –

[1]Busoni had played this work in Boston, under Nikisch's direction, on 13 and 14 November 1891. The cadenzas were composed in 1890 and entered for the Rubinstein prize.
[2]*Konzertstück*, op. 31a. Completed in June 1890 and also entered for the Rubinstein prize.

31   TO ANNA BUSONI
in Italian

New York 24.9.1893

[. . .] Two things are on my mind today. I. Thanks to an excellent pupil whom I taught in Boston, I find myself in possession of some rare and highly interesting *first editions* of the works of *Liszt.* – These, together with other more recent editions, constitute a 'Lisztiana' of nearly 50 volumes.

There arose in me (as usual) the mania to complete this collection of the great master's piano works as far as possible★ and, knowing that you possess a goodly number of items *published during your youth*, I would ask you:

to be so kind as to draw up an *exact list* of *those works of Liszt* in *your* possession and to send it to me as soon as possible. –
NB. The Liszt *original* editions are valuable! 1) because they are no longer *available*, secondly because they *differ greatly* from the new editions and are more difficult.

══

★a difficult undertaking, as there are no opus numbers and many have vanished from the market, while others are forgotten or indeed unknown.

II. Having acquired a reasonable knowledge of world literature, I note with regret that I am entirely unacquainted with the works of *Mazzini* and with Guerazzi's *L'Asino*. These two works, the one of the heart, the other of the *head*, must be read. Let me know how much they cost and I shall send you the money. How are things with Carducci? –

For today, in haste. –

Monsieur le père, écrira-t-il?

III

1894 – 1904
The Virtuoso

32 TO GIUSEPPE VERDI
in Italian[1]

[Berlin undated][2]

Long have I felt and nurtured the desire – which soon became necessity and now irresistible compulsion – to open my heart to you, to make some kind of contact with Italy's leading composer, with one of the noblest persons of our time.

But my diffidence, the scant reputation on which I could pride myself, the insignificant tokens of talent which I may have been able to offer as justification for so honourable and singular a connection had always served to restrain me. I felt unable to take a step which could so easily have appeared presumptuous and would certainly have been considered as such.

My childhood was occupied with serious study, diligent perseverance and reflection, nourished and supported by the arts and sciences of Germany. But scarcely had I developed beyond the theoretical stage, in that period between youth and adulthood – in which I now find myself – than I began to grasp the *spirit* and the *soul* of art, to comprehend and draw closer to it. So it was that I came relatively late – please forgive me – to an admiration of your master-works, with which I became enraptured. Finally 'Falstaff' provoked in me such a revolution of spirit and feeling that I can with ample justification date the beginning of a new epoch in my artistic life from that time.

This event made me sad at heart; for I realized how great was the distance separating me from a loved and honoured master, almost beyond the reach of so insignificant a person as myself. Yet the consciousness of having at last arrived at an understanding of your genius would not have presented sufficient justification for an attempted approach, had I not at the same time succeeded in writing a work in which I believe I have achieved a legitimate recommendation of myself to you.

Permit me, renowned master, in all humility to submit this work to you for your appraisal; it will arrive together with this letter.

I tremble and hope: my heart will not rest until some sign has been sent from you. I dare not demand or beg you for a word. But, should you do me the honour of such a distinction, it would be a deed of inestimable goodness and would perhaps give me consolation and encouragement, fill me with self-confidence and enrich my insight.

[1]The Italian original is untraceable; this translation has been made from Dr Friedrich Schnapp's published German rendering (see Sources).
[2]The letter was written in 1894 to accompany the score of Busoni's *Symphonisches Tongedicht*, op. 32a. Neither score nor letter were ever sent.

33   TO LUDWIG VON BÖSENDORFER
         in German

Berlin 14.12.1895

[. . .] I cannot find the words to express the surprise and joy which your telegram signifies to me,[1] nor to thank you adequately for your trust in me and for your swift, honourable and hence successful manner of dealing. Let it suffice to say that I have fully comprehended the significance of your cable and that I am making myself ready to match my accomplishment to the level of the occasion on which it is to be presented. – As for the programme, I recall firstly that 'solo items' have been banned from the programmes of the 'Philharmonic'. It is therefore a matter of finding a concerto (with orchestra) which would present as complete a picture as possible of myself as a pianist. On the other hand, I doubt whether it would be wise to make one's Viennese début with a work by *Liszt*.

The concerto no. 5 (in E♭ major) by Rubinstein would have the virtue of combining many pianistic constituents. Incidentally it will have been played only very occasionally (perhaps only by the master himself). Apart from which it is one of Rubinstein's best works, certainly his *best piano* work, and for this reason worth hearing.

Therefore I would like to suggest this piece and ask you kindly to make a decision about it.

If there are reservations – what attitude would one take to Liszt? If he is also held in disdain – what then?

I am (frankly) reluctant to introduce myself with Beethoven. I would have to suppress my individuality and also my virtuosity too strongly. These reservations only hold true in the case of a *début*.

Please excuse my ending abruptly, for I am about to set off for Belgium.

[1]Busoni had been invited to play a piano concerto with the Vienna Philharmonic Orchestra.

34   TO ANNA AND FERDINANDO BUSONI
         in Italian

Berlin 27.2.1896

You will certainly be not a little pleased to hear that, after many years' preparation and waiting, I have succeeded in vindicating myself in Vienna.

My success on 16 Feb. was extraordinary. All my old *'friends'* were present. Leschetitzky, Brahms,[1] Hanslick, Epstein, Rosenthal,[2] Gutmann[3] and a thousand others.

Hanslick wrote more or less as follows:

'It was with something between anxiety and expectation with which we prepared to hear Busoni again after 20 years, having already admired him as a boy of nine. Let us say at once that he has fully realized the great hopes which we had founded upon him as a child. Busoni is now one of the foremost pianists and the one who comes closest to Rubinstein. We found that Busoni commands the same great touch, enormous confidence, extraordinary suppleness and unparalleled bravura of Rubinstein.' –

(I am translating from memory, as I don't have the article by me, which incidentally was published in the edition for Sunday 23 Feb. of the Neue Freie Presse.)[4]

=====

Unfortunately I am ill with influenza and with this trifling complaint I have to play tomorrow in Dresden. My finances too have their ups and downs, and it was with great reluctance that I was *obliged* to send you the telegram on the 24th. –

I hope that the rent can wait a little while, especially as you have always been punctual with it. –

If my successes continue in this fashion, I hope to be rich in a few years, or at least comfortably off, and then, for you too, better times will come. [. . .]

NB. I wrote to Bösendorfer for a piano to be placed at Mamma's disposal. I was told that all the instruments are at present reserved, but that he should soon be able to reply more favourably.

I enclose his letter.

---

[1]Brahms died only five weeks later, on 3 April 1896.
[2]Moritz Rosenthal, 1862–1946, the celebrated pianist.
[3]Albert Gutmann, Viennese publisher and concert agent.
[4]Hanslick actually wrote the following:

> It is well known that the promise of infant prodigies is deceptive, hence we looked forward to the 29-year-old artist's performance with a mixture of anticipation and anxiety. He has entirely fulfilled our former hopes. As a virtuoso namely, for we have heard nothing of his compositions. Busoni is now one of the foremost amongst pianists. I know no other who so strikingly reminds me of Rubinstein. The same sonorous touch, the same massive strength, endurance and assurance, the same wholesome suppleness of interpretation. In the unbelievably difficult and taxing Eb major concerto (no. 5) of Rubinstein, Busoni was able to let his technique triumph. As a good musician, he certainly did not choose this work on account of its beauty but rather in spite of its hideousness. The Adagio cowers between the

first movement and the finale like a sick sheep between two cannibals . . . Busoni's
agent in Berlin, Hermann Wolff, had Hanslick's review reprinted as a publicity
hand-out.

35   TO HENRI PETRI
         in German

Berlin 3.1.1897

Man proposes and God – sometimes leaves him in the lurch. This is
particularly forgivable at the turn of the year, when a million demands and
wishes have to be noted and fulfilled.

My concert of [original] compositions will not be taking place until March
the 19th – for a number of reasons, pointless to enumerate here. My New
Year's wish for myself is: that you will find pleasure in my Violin Concerto,[1]
and that you will honour and delight me by playing it on the 19th. I hope it
comes true!! To you and your family I wish peace and contentment,
prosperity, joy with your children, artistic fulfilment and worldly success, at
least for the next 50 years, i.e. until 3 January 1947. By then one or two
things will probably have changed and we shall have to think up new
formulae for our good wishes, appropriate to the circumstances. –

[. . .] Some time in January I must come to Dresden and demonstrate the
concerto (of which only the Finale has still to be orchestrated) to you.
Perhaps in the very middle of the month. –

Greetings, greetings, greetings.

Your old
F B Busoni
Pianist and composer.

[1] Violin Concerto in D, op. 35a. The work is dedicated to Henri Petri.

36   TO HENRI PETRI
         in German

Berlin 9.3.1897

I don't know how it happened. For months I had been firmly counting on the
19th when Wolff[1] suddenly announced that this was a mistake and pressed
the 20th upon us. I rather suspect that they had made other plans for the 19th
and changed the date. But now you are not free on the 20th; and this has
decided me to postpone the whole business, which was anyway rather hasty,
until early in the coming autumn, when I shall *definitely* be counting on you,
should your favourable impression of my piece also extend to the orchestral
contribution (which is certainly no subordinate one). I think there is some

worth in the thing and was glad that it didn't daunt you. In my haste I was unable to complete the piano reduction, the score was at the copyists'. – The Finale gives the general impression of a sort of 'Carnival' and should make a pretty unusual effect as the closing movement of a violin concerto. – On top of all this I was wanting to publish the work (as well as an orchestral suite)[2] but could not risk doing so without at least having had a rehearsal of it.

Could you sacrifice the time to be there? (Your expenses would be covered.) I have to learn an *entirely new programme* for Berlin by the 16th,[3] which gives me only 6 more days. Am therefore out of commission until then. My congratulations on your success in *Vienna*.

[1]Hermann Wolff, 1845–1902, celebrated Berlin impresario, formerly secretary to Anton Rubinstein.
[2]*Geharnischte Suite*, op. 34a, composed in 1895, revised in 1903 and published in 1905.
[3]On 16 March 1897 Busoni played the following progamme at the Singakademie, Berlin:

Bach–Busoni	Chaconne
Beethoven	*Eroica* Variations
Weber	Sonata no. 1 in C
Meyerbeer–Liszt	Fantasy on *Le Prophète*
Mozart–Liszt	*Don Juan* Fantasy
Liszt–Busoni	Fantasy and Fugue on the chorale 'Ad nos ad salutarem undam' from Meyerbeer's *Le Prophète*

37   TO HENRI PETRI
in German

Berlin 13.10.1897

Once again I thank you from the bottom of my heart for your artistically perfect performance of my concerto, which you accomplished with such warm, generous, truly staunch devotion.

The evening of 8 October[1] is a landmark in the development of our artistic and human bond: an alliance originally formed between *three* of us, and now drawn even closer through the affiliation of Gerda and Egon's growing up.

The concert was like a double-bar in the great symphony of life and – as fate uncompromisingly forbids us to take the repeat – we would at least wish to sustain a good long pause over it!

As for Egon, it is a good thing that the difference between his age and mine is almost exactly the same as between mine and yours; hence I can understand and share the feelings of both of you. Where I have the lead over Egon in some things, he will soon be keeping pace with me and who knows if I shall eventually be left well behind!

May he be fortunate in life, let him contribute his stone as an artist to the

1 Busoni with his elder son, Benvenuto, at the quayside in Trieste, *c.* 1897

2 Busoni *c.* 1898. He wore a beard until 1903, when he surprised his friends by appearing clean-shaven

3 Henri Petri, leader of the Leipzig Gewandhaus Orchestra and a close friend of Busoni

4 Egon Petri as a boy *c.* 1890. Like his father, he played the violin but later became the foremost of Busoni's piano pupils

great monument which we are all carving, shaping, building!——

    The critics have treated me as 'one among many'. One of them has gone so far as to assert that I have no idea of symphonic structure! All of them introduce me as an 'acknowledged master of the pianoforte', so at least that much has been achieved! [. . .]

[1]Busoni had conducted the Berlin Philharmonic Orchestra in a concert of his own works at the Singakademie, Berlin. Apart from the Violin Concerto, the programme included the *Comedy Overture*, op. 38, the *Symphonisches Tongedicht*, op. 32a, and the *Geharnischte Suite*, op. 34a. All except op. 32a were first performances.

38   TO HENRI PETRI [facsimile on facing page]

Berlin 26.3.1898

    First Tutti.
second bar.
second crotchet.

Would you be so very kind as to send the *piano reduction* of the Violin Concerto to *Breitkopf* as well as the corrected *violin part* with the alterations you consider necessary, together with a note to the effect that the alterations in the solo violin part must be incorporated in the score as well as the piano reduction? The thing is now being engraved, indeed in great haste.

39   TO ANNA BUSONI
in Italian

Berlin 7.5.1898

There is seemingly no end to my *stagione* this year; on the 14th I shall be playing in Gotha again, after which I am off to London for the big season (May and June). My career is going well, successfully and also profitably – but mountains, too, while they may from afar give the appearance of being blue, hazy and ethereal – from close up are made of the commonest earth and stone, with a few trees planted here and there. Which is to say that my earnings, while appearing lucrative, are in actual fact only modest, indeed too much so.

    Of my takings,
        10% goes to Wolff
         5% for tax
        20% for travelling expenses
        20% to you
        25% for household and living expenses.

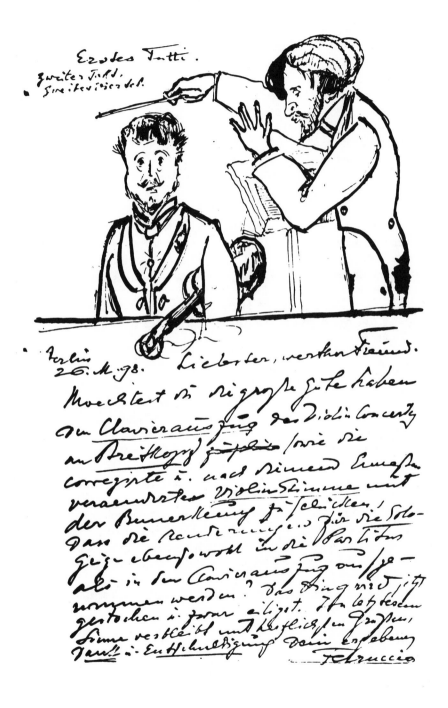

Thus 80% of my *regular* income is taken care of; of 15,000 Marks, 12,000 are hence consumed, without counting any extra expenses. In April I paid out 2,400 Marks in cash.

Rent	300
Debt to Petri	300
to you	200
Furnishings	100
Music	100
Pictures	180
to Wolff	1,000
Bookseller	100
Tailor	100
	2,380

And now I am literally penniless, with no hope for the summer, especially as London doesn't pay anything! Usually I was obliged to ask Steinway for an advance at the end of the season. This time I had no wish to do so, and this is why. Next autumn I am involved in a major project. I am to give 4 concerts with orchestra in Berlin, in which I shall play *all the concertos* for piano and orchestra from *Bach to Liszt*.[1] I shall need to set aside the money from Steinway to cover a part of the expenses. The idea is monumental, it will make a great effect and a lasting impression, I hope. Do you agree?

Now I am composing a new violin sonata[2] and it is almost finished. The [Violin] Concerto is being engraved. You have said nothing about the Bach chorale preludes,[3] don't you like them? I find them incomparable! Our plans for the summer are still uncertain and will depend on our finances. Besides, we have been invited to Habrovan (Frau Caroline)[4] and Oppenheimer[5] has invited us to Aussee. The former asked me to pass on her kindest regards.

Here I have met a nephew of Anzoletti[6] from Bolzano, the one who at the time presented me with the old editions of Schubert–Liszt. He is a splendid youngster, intelligent, cultivated, very placid and very well brought up (too well); he was born and lives in Bologna, where he is studying at the Polytechnic. With him I met the son of *Serato*,[7] who has made a good name for himself as a violinist. He, on the other hand, is a carefree, lighthearted, handsome young fellow (with a face to grace a barber's show-case).

Ask Babbo if I could have some wine from Zio Alfonso – I have a great need and longing for it.

If Babbo no longer needs the Fétis,[8] it would be useful to have it here. [. . .]

---

[1]The concerts took place on 29 October and 5, 12 and 19 November in the Singakademie, Berlin, with Franz Rebiczek conducting the Berlin Philharmonic Orchestra. The programmes were: 1. Bach Concerto in d, Mozart Concerto in A, K.488, Beethoven Concerto no. 4 in G, Hummel Concerto in b, op. 89; 2. Beethoven

Concerto no. 5 in E♭, Weber Konzertstück, Schubert–Liszt 'Wanderer' Fantasy, Chopin Concerto no. 1 in e; 3. Mendelssohn Concerto no. 1 in g, Schumann Concerto in a, Henselt Concerto in f, op. 16; 4. Rubinstein Concerto no. 5 in E♭, Brahms Concerto no. 1 in d, Liszt Concerto no. 2 in A.
[2]Sonata no. 2, op. 36a.
[3]Ten chorale preludes, transcribed for piano, published 1898.
[4]Caroline Gomperz-Bettelheim (see footnote to letter no. 14).
[5]Jella Oppenheimer (see p. 427).
[6]Presumably Emilio Anzoletti (see p. 424).
[7]Francesco Serato, 1843–1919, cellist, professor at the Liceo Musicale, Bologna. For his son Arrigo see p. 428–9.
[8]Either François Joseph Fétis *Biographie universelle des musiciens*, 8 vols., Brussels, 1833–44, or *Histoire générale de la musique*, 5 vols., Paris, 1869–76. Busoni made frequent reference to both these works in later years.

40 TO ROBERT FREUND
in German

Budapest March 1899

[. . .] I have received your letter, together with Huber's concerto[1] and the magnanimous consignment of wine, whose value I fully appreciate. I am less certain whether I shall come adequately to appreciate your friend, the esteemed composer Huber's piano concerto. The author's name and the fact that *you*, dear friend, are advocating the piece, speak for its qualities – which are undeniable – but give rise to too many expectations whose fulfilment is not conclusively proved. Above all, the surefire power of genius, which compels one to ignore lesser deficiencies and silences criticism, seems to me to be lacking. – The piano writing vacillates between musicality and virtuosity which, while not detracting from the one, seems to hinder the other. For a composer with such inexhaustible imagination it was most certainly a mistake – (this seems the most conspicuous one to me) – to open the work with a set of variations. Huber seems to have made use of every rhythm and motif he could think of, without any sense of economy towards the rest of the piece. Like a paterfamilias who squanders his whole annual income in six months, Huber has entirely spent himself in these nevertheless *significant* and altogether noteworthy variations. You must admit that the scherzo and finale present nothing particularly new and are also disturbingly *alike*. – The grave consequences of variation form could have been avoided if [the movement][2] had come at the *end* of the work.

The repetition of already stated rhythms and motifs would then have acquired the character of an *epilogue*, whose effect would have been altogether satisfactory. Perhaps the sole deficiency is that, instead of being restricted to exhaustive investigation of *one* state of mind, as is the case in Beethoven's A♭ major Sonata [op. 26], the Appassionata or the Kreutzer Sonata, the variations are too *heterogeneous* in character; variation movements of a *universal* nature appear at the *close*, as in the Eroica, in Brahms's Fourth Symphony, [Beethoven's Sonata] op. 109 and – <u>last not least</u> – the Choral Symphony!

Not wishing to overlook the good impression which the work made on me, I should mention that it shows evidence of great musical competence, fluency of form in the structuring of the movements, good taste, seriousness and a welcome absence of extravagance; – these are all my *personal* impressions – written, furthermore, in recollection of a first play-through and without purporting to be a definitive criticism.

If I have expressed anything with undue haste or with demonstrable lack of justification, then I ask you to forgive me and ascribe it to pressure of work.

I am distracted, exhausted and truly not in full possession of my perceptive faculties.

═══

You will be interested to hear that I found six volumes of the 1st Edition of Liszt's [Hungarian] Rhapsodies in Strasburg – in a junk shop; a seventh volume in Stuttgart; they are numbered up to *eight*, so I am *certainly* lacking *one* book, but it is also *possible* that a ninth or even tenth might also exist. I already possess *three different* earlier versions of the 6th Rhapsody, and I can also remember a *fourth* which I played as a child and was slightly different from the above-mentioned three.— [. . .]

[1]Hans Huber (see p. 426), Piano Concerto no. 3 in D, op. 113. Dedicated to Robert Freund, who first performed the work in 1899. Published by Kistner, Leipzig. The work has four movements: Introduction (Passacaglia on the bass of the 1st theme in the finale), Scherzo, Intermezzo and Finale.
[2]Original partly illegible here.

41　Recipient unidentified[1]
　　in German

Berlin 5.10.1901

[. . .] Let me thank you for your confidence in me and for the aid you are giving my young friend. I have always been interested in D. and I shall be only too glad to watch over his further studies and guide them to the best of my ability. He possesses many of the qualities which go to make a good artist. Above all talent in his chosen field and general intelligence.

The factors which constitute a great artist are, however, more numerous. The chief ones are perhaps: character, individuality, personality and a true vein of artistry. In the case of a virtuoso who appears before the public, one must add: the ability to dominate and persuade a crowd of persons unknown to him, and active but not passive nervousness. That is: to develop nervous energy without succumbing to one's own nerves. Please also consider, dear

Dr X, that even when all these qualities are in evidence, *external influences* play a role which is important and not easily foreseeable in one's development or decline. The surroundings in which the budding young artist lives, his life-style – physical and moral – his ability to absorb impressions and mould them into an individual intellectual entity – thousands of unforeseen circumstances – all these things have some effect. Probably no one succeeds in remaining on the absolutely straight road, the majority ends up somewhere not originally so conceived, many are cast hither and thither, change their direction or lose their track altogether. He who steadfastly pursues his goal, or finally ascertains what it is, will find his thirtieth year the most decisive. Until then, hopes and doubts as to a successful outcome are equally justified.

If you, dear Dr X, have been following these remarks with ready attention, as I assume you have, then you yourself will probably be somewhat taken aback to have been expecting our young friend to complete his studies within a maximum of 1½ years. But the moment is important for D. and every encouragement or disencumbrance could have the happiest results, either during the limit of 1½ years or later on. But if one expects 'to be able successfully to recommend D. for an adequately remunerative post', the case is different. Suitability for such a post has little to do with the inner development of an artist and, even if a more extended period of freedom were desirable for D. to develop in such a way, he should be able to occupy a good post in two years or even sooner. As an aid to understanding these last sentences I must add that that which, in ordinary life, counts as an independent position becomes, in artistic parlance, a dependent one. But this is, all in all, another story and has at present nothing to do with our case.

With kindest regards and, in the light of this discussion (which is intended to make clear to you how many difficulties stand in the way of a young artist), with the sincere request to abide all the more by your noble-minded decision, I assure you once again of my devotion to D.'s cause and of my thanks.

---

[1] This letter, published in 1936 (see Sources), is addressed to an unidentified benefactor. The pupil in question could be H.W. Draber (see p. 425), who studied in Busoni's master-class at Weimar in 1900.

42 TO HENRI PETRI
in German

[Berlin] 23.12.1901

[. . .] Egon's quick understanding of everything intellectual and artistic has made my task considerably easier.

Not only is he naturally blessed with talent, but also his honest, attractive personality helps him to win people over at once. In effect, between myself and Egon it is not so much a continuation of the old avuncular relationship as a *completely new* friendship, mutual investigation and submission, mutual gaining of confidence. I now know an Egon of whom I was not previously aware, while he has made the acquaintance of a teacher who had been a stranger to him.

Beside your son's excellent qualities, which will help him on his way, he has others – one should not conceal this – which could be an obstacle. I am as yet unable to perceive how far the German atmosphere, the provincial milieu and the musical bourgeoisie with which he was surrounded as a child are to blame for this; – or how great a part his own personality plays. But it is certain that his decided *talent* for music is not matched by an equal degree of artistic *temperament*. The electricity, bohemianism, 'vitality' of the art is still dormant in him; without which it is impossible to project oneself on people, especially on a larger group of *strangers*, as with an audience nowadays. He still has the greatest respect for everything 'staid', 'official' and 'generally accepted'. This, for example, has recently prompted him to register at the university ('matriculate'); a fine achievement for the average German youth of good family but, as I somewhat curtly remarked when he told me of it, not so for Bach or Beethoven.

I hope that experience, his *own* observations and greater maturity will modify the balance which at present prevails in him between citizen and artist, German and cosmopolitan.

All this would have a clearer and perhaps more cordial effect in conversation than it does in a letter. At any rate let me assure you, both you and Kathi, that I love Egon – as human being and artist – and also that I shall certainly be able to develop his talents: I found it necessary to confront him somewhat forcibly with my views, so that he might eventually come to find a logical combination of old and new. Maybe Egon, with his own militant way of expressing things, will already have made a somewhat radical impression upon you; – let it be; as one grows up, everything falls into place.

43 TO FERDINANDO BUSONI
in Italian

Berlin 2.6.1902

I cannot tell you how sorry I am to hear that you are unwell. If I had been able to rid you at a stroke of your moral and physical sufferings, I would have done so long ago and without being asked. But unfortunately my means are limited and even if my earnings are satisfactory, they are counterbalanced by incurred expenses, so that I am obliged to borrow money at the end of every summer. My regular expenses, which cannot be avoided, are 1. rent for the apartment, 2. travel, 3. agents' percentages, 4. taxes and duties, 5. your monthly allowances. I do and always have done my duty to you and I am glad to be able to do so, but there is no point in your afflicting me every six months with impossible demands. I assure you that your continual requests for money, amongst all the many moral, artistic and material problems bearing on my labours, are not a little aggravating.

I hope that I shall soon (i.e. in one or two years) be making a major tour of America. Until then it will be impossible for me to alter my budget. And even if it is possible to make a few small exceptions during the winter months, there is no likelihood at all in the summer. This is the honest truth.

44 TO EGON PETRI
in German

Berlin 5.9.1902 [postmark]

From your pater – and your mater – your long-suffering procreator – came an epistle – and a parcel, made me whistle – the former was to me directed – the latter well-packed and protected; – knowing little more than less – they asked me for your address – so urgently did they inquire – I bowed to their desire – and answered forthwith by wire.

As a bell I'm feeling sound – though in my head much is going round; – for concert projects: clarity – for piano effects: particularity – for lesser intellects: charity – for human affects: solidarity – for my infants' defects: liberality – for all good things one expects: jocularity – for those unrespected, with envy affected or utterly rejected: civility – for things projected, prospected, concocted, by patent protected: sensitivity – for things brightly confected: every modality –

    for things unconnected: perspicacity,
    for things ill-selected: unambiguity,
    for things far deflected: scrupulosity,
    for things near-neglected: curiosity,
    for things misdirected: perspicuity,
                      Ugh!
    for those with the style of Rückert 'infected': greater tenacity
– will be needed.

I shall do the Bach myself.[1] Thank you for your kind offer.

[1]Probably a reference to a revised edition of four Bach chorale preludes, which was published in 1902.

45 TO EGON PETRI
in German

Berlin 10.6.1903

Some sort of influenza or nervous exhaustion has kept me in bed for four days; – your letter came as an effective tonic for such depressing circumstances. My familiar spirits, the gremlins of good and evil humour, are waking up, stretching themselves and trying out their old knavish tricks again. But today I shall send the evil ones packing – for your well-intentioned letter makes an effect comparable to a narrow, cold stream which initially flows between mountain crags but eventually broadens into quite a substantial river, leading to a green valley. How often does your intentionally defiant attitude eventually modulate to one of openness and sincerity, and so it should remain. For you feel instinctively that we are both very fond of each other and are vexed by weaknesses in the other which we would prefer not to detect.

But of the two us, you will have to accept me as the maturer person, talis qualis, willy-nilly; whereas I may, can and in certain matters *should* expect changes in you – i.e. this has been my opinion until now. But I understand that you now wish to be considered as an equally mature person or as one in whose process of maturation my participation strikes you as being un-desirable or indeed unsuitable.

Just as you expected 'technique' from me as a teacher (as you yourself have admitted), instead of which you were taught matters of greater consequence, so it was my wish to indoctrinate you as a person not into a 'career' but rather into ideas and values of greater mystery. For this I considered your ability sufficiently great. Here, however, our ideas differ vastly, for you will often gladly lay yourself bare in situations where I would cover myself up; you knock at doors which – even if they were opened to me – I would furtively pass by; you unpack your wares and indeed extol their virtues, where I – even upon inquiry – would conceal and disavow them, proclaim their worthless-ness and finally, in my heart of hearts, not even look upon them as merchandise.

I could outline and embellish our mutual differences with a thousand small details; but this is not the moment.

Someone told me how Liszt, when asked to play at a social gathering, was as usual only too pleased to oblige. On his way to the piano he passed a friend, to whom he gave his hand. – 'Just feel,' he said – it was cold and sweaty. 'This', said Liszt, 'is a habit I have not yet learned to break.'

That a master, certain of his triumph, should have these cold, sweaty hands signifies: contemplation of the inadequacy of his achievement in the face of the possible ideal, resultant timidity and diffidence; no matter whether a Beethoven or some quite ordinary individual should be listening. Signifies: indifference to a certain triumph before a throng with no defined ideals, in consideration of certain defeat in the face of the flawlessness for which he yearned.

I shall finish here. I know what retort will be on the tip of your tongue and, for the sake of us both, I shall not enlarge upon it.

You will also secretly be thinking: *idealism* alone cannot make a Liszt of you and will only cause you to lose sight of other things.

But *should* anything lead us into *higher* regions – (*how far* is immaterial) – then it is this, unfortunately prostituted, concept. The fact that you, young and talented as you are, simply discount it and thereby feel conscious of doing a good deed, has provoked these sneering sarcasms from me, but the serious underlying idea is one which you will not readily admit to having digested and even to having found daunting.

It would be a *great pleasure* to see you, to talk of this and other matters and to maintain our friendly relations.

46 TO EMILIO ANZOLETTI
in Italian

New York[1] 23.2.1904

Your letter, which arrived today – even if not intended to bring me solace – has nevertheless warmed my heart; if for no other reason than that it speaks a European tongue, that is, one of mind and soul. Such a chimera is unknown here and, even if a trace of it was once in circulation, today it has been replaced by a vocabulary of commerce, which speaks of facts but never of feelings.

Indeed I am beginning to have my doubts about the 'future' of America and the development of the nation in the sense of the blossoming of the arts in the 'old' world. During my ten years' absence there has been no change – the American way of life was formed virtually at a stroke from a brilliantly practical idea and has remained so – imagination seems only to run to the superlative fulfilment of community needs.

Let me summarize this in the following sections:

The means of transport aim for speed and comfort;

Domestic comforts are practical, but neither aesthetic nor poetic; i.e.: elevators from the kitchen to the dining room, bathrooms adjoining the bedroom, recessed cupboards and similar tomfoolery.

Thirdly: the patenting of inventions for practical and domestic life, mechanical kitchen gadgets, pressure cookers,[2] powders for polishing metals and shoes, etc.

Fourthly: *publicity*, pushed to its limits, the importance of the press (for this sole reason), its impudence towards any possible rivals, its exaggeration, untruthfulness, '*sensationalism*'. The *result*: *success* (a concept which has a purely financial meaning here.) And now success has to be mass-produced, thus the object of any sort of success must be such that it can be *within the reach of all,* even the lowest.

The outcome: success and the means of achieving it can be the subject of an exchange of ideas, of a conversation between persons superior and inferior (at least in rank), without any difference of intellect becoming apparent.

All America has founded its ideal on
Quantity
and not on quality, about which everyone is in perfect agreement.

It seems to me that the American character is now completely formed and has perhaps arrived at a point of stagnation. The Americans have learned *everything* from Europe, but they are convinced they have surpassed it in everything. This conviction has a fatal influence on development and could have serious consequences. In fact it seems to me that even in those things which one could call American *specialities*, Europe is beginning to leave them behind. French automobiles, the underground railway in London, the electric train at Zossen,[3] the factories of Essen and Stettin have already overtaken the wonders of the United States. As for the Untergrundbahn in Berlin, an American could never have dreamed of finding such an elegant way of combining technology with aesthetics.

Here is the essence of my observations, influenced perhaps by momentary antipathy but otherwise intelligible enough.

It is not 'the frailty of memory' in the old world which I seek and with which you reproached me, but rather the desire for a future which awaits me there.

And to this I reach out with all my soul, so that I may once again 'rejoice in the dawning day', as is my nature; a faculty which I cannot exercise here and have almost lost.

I am glad to have unburdened myself a little and taken a weight off my mind, and thank you for your kind letter, which gave me a good opportunity of doing so.

[1]This letter marks Busoni's first extensive American tour. One of its high spots was a recital in the White House on 29 January 1904.
[2]Orig. literally 'ovens with valves'.
[3]An outlying suburb of Berlin.

47   TO EGON PETRI [with facsimile]

On Earth.
In Berlin, 27 August
1904.
Augsburgerstr. 55.–

My Egon

Here I stand and long for stars and star-songs.[1] Let the rays rain down, let them break on divided strings, transforming them into notes; write these down and entrust what you have written to the earthly post, so that they should reach me and be able to rise once more, to be converted from sound back into light.

[1]This letter alludes to an unpublished orchestral tone-poem by Egon Petri which he originally entitled *Sternenlied* (Song of the Stars). Busoni persisted in teasing him about this title, with the result that when Petri made a revised version, he now simply called it *Notturno*.

Auf der Erde.
in Berlin den 2? August
1904.
Augsburgerstr. 55. –

Mein Egon

Hier stehe ich und
sehne mich nach
Sternen und Sternen
liedern. Lass Strahlen
regnen, lass sie durch
getheilte Kreisler brechen
und verwandle sie in
Toene; diese schreibe
wieder, vertraue das
Geschriebene der indischen
Post an, dass sie mich erreichen
und sich wieder erheben koennen
und sich zurückverwandeln aus
Klang in Licht.

48   TO ROBERT FREUND
in German

Berlin 16.11.1904

I can scarcely express my regret that you were unable to be here on the 10th[1]
– you would have numbered amongst the chosen few upon whom I could
have relied as artists and human beings.

Now – until I am in a position to send you my score – you will have to base
your impressions on the utterances of Dr Schmidt,[2] whom you esteem so
highly – but who has published the nastiest of all the nasty things which
appeared in print on this occasion.

Criticism, it seems to me, is like a breaking wave: it can knock a man
down, but the water is dashed on the rocks and the man picks himself up
again.

In the face of all you must have heard – more or less directly – about my
concerto, I feel the need to assure you that I have created a work for every
note of which I can answer, and which will endure, inasmuch as human
achievements are at all durable.

I look forward to the moment when I can show it to you; for I know you
will approach it with the balance and clarity of your judgement, and that you
will find pleasure in some of it. –

Maybe I shall bring it to Switzerland with me.

[1]On 10 November 1904, in Berlin, Karl Muck conducted the world première of
Busoni's massive Piano Concerto.
[2]Leopold Schmidt, 1860–1927, the much feared music critic of the *Berliner Tageblatt*.
Here is an extract from his review (11 November 1904) of Busoni's Concerto:

A lively, primal musical imagination is at work in Busoni; but it is the imagination
of a gifted technician, not of a truly creative spirit. Above all, the wealth of material
is not shaped into any architectural structure. And here it becomes evident that
there is a lack of true mastery and that uninhibited rhapsodizing on poor models has
exerted its influence.

. . . I fear that Busoni has revealed his innermost musical nature in this curious
creation . . .

IV

1905 – 1909
Berlin (I)

49 TO EGON PETRI
in German

Berlin 10.7.1905

Mengelberg has been here and a plan has been drawn up for me to *conduct* my 'Concerto' (everyone stubbornly retains the final o) in Amsterdam, and for you to play it. I had been engaged as piano-player for the concert – when M. suddenly received an invitation to America.

The programme would be

1) Concerto
   Interval
2) [Liszt's] Concerto pathétique for 2 pianos
   (you and I)
3) Suite from the music to 'Turandot'.

This twice on succeeding days, probably at the end of October.

Before I finalize, scribble your assent.

Financial outlook poor – they only want to pay for a head-waiter – who is then supposed to tip the kitchen boy out of his own pocket.

Should the idea appeal to you, I can offer you one third, which amounts to 200 fl.

'Vater' wrote that you had received an advance on the Rubinstein Prize. Couldn't we two paint the town red with the whole bagatelle?

Your bribable adjudicator, i.e. one who lets himself be judiciously bribed.

11 July 1905. Gerda has driven off to Ysaÿe[1] with the 'kith'. The 'kin' remains at home.

27th postscript.

Please remind me of the cities in which I wanted to try to find you an engagement. –

(Actually the page is not yet full, but I shall finish.)

27B. Greetings to Draber, the 'Robinson' [Crusoe] of Worpswede.[2] (Ouch!)

---

[1]Eugène Ysaÿe, 1858–1931, Belgian violinist and composer.
[2]Draber and Petri were both resident at the artists' colony in Worpswede, near Bremen.

50 TO ANNA BUSONI
in Italian

Berlin 21.8.1905

I have remained in Berlin all the time and have, as always, been very busy. On this occasion with a new score which I completed *the day before yesterday*. Babbo will perhaps be pleased to hear that I have made a new attempt at a theatre work, but in an unconventional way; not with an *opera* but with descriptive music for a spoken drama.

The play I have chosen for this purpose is an old dramatized fairy tale, a tragicomedy by our own Carlo Gozzi. Nothing would be more natural than to attempt to put on a play by an Italian writer which has by now become a classic (and yet, because it has been forgotten, remains a novelty), but unfortunately the state of affairs in our country gives no cause for hope.

For the production one would require not only an élite theatrical company but also great opulence and excellent taste in the design of costumes and scenery and, furthermore, a first rate orchestra. Gozzi is the author of the fairy tales which Mamma's grandmother used to tell her. *L'amore delle tre melarance*, *L'augellin Belverde* and others were greatly in vogue in rococo times, but then they vanished without trace. I have chosen the tale of the cruel, seductive Chinese princess (or Persian, who knows) Turandot, who demands of her suitors the solutions of three riddles, at the risk of their losing their heads if they fail. As well as the heroic and oriental characters, the old Venetian masks also appear in comic roles: Pantalone, Brighella and Truffaldino.

The task absorbed me completely for two and a half months, during which I was unable to concentrate on anything else. Now it is finished and I must attend to other interests and endeavours.

Benni[1] is showing decided talent for drawing – Lello[2] remains for the time being a charming little rascal.

Thus, as we observe the new generation growing before our very eyes, we are constantly being reminded of the passage of time and the transitory nature of our existence. Also as an artist I am being counted amongst the 'maestri' or the *fathers* of the art, and here too new twigs are sprouting from every branch, covering it and soon obstructing the view.

Immutable laws! Let us bow before them.

---

[1]Benvenuto Busoni, 1892–1975. The text of this passage was originally longer. Unfortunately the original letter is lost and Dent's typescript offers only a précis of the sentence.
[2]Raffaello Busoni, 1900–1962.

51 TO EGON PETRI
in German

Leipzig 6.9.1905 [postmark]

Polemical national letter to E.P.

My dear Egon. Are the Germans musical? A discussion of this hitherto unimpeachable and unimpeached question would for once indeed be worthwhile.

Supposing a traveller were to come to some Wonderland, where the first question the hotel porter, the landlord, the police should ask him was: 'Do you have 5 fingers on each hand too?'; and the lady of the house were to introduce him in society as: 'Mr What's-his-name, who has 5 fingers on each hand'; and one bowed before him with a smile of admiration. This traveller would eventually become suspicious and allow nobody to 'slip through his fingers' until he had convinced himself that, in that land, to have 5 fingers was something very rare and highly regarded.

So it is in Germany with being musical. Here too, the lady of the house presents: 'Mr What's-his-name, a very musical gentleman', and the police registers the fact with satisfaction; for in Germany they have gone as far as to organize a music-police. – It is well known that this high regard for 'musicality' goes hand in hand with a contempt for technical matters: which leads us to another topic, the congenital clumsiness of the Germans. Thus we suspect them of being unmusical and definitely find them clumsy. What remains of the ethical side of our German? He is sober, sentimental and inflexible. All anti-artistic qualities. Someone like Menzel[1] – or Ludwig Richter[2] – is 'just the thing' for the Germans. The Germans' most frequent emotion is homesickness, they delight in writing poems about it. But art is at home everywhere. The Germans are bourgeois, art is aristocratic.

And then 'profundity'. To be 'profound' is the greatest praise one can give a composer. Something which sounds deep, cautiously creeps or obstinately scowls, is profound. This is what the Germans detect and nervously admire in Beethoven. He who has clambered, jumped or dived into the depths is no longer impressed by profundity. Only he who remains at the surface and lacks the courage to descend.

Well then, are the Germans musical, technically adroit, artistically inclined, profoundly sensitive, nonchalant conquerors of the depths? – Music, a bird on the wing, if it remains in German regions, is in danger of ending up in a cage. And the Germans will become museum janitors. Lex Heinze vitalized and applied.

We are already seriously behindhand. Music is like a brilliant boy who, as an adult, has not quite fulfilled his early promise. With superhuman energy and renunciation, such a man could regain the genius of the child.

Written by myself in German. Ferruccio Busoni.

---

[1] Adolf von Menzel, 1815–1905, celebrated German painter. Music lovers will know his picture of Frederick the Great playing a flute concerto at Sans-Souci.
[2] Adrian Ludwig Richter, 1803–1884, popular German painter and lithographer.

52   TO EMILIO ANZOLETTI
in Italian

Berlin 10.5.1906

[. . .] Every seed contains a flower, and my journey to Italy[1] has brought forth several ideas. I would like to pass one of these on to you, which sprang to mind yesterday evening during one of those strolls for which Berlin offers more incentive than elsewhere, especially 'im wunderschönen Monat Mai', as Heine says. – Scarcely any Italian cities have systematically organized orchestral concerts. And of these centres, none would satisfy me to such an extent that I would prefer it to any other. Therefore I have conceived the idea of an Italian orchestra which would regularly serve all the principal cities, following a carefully matured plan.

A full-time orchestra, well-paid, better than average, also as guarantee of its stability, well-prepared and equipped, with programmes unprejudiced in matters of period or nationality.

It wouldn't take much. A subsidy and an intelligent, active secretary. The rest would come of its own accord. Bologna seems propitious to me, Rome would provide an international public and one would also be certain of success in Trieste. Florence and Milan would have to join in, while Turin would be best left out of it, for it already has its own traditions, apart from which they have no particular desire for me there.

But the question of finance is difficult, for one would need at least 200,000 Francs 'starting capital'. But this is a daydream, every 1001 Lire is comparable to the 1001 Nights!

Good. I pass the idea on to you.

[1]Busoni had spent several weeks in Italy, with a recital in Trieste on 5 March and the first Italian performance of his Piano Concerto at Bologna on 29 April.

53   TO EGON PETRI
in German

Trent 30.7.1906

What a shame you aren't here; I am *entirely* on my own and we could have spent two fruitful and memorable weeks together. Picture if you can an old renaissance principality, pronouncedly Italian, surrounded by epic landscape, mountains and hills with old towers, monasteries, vineyards, walled stone pathways, sun and wine. If only I were not so isolated! *Entirely* alone, for as a result of the uneventfulness of my surroundings, even my zest for work has abandoned me, my character, which is not as strong as I thought, having so decided! –

While still in Berlin I finished my new libretto[1] and composed the *whole* of

the longer half of the 1st act. But then things came to a 'stop'. —
And why am I here? Gerda said I needed it —

> 'ich bin ein weicher Vater,
> mag keine Tränen leiden'[2]

as my Kommissionsrat[3] says — and I gave in. —

Before setting out I sent you the proofs of the last two movements of the Concerto. Thus you will have noted that this load too has been taken from my heart and shouldered by the bright and hearty copyright holders[4] of Leipzig — without stirring them in the least, by the way. For, since they at last paid something out for Turandot, they have assumed a proud, dissatisfied cast, fitting to such a distinguished dynasty.

> ('Sie sind gewiss aus vornehmen Haus,
> sie sehen stolz und unzufrieden aus.')[5]

Are you coming to Berlin and, if so, when? I shall definitely be staying here until Sunday and would be very, very pleased to hear from you. Greetings to Mitta.[6]

---

[1]*Die Brautwahl*, adapted by Busoni from a novella of E.T.A. Hoffmann.
[2] I am a soft-hearted father,
  who cannot suffer tears.
[3]Kommissionsrat Voswinkel, character in *Die Brautwahl*.
[4]Play on the name Breitkopf und Härtel. Orig.: '. . . daß auch dieser Stein mir vom Herzen und auf die breiten und harten Leipziger Köpfe zurückgefallen war.'
[5] Such a proud and dissatisfied cast
  Gives token of a most distinguished past. (Unidentified quotation).
[6]Egon Petri's wife.

54 TO EGON PETRI
in German

Amsterdam 6.10.1906

Your most appreciated letter reached me here — many thanks; it bears witness to your great powers of galvanizing corpses.

The formulation: Serapiontic-Pantagruelistic-Shandyish pleases me so much that I consider the suffix 'Busonian' an honour.

Oehlenschlaeger once wrote a letter to E. T. A. Hoffmann and signed it: A. Ö. Serapionsbruder. (By the way, did you know that E.T.A.H. once received a most beautiful letter from Beethoven?)

And as regards[1] Oehlenschlaeger: for four days I have been sitting around in the capital of Holland, where I am giving 3 piano recitals (Drie Piano-Avonden) and, instead of practising, I have written down the whole first act of an Aladdin adaptation.[2] About 50 vocal score pages of 'Die Brautwahl' have already been composed. Lo, we make use of our allotted time.

And the words 'vocal score' bring me to the next point. Couldn't you bring yourself to pick up '*my* heavy load', i.e. finish off the [2-piano reduction of the] Concerto? The full score has been published. But who's going to buy such a folio volume of more than 300 pages and at a price of about 50 Marks? The piano reduction would find a good market. – The Deutsches Theater wants to perform Turandot in the spring.[3] An attempt at this Chinoiserie in London has been abortive.[4] The abortion of my heavy load![5]

My plans for the future are as follows: with the Concerto I have for the time being completed my orchestral essays and have had the provisional 12 works bound in 5 volumes. Next summer I want to publish the three libretti ([Der mächtige] Zauberer, Brautwahl, Aladdin) and then set to work on music for the stage. Turandot inaugurates the series, then follows 'Die Brautwahl'. I also have other plans, but these are secondary. – The volatile vapours of the love-god are no hindrance, at least not morally – (I have, thank goodness, no lack of them) – but the flatulent filth of piano teaching most certainly is. – In Berlin I was engaged in this activity for 5 afternoons; Beklemishev,[6] Zadora[7] and a youngster from Trieste[8] were stimulating. There were between 25 and 30 others present. – *All* the women were pretty. I had sent one of these on to you, she had made up her mind and was ready to depart, when her sick mother ('The Mothers, the Mothers' – Faust II) wired that she should return to Switzerland.[9]

Whatever I have omitted here can be communicated orally. Am tremendously looking forward to seeing you again, you and your wife Mitta.

Scattering flowers on your connubial tomb,

Yours,

Ferruccio B.

Amsterdam,
now 8 Oct. 1906

[1]Orig. À popò. German Popo colloq. = backside.
[2]The Piano Concerto ends with a choral setting of verses from Adam Oehlenschlaeger's play *Aladdin*. Busoni's stage adaptation of the play is unpublished.
[3]Max Reinhardt staged a production of *Turandot* with Busoni's incidental music at the Deutsches Theater, Berlin, in 1911.
[4]*Turandot* was staged at the St James' Theatre, London, but only in 1913.
[5]Orig. Ein Durchfall meiner Leibesfracht. Pun on the word Durchfall = flop, failure *or* diarrhoea.
[6]Gregor Beklemishev, 1881–1935, Russian pianist, dedicatee of Busoni's third Elegy for piano.
[7]Michael von Zadora, 1882–1946, Austrian pianist, dedicatee of Busoni's fourth Elegy for piano, later collaborated with Egon Petri on the vocal score of *Doktor Faust*.
[8]Gino Tagliapietra, 1887–1954, pianist and composer. Later professor at the Liceo Benedetto Marcello, Venice.
[9]Alice Landolt. In November 1906 she went to Manchester, where Egon Petri was teaching, and studied with him.

55 TO LUDWIG VON BÖSENDORFER
in German

Berlin 22.12.1906

While not as yet having received an 'official' invitation from any quarter, I have been approached 'confidentially' by several gentlemen with the idea of my taking over the 'Master-class' at the Vienna Conservatoire, and thus I can well assume that some response is expected from me.

Of all these people, it is to you that I can speak most freely and therefore I would ask you to be the addressee of these comments, first of all to pass your opinion of them on to me and then to make whatever use of them you may consider beneficial.

Accepting an 'office' has always aroused in me a feeling of something constricting. The change of city, country and habits, the interruption of diverse activities would – in our case – play a considerable role in my life, at an age when it should begin to direct its course according to a clearly forged plan, and one would have to make it clear to the gentlemen that, even in the case of a favourable decision on my part, of the steps which I and Vienna would be taking towards each other, mine would morally always be the larger.

Since leaving the Boston Conservatoire – about fourteen years ago – I have come to enjoy and love almost unlimited freedom and independence. In this sense as well, even 'favourable conditions' would never quite subdue a feeling in me that I had sacrificed my freedom of action – I say this, once again, only so as to make it clear to those concerned that I would be losing just as much as I would be gaining through them. On the other hand, I am well aware of the honour which such trust signifies for me: I also value the artistic possibilities offered by such a position very highly and set great hopes on an outcome in this direction.

I love your city, to which I am still connected by indelible memories, good and bad, of my early days and by the maintenance of relations with distinguished friends; but I am as yet unable to perceive whether it has progressed musically in the same direction as I, how far twenty years have separated Vienna and myself from one another and to what extent a sojourn in the city could reconcile me with it. I am no longer at the 'acquiescent' stage and, should I find myself alienated from musical Vienna, I would either have to make a great effort to draw it towards me or – remain an outsider. You can see, my dear friend, how significant a decision could be for me; felicitous and fatal. I am still considering the favourable aspects and, bearing in mind that good can be done for me and through me, I have decided in principle, but with some reservations, to submit some suggestions to you, the acceptance of which would win me over completely to your side.

If the gentlemen who make the decision about my election have placed so much trust in me, then they would have to make a categorical declaration of this trust by conceding me absolute authority over my own actions. The prime consideration would have to be that I *reject* any official or moral subordinacy to the Director.

The class would meet *as a group* and no pupil would have the right to a specified period of tuition for himself alone. The time would be self-regulating and proportionate to the talent and diligence of the pupil. – Intrinsic to *group* tuition, moreover, is mutual competitiveness and criticism, and each individual pupil would have the benefit of the instruction given to his comrades. Hence the teacher's expositions, which every pupil should hear. –

I would schedule this class tuition for two afternoons weekly. As I do not know how long the terms last, nor how many pupils there are to be, an agreement would still have to be reached about the duration of these group afternoons.

This agreement would have to be based on the approximate establishment of the number of pupils. I consider *artistic* tuition impossible if the number of students exceeds a certain limit. Also, if the number were to be increased above this limit, the agreed tuition times would be exceeded.

I would suggest that one accept non-participating students, for a certain admission charge, as *listeners*.

In the past years I have made a reputation for myself abroad, and it is to be expected that a preponderant number of pupils would be foreigners. – When I held a summer-school in Weimar, 8 youngsters attended it in the first year, in the second something over forty.[1] Who sets the limit here, and what relation would it have to my fee?

At present I am at the height of my career as a pianist and, happy as I would be that the post in Vienna should give me the opportunity to limit this career to the best and most artistic purposes, it would be impossible for me to interrupt it completely at this juncture. Therefore the question of leave of absence is very important and would have to be so determined that, on condition that the compulsory number of pupils should not have to be reduced and that my absence should not exceed a certain duration, in such a way – as I say – on these conditions, that I would be free to take leave of absence at any time and without complicated formalities. – An American tour is probably going to be arranged in the immediate future; if this were to offer the opportunity for a decisive improvement in my career, my contract would have to allow me exceptional leave of absence for this purpose.

I feel it my duty to declare herewith my belief that this letter is seriously intended and that I would also pursue my duties with all seriousness and ability, making every effort to create a significant centre of piano playing, while also having sufficient trust in my abilities to achieve this to an uncommonly high degree. I would like to be assured that consideration is given to the idea that a mutual trial period of one year might be advantageous before any longer contract be drawn up.

For the time being this is about all which I feel must be written by way of preliminary discussion. There will be further, more specific matters to discuss when I have received your reply.

5 and **6** Busoni's parents, Ferdinando and Anna (née Weiss). In *Arlecchino* Part II the hero's parents are modelled on these pictures: the father with 'a flowing beard and long hair, a Turkish fez on his head; close beside him a flask of wine, behind him, on a perch, three cockatoos', the mother 'snow white and wearing a crown with a halo'.

I hope to receive this in the course of the next two weeks, which I shall be spending quietly in Berlin before setting off on a new tour.

[1]Busoni's Weimar master-classes had taken place in the summers of 1900 and 1901.

56 TO EGON PETRI [postcard]
in German

Marseilles 13.3.1907

Life is really too short for such remissness! Where have you been? – I had so much been hoping to see you! – Enfin! – The first act of Die Brautwahl is complete, as well as a good deal of the two succeeding ones – in particular the scene with the church vision. – Vienna has been settled for a trial year. Meanwhile I have been everywhere and nowhere and am at present in Marseilles, from where I send you and Mitta my kindest greetings.

57 TO ROBERT FREUND
in German

[Berlin] 25.4.1907

Your excellent letter was the *first* reaction to my scribblings[1] and important not only for that, as I have always valued your judgements and opinions particularly highly.

You are right – where I took great pains in adapting the Zauberer to *unify* the action and to limit it to a *minimum* of *characters*, I have laid less stress on this in Die Brautwahl. However, the predominance of dialogues made me anxious for the music and resulted in the need for *periods*, for musical paragraphs. Incidentally, for a beginner like me it was a challenging task to adapt this thoroughly chaotic short story for the stage; however I felt irresistibly attracted by the atmosphere and the characters of Leonhard and Thusman. I also recalled Mozart's Don Giovanni, Falstaff and other highly successful operas which are not spoiled by the scenic deficiencies you rightly mentioned. And don't forget that 'the libretto is merely part of a work and is rounded off only by music'.

The whole first act of Die Brautwahl has already been set to music, as well as enough of the rest of the libretto to make a further act!

I hope that this music has turned out well; I have profited mostly from Mozart and Verdi, but it will have an independent style.

I was particularly glad that you devoted so much attention to the essay.

I am not speaking of formlessness but rather of traditional forms, which should be cast off, and I maintain that every new idea calls for a new structure.

Is this not expressed clearly?—

Anyway: many, many thanks for reading and discussing it so carefully and patiently, and for your frankness.

======

The Vienna affair has been settled for a preliminary trial year. My conditions of leave necessitate arranging my concert schedule as soon as possible, and I would therefore most appreciate it if the Zurich business could also soon be booked. As programme I thought of suggesting: the 'Concerto' – Chopin's 24 Preludes and the Totentanz.

¹*Der mächtige Zauberer*, the libretto of *Die Brautwahl* and the *Outline of a New Aesthetic of Music* had recently been published in one volume by Schmidl, Trieste.

58 TO CARLO SCHMIDL
in Italian

[Berlin] 28.5.1907

The following shall we say 'public' persons should receive a complimentary copy of my little book:

[Alexis Zdislaw] Birnbaum, concert conductor, Lausanne;

Dr [Hugo] Botstiber, secretary of the Gesellschaft der Musikfreunde, [Vienna];

Oscar Bie, editor of the Neue Deutsche Rundschau;

Dr [Gustav] Altmann, critic of the Nationalzeitung [Basle];

[José Vianna] da Motta, who will write;

[Hippolyt von] Vignau, Intendant of the theatre at Weimar;

Dr [Franz] Beier, municipal theatre in Kassel;

[Otto] Lessmann (Allgemeine Musik-Zeitung);

A. [?] Hensel, Munich [Schmid];

[Felix] Weingartner;

Robert Freund, leading musical personality in Zurich;

Count Moltke, Commandant (close friend of the Kaiser);

Mr [Lazare] Ponnelle, who is to make the French translation;

Wolff Agency;

Schulz Curtius Agency, London;

My friend Draber, who will write;

The rest go to personal friends.

I send you my warmest greetings.
If there is anything doing in Trieste, it will be
necessary to decide *in good time*.

59   TO EGON PETRI
          in German

                                                        Berlin 9.8.1907

Your card did not surprise me in the least, indeed – what you wrote – I had
been sensing it for the last two days, almost knew it. Your sane outlook and
great talent will certainly bring you on to the right track – if not all that
quickly. But this is no reason for avoiding me and I protest in the name of the
love that binds us. –

I was very excited by what you told me about B. Shaw; it so happens that
'Der *Morgen*' is starting to publish one of his plays, 'Der Liebhaber',[1] which,
with its uncanny knowledge of human nature and its dazzling virtuosity, once
again fascinates me.

This new impression and the fact that Shaw was (and is?) part musician
gave me the idea of prevailing upon him to write something for music. He
would certainly create a new direction in music-theatre, even if unintentionally,
and something could well come of it. I am thinking of myself as the
composer; but he doesn't know me at all, so how am I to convince him of my
ability?

You have spoken to him; perhaps it would be agreeable to you – as
representative of this idea – to get to know him better.

As you have unfortunately cut off all contact, I am sending this letter to
Worpswede.[2]

---

[1] *Widowers' Houses*. The play was translated by S. Trebitsch in 1907 but actually
entitled *Heuchler*, later altered to *Die Häuser des Herrn Sartorius*.
[2] Petri was on holiday in Airolo; the letter was forwarded to him there by
H. W. Draber.

60   TO EGON PETRI
          in German

                                                        [Berlin] 26.8.1907

Your letter was also kind. But it's a pity, if you decide to travel on my
account (and prolong the journey by a month), that I shall only get to see you
for *one* day!

I shall discuss my idea about B. Shaw with you and then attempt to carry it
through.

Meanwhile I have an abundance of working materials. Singular circumstances recently made it possible for me to track down four lost pieces by
Liszt, which had been printed but never published;[1] evidently the original
version of the later Venezia e Napoli! The pieces are brilliant. The first
incorporates the 'Tasso' theme:

I believe (judging by contents) that the Shaw play in 'Morgen' must be 'Widowers' Houses'.

I would be delighted to arrange things in such a way that I can be with you both in Manchester.

As yet I can say nothing definite.

[1]See letter no. 215.

61 TO EGON PETRI
in German

Vienna 2.12.1907

I am sure you will be glad to hear that I completed my series of piano pieces yesterday.[1] There are *five* of them now, of which I took the liberty of dedicating the second, 'all' Italia', to you. Accept it with the affection with which I present it.

You shall be sent the printed score, soon I hope.

It seems to me to be my maturest achievement so far.

[1]Elegies: Six new piano pieces. 'Die Nächtlichen', the fifth of the series, was composed later in December 1907, adapted from the *Turandot* music. The whole group was published by Breitkopf und Härtel, Leipzig, 1908.

62 TO EGON PETRI
in German

Vienna 2.5.1908

Your letter was as refreshing for me as for you. That you are facing up to the situation, seeing your environment in its true light and arming yourself with decisions, that you 'definitely' wish to come to Berlin, that possibilities are opening up for you, all this is very gratifying! Thanks to your youthfulness, these joys of spring affect you twice as strongly.

Basle – Dresden – Berlin then. I have initiated the latter with a view to our working together.

Thank you for your kind words about the Elegies. On several occasions I have now found that they appear infinitely simpler to the *reader* than to the *listener*. In these pieces I am particularly proud of the form and clarity. For instance, the structure and proportions of the 'Erscheinung'[1] seem exemplary. –

Excuse me for showing you round my own house. – Now and then one has an urgent need for it.

Here in Vienna I have discovered a music dealer where many old volumes of Liszt are still to be had. (The very rare [Réminiscences des] Hugenots I). Maybe you have some gaps to fill. I snapped up two really clear, unused copies of the untraceable first edition of Schubert's Ständchen, one for you. If I am not mistaken, you wanted to complete the [set of] 12 Lieder (published by Diabelli). They have several. So send me your order.

=====

I also sent the Elegies to Kindl – am glad that you were able to spend 3 enjoyable days together and said nice things about me.——

I have been here for more than 2 months – am teaching and have plunged thirstily into 'Die Brautwahl'. I think it will be very good.

Meanwhile I also quickly made a concert ending for the overture to Don Giovanni[2] – this too, it seems to me, has turned out well.

In April I had extraordinary successes in Berlin, Rome, Milan and Paris, I was moved to gratitude. In these cities I had the pleasure of counting Lamond, Godowsky, Gabrilowitsch, Lhévinne, da Motta, Ansorge (Berlin), Sgambati (Rome), Boito (Milan), Saint-Saëns, Diémer and Fauré (Paris) amongst my listeners. Excuse me again, but I like to share my joy. Not with everybody.

P.S. In Berlin your father played Beethoven's C♯ minor quartet *most* beautifully. (The work is miraculous.) 'Vater's' interpretation was noble, considered, tasteful and clean as a whistle. One could make something else out of each piece – something more psychological – but, as it was, in *that* style, it was perfect.——

---

[1]'Erscheinung' (Notturno), the sixth Elegy.
[2]Busoni's concert version of the overture to *Don Giovanni*, dated Rome, 7 April 1908, was published by Schirmer, New York, in 1911.

63   TO ROBERT FREUND
in German

Vienna 7.5.1908

Your opinions have always been a guide to me, and I would ask you to have the patience to carry on following – and criticizing – my progress. [. . .]

The Elegies – permit me to talk about myself a little, my reasons are not egocentric – the Elegies signify a milestone in my development. Almost a transformation. Hence the title 'Nach der Wendung'.[1] And this is most completely apparent in nos. 1, 3 and 6. – Of these I am fondest of the third.

The 'Erscheinung' is the condensed paraphrase of a scene from 'Die Brautwahl', the *'vision at the town-hall window'*. From the point where you found it pleasing, it follows the text of the opera almost exactly.

You see that an individual style is superimposed upon Verdi and Mozart who (as I have already told you) will prove to be my models in this work.

Please forgive this self-observation, which must be of greater interest to me than to you, at a time when I am engrossed in my work.

My voluntary activity in Vienna affords me a measure of tranquillity; but the uneasy atmosphere – in a strange house and a peculiar city – cannot easily be banished.

Today – in one hour – the Brahms monument is to be unveiled. I know how fond you are of this composer; I am irritated by his facility and his Germanism. By facility I mean: his avoidance of every new problem. An exception to this is perhaps to be found in the Paganini variations. Only in the introduction to the finale of the C minor symphony is music, according to my ideals, to be found. Incidentally, did you know that its theme is the bell motif of the London church towers? Of course you did.

[1]After the turning point. The first Elegy is entitled 'Nach der Wendung. Recueillement.'

64 TO CARLO SCHMIDL
in Italian

Vienna 2.6.1908

This is what I want to discuss. Towards the end of the summer I would be glad to publish a new revised and expanded edition of my book.[1] The volume would republish

1) Der [mächtige] Zauberer;

2) Die Brautwahl,

corrected and altered to correspond with the music. I would here include

3) introduction to Aladdin or the magic lamp

(this too is a kind of libretto).

There would follow 4) the *Aesthetic* (greatly revised and enriched)

5) Aphorisms on Mozart (already published with great success in the Local-Anzeiger on the 150th anniversary of Mozart's birth).

6) An essay on Liszt, the introduction to the complete edition of Liszt's piano works (Breitkopf & Härtel)

and finally

7) a brief satire published in the Carnival number of 'Die Musik'.[2]

What do you think of this?

What would be the best and – fairest terms you could offer me? Please let me know. Meanwhile I hope to have the music for Die Brautwahl finished by the autumn. [. . .]

---

[1]The book Busoni was planning never appeared. Items 5, 6 and 7 were published in 1922 in *Von der Einheit der Musik*, Max Hesses Verlag, Berlin; the revised edition of the *Outline of a New Aesthetic of Music* appeared in English in 1911 and, further revised, in German in 1916.
[2]Ino Sub-F (anagram of F. Busoni), 'Aus der klassischen Walpurgisnacht' in *Die Musik*, vol. 1, February 1908, pp. 165–7.

65   TO EGON PETRI
in German

Vienna 3.6.1908

Why haven't you answered my well-intentioned letter? I was also expecting an order for Liszt sheet-music. But now the Complete Edition is on the way. Yesterday I sent off the 'Preface'. It has turned out a fine essay. Schumann gets something of a knocking. He deserves it. Occasioned by my discussion of Liszt's études. As for that Protestant parson, that Saturday-evening stay-at-home, Sunday-afternoon sonata-player, stubbornly tedious sequence-repeater! On the war-path against the Philistines! Wasn't the imaginary inauguration of the Davidsbündler an act of Philistinism of the first order?! The amateur of Zwickau! His inane infatuation with Clara Wieck places him at as great a remove from Liszt as the problems of a rural dean from those of the Pope. Takes it upon himself to pronounce upon Liszt and does so, furthermore, with dispproval! Shakes his head until you can hear the grey matter slopping about!

Yes, why shouldn't I speak it out for once? But, let me reassure you, my preface is not written in *this* style. –

Pity you aren't here. My group of pupils is delightful – the men, at any rate – with many a fine young head. Very able. One of them recently played the Liszt sonata so well that I struggled to restrain my tears.[1] There is no rivalry amongst them, they are all good fellows. We carry on until mid-July. –

Die Brautwahl has put on seven-league boots; or in modern usage: is driving an automobile. I have every hope of finishing it in the autumn.

Then I want to work on an *Italian* opera. Would like to sing with my full voice. And then I look forward to seeing you, from whom I am only too far removed in time and place.

Goodbye then. I am living at Wallfischgasse 4. Please note the second *L*.[2]

---

[1]Evidently this was Louis T. Gruenberg, 1884–1964, Russian-born pianist and composer.
[2]Walfisch = whale.

66 TO EGON PETRI
in German

Vienna 13.6.1908 [postmark]

I had really been looking forward to the letter heralded by your telegram and today – the 13th – it arrived.

Your introspectiveness leads you to inappropriate extremes; only a conversation would prompt me to fitting arguments. But I hope that October in Berlin will fully restore your morale, indeed I am banking on it. Things are also very unsatisfactory for you where you are. When I was in Helsinki, and younger than you are now, I had Sibelius and the Jaernefelt brothers for stimulating company; I learnt a few things from my director, Wegelius, an extremely fine and cultured man. The country too was delightfully exotic and, despite the Nordic way of life, more cheerful than Manchester. That must have an effect on your frame of mind. Weren't you satisfied with your Beethoven sonatas? I consider them a splendid achievement. Now it is your goal to prepare yourself for Berlin: time flies and in September I shall certainly be seeing you. –

I have promised my pupils to adhere to the Conservatoire's absurdly organized academic year, which is why I am here until the middle of July, loved but also personally and financially victimized. However, it has its agreeable side as well. Enough for today.

[P.S.] I have read [Bernard Shaw's] 'The Sanity of Art' with delight.

67 TO LUDWIG VON BÖSENDORFER
in German

[Vienna] 13.7.1908

Today my unofficial 'Master-class' in Vienna comes to an end and I feel the desire to send you a brief report.

A total of 25 pupils attended, together with a dozen listeners, and twice-weekly tuition was regularly observed.

Apart from these periods, some afternoons were devoted to performances, at which I myself played three times and Professors da Motta[1] and Bartók[2] once each. – Lesser-known symphonic poems by Liszt (his Faust symphony) were performed on two pianos in carefully prepared interpretations.

Distinction was won by the pupils Sirota[3] (Kiev), Gruenberg (New York), Closson[4] (Liège), Turczynski[5] (Warsaw) and Friedmann[6] (Vienna). The company was cordial, convivial and unclouded.

If I add that I for my part was able to work hard and successfully and have all but finished my opera; finally also that the weather was consistently good and the city beautiful and festive, then one can see that I can look back in joy on a most memorable experience.

I would like to thank you for supporting me and some of the students with your magnificent instruments and your kind interest, and I assure you that I am leaving Vienna reconciled and with regret.

[1]Text unclear. Probably José Vianna da Motta.
[2]On 29 June 1908 Bartók played his 14 Bagatelles, op. 6 to Busoni's class, as we learn from a letter of Bartók's, dated 28.6.1908, to Etelka Freund (herself a former Busoni pupil and sister of Robert Freund). 'At last something really new,' was Busoni's comment on Bartók's music.
[3]Leo Sirota, 1885–1965, Russian pianist, dedicatee of No. 3 of Busoni's *An die Jugend*.
[4]Louis Closson, ?–?, Belgian pianist, dedicatee of No. 4 of Busoni's *An die Jugend*.
[5]Josef Turczynski, 1884–1953, Ukrainian pianist. Later a celebrated pedagogue and Chopin editor in Poland.
[6]Ignacy Friedman (sic), 1882–1948, who had also studied with Leschetitzky.

68   TO CARLO SCHMIDL
in Italian

Berlin 17.7.1908

[. . .] The '*Allgemeine Musik-Zeitung*' has published an extensive leading article on the Aesthetic[1] (next Christmas the '*Signale*' will do the same) and this will be a great help in circulating the pamphlet. Maybe you have not yet seen the results. I repeat that one of the leading English critics (perhaps the most capable) has dedicated a very interesting article to it in the 'Birmingham Post'[2] – I have a copy of it.

The idea of Breitkopf seems a good one to me, as they have the rights of my best compositions – therefore I would try to make a contract with them. One would have to make them understand that it is not just a question of a new printing but of a book with twice the amount of material.

I have completed the first 3 acts of the *Brautwahl*, and all that remains to be done is the final scene. The libretto has undergone relevant alterations during the course of composition.

But I fear that the rights of the libretto would be a grave hindrance in selling the score to a publisher.

They would certainly share your opinion, i.e. that the libretto is an effective source of revenue, and I am not sure (please understand me) whether this sort of *rift* between the libretto and the music will be successful.

In general I am fairly ignorant of the manoeuvres necessary for the *opera* and would be grateful for your advice.

[1]Paul Bekker reviewed the *New Aesthetic* in the *Allgemeine Musik-Zeitung*, July 1908, pp. 541–6.
[2]Ernest Newman, whose review in the *Birmingham Post* appeared on 24 August 1907.

69 TO EGON PETRI
in German

Berlin 29.7.1908

An idea I have so often ruled out, that of opening an 'Emergency Exit' for the 'Concerto', i.e. of an edition in 4 sections and without chorus, has once again occurred to me. It still goes against the grain but could very much help to propagate the work, and Liszt, as well, did not disdain such a procedure in the case of his Faust [Symphony].

The plan, which I drew up today and am passing on to you at once, is very simple.

To the last $\frac{12}{8}$ cadenza one adds an orchestral accompaniment, i.e. thematic, as originally intended. The orchestra has the Church theme in unison (one octave). After the final run of the cadenza (dominant of B) the closing section in $\frac{9}{4}$ (in whole tones) follows immediately, *pianissimo* then swelling; and the succeeding music. –

I think – it would be good.

Before beginning (as the notation might possibly cause difficulties) I would like to ask you 1) for your opinion; 2) if at the end you would like to play the Concerto *here* in this form?!?!?! In your first concert?!?![1]

(*Without your feeling importuned*, answer me with absolute frankness.)

[1]Busoni's revised version of the Piano Concerto, omitting the final chorus, was made in August 1908 and Egon Petri played the work in this form, with Busoni conducting, for his Berlin début on 3 October 1908. Later Busoni changed his mind (cf. letter no. 310) and this abbreviated version remains unpublished.

70 TO EMILIO ANZOLETTI
in Italian

Rome 1.3.1909 [postmark][1]

Preface to the Italian edition. On my return to Italy I shall first have to narrow the limits of what my little book sets out to overthrow in that country. Like a man who, having long studied the heavens, lowers his gaze and directs it towards the earth, of which he only perceives the narrow horizon surrounding him.

The development of the art of music in our country hovers on the one hand between recent influences of Wagner and even more recent ones of the French school – while, as a counterbalance, the famous words of a famous man insinuate themselves into the Zeitgeist, while only touching its surface: 'Torniamo all' antico' – let us return to the past.

While gladly acknowledging the great uproar which Wagner produced in Italy, it does not seem to me that one can likewise acknowledge that his music is congenial, and our composers have only apparently gained from him. Closer at hand – due to a similarity of race – the French have succeeded better in dominating, proof of which is to be seen in the most celebrated of our living composers. It is a certain loss of self-confidence in the face of the foreigners' astonishing *technique* which leads us to appropriate these qualities. Whereas nature in fact rebels against a means of expression characteristic of another race, of an alien race.

While not succeeding in being German, we are hence afraid of being Italian; and however much we may gain from the French, it will never exceed the value of an imitation, always a negative value; this influence thus makes us less sincere and less strong and substitutes an artificial perfume for the wholesome smell of earth.

The other school, which looks towards Verdi's catchphrase, has not yet achieved anything – it seems – other than pure theories. It is the war-cry of the self-possessed. And what is actually the meaning of such a slogan: torniamo all' antico? In Cherubini's book on counterpoint he spoke of the rules 'degli antichi'. And now he himself has become 'antico'. To which point in history are we supposed to turn our attention? To Palestrina? Cimarosa? Donizetti?

Those who have a taste for old music are at liberty to re-read, re-hear and re-admire the works of former times, and the first step would be to revive the scores of such composers as Monteverdi and Caccini and produce them on stage.

Such an experiment would certainly be useful: we shall not return to the past; but in the ancient sources one could seek a new art, an art which would remain Italian. The catchphrase we need, now and always, must be: 'Let us progress, and let us remain Italian.'

[1]This letter was written in Nice and posted in Rome.

71   TO EGON PETRI
        in German

                                              Berlin 26.6.1909

[. . .] The misprint is in the Adagio after the cantabile 'lyra' passage (as da Motta described it in his review);[1] the three sustained Dbs – where the orchestra re-enters – have a treble clef (instead of bass) and look as if they are *C's* [sic].

Have you also received the *new cadenza?*

'As for the well-tempered', I meant that you should publish the incorporated *piano études* separately, complete the suggested ones and add a few of your own.

Take for a start the first Prelude.

The second is in double-stops.

The third is already complete, so just paste it in.

The Prelude and Fugue in D major *superimposed* make for an amusing study. The first 5 bars are in the footnote. The following ones could run:[2]

Prelude No. 6 calls for wide leaps.

Include the appendices to Fugue X and Prelude XI. –

Fugue in G major for 2 pianos. – B minor Prelude & Fugue (organ transcription).

And so on, with whatever occurs to you. – It could be entitled:

Studies from J. S. Bach

taken from F. Busoni's

edition of the

Well-tempered Clavier

edited

(partly completed and augmented)

by

Egon Petri

Schirmer would take it (I am fairly certain) and would pay well, maybe 500 Marks.

Be of good cheer, Egon, life will still treat you very well – even now things are not too bad. – I have written a Berceuse for 'Peter Pan'[3]. Then 3 piano pieces 'An die Jugend'.[4]

I dedicated a major concert work for piano, 'Fantasia nach J. S. Bach' (one of my best) to the memory of my father, who died on 12 May. Had you heard about it?

Furthermore the first volume of Liszt Etudes for the Complete Edition is ready for the press. Have written about 50 pages of score for the opera. All in one month! That really is well done.

Looking forward to Newcastle.[5]

Greetings – greetings – greetings.

[1]Reference to the two-piano arrangement of the Piano Concerto, which had been prepared by Egon Petri. (The misprint is corrected in the published score.) José Vianna da Motta published a long review of the Piano Concerto in the *Allgemeine Musik-Zeitung*, September 1908, pp. 670–1.

[2]Busoni was soon to use this idea as the basis for the 'Preludio, Fuga e Fuga figurata', No. 2 of *An die Jugend* (cf. letters nos. 72, 73 and 75).

[3]'Berceuse pour le piano'. The MS is dated 5 June 1909. 'Peter Pan' was the nickname of the dedicatee, Johan Wijsman, evidently on account of his ample girth.

[4]No. 1 of *An die Jugend*, 'Preludietto, Fughetta ed Esercizio'.

[5]On 22 October 1909 Egon Petri was to play Busoni's Piano Concerto in Newcastle with the composer conducting. This was the first British performance of the work.

72   TO EGON PETRI
in German

Berlin 19.7.1909

[. . .] Your idea for piano recitals is most exciting. It gave me the idea of the following outline for a *dance programme*. Please consider that my name appears so frequently only because I found it amusing to see how much I could personally contribute to such a programme. – Actually 2 recitals.

I

1. Bach:– French or English Suite
           (or the delightful transcription from the violin
           sonatas by Saint-Saëns)
2. Mozart–Busoni:– Giga, Bolero e Variazione (my latest)[1]
3. Beethoven:– Ecossaises (Busoni)
4. Weber:– Invitation to the dance
5. Schumann:– Carneval
6. Schubert–Liszt:– Soirées de Vienne

II

1. Chopin:– Valses, Mazurkas, Polonaises
2. Liszt:– Valse mélancholique
           Valse de Bravoure
           Mephisto Waltz [No. 1] (Busoni)[2]
3. Debussy:– Danse sacrée
           Danse profane
4. Saint-Saëns:– Danse macabre (Liszt)
           or: Étude en forme de Valse

5. Busoni (yet again!):– Ballet-Scene [no. 4][3]
6. Strauss–Tausig:– Waltz.

For America – (I am going there at Christmas time!) – I have assembled a *Bach recital using my own transcriptions*. I recommend it to you:

1. Chromatic Fantasy
   Preludio, Fuga e fuga figurata (D major)
2. Toccata – Adagio – Fugue (C major)
3. Three chorale preludes
   Fantasia on motifs by J.S.B.
4. Chaconne

It is well contrasted and appealing.

Please, dear Egon, in the Chorale prelude from the Elegies – from bar 4 in the right hand – play as follows:

The *left hand* remains unaltered. –

In this way the line is more perfectly expressive. It is also more 'Beklemmisch'.[4]

——Your sympathetic description of Vogeler[5] gave me the idea of sending Benni to Worpswede for the holidays – he is now attending the Academy.

——In my spare time I have, for a joke, been writing an operetta libretto – *Frau Potiphar*[6] – which includes very many comic ideas. – Very indecent.

When is 'Peter the Small' going to appear?[7]

PS I The painter [Karl] Walser is designing the sets for Die Brautwahl.
PS II I have been sent a *rounded keyboard*.[8] The thing has deficiencies which seem to me to be insurmountable. As yet I can say nothing binding.
PS III Have you thought about the analysis of the Concerto for Newcastle?
PS IV This letter has no form.

---

[1]No. 3 of *An die Jugend*, completed on 13 July 1909.
[2]Busoni's edition, published in 1904, draws on the text of the orchestral version, *Der Tanz in der Dorfschenke*.
[3]*Vierte Ballett-Szene* (Walzer und Galopp) op. 33a. Published in 1913, but written as long before as 1894. A passage from this work is also quoted in *Die Brautwahl*.
[4]Pun on the German word beklemmt (= anxious, oppressed) and the name of the dedicatee of this piece (the third Elegy), Gregor Beklemishev.
[5]Heinrich Vogeler, 1872–1942, distinguished painter and graphic artist. He engraved the title page of Busoni's Piano Concerto.
[6]The manuscript of *Frau Potiphar* is preserved in the Deutsche Staatsbibliothek, Berlin.

[7]i.e. Johan Wijsman (see letter no. 71)

[8]F. Clutsam patented his rounded keyboard, on which the keys are arranged in the shape of a fan, in 1907. It was intended to facilitate playing at the extreme upper and lower ends of the instrument. Busoni wrote an article on the invention in *Signale für die musikalische Welt*, No. 35, 1909.

73   TO EGON PETRI
          in German

Berlin 16.8.1909

On returning from a brief holiday[1] (during which I recovered from a substantial depression caused by exhaustion) I found your very kind letter, which I had almost been expecting and whose arrival caused me redoubled pleasure. – I rummaged amongst my old scraps of manuscript paper (don't ever try it, it's the 'morning after' without the 'night before'!), rummaged and found the long-lost first pages of the Well-temp. Cl. *part two*. I am sending them to you because they have a bearing on our current correspondence and will be in good hands. Should I persevere with it, I shall be happy to accept your obliging offer to 'do the dirty work'. You are the *only* one who can help me: there is nobody else to whom I could entrust a single bar. Sometimes I have run into such difficulties and found myself helplessly isolated.

To test yourself (i.e. to see if you can stand so dull a task) you can begin the spadework with the already started C♯ minor Prelude. For this you will need two copies of the Steingräber edition[2] for cutting and excavating.[3] A certain amount of bookbinder's know-how will be required, for which you have an expert in the house, whose duties at the moment are however rather the opposite of 'binding'.[4]

Your suggestion for a third volume is excellent, but I think – this was my intention – that I shall not further enlarge on matters of piano technique in the 2nd [part]. It should rather immerse itself in the mechanisms of *composition* and bring all manner of dazzling things to the surface. The combination of D major Prelude and Fugue is to be provisionally published in a newly inaugurated collection 'An die Jugend' (3 volumes).[5] Since it will be included as a comprehensive piece (preceded by the original Prelude and Fugue, with a transition), nothing would prevent the example being included in the Etudes.

Meanwhile Galston[6] – who is almost your peer in questions of culture and understanding – has written a book, about 200 pages long, recording his experiences in preparing for his five historical programmes. He makes frequent reference to me and I have also contributed two little aphoristic word-chains: about the piano and its pedal, and about Liszt. When you see the book, you might perhaps feel inspired to some sort of essay yourself. You have indeed observed and experienced a good deal; why not write the most important things down? [. . .]

When are you expecting the 'new arrival'? – My greetings to your dear wife Mitta who, I hope, will have an easy time of it!

[P.S.] This page of music, printed from the plate on fine paper, is a small contribution to a composite work. It was the work which gave me the idea for the Chorale prelude 'Meine Seele bangt und hofft zu dir'. For that reason, and because I think highly of it, I am sending it to you.

[1]Busoni had spent ten days in Italy.
[2]Dr Hans Bischoff, 1852–1889, had edited the complete keyboard works of Bach which were published by Steingräber, Hanover, between 1880 and 1888.
[3]Pun on Steingräber = stone-digger.
[4]Pun on the words binden = to bind, and entbinden = to give birth.
[5]A fourth volume, 'Introduzione, Capriccio (Paganinesco) & Epilogo', was completed in the autumn of 1909.
[6]Gottfried Galston, 1879–1950, Austrian pianist and pupil of Leschetitzky. His *Studienbuch* was published by Bruno Cassirer, Berlin, in 1910 and reviewed by Busoni for *Signale* in the July 1910 issue.

74   TO H.W. DRABER
in German

Berlin 24.8.1909

[. . .] Gruenberg[1] has the idea for 'Signor Formica' from me. I have a volume of Italian poems by S[alvator] Rosa in which is included a biography of the painter (or poet in this case). The events in E. T. A. Hoffmann's tale – when compared with this account – are *historically exact* and it is almost baffling how the author, despite his pedantic accuracy, unfolds an aura of the fantastic and improbable over the events like a magic cloak.

Gruenberg is a pleasant, talented fellow.

But as an artist he gnaws doggedly at himself and feeds on his own blood. He considers himself a fully fledged master and this prevents him from transcending his own limitations.

Therefore he is discontent – although 1,000 elemental spirits would never persuade him to admit it – and in danger of developing into a misunderstood genius. I am very fond of him and it is my wish that 'Mr Ant'[2] should bring him good fortune. I myself would be very interested in your scenario, as I have long been considering the subject as material for an opera. The 'Brautwahl', however, has deterred me from such partial repetition. –

I have been working very hard. Amongst other things six not insignificant piano pieces, the fruit of this summer, are soon to be published. [. . .]

[1]Louis T. Gruenberg.
[2]i.e. 'Signor Formica'

75 TO EGON PETRI
in German

Berlin 29.8.1909

Before very long, I hope, you shall be receiving a series of piano pieces which I have written this summer. Slight and not so slight, original works and transcriptions, all in all *nine* items.

Berceuse	I can answer for all of them,
Fantasia (after Bach)	but the first and the last are my favourites. Particularly
Preludietto	in the Epilogue I believe I have
Fughetta	taken the first step towards heights which I can visualize
Esercizio	but which it will not be given
Prel. + Fuga figurata	to me to attain.
(Bach D major) Giga, Bolero e Var.	
(Mozart) Introd. e Capriccio	
(Paganinesco) Epilogo	

Simply on the *piano* and with *12 semi*tones one could go infinitely further; and how much further still with a new tone system and an orchestra! But what a technique and what a long life one would need for that!!

I hope you received my last letter and the page of Bach. – I do understand that more important things will soon be arriving in your household (or have already arrived?), and that your thoughts are at present concentrated on nothing else. –

Benni has set out on his first unaccompanied journey (to Worpswede).

My opera has today been accepted in Prague for its first performance: I myself have not quite made up my mind. [Karl] *Walser* is designing the sets.

76 TO HENRI PETRI
in German

Berlin 10.9.1909 [postmark]

In my last letter I forgot to discuss the programme planning for the quartet concerts, as you had requested.

Unfortunately four of them – apart from their differing spiritual strengths – belong to the same colour range, namely Schumann, Brahms, Reger and the Busoni of the 2nd quartet. *All four are by Schumann*, i.e. are dry in sound quality, confined to the middle registers and short-breathed, even when – as in the case of Reger and myself – they apparently transcend 8-bar periodic structure. – So let us take the two D minor ones, each as the central item of a programme; Haydn and Beethoven as the respective closing items of each programme. Thus we arrive at:

2. Busoni	2. Reger
3. Beethoven	3. Haydn

The Brahms and Schumann remain as the opening numbers.

But here I am 'Hercules at the crossroads'[1] (pardon!). So I shall leave it to you to decide between the two no. 1s and the two no. 2s.[2]

Eulenburg's Score Library has just advertised a quartet by Sibelius (op. 56) with the promising title: Voces intimae, inner voices. I expect beautiful things of it.

I myself have long been planning to write a quartet in one movement, which should be *my* masterwork and really stir up emotions.

If only I had a few years of peace! Peace, peace, peace!

This summer I have scored the 1st act of the completed opera and written 9 piano pieces. That was my holiday.

Thank you for your kind words and sentiments with regard to the quartet.

[1] Orig. Herr Kules am Wege der Scheide (indecent).
[2] i.e. op. 36 no. 1 or 2 of Schumann, op. 51 no. 1 or 2 of Brahms.

77 TO HENRI PETRI
in German

Berlin 10.10.1909

I do now believe that one can bring the dead back to life. Last Thursday you performed such a miracle.

I thank you with all my heart for your loving, perfect and understanding performance of my 2nd quartet on 7 October 1909 in the Klindworth Saal, Berlin – and I would ask you to pass on my thanks to your quartet colleagues.

78 TO EGON PETRI
in German

Manchester 4.11.1909

If you are seriously proposing to prepare the vocal score of Die Brautwahl, I shall depart to America with a considerable weight off my mind.

But can you take on so much without sacrificing yourself?

I would not have had the courage to suggest it to you.

V

1910 – 1914
Berlin (2)

79 TO EGON PETRI
in German

New York 19.3.1910

Your silence and evanescence is equal only to that of my son Benni, who took 2½ months to write me a letter and then only <u>at my own suggestion</u>, as in Bernard Shaw's play. You don't consider how much one values the memory of dear friends in a far-off land, when one has irksome duties and is separated by an apparently measureless distance. [. . .]

I have achieved much, travelled far and played a good deal, have practised counterpoint and harmony, have worked at various compositions.

Six weeks more!

The most pleasant encounters were with: Gustav Mahler; my old publisher Schirmer; Wilhelm Middelschulte,[1] Gothic master of Chicago, Illinois; O'Neil Phillips[2] in Montreal; my ex-colleague Stasny[3] in Boston; the most delightful experience: an incomparable performance of the Turandot [Suite] under Mahler; the most interesting impression of the journey: New Orleans in the Gulf of Mexico.

Gerda left N.Y. on 24 February, whilst I was in Kansas City. She has already arrived home safely.

It has been arranged that Mark Hambourg[4] should play my Concerto in London on 8 July and I have been asked to conduct. I didn't say no, although my conscience about you was whispering in my ear. But I thought it better for *me* to conduct and perhaps a good thing if someone else takes care of my piece for a change.

In Basle they obstinately insisted that the Swiss Generalmusikdirecktor Suter[5] should conduct and I myself should play. – Sometimes one is helpless. I had suggested you on both occasions. (Moreover the telegraph wire is such an unmanageable means of communication. One does not express oneself or even reflect at any length.) [. . .]

At least I have mentioned your name and spoken highly of you on every more or less appropriate occasion. My agent Hanson is also very interested in you but has simply not yet found the right line with which to bring you here.

I would advise you to write to him, but while I am still here; he is very impulsive, if the tone of the letter were to please him, he could well become enthusiastic: he is also not timid and glad to take a risk. Do you want to try? [. . .]

Mr M. R. Hanson, 437 Fifth Ave., New York. This is also *my* address.

[1]Wilhelm Middelschulte, 1863–1943, German virtuoso organist. Settled in Chicago in 1891, remaining there until 1914.
[2]O'Neil Phillips, ?–1911, pupil of Busoni's in Berlin.
[3]Carl Richard Stasny, 1855–1920, pianist and Liszt pupil. Professor at the New England Conservatoire, Boston, from 1891.
[4]Mark Hambourg, 1879–1960, well-known pianist of Russian origin.
[5]Hermann Suter, 1870–1926, Swiss conductor and composer. Director of music at Basle from 1902. In the event, Petri did play in Basle (see letter no. 88).

80   TO H. W. DRABER
in German

New York 24.3.1910

[. . .] Mahler is doing the Turandot [Suite] on 1 May in Rome. This is the reply to your 'peace news'. It was a *great* success here and *ideally* played.

I gratefully agree to what you wish to do for the *Notation*,[1] you will certainly do the right thing and well. It is, I presume, already published and can certainly be seen at Spanuth's,[2] to whom I sent it.

Mahler himself has no wish to make anything out of the Mahler festival. Can there be such a thing as a Reger 'festival'? Where is the festive spirit? – When will there be a decent Liszt festival? With the oratorios, symphonies and complete works for piano and orchestra, interspersed with works for two pianos and a Lieder recital? – I believe that 1911, the hundredth anniversary of his birth, will bring forth something of the sort.
[in the margin:] NB I believe you could coordinate something here.

[1]Busoni's *Attempt at an Organic Piano Notation*, a strange and short-lived endeavour to simplify sight-reading and transposition at the keyboard with the aid of a multilinear system of notation. It was published in 1910.
[2]August Spanuth, 1857–1920, music critic. From 1907 the editor of *Signale für die musikalische Welt*.

81   TO EMILIO ANZOLETTI
in Italian

Colorado Springs 1.4.1910

The mountain range which I can see from my window reminds me in its outline, colouring and atmosphere so much of Segantini's[1] pictures that I could truly imagine the city of Varese beyond it. On the contrary . . . I have never been further from you. The clock indicates a difference of eight hours between you and me, precisely the equivalent of one third of the earth.

A great confusion of memories and wishes, governed by emotion rather than intellect, is seething in my brain – it is my birthday – for this was a strange and decisive year, sad[2] and important: – the situation in which I am entering my 45th year is new to me, not because of my remoteness but rather on account of my *complete* isolation.

There is scarcely a single American city in which I cannot count on at least *one* person I know – here, on the other hand, there is nobody.

Even without Segantini's mountains, it is only natural that I should think of you today[3] and feel the need to send you my warmest greetings. I do so with all my heart across the American continent and the Atlantic ocean.

[1]Giovanni Segantini, 1858–1899, Italian painter, particularly celebrated for his Alpine landscapes.
[2]Both Busoni's parents had died in the preceding ten months.
[3]cf. letter to Gerda, written the same day:
>. . . I can see the white and brown mountains etched against Segantini's grey-blue sky and become conscious of *where* I am – but if I stare longer, I forget it again and feel myself actually in the Engadine and think: beyond the mountains, there lies Italy.
>
>And I knock on the mountains as on a wall and from the far side (as if behind a door) I hear Anzoletti's voice: Che c'è!? Oh, Ferruccio!

82 TO EDWARD J. DENT
in Italian

Chicago 23.4.1910

Bless you! But what was the intention of your making my mouth water by torturing me with your sublime description of a ramble in Tuscany? One might just as well have discussed freedom with a prisoner or health and youthfulness with a dying man.

While you have been enjoying the pleasures and the wine of my home country, I have had to cover 35,000 miles of the Wild West. Unmerciful Dent!

All this is indepen-dent[1] of the main question of your kind letter. I am sorry to have to admit that neither the Franck variations nor the Brahms B♭ major concerto are at present in my repertoire. Were my strength not so exhausted, I would be glad to prepare one or the other for Cambridge. But I find myself absolutely at the limits of my physical and mental powers, which amounts to the same thing. Instead I would like to play the *fifth concerto of Saint-Saëns*, a composer whom I value highly as an artist and who is a personal acquaintance of mine, if you consider it suitable. But I would be happy to rehearse the orchestra; and before choosing one of my compositions – which I consider an honour to perform – I shall have to know roughly the size and quality of the orchestra which you have at your disposal.

You have regained your strength and I am exhausted!

Therefore I assure you that I shall have to forgo any new activities until the autumn. Time is pressing for the completion of my opera, whose full score is still unfinished, and I am unfortunately almost certain that I shall not be able to meet the deadline which has been agreed for its completion (which should be November at the latest – for Hamburg).

For this second reason, I would be grateful for any simplification of my Cambridge programme and am certain that a concerto by Beethoven or Liszt would save me much work. So please decide, and let me know what you have decided when I return to Berlin around the middle of May, since a reply will no longer reach me in America. [. . .]

I met [O'Neil] Phillips twice and we have also had a fairly extensive exchange of letters. It looks as if he will decide to remain in M.R. [Montreal] for a further year.

[1]orig. prescen-dente (sic).

83 TO EGON PETRI
in German

Berlin 12.7.1910

My memory cells have just reminded me that you wrote: you would find *new* principles for a Bach edition unthinkable. So I would like to record at least some idea of what I had been envisaging for the second part of the *Well-tempered Clavier*.

This 2nd part – according to my plan – should signify just as much for the study of

composition

as did the 1st part for that of piano playing. Thus I recall, for instance, that I had sketched out, as *one* of the chapters, the theory of *varying* the theme, which Bach developed very nicely, and I wanted to introduce examples from the chorale preludes.

In the case of Bach, as I said, this art of variation – controlled by feeling – is elevated to the level of Gothic decorative art. There are countless examples and they are absolutely valid as the basis for a theory of the *formation of melody*. – This example occurs to me:

Variations of this kind are also applied to *fugue themes*.

Furthermore, all the contrapuntal possibilities which Bach did not apply to a theme should also be introduced.

Reflections on *expression* by means of polyphony. – The new prospects which Beethoven opened for us in this direction (which received no further development in the ensuing *un*polyphonic era) should also be seriously considered. (e.g. the mocking fugue from the Mastersingers

is an isolated instance of this sort.) The decay caused by the 'pianistic' fugues and fugatos of Brahms, Liszt, Sgambati etc. should be held up as a warning. Attempted revivals by Franck and, recently also, Reger.

The main principle: not to look upon counterpoint as dry 'academic' 'labour' but as the instrument of individual, further developed expressive faculties. Its highest form: the dissolution of fugal form through the employment of polyphony as one of the most important elements of 'great' music (see the 'New Aesthetic').

And so on!

Part 2 of the W. Clavier offers the most diverse *starting* points for comments on all aspects and the entire future of music.

Did you receive the first sheet at the time? At the end of the 3rd Prelude there was – (I believe) – a composition model.

The 'Art of Fugue' will help to explain my words; I hope this will be in order with *Br. & H*. That even Bach did not exhaust all the possibilities with his 16 fugues on the same motif is proved by my 'Grosse Fuge'[1] which, when you compare it, introduces something like 20 pages of new combinations.

This is only intended as a theoretical letter.

---

*In my 'Grosse Fuge' appears, amongst others, the following variation:

Theme.

Var.

I forgot to mention the expanded harmonic and contrapuntal objections and particularly the symmetrical inversion of intervals (introduced by Bern. Ziehn[2] in Chicago), which opens up a new field.

These examples, on a half sheet of manuscript paper, have been lying aimlessly on my desk for some time. Here they are very much to the point. Please preserve them.

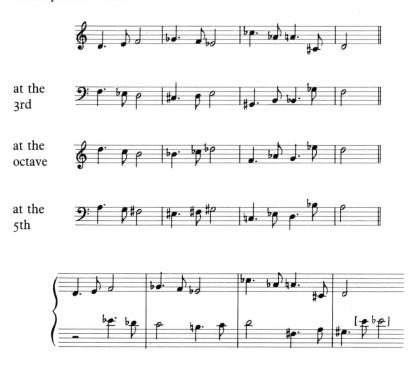

at the
3rd

at the
octave

at the
5th

good!
Symmetrical inversion at the
minor 2nd in stretto.
In the last bar the answer
is introduced as follows:

---

[1]'Grosse Fuge. Kontrapunktische Fantasie über Joh. Seb. Bach's letztes unvollendetes Werk' für Klavier ausgeführt. The original version of Busoni's *Fantasia Contrappuntistica*, written during his American tour of 1910 and published privately in New York in April 1910.
[2]Bernhard Ziehn, 1845–1912, German musicologist. Author of *Canonical Studies*, Milwaukee and Berlin, 1912. He settled in Chicago in 1868.

84   TO EGON PETRI
in German

Berlin 15.7.1910

Immediately after sending off my 'theoretical' letter, I received the second of yours, which gave me particular pleasure.

We have inaugurated an edition of Bach's keyboard works with Br. & H., for which I have proposed Petri and Mugellini[1] as collaborators.

My edition of the Inventions, which is to be incorporated, should indicate approximately the form of the new publication. The Art of Fugue has nothing to do with the organ. The fugues are actually intended for no instrument at all, but one of them is for *two* keyboards. They simply have to be divided up between two hands and, as you say, analysed with an aesthetical commentary. The fee I have been promised (I believe 2.50 Marks or more per page) will go to you. I enclose my first attempt at the 'grosse Fuge'. The pencilled notes are *not* valid.

Have re-opened the letter.

It occurred to me that a reduced version of the 'grosse Fuge' would have to be included at the end of the Art of Fugue. Omitting the variations and cadenza.

'For school use'

How do you think? I have already finished the plan.[2] – Did you receive my theoretical letter? Then you will, for the time being, have heard enough about editing Bach.

[1]Bruno Mugellini, 1871–1912, pianist and conductor. Became Director of the Liceo Musicale, Bologna, in 1911.
[2]This simplified version of the 'Grosse Fuge' served as the fugal part of the *Edizione minore* of the *Fantasia Contrappuntistica* which was published in 1912, preceded by a new chorale prelude.

85   TO EGON PETRI
in German

Berlin 23.8.1910

The Bach Edition is now to come into being and we have the task of dividing up the work between the three men whose names end with i.

I had reserved for myself:
– *the Inventions and Little Preludes*
– *Chromatic Fantasy [and Fugue] – Italian Concerto –*
  Capriccio on the departure [of a beloved brother] –
  Goldberg Variations

– Four Duets – and *The Art of Fugue* together with you.

You could also prepare the two interesting *Toccatas in F♯ minor and C minor* for me and, also following on from the A. of F., the *Musical Offering'*.

You should do the English and French Suites and the Partitas entirely on your own, for which the letter from Br. & H. gives you the explanation.[1] – Would you – to save me a little work, with which I am overburdened – write to Br. & H. about it yourself! – The A. of F. would have to be published first. How is your work progressing?——

Today I shall hear whether the score of Die Brautwahl is first to be *engraved* or *arranged*. In the latter case you shall receive the first two volumes straight away.

The rehearsals for the opera have definitely been scheduled for the beginning of May.

A harmonium with a new system of tones is being built.

The Fantasia contrappuntistica and the Sonatina[2] are at the printers.

On the 28th I have to leave for Basle – 35 pupils.

The engraving of *three* volumes of the Liszt Edition (the complete Etudes) is now finished.

Then comes America, followed by a year to catch my breath, should I have any left to catch.

---

[1]The letter was accompanied by a note from Breitkopf und Härtel, explaining that Mugellini had already edited the works in question for Ricordi (as well as various others which Busoni himself was planning to edit).

[2]Sonatina (no. 1) for piano, completed on 4 August 1910, a re-working of the original sections of *An die Jugend*.

86   TO EGON PETRI
in German

Berlin 29.8.1910

I am leaving for B[asle] today and have no paper left at home; excuse these scraps, but your letter gave me such pleasure over breakfast that I must convey my thanks to you while they are still fresh.

Yes, there are a few pianified editions of the Art of F. *Peters*, and more recently a dryly analytical one by some provincial organist. But would they help or hinder?

There is Riemann's analysis in book form, which is most amusing on account of his completion of the unfinished fugue (*the same one!*). Retail price: 1 Mark. – My own solution to this problem (for our new Edition) is *complete* in sketch. I would have to write it out or you will otherwise have to be content with my annotations to the confusing manuscript. Isn't November too late for that? Please give me your opinion.

Today the final proofs of the Fantasia contrappuntistica are to be despatched to Leipzig. This work has now been running through my head and fingers for at least half a year! It is my most significant piano work and one of the most important in modern piano literature. In print it extends to 45 pages of continuous music. I also know what its weakness is: it is too tightly corseted. For you it is basically nothing new, the marriage of the Chorale prelude from the Elegies with the Grosse Fuge, very carefully revised. – Also the Sonatina is merely a re-working of the Preludietto, Fughetta, Esercizio and Epilogo from 'An die Jugend', organically condensed. Perhaps the maturest of my piano pieces.

The first act of Die Brautwahl is – being engraved! After careful consideration, we – the publishers and the conductor – have decided on this course of action. The plates should be finished by 1 October and an impression of them shall be sent to you immediately.

I have written too much about myself. Thank you for your faithful devotion. [. . .]

87   TO HANS HUBER
in German

Bottmingen 17.9.1910

If you were hoping to find sympathy for your retreat,[1] you could have turned to no person more receptive than myself. I approve all the more enthusiastically of your seclusion in that it affords me the opportunity of seeing the development of your piano concerto, from which I expect some satisfaction. I have the greatest understanding for your situation, as I find myself in a similar, unfortunately more urgent one. The scoring of my opera has been interrupted once again, instead I have to toil away at the Chopin Etudes, which I believed myself to have mastered 25 years ago, yet always have to conquer anew. But this is no new or fruitful nourishment for the soul and I am seriously considering abandoning my finger- and hand-work. The book by Saint-Saëns, which you so kindly sent me, has not exactly encouraged me! The chapter about Liszt and Rubinstein makes the pointlessness of all further piano playing brutally clear. Nevertheless, I have been able to penetrate so far into the profundities of this minor art as not to believe in 'miracles'. Liszt made his effect through contrast with his predecessors and Saint-Saëns reports on his 'youthful' memories from his recollections. I myself heard Rubinstein play. What direction is piano playing now taking? If anything further is to come of it, we need new literature and an improved instrument. While the organ builders are making improvements and modifications to every new instrument, the piano has made no progress at all in the last 50 years. My suggestions to piano manufacturers have all been imperiously rejected. Enfin! – [. . .]

[1]Busoni was giving a piano master-class at the Conservatoire in Basle. Hans Huber, the director of the Conservatoire, was meanwhile on holiday in Vitznau, where he was working at his Piano concerto no. 4 in B♭ (without opus number).

88 TO HANS HUBER
in German

Berlin 12.10.1910

I missed you sorely at the final concert[1] but I can understand only too well! Everything went well, thanks to the eager willingness of all concerned. I have the most exquisite memories of the occasion, as of the whole September 1910 in Basle!

The critic of the Basler Nachrichten thinks that one should not look for German profundity in my Italian work.[2] If only I knew what was meant by German profundity in music. I am quite at a loss! In Beethoven I hear great humanity, freedom and originality, in Mozart joie de vivre and beauty of form (actually Italian hallmarks), in Bach feeling, devotion, grandeur and skill. The German, typically German manner, which is transcended by Beethoven, Mozart and Bach, is actually restrictiveness and provincialism. Lohengrin, Freischütz, male-voice choirs and our celebrated contemporary Max Reger, these are German. Schumann too. But where here does one find a profundity not possessed by Dante or Michelangelo? Wagner's Meistersinger is German through and through (without necessarily being restricted); is it therefore profound? The 'profundity' of Parsifal is less German. And *were* such a thing as German profundity to exist, would it really be so necessary for the appreciation of a work of art? Shouldn't an artist surmount the problems and make them dance, as if he had to conduct the Universe, altogether at his own tempo? Tell me!

[1]The concluding concert of Busoni's Basle master-class, on 4 October 1910, was devoted to a performance of his Piano Concerto, conducted by the composer and with Egon Petri as soloist.
[2]Karl Nef wrote in the *Basler Nachrichten*, 6.10.1910: '. . . One may not look for German profundity in the Concerto, but it is true Italian, sensuous music.'

89 TO ROBERT FREUND
in German

Berlin 8.11.1910

I find your 'appraisals' extremely valuable and tacitly expect one on publication of every new work.

The Sonatina has been panned here, the mildest critics found it an imitation of *Debussy*!

I shall have to revise my little Aesthetic, in which not everything seems to have been expressed with sufficient clarity.

I am a worshipper of form!!

This is a matter about which I am hypersensitive; it is a weakness in me that our frequent profanation of form causes me distress – even in everyday things: in paying a call and taking one's leave, in pouring out a cup of tea or planning a programme, in gestures, words and deeds.

But I reject *traditional* and *unalterable forms* and feel that every idea, every motif, every object demands its *own* form, related to that idea, to that motif, to that object.

In nature this is so: the *bud* already contains the fully grown plant.

Although I could write in great detail, these words will convey my meaning to you.

I would like to draw your attention to a little piece by *Arnold Schoenberg*, reshaped for piano by myself, which has just been published by Universal Edition, Vienna.[1] (Unfortunately I have no spare copy.) You will find it hateful, particularly the sound of its harmonies, but it has its own individual feeling and seems to be perfect in *its* form. –

The architectural frame of music is the 'sphere'; it is simply a matter of correctly apportioning the content within it.

In a symphonic poem (Pelleas und Melisande) which was recently performed here,[2] the same Schoenberg had *not* understood this.

It is like a sack crammed with angular objects. – But this work too has its individuality, independence and, in places, beauty as well. (He composed it at the age of 29.)

I could go on waffling for quite some time——

[1]Piano piece, op. 11 no. 2, by Arnold Schoenberg. 'Konzertmässige Interpretation' (interpretation for concert use) by Busoni. See Appendix.
[2]The work was conducted by Oskar Fried on 31 October 1910.

90   TO EGON PETRI
in German

Berlin 11.12.1910

I have to travel to America 10 days *earlier*; therefore I shall be in *London* on 20 December and sail from Southampton on the 21st. – This upsets my work schedule, which I had pre-calculated to the day and hour, quite appreciably.

Today I am off to Vienna to perform my Concerto with Sirota.

In the meantime I sent you some relatively important information about an appointment for you, which should coincide with your arriving and settling in Berlin.

Have you brooded over the arranging of Die Brautwahl and made any sort of decision?

If you should meanwhile have been thinking about the analysis of my 'Grosse Fuge', I take the liberty of noting the following: I have evidently borrowed the motif for the Stretta from the 10th Fugue; without an inner motivation, this procedure would however be meaningless. The genealogy has the following pedigree:

3rd subject

2nd variation

Stretta

In this sense (Bach seems to have arrived at it fortuitously) the figure has a logical evolution.

Steuermann[1] surprised me with a piano sonata of his own composition, which testifies to exceptional talent and great originality. – He is 18 years old and has not yet 'learnt' – it gave me great joy.

On Thursday I shall be back from Vienna and would be grateful for some news around that time.

---

[1]Eduard Steuermann, 1892–1964, studied with Busoni in Vienna. Later famed for his interpretations of the piano music of Schoenberg, Berg and Webern.

91   TO EGON PETRI
         in German

New York 30.12.1910

The crossing was good, better than all previous ones; it was already my fourth.

Immediate impressions of New York are always barbaric; one would like to return home on the next boat available.

Gradually one grows accustomed to it – (i.e. lowers one's standards appreciably) – and in the end, as when constantly in the company of unsightly people – one does find a few attractive features. – I have to consider this period as lost time and do whatever I can for my own gain with it. The 39 scheduled concerts (in 11 weeks), together with the accompanying coupé sittings, give me little hope for work. And even if the time should occasionally be available, where can one suddenly find the peace of mind? Nevertheless I am banking on curtailing my sufferings and shall attempt to call a halt at the beginning of April.

Meanwhile I shall at least be *thinking* about my work and expect that, after such preparation, I shall be able to complete Die Brautwahl all the more speedily. The remaining portions are all *better* than those you have by you.

Please work hard, for much material has to be produced: several vocal scores (one for each singer) and orchestral parts.

Always check against the manuscript. – I hope it also gives you a little pleasure. [. . .]

On 13 January I am to play my Concerto in Chicago. (I am sick and tired of it.) [. . .]

I shall, of course, be putting in a word for you and America.

92   TO EGON PETRI
in German

Chicago 25.1.1911

In the engraved full score 3rd bassoon and contra-bassoon, 3rd clarinet and bass clarinet have frequently been *confused*; the latter also *in the clefs*. Please watch out for this.

It really is ridiculous to send such details across an ocean, but in this way I preserve the feeling of continuity in my work.

I have been unable to resume it, as it has been impossible to find peace and quiet. The next two months are fully occupied with travelling and playing; it was only with the greatest firmness that I was able to settle 1 April for my *final* date and the 8th for my departure. In exchange I have to set up a hasty tour of California between *7 and 31 March*! (It should have begun after 1 April.)

Please understand that, under these circumstances, my humour has abandoned me and my letters appear brusque. It takes the greatest effort to keep my thoughts *set* on my *goal*, yet without putting them into practice.

I am amazed at those people who find America desirable. It is actually only made for those who know no better than to play their instrument, and know *no modesty*.

A *celebrated* confrère of ours has offered his services to play *as often as required* (!) for a fixed sum (Hanson tells me).

Yesterday I made friends with a splendid young lady. The first <u>American girl</u> who meant anything to me. For the present, such specimens are quite isolated. Perhaps the species will occur more frequently in later generations, which would bode well for the future here. Big, healthy, normal, very bright, entirely natural and human; a beautiful person without being a 'beauty'. –

Let us close for today on this major chord which includes – as major sometimes does – a melancholy note. – [. . .]

93   TO EGON PETRI
in German

Minneapolis 27.1.1911

Why am I writing to you again? Because I feel the need to communicate. And you are the aptest partner, so please have
Patience!
Should I ever be 'knighted', this would be my motto. Perhaps more accurately:
In activitate patiens.
Coat of arms: an ass's head crowned with a laurel wreath, and two claws.

I for my part am finished with America – the interest which was kindled anew last year has died out, because it has found no new fuel. Therefore large doses of patience will have to be stirred into two full, arduous months; my nerves will have to knuckle under if they show any sign of getting out of hand.

Then I shall open the score of Die Brautwahl and make plans. It is remarkable that the last act – which is musically the most daring – has the most concise forms. (I consider this an indication of my maturity.)

1. Entrance of the three suitors
2. The Komissionsrat's speech
3. Terzet of the suitors
4. a) b) c) The three caskets
    (-a Thusmann with female chorus
    -b Bensch with male chorus
    -c Edmund with mixed chorus)
5. Scherzo for 4 voices 'Alles hat sich wohlgefügt'[1]
6. Hasty coda.

The scherzo is 'ad libitum' – 'you can play it, you can leave it out', as someone taught us. –

The second act (on the contrary) will give me difficulties; I am saving it up for last.

Mahler is performing the Berceuse élégiaque.[2] Chicago is doing the Concerto.

Middelschulte's organ transcription of the Fantasia contrappuntistica is a feast for organists. The triplet variation on the pedals! –

'903 bars long,' he said with pride, looking round the assembled company.
Today over 2,000 tickets have been sold.

Strange place! The town is just 51 years old and has 300,000 inhabitants. Their one concern is to outdo (to beat . . .) the older neighbouring town of St Paul. In the end they will be amalgamated (this is unavoidable) and, in their union, will detest each other.

I must pass on to you a report from a New Orleans paper, which is typical of the state of civilization.

'A group of high-spirited youngsters behaved in *very unfriendly* fashion

(sic!) towards some coloured people yesterday. On the way from their homes to the theatre, the former came upon three minstrels (roving folk-musicians), hurled abuse at them and killed one of them, seriously wounding the others.'
– This in January 1911.

Good luck for your American tour in 1913. –

[1]All has turned out for the best.
[2]*Berceuse élégiaque*, op. 42, composed in October 1909 and dedicated to the memory of Busoni's mother. Mahler conducted the world première of the work in Carnegie Hall on 21 February 1911.

94 TO EGON PETRI
in German

New York 6.2.1911

Today I have an afternoon's peace and quiet, insufficient to start on new work; so I am writing letters. The last three days were arduous; I am glad they are over, although it is blasphemy to admit to such gladness. For, no matter how arduous they were, they are irrevocable.

Does it interest you? Then look at the following sheet.

3 February	12.00 midday	Depart for Philadelphia
	2.00	Arrival
	3.00–5.00	Concert (public rehearsal)
	6.00–8.00	Return
4 February	3.00–5.00	Recital New York
	6.00–8.00	Journey to Philadelphia
	8.15–10.00	Concert
	10.30–1.00	Return
5 February	12.00	Rehearsal
	8.00 p.m.	Concert
	in New York	

Thus two concerts and two journeys on the 4th!

In these three days I have played to about 10,000 people! (Yesterday evening there were 4,000 in the Metropolitan Opera House.)

This is all very fine and gratifying *at the time*, but actually a feeling of shame prevails.

I expressed this feeling in a brief article, 'Wie lange soll das gehen?'[1] (Signale); it has already been attacked from two sides, has hence been misunderstood.

Maybe the English translation of the Aesthetic (slightly expanded), which is being published this week, will achieve greater clarity.

To turn to something else. All my life I have failed to understand the passage with the

'Mothers'

in Faust, Part II, and nobody ever succeeded in giving me a satisfactory explanation of it.

Faust wishes to behold Helena (clearly the culture of antiquity). Do not the *Mothers*, to whom he must descend, represent the oldest cultures, in which he must steep himself in order to grasp Helena?

It would be a solution.

To continue with literature. Have you noticed how the *English* – despite the high-flown gestures of their writers – are crippled by 'decency'? Every entanglement with a girl leads either to marriage or to renunciation. I am now examining every English book from this aspect and it is beginning to vex me. Even as simple a story as G. Keller's 'Village Romeo and Juliet' would be unthinkable as the work of an English author. The apparently illegitimate child in B. Shaw's 'Man and Superman' is ultimately explained away by a clandestine marriage! – To express it artistically: it seems to me that the Anglo-Saxons are at the *second* stage of their development (in contrast to the *third* and highest). They are still anxious to cast off or conceal their animal instincts. The third period would then represent the victory of the laws of nature over convention; not through primitivity but with greatest refinement.

'For a man stands differently on the same side of the river' etc., as I wrote in the introduction to Liszt.

Yesterday I met my countryman *Toscanini*. He is uncomplicated, agile and quick-witted. – Pleased me. –

Mahler is always inspiring. Yesterday I heard (between everything else) his Schubert Unfinished and some fragments of Wagner. He is a creative musician.[2]

Die Brautwahl is *lying* here – how do things stand with you? Please excuse the astral bell.[3] –

Enough of this prattle. Sorry.

---

[1]'How long must it go on?' The article is dated 'on board M.S. *Oceanic*, 23 December 1910'. Subsequently reprinted in *Von der Einheit der Musik* in 1922.
[2]Orig. ein Gestalter.
[3]The 'astral bell' was evidently a private joke between Busoni and Petri, founded on an American Indian folk legend. Busoni would 'ring' the astral bell across the Atlantic to remind Petri to keep working at the vocal score of *Die Brautwahl*.

95 TO H. W. DRABER
in German

Sedalia Missouri 10.3.1911

[. . .] I am making my way to California, on a detour from Kansas City where I shall catch the main-line train again tomorrow. It will lead me not to rose cavaliers but to rose-fields – a little beauty once in a while will do me no harm, particularly when one has long been travelling through lark-less ox-fields, as I have.[1]

Only Mozart and Verdi have until now found the true 'Cadenzare' of their texts. – It incorporates many factors: mood, tempo, pitch, chiming in with a response, the support, discreet falling back or complete silence of the orchestra. Changing the subject of the conversation, expressing a parenthesis and what know I. 'Falstaff' is the absolute paragon of such things. I can think of hundreds of examples. In 'Der Rosenkavalier' I found not one. Wagner laid too much emphasis on 'declamation' (longer and shorter syllables, the longer ones generally higher) and too much literary illustration. –

Let us take the sentence (which I have just written)
'the longer ones generally higher'.
You could bet that Wagner would have set the word 'longer' to a longer note, the word *higher* to a higher one. But in conversation the inflexion comes on *generally*, the word 'higher' *falls* in pitch.

Please excuse these lectures, I always gallop straight into them.

I heard Don Quixote from the Boston Symphony with great enjoyment. Perhaps Str.'s best work. – I cannot write much, I am convalescing and constantly on the point of changing from travelling clothes into tails. – I would have liked to avoid it, but have to inform you that my dear friend O'Neil Phillips has shot himself. It sounds so abrupt, but it has given me a very trying time.

He no longer had any peace of mind, was virtually hounded by his nerves and often went for weeks without sleep.

At dawn he leaped out of bed and did it. The effect was frightful. Let us rejoice in life, let us remain faithful – every hour is a gift.

[1]Orig. lerchenlose Ochsenauen. Pun on Baron Ochs von Lerchenau in *Der Rosenkavalier*. The opera had been performed for the first time, in Dresden, only a few weeks before, on 26 January 1911.

96 TO EGON PETRI [postcard]
in German

Los Angeles 14.3.1911

Shall open by ringing the astral bell a while. Don't fail to read *Wells'* book 'The new Machiavelli'. It is A1. –

Best wishes and greetings.

97   TO EGON PETRI
in German

San Francisco 20.3.1911

Your letter came like a consoling angel – I am at the end of my tether: have
been unwell for more than 2 weeks, travelling for 3 days, then another 20
hours, then another 30 hours, then another 3 days; am confronted in every
city with a sort of début and, to crown it all, have heard no news from Europe
for ages! At last, at the same time as yours, a letter from Gerda arrived (only
the 2nd from home, today on 20 March).

What you are doing for me is a considerable task; if you have ever owed me
anything, you have amply repaid it and I must *thank* you for the surplus.

But you have not written of your further impressions of Die Brautwahl.
Have I been wrong in thinking that the later work is also an improvement? – I
still hope for sure that this is so.

Before I had begun to ponder over changing the title, Dr Anzoletti[1] – in his
Italian translation – had rendered it (most meaningfully and also beautifully)
as

la sposa sorteggiata.

Sorte means (as you know, or will immediately understand) *fate*, in a moral
sense. – [. . .]

Gerda is looking for an apartment for you – I assure you, dear Egon, that
you could support yourself very well in Berlin even from private English
tuition. How can you feel so uncertain?

Before you receive this letter (yours, dated ?, arrived on the 20th, mine is
unlikely to reach England before 5 April) – you will already have heard of the
death of O'Neil Phillips.

It has distressed me greatly.

He shot himself through the temple and the bullet emerged through the
top of the head: his maladjustment drove him to the idée fixe that it would be
a ridiculous disgrace to have to wear a wig. Don't laugh, it is macabre. – How
one piles up gloomy memories as life goes on!

I should like to close this letter with something more attractive – springtime, the journey home, perhaps our meeting up in England.

I would like to make you conscious of the fact that the best part of your life
is just *beginning*. From 30 to 40 comes the richly flowering tableland, still
gently rising, and only then follows the open summit! – One's children grow
up, one's works abound and ripen, one's outlook grows steadily broader. For
the best of us there is no descent, one is drawn ever higher until – one is lost
in the clouds.[2] –

---

[1]Augusto Anzoletti, Emilio's brother, who was a doctor.
[2]On 24 March 1911, Busoni wrote to Petri as follows:
    When I wrote to you from 'Frisco' 2 or 3 days ago, I was not at all well, and I fear

that the letter came out accordingly; weak and indistinct and formless. Towards the end I clearly remember my feverish attempt, with sickly, uncertain steps, at spiritual mountain climbing, the caricature of a style into which I have been slipping in recent essays, but from which I shall be cured.

98 TO EDWARD J. DENT
in Italian

Berlin 10.5.1911

Your letter gave me immense pleasure. The return to culture, heralded by the refined intelligence which emanates from your words, is a moral favour which only a traveller just returned from America knows fully to appreciate!

Your review of Turandot is the most prudent to have been written about this work and – as overall proof of its accuracy – it is a curious fact that most of the opinions expressed in the article could have a prophetic relevance to the opera 'Die Brautwahl'.

None of the Berlin critics understood that which you correctly call '<u>the Mozartian framework</u>', nor did they understand its clearly defined heredity from Liszt, nor did they discover its origin in L'Enfance du Christ.

As for the rest, should you desire to study the Berceuse élégiaque, you will discover in it that same 'polyphonic logic' for which you have so finely praised me. So I thank you for all the good words you have devoted to me.

You have, as one sees from the brief psychological study of Phillips, reached the same conclusion as I. Poor boy! He suffered and made us suffer, more than you can imagine.

Schirmer (good friend that he is) *surprised* me with his English edition of the Aesthetic.[1] I have *full* trust in you and will accept whatever you decide (with Heffers,[2] or what you think) and gratefully!

I too have had to correct, modify and add various things (the last 5 years have made a man of me, at last) – but this summer I am unable to think of anything but the *opera*, the creation of which is threatening to turn me grey.

For this reason I have to relinquish teaching commitments and every other diversion. Young Browne[3] will always be very welcome when I return to an 'attitudine pedagogica'.

---

[1]Dent had himself made a translation of the *Outline of a New Aesthetic of Music*, which has never been published.
[2]Booksellers and publishers in Cambridge.
[3]William Charles Denis Browne, 1888–1915, composer and critic, close friend of Dent.

99 TO EGON PETRI
in German

Berlin 12.5.1911

I read your letter, yours and Fried's,[1] with feelings of great joy and gratefulness; I thank you in particular for this new token of love!

À propos Fried, England and myself, the preceding day I received – as if by unwitting coincidence – a review of Fried's performance of the Turandot [Suite], written by *Dent*. It is the most intelligent review of this work I have ever read. Published in 'Monthly Musical Record' for 1 February.

Dent himself further sent me a delightful letter (he has a perfect command of Italian). In it he told me, amongst other things – that [Ursula] Newton[2] and [Rosamond] Ley[3] played a 2-piano recital in Cambridge!! The programme included the Berceuse élégiaque, presumably in your arrangement.[4] – Dent's comment (in Italian): I tell you frankly that the B. speaks to me in a completely unknown and remarkable language, and if I – who know and admire your Concerto, Elegies etc. – gained *such* an impression of the work, you can imagine how it struck the other listeners. –

Yes, I can imagine it. The dear girls! <u>They meant it so well</u>. But in Cambridge of all places!

Now I must return to the score. –

[1] Oskar Fried, 1871–1941, conductor and composer, pupil of Humperdinck. Dedicatee of Busoni's *Nocturne symphonique*.
[2] Ursula Creighton (née Newton), 1881–1974, pianist and writer on music. She studied with Busoni at Basle in 1910.
[3] Rosamond Ley, 1883–1969, pianist and writer on music. The English translator of Busoni's *Letters to his Wife* and *The Essence of Music*.
[4] Petri's transcription of the *Berceuse élégiaque* for two pianos has never been published. The MS is the property of Mr Daniell Revenaugh.

100 TO IRMA BEKH
in German

Berlin 25.5.1911

[. . .] Yes, I shall be here for the whole summer (and am finishing off my opera) and I look forward to your arrival with great joy! Perhaps at the moment there is enough in Berlin to keep you away from Paris; on the other hand, it is certain that if you were to see Paris first you would no longer have any interest in Berlin.

Since 1 May (I returned at the end of April) I have been working hard on my own account. It is the finest time of my life; the spring has come, I am free and healthy and deeply, profoundly grateful to fate.

This seemed almost *unjust* to me whilst Mahler was lying on his deathbed; I had an uneasy conscience. I sailed back from America on the same ship as he and already then had no doubt as to the outcome. It had a dampening effect on our little party of travellers (Stefan Zweig was amongst them) and in the midst of conversation we were often silent. Now that he is no more,[1] he seems to me to grow ever more beautiful. A true artist and a character of gold. What purity in that soul!

Enough, I weep. –

(Yesterday Benni became all of nineteen years old!)

[1]Mahler had died on 18 May.

101 TO EGON PETRI
in German

Berlin 4.6.1911

'Soon the gruesome and ghostly old Jew will at last be dislodged . . .'[1]

═══

Yesterday Brecher[2] called (and incidentally used the libretto of 'Lohengrin' as a yardstick with which to measure mine – with such 'theatre people' who see everything *from the rostrum, looking into the auditorium* and believe they have the only viable perspective, I was made to think of Poe's: 'The system of Doctor Feather'[3] – a long parenthesis! – so Brecher called and said,
and said:
it would be absolutely necessary to have *three acts complete in orchestral and vocal score* by *1 August*. – Well, we can surely achieve *that*! I myself hope to get even further.

═══

I was delighted to make the acquaintance of Mussorgsky's opera Boris Godunov (pronounced: Báris Gadūnôff). Fresh, genuine, Russian in the best sense, artless, original, often astonishingly expressive.

═══

31 May, a red-letter day for me. Discovered weaknesses in Wagner scores for the first time. Made me a little nervous.

═══

Today, 4 June 1911, the unveiling of the Vittorio Emmanuele monument in Rome. Consumed 25 years' work and about 11 million. But it is a 'monument' for centuries. Oh, victory avenue! There they stand in endless rows, as if in a bad dream, these benches and figures pulling faces; one has no neck, the next an over-sized head, another seems to be reflected in a distorting mirror – and there are ever more of them, to the right, to the left – without rhythm, equally spaced, equally tall, equally wide – just as in Little Nemo in Slumberland.[4]——

Now I have landed in a marble cul-de-sac; if there is an exit, I am quite likely to arrive at the Zelten:[5] there we are reminded of Die Brautwahl and – God be praised! – the form of my letter is redeemed.

[1]Reference to Manasse, one of the chief characters in *Die Brautwahl*.
[2]Gustav Brecher, 1879–1940, conductor of *Die Brautwahl* at the Hamburg world première and dedicatee of the opera.
[3]Actually 'The system of Dr Tarr and Prof. Fether'.
[4]*Little Nemo in Slumberland* strip cartoon series by Winsor McCay depicting the dream-adventures of a little boy called Nemo. Published in the *New York Herald* 1905–10, republished in book form by Nostalgia Press, New York, 1969.
[5]Park in Berlin, scene of Act I part I of *Die Brautwahl*.

102 TO EGON PETRI
in German

Berlin 9.6.1911
Letter No. 115?[1]

Thank you, first of all! for sending the MS – for completing the 3rd act – for the sensitive and entertaining letter. It calls for a reply; and then I also need to prepare you for the 4th act.

The 3rd part of Act 3 is one of the *earliest* sections of the opera, which is at this stage no longer a 'comedy'. Therefore I was somewhat wistfully gladdened to hear that it is your favourite. One really prefers to have one's later work recognized as being superior! – The beginning (Albertine) was inspired by a recitative of Carissimi (from La figlia di Jefte). The situation (that of a daughter betrayed and sold by her father) is to an extent parallel. Carissimi begins:

Heu, ___ heu mi – hi   fi – lia   me - a!

Of course the harmony, pounding temples, the interweaving of the Erscheinung motif render the model unrecognizable.

(I have not been sparing with quotations: Gregorian chant, the Polonaise, the Jewish motifs – these are all transcriptions.) – [. . .]

And now to Act 4.

It is nearing completion and is the *latest* creation for Die Brautwahl. It will probably be its downfall.

The act is subdivided as follows:

Lighthearted:

> Prelude
> Arrival of the suitors (1st)
>   (2nd)
>   (3rd)
> The father's speech (to I.II.III.)
> Agreement (4tet) (also conclusion of the Prelude)
> Terzet of the suitors

Mystical:

> Commencement of the casket ceremony
> The three caskets (1st)
>   (2nd)
>   (3rd)
> Quartet-scherzo for the remaining characters ('Alles hat sich
>   wohlgefügt')
> Leonhard carries Edmund off to Rome

Formally speaking, everything has really turned out for the best and in my maturest vein.

It happened *unintentionally* that the 'commencement of the ceremony' and the three caskets formed a theme and three variations. I myself only noticed it subsequently and found it the correct reaction. Naturally: variations in the fantastic sense. – I reworked the quartet-scherzo three times until it became crystal clear; just as I have indeed been continually revising (with a view to conciseness rather than breadth). – Excuse this rather pedantic address; but *I* am most fond of this section. –

And now 104 pages are already at the engraver (the act runs to about 150) – so that material will soon follow; meanwhile you are reading proofs. –

Thank you again!

---

[1] During the summer of 1911 Busoni began to number his letters to Petri, beginning with this, No. 115. The idea, possibly a private joke, was soon abandoned.

103 TO EGON PETRI
in German

Berlin 27.6.1911
(119

At the same time as your kind letter I have just received the first 88 pages of
Act 4 from the printers. I shall send them on to you tomorrow together with
the manuscript. It is *two thirds of the whole thing*, and that is merely the
postlude. –

I also received the finally corrected 3rd part of Act 3 (but not the 2nd part).
(Probably because of the addenda.)

Further, from you, part 1 in vocal score, which seems to be masterfully
done and well engraved. (It is somewhat confusing and I shall be glad when
everything has been assembled!)

Meanwhile the first 25 pages of MS for *Act Two* have been written, the last
task that remains.

My admiration and gratitude for your work are not in the least prejudiced
by the fact that there are still misprints everywhere. Of course I am reading
everything through, if only for the sake of checking my own work.

I also forgot to answer that I have *heard* the Liszt sonnet:[1] I performed it
with Senius[2] in my orchestral concert.[3] Does one say 'die Sonette' or 'das
Sonnett' in German? 'Sonnette' sounds like 'a bell' and is sometimes more
appropriate. The German translation is then 'Reim-Geklingel' – 'rhyme-
ringing'.

Unfortunately I am beginning to feel tired: it's all a little much.

All praise to your grandfather Tornauer!

French humour has a different nuance. I read, for example, that Gavarny
said to the Goncourts, 'I cannot admit that "la pensée" is a gift of God. It
reacts to a kick in the pants!' Or: 'Science eats away constantly at the gods.
Now they have trapped Jupiter's lightning in a Leyden's jar!'——

(More about books:)

When I bought a book by Fouqué some time ago, because of the beautiful
First Edition, I didn't look inside it. The day before yesterday I thumbed
through it (it is called 'Sigurd der Schlangentöter') and was astounded to
discover a dramatization of the Siegfried saga, indeed with *exactly the same
scenic disposition* as in Wagner's Siegfried and Götterdämmerung. The
language (with alliterations) is also very similar. The book was published in
1808. One could well hold it against Wagner that he first sketched out these
two pieces as an independent work and also that Fouqué's book is part of a
trilogy (Der Held des Nordens).[4] – Fortunately with Fouqué we are back in
the 'Zelten';[5] otherwise I would have been lost.

---

[1]Liszt's Petrarc Sonnet no. 104, 'Pace non trovo', which Busoni orchestrated in
December 1907.

[2]Felix Senius, 1868–1913, celebrated German concert singer.
[3]The concert had taken place on 3 January 1908 in the Beethoven-Saal, Berlin.
[4]The other two books, published by Hitzig in 1810, are *Sigurds Rache* and *Aslanga*.
[5]The scene in *Die Brautwahl* to which Busoni here refers includes a setting of a Fouqué sonnet.

104 TO EGON PETRI
in German

[Berlin 12.7.1911]

Last Friday we met up with Schirmer[1] (from New York) and Oskar Fried for a frugally aristocratic meal at the Kaiserhof.[2] It was a most memorable, undissonant evening. Firstly we were united in our allegiance to Gustav Mahler (we three happened in fact to have been his true friends) – further we were associated by matters of mutual interest which, thanks to Schirmer's predilection for me, were helped to a speedy and fruitful conclusion.

Fried has – with the greatest probability – fulfilled his most passionate wish – (just see how human passions can be misled) – America.

Schirmer has decided to buy up the complete works of Delius.

Also: to rescue me and Die Brautwahl from Harmonie Verlag;[3] like the knight, the virgin and the dragon.

All this was most pleasing and on top of this came a further pleasure.

A Gustav Mahler Foundation (for the support of talented musicians) has been inaugurated. It was the wish of Frau Mahler herself that I should be one of *three* people who should have a sort of tutelary function. This made me realize how high I stand in the estimation of this outwardly and inwardly beautiful (almost noble) woman. I hope you will meet her sometime and make friends with her. (She is not yet thirty years old.)[4]

You were also a topic of the conversation with Schirmer, as Fried volunteered some illustrations of his 'sentimental journey through England'.[5] Should you eventually get to America, I can guarantee a good friend in this Schirmer fellow.

My opinion of that country has once again changed remarkably. Not only do I hold no brief for its cultural ascent but I also believe it has already passed its zenith. What the Americans have done since crossing this line is leading to a moral desert. Which is to say: practical exploitation (for its own sake) and coarse luxuriation. As other problems (moral, religious and artistic questions) are not being considered, America presents itself as the Middle Ages equipped with machines and electricity! 'A great country!' – Yes, by God, and as *He* created it; even if it has no nightingales and no wine. One could be reconciled through their naïvety if they were not so impertinent. – But enough.

====

I am writing this in expectation of your promised letter and in a pause in the score. And recall that this letter has not yet been numbered. Therefore:

~ 123 ~
=====

Meanwhile I have circumnavigated the worst rocks in the score. The first part of the 2nd act was deformed. Plastic surgery came to the rescue, provoking more groans from the doctor than from the patient.

'La Génie c'est la patience,' says Flaubert, who almost proved the point. –

As today, 12 July, 1911, your letter has not yet arrived, I shall close mine without further ado.

[1]Rudolph Edward Schirmer, 1859–1919, American publisher. Was acquainted with Liszt in Weimar 1873–5; president of G. Schirmer Inc. from 1907.
[2]Pun on Hotel Kaiserhof = imperial court.
[3]A new publishing house in Leipzig. Busoni had begun to have legal and financial difficulties with this short-lived concern. Several works of Delius had also been published by Harmonie Verlag.
[4]Alma Mahler was in fact 32 years old.
[5]Allusion to Laurence Sterne, *A Sentimental Journey through France and Italy. By Mr. Yorick*, 2 vols., London, 1768.

105 TO EGON PETRI
in German

Berlin 16.7.1911
124

I was indeed surprised when the roll [of manuscript] – proof of a completed task – arrived yesterday. I took my best hat and put it on, so as to raise it – to you. – I too shall have to resort to the evenings in the coming month; how shall I otherwise finish the task. (But around 7 o'clock I actually feel drained.) Meanwhile 70 pages of manuscript score (2nd act) are ready for engraving.

I believe the most difficult knot has therewith been partly untied and partly cut asunder. Once I brought out my 'broad brush' and daubed the outer wall of the 2nd act, namely the Prelude, quite thickly. I myself am curious as to the effect. The outline of the scoring is as follows: full orchestra and fortissimo; but all strings, the horns and full brass with mutes. Liszt would have dubbed it 'Valse chromatique'. – In the interest of good musical proportions I have had to condense Thusman's dream narration. So it is now: March – Waltz and March.

Geometrically illustrated:

□ △ □

(I have bought myself three Indian temple figures, which are my greatest joy and the crowning glory of my apartment. The central one is a dancing Buddha, richly clad – almost Spanish – and wellnigh a Don Giovanni.

To his right and left kneel two praying youths. They all look as if of solid gold and are inlaid with coloured stones, half life-size.[1]

Your letter did not arrive until the evening. I had really been longing for it. Such a conservatoire involves you in a pile of work, which one overlooks when signing the contract! I too had to attend two examinations as 'jury' and thanked my stars (on the two mornings) that I didn't have to rush off to school after breakfast every day – as I did earlier in Boston. – But I get no picnics and also no farewell parties (have not practised for just as long – since 1 April).

Many thanks for your kind sympathy and friendly words about the 4th act. May God grant that the 'mystical' section expresses what I wanted.

Draber has undertaken the final proof-reading and I shall send him your questionnaire, with which I agree, except for the heading: IV. Act. This should be replaced by 'Nachspiel'. (Previously it was part of the third act, I have subsequently separated it.) –

How is Frau Mitta? – The story is told that – as Bismarck and his architect were discussing the plans for a new west wing for Friedrichsruh' – the 'princess' came on the scene, looked over the area which had been staked out and exclaimed: Oh dear, and what about my lovely sunsets! – 'You see,' – Bismarck turned to his architect – 'our scheme has been rejected.' –

Middelschulte is in Germany. At the end of August the first performance of the *Fantasia contrapp.* (for organ and orchestra)[2] is to take place in Dortmund.

Maybe I shall go there. (Instead of to Italy, bon Dieu.) – And how much else I am supposed to do this autumn! – To see you again will throw a more pleasant light on many things. [. . .]

---

[1]See plate 7. The figures are clearly visible over the grand pianos.
[2]The arrangement for organ and orchestra, entitled *Sinfonia Contrappuntistica*, was made by Frederick Stock (between 24 July and 11 August 1911!). See also letters 107, 108 and p. 429.

7 Busoni's music-room at Viktoria-Luise-Platz 11, Berlin. The wooden organ benches at the pianos are no less unorthodox than the combination of Oriental figurines (cf. letter No. 105) and a bas-relief of Donatello (extreme top left corner)

8 (from l. to r.) Busoni, Frederick Stock, Wilhelm Middelschulte, Georg Hüttner in Dortmund, August 1911, on the occasion of the first performance of Stock's orchestration of the *Fantasia Contrappuntistica* (cf. letters No. 105, 107 and 108)

9 In Busoni's library, Berlin, September 1911 (from l. to r.) Oskar Fried, Busoni, Frederick Stock, Egon Petri, Arthur Bodanzky, Wilhelm Middelschulte, Arrigo Serato, H.W. Draber. These musicians are all mentioned in Busoni's letters, and four of them were recipients of letters included in this book

106 TO EGON PETRI
in German

Berlin 4.8.1911

It was a great pleasure to read your letter; I have rather a bad conscience that I am taxing you so severely (Gerda says: Gewissensgebisse[1]) but I myself – in dangerously hot weather – have not relaxed for a single day. – Draber is checking the final proofs. He is becoming a little familiar and making suggestions for the orchestration. For the banjo imitation it would be effective to slip a piece of paper between the strings of the harp (his own criticism) – well, you know him. He does not possess what I would call a 'delicate touch'.

When someone recommended a still inexperienced 'but modest' young musician to Mahler, the latter said: 'In what sense is he modest?' (You can make the connection with the previous paragraph yourself.)——

The end is now approaching but I still have to negotiate a few tricky problems. This section is theatrically important and should not be a failure. Moreover I had not looked at it *for over three years*! So some rewriting will be necessary.—

The end of the 2nd half-act is being engraved, the first 70 pages are already finished. I shall send them to you tomorrow.

Should the *Vorspiel* be arranged for *four* hands? – Now you hold the strings in one hand. The first scene – as you can see – is the amiable original which is later caricatured (die erste Gefahr).[2]

Also other passages correspond to later ones, as for example:

Komissionsrat (Act 2) Leonhard (Act 3)

nahm gar kein Geld   mit Geld ist hier nichts_ an - zu -fang- en

The dream narration[3] has turned out well. In the later section Manasse's entrance is the best piece in the half-act. Here you will find a connection with the 2nd casket (chorus).

For your amusement I am sending you the programme for Heidelberg. The revision of my 6 Liszt programmes is all but complete.[4]

I strongly recommend the Goncourt Journals to you. (One of them meets his former mistress, who is now married: 'Actually she had not changed at all, mais la caisse d'épargne lui était écrite sur le front.)'[5]

[1]Non-existent word. Gewissensbiß = pang of conscience; Gebiß = denture.
[2]The first danger, section in Act III part 2 of *Die Brautwahl*.
[3]Scene 18 in Act III part 2.
[4]In the autumn of 1911 Busoni gave six recitals in Berlin which presented virtually all of Liszt's major works for piano.
[5]But the savings bank was written on her forehead.

107 TO EGON PETRI
in German

Berlin 15.8.1911

Yesterday I received your eagerly awaited, *semi*-humorous letter. We two are now handcuffed together; let us endure to the end!

I have been prostrated by a sudden violent attack of influenza – in the hottest weather – which robbed me of three days!! Today I resumed work and the end is coming into sight. I ask for no letters, by God; but just to reassure me, I would like to hear from you whether you find the 2nd act just as good. I noticed that you wrote in considerable detail about arranging the Vorspiel, without a word about the impression it made. We women in confinement are sensitive creatures.——

Yesterday I was visited by *Stock*. He has completed the instrumentation of the Fantasia contrapp., the thing is being performed in Dortmund on 21 August and I am going there to hear it. It is with organ ad libitum and Middelschulte is playing, Stock is conducting. As he was at a loss for a pianist for an East[-coast] tour (with the Chicago Thomas Orchestra), I suggested *you* and he wrote to America straight away. – Nous verrons.

At the same time I made the acquaintance of Ludwig Rubiner,[1] a *highly* intelligent young Jew with whom you could become friends. [Alice] Landolt was also here and a delightful, very young, yellow-skinned *Japanese* girl,[2] who didn't come from Tokyo on foot. – Moving house is a distressing state of affairs, but so full of indeterminate light reflections whose sources one does not recognize. The most valuable things in life are its uncertainties. In contrast the clearly defined screaming of children, shifting of packing cases and hanging of curtains is admittedly trite, simply because it obscures every intuition of what is to follow.

But everything runs its course and how soon does it belong to the past. 'Weg, weg,' barks Andersen's watch-dog.[3]

So let us look forward to Berlin, where you will undoubtedly feel happy, inspired, free; not the Berlin for tourists on the bummel, but rather the city which compels creativity, promotes and isolates, luxuriates and socializes, the important centre [4]

[1]Ludwig Rubiner, 1881–1920, socialist author.
[2]This was Hide Kasiwa-Mura. In 1922 she married Raffaello Busoni; she died in 1931.
[3]Weg = away. Reference to Hans Christian Andersen's story 'The Snowman'.
[4]The note E^b is called Es in German; Es = it.

108 TO EGON PETRI
in German

Berlin 24.8.1911

[. . .] I have become rather weary and been *forced* to interrupt the business.
'So nah am Hafen' –
or however it goes in the 'Flying Dutchman'.[1]

I am going to travel and shall have to leave 60–70 pp. of MS unfinished. In asking you for your opinion, I did so chiefly because I feared that – due to over-tiredness – my critical faculties had become unreliable.

Now, to my joy, I have received your very kind and rich letter – which triumphantly braved the strike.

I really should have provided an impulse for the trip to Dortmund. But (firstly) I didn't dare tempt you into a journey in the midst of your moving house, secondly I was not certain enough of the value of its motive. The greatest event[2] of the little festival was Middelschulte's superhumanly beautiful organ playing. What the layman understands by 'music of the angels' was realized. The transition to the 1st fugue, the Intermezzo, the Cadenza (particularly the march-like section) were artistry of the highest order and sounded as if from another world. (Both M. and Stock are remaining in Europe for two further weeks and hope to meet you in Berlin.) Stock's orchestral transcription is un-mystical and, for my taste, lacking in fragrancy and transparency, though in some parts brilliant work.[3]

From here to the 'Berceuse [élégiaque]' is the difference between Sancho Panza and Don Quixote (to be taken with a grain of salt). I think: Sancho is also entertaining and often in the right.

======

Draber and Fried came with me.

======

My journey is intended to divert me ('abstraction') and simultaneously bring Benni to Italy. For the time being I shall leave him with Anzoletti (one hour from Milan), who serves as a bridge: the only one which this engineer shall ever provide for mankind.

======

Well, I have gleaned *one* criticism from you: the discrepancies of style in the opera.

But – *pace* Ludwig of Bavaria – can one not sense them in the 'Ring'?

However, only in an *ascending* line, whereas I did not proceed chronologically.

I am very pleased at this admission.——

Dear Egon, if I were you, I would not play on Ibach [pianos] without making an agreement with them. Steinways have indeed turned down Carreño[4] point blank; they are much superior. Nevertheless, every step back would become more difficult. In Dortmund I took the liberty of arranging something for you (Kapellmeister Hüttner.)[5]

Your prospects seem certain to me, even if lacking in explosive immediacy. Everyone with whom I have spoken knew your name and reacted respectfully.

---

[1]'So nah dem Ziel nach langer Fahrt' = so close to port after a long voyage, *The Flying Dutchman*, Act I.

[2]Busoni writes Ergebnis = outcome, but evidently means Ereignis = event.

[3]cf. Schoenberg's letter to Busoni, Appendix No. 26.

[4]Teresa Carreño, 1853–1917, Venezuelan pianist, opera singer and conductor. It was

customary for celebrated pianists to make exclusive contracts with piano manufacturers, e.g. Busoni had a contract in the United States with the firm of Chickering.
[5]Georg Hüttner, 1861–1919, conductor. Concert director and Director of the Musikhochschule in Dortmund from 1887 (see Plate 8).

109 TO EGON PETRI
in German

Varese 9.9.1911

Now you are in Berlin and I am going to write to you after all. Anzoletti sends you his best wishes. I call him Robinson deux; firstly because he resembles his namesake,[1] secondly because he too does everything himself; the cooking, the electrical wiring, the shoe-buttons (as engineer, director, book-keeper and paymaster, traveller), the soda water and the bathroom fittings; makes his own cupboards and his single bed; has in fact lived all alone for years without exchanging an opinion with anybody.[2] While he was recently attempting to explain to Benni that there is a club here – as he said – 'for the elevation of the middle-class point' (for the improvement of the working classes), I thought to myself that he would on no account be a member of it.

The following is curious. Today I met an (Italian) conductor from the Metropolitan Opera House in New York who is holding chorus rehearsals for the forthcoming American season *here* (in a circus). 'The flying Dutchman' (not to be confused with Wijsman – nor with an aviator) and . . . 'Lobetanz'.[3] (Was performed in Germany as a 'Wald-Oper', which gives you some idea). – Incidentally tonight there is a performance of 'Madame Butterfly' (for the last time this season) and – I shall attend it; for 'if need be, the Devil feeds on flies'[4] (in French: faute de mieux on couche avec sa femme).[5] (Well, I don't have any *flies* to feed on; they are feeding on me!) – Moreover I long for sounds of music, and a poor orchestra is instructive: sound gives birth to sound and I hope it will help me break the deadlock in Die Brautwahl. 50 pages are lacking and I can get no further!! And you?

On Monday I shall start to make my way home and shall see you – God willing – around the middle of the month. I can visualize you (like Thusman's narrative, framed by two fairy tales), flanked by Kestenberg[6] and Draber: (would have liked to have a report from you; now it is too late, instead we shall have to get together one afternoon). – I could also imagine you three in the style of my Indian figurines, my golden ones! Or singing angels.

NB When I arrive, the get-together will be accompanied by Istrian wine.

[1]i.e. H. W. Draber.
[2]Emilio Anzoletti married in 1918.
[3]Opera in three acts by Ludwig Thuille, first produced in Karlsruhe, 1898.

[4]Orig. In der Not frisst etc. [sic], i.e. 'In der Not frißt der Teufel Fliegen'; a proverb equivalent to 'Beggars can't be choosers'.
[5]For want of anything better, one sleeps with one's wife.
[6]Leo Kestenberg (see p. 426).

110 TO EGON PETRI
in German

Berlin 19.9.1911

Without in the least wishing to be importunate, permit me to ask you what you still have of the opera, where the key to my writing desk is, and when you are coming. –

Today Frau Jella (Baroness Oppenheimer) is here with Hofmannsthal; we would have liked to have you here too. –

111 TO EGON PETRI
in German

Cologne 20.12.1911

It was unavoidable. I was discovered in the hotel by Frau and Herr Cahier,[1] the latter 'K. und K. Hofopernsängerinsgatte'.[2] 'Herr Cahier' – in his idle hours – which are all the hours of the day – likes to strike up a conversation with people he knows and doesn't know. As the addressee never remembers his face, the young man introduces himself; the addressee being still just as mystified at the unfamiliar name, our K. und K. spouse hastily adds that he is 'the husband of Frau Cahier'. He is prepared for this and has the brief introduction at his fingertips. – He and I had already played the same scene in Heidelberg and yesterday it was repeated precisely and smoothly.

===

Now, some days ago, in Berlin, Weingartner had invited me, through Frau Klinckerfuss,[3] to listen to his quintet.[4] At the time I had been able to shirk it; but yesterday I could not refuse to attend the performance of his symphony.[5] Thus it became unavoidable, and I went to the 'Gürzenich concert'.

How can I convey my impressions to you? It was a perfectly normal 'symphony' concert and became for me quite an experience. I rarely find time to sit in the audience, and simply observing the public gave me an unaccustomed sensation. An uneasy, oppressive sensation which deeply dispirited me. These two groups of people, of which the one below has the other demonstrate something to them: there was something grotesquely ghostly about it.

Let us forget the 'high society', we all know about them. But have you ever had thoughts about an 'orchestra'? Each individual is a disappointed person, a poor devil; as a group they are a suppressed rebellion and as official 'body' they are vain and conceited. Routine bestows upon their performance a veneer of perfection and reliability; otherwise this throng hates its profession, its situation and, as often as not, music itself.

Now Steinbach[6] comes on.

Every line of his face and his body is inartistic. His attitude, which wavers between gravity and vanity, and, with the aid of ugly and offensive movements, is intended to simulate meaningfulness and enthusiasm in his actions, banishes any aesthetic pleasure on the part of the spectator from the outset. But also on the part of the listener. I shall not embark on a further lecture on this point. Nor would I be telling you anything you did not already know.

Of the programme, individual passages of 'Leonore No. 2' thrilled me. It has moments of genius, at times more original than the 'third': I was also moved by the imperfections of the second; for it made clear to me the agonized searching and touching helplessness in the face of such mighty intentions and feelings. – The succeeding items in the 1st part – I cannot help it – left me with the impression of an inquest. Every item had something defunct or moribund about it, and within me, too, something gave up the ghost. I listened with the greatest attention while the various structures crumbled away in eight-bar periods.

Where in the Beethoven the music had held *me* in its grip, in the others I held the pieces in my hands, looked them over and threw them on the heap.

It is difficult to describe such a thing; and even harder to experience it.

The aria from 'La Clemenza di Tito'[7] is more of a ghost than a corpse: rather a shadow of (perhaps) a more fortunate age.

Five Lieder by Brahms! – and accompanied at the piano by a Court Director of Music![8] They never did live. Harmony exercises interlarded with platitudes. Nor could I find any relationship between the words and the music. –

Siegfried Idyll:

> 'Erscholl ein Ruf da froh in meine Weisen:
> "ein Sohn ist da!" – der musste Siegfried heissen.'[9]

(The poem is – by your leave – Wagner's own.)

This music is very attractive. It is clear that it has been pieced together and has a serious imbalance between content and duration. Moreover the style of fragmentary repetition and hypnotic persistence obtrudes too strongly.

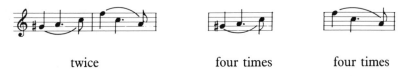

| twice | four times | four times |

and once more from the beginning. – But this is a corpse that is beautiful to behold even in death.

Weingartner's symphony is a theatre cloak-room. I left after the second movement, all the more decisively in that my bladder was no longer holding its own.

My spirits had sunk terribly low. When that acknowledged as the best fails, what remains? And this manner of dishing up art which we call a concert; it had never so discouraged me!

I paid 6 Marks for my ticket, 50 Pfennigs for the cloakroom and 1 Mark for the cab. – Otherwise it cost me very dearly, but in exchange I acquired new knowledge; – nobody can take that from me.

If you find this letter distasteful, then tear it up. I felt the need to write it, and to you.

[1]Madame Charles Cahier was the artist's name of the mezzo-soprano Jane Walker, 1870–1951. Born in Nashville, Tennessee, she married Sir Charles Cahier in 1904. From 1906 she sang at the Vienna Hofoper; in 1908 she sang in the world première of Mahler's *Das Lied von der Erde*.
[2]K. und K. (Austrian) = royal imperial; Hofopernsängerinsgatte = Court opera singer's husband.
[3]Margarete Klinckerfuss, 1877–1959, German pianist, pedagogue and writer on music.
[4]Felix Weingartner, Quintet, op. 50, for clarinet, violin, viola, cello and piano. Published in 1911.
[5]Symphony no. 3 in E, op. 49. This was the first performance, conducted by the composer.
[6]Fritz Steinbach, 1855–1916, conductor. He was 'Gürzenich Kapellmeister' from 1902 to 1914. A noted Brahms interpreter.
[7]'Parto, parto', with obbligato clarinet.
[8]The songs were 'Weit über das Feld', *Spanisches Lied*, *Sapphische Ode*, *Der Schmied*, *Von ewiger Liebe*. Arnold Kroegel, 1857–1923, Königlicher Musikdirektor, played the piano.
[9]'A son is born!' – the joyful cry resounded;
On Siegfried's name his fortune must be founded.

112 TO EGON PETRI
in German

Hamburg 28.3.1912

When a work, which (until its completion) has been entirely occupying *one* brain, is subsequently divided out between 100 brains and more, it is only natural that some of its content should be spilled during re-loading.[1]

However, it will be possible to gain an impression of 'Die Brautwahl'.

As always, the orchestra is the composer's strongest adversary. (I *don't* mean this *personally* but rather in the problem of artistic manipulation.) It is a myth (which is passed on thoughtlessly from one person to the next) that nowadays everyone is a good orchestrator. The moment it becomes a matter of personal expression and new goals, one is repeatedly confronted with problems. Mahler and Strauss both admitted that to me!

On the other hand, in *theatrical* matters – where I really am more of a novice – I feel entirely *uninhibited*. This is no doubt due to my Italian blood. Here I feel almost at home and have command of the situation. – I am exhilarated by the 'experience' and 'routine' of a stage-director, everything has a child-like air: the apparatus is large without being overpowering.

I do believe – if it is not too late – that I shall still accomplish good things in this field. [. . .]

---

[1]Busoni had gone to Hamburg to supervise the rehearsals of *Die Brautwahl*.

II3 TO EGON PETRI
in German

Hamburg 4.4.1912

My thoughts have frequently returned to our conversation about literary matters. – I had not quite understood you and wished to clarify my own thoughts. In saying that I had not understood you this is not, in this case, the polite phrase one substitutes for
                                   'you were wrong'.
The phrase is to be taken *literally*.

As soon as one commands and can correctly apply a language as well as you do with German, there is no obstacle to writing.

If you have clear thoughts, you will express yourself clearly; if you have an original idea, it will sound original; if you have taste (which is an indefinable term), then nothing tasteless will emerge from your pen; finally, if you have personality, it will be bound to radiate in every sentence.

Your systematic manner of thinking enables you to perfect *your technique*, *should you attach importance to this*. But it will not generally emerge as a matter of course from your idea. It consists of a degree of expertise, as for example: expressing yourself as succinctly as possible, using diverse words to express the same idea, choosing the appropriate form in which to express yourself, etc.

If you are master of your *subject* (as *is* the case in matters of musical theory or musical aesthetics), this sleight of hand will suffice.

Should you be, for example, a *playwright*, then you would have to devote yourself to other exercises and observations – in which no 'man of letters' could be of assistance.

Should you have the inclination and ambition to become a *virtuoso* of language and style, then you will have to go beyond the norms of the literary world. In this case your talent and continuous practice would be decisive.

But thought, feeling and originality will always remain the most important, dominating and outstanding factors.

Vide Schopenhauer, Heine, Kleist and even Goethe. They seem to write merely

'correctly';

that which makes them what they are is, in the case of the first, clarity, precision and power of analogy; of the next, humour; of the third, strength and intensity; and, in Goethe's case, calm superiority and comprehensive understanding. Are these qualities

'literary'? ?

Compare, if you will, an 'uneducated' letter of Beethoven's with a feuilleton by the erudite Leopold Schmidt[1]: which is the greater writer?

[1]See footnote to letter 48 on p. 72.

114 TO EGON PETRI
in German

Hamburg 5.4.1912

A Good Friday without a hint of magic. Grey and rainy. However:

'Et resurrexit tertia die'.

(Did you know that I was born on Easter Sunday?)

Many things are depressing me.

The *Nachspiel* is still misunderstood. The dear 'theatre people' cavil.

At present I am, quite unnecessarily, reading a book – a book! (called: *L'Ève future*) which is 'getting me down' completely. It's the most wicked book ever to have been written and, were it not for passages of outstanding brilliance and 'literariness', it would deserve the censor's anathema. It is by my much admired Villiers de l'Isle-Adam.

In this book, where an 'idealized' Edison speaks uninterruptedly for 300 pages (a dialectical feat of virtuosity which must be unique), the advantages of a 'surrogate' woman are proved against those of a real one.

The appalling theories which are proposed in the course of the dialogue are discouraging to the point of resignation.

The tragedy for me is that I am finding my own opinions in this devilish work carried through to their final – unexpected – conclusion, and that I myself am horrified at the prospect.

Maybe its effect on many, on most people is humorous.

But life is brief and insignificant: Why should one take things seriously?

═══

On Thursday the *preliminary* dress rehearsal. – Excuse this explosion.

115 TO EGON PETRI
in German

Hamburg 6.4.1912

You're all letting me down (strains of the egoist in me); Gerda hasn't written me a single line, dear Egon is equally silent, even if he may have something to report. –

The rehearsals are getting worse. The more forces (weaknesses) come together, the greater the sum of inaccuracies becomes.

I am beginning to lose confidence; without in the least becoming 'nervous'.

I have read to the end of that diabolical book. It has taken more toll on me than the rehearsals!

A mythical inventor constructs a synthetic woman and proves that she is preferable to any living one. Every objection is anticipated and exhaustively countered – and finally mysticism also enters into the action, completely confusing one's disordered reason. One wrings one's hands and loses all foundation and belief. An abominable book and of such deceptive persuasiveness that the reader abandons his own viewpoint.

I must say it again: if only I could compose like that! Despite obvious reminders (of Poe, Hoffmann and R. Wagner)[1] it is uniquely original.

How remarkable that such a work should remain almost unknown! Has anybody discussed why one work should become more *popular* than the others? – A subject for H.W.D[raber]! An intrepid man! A bold seizer of opportunities! Always 'au fait'.

Auf Wiedersehen, but when?

[1] A letter to Gerda, dated 2 April 1912, gives more specific information on this point. Busoni meant *Ligeia* by Poe, *Der Sandmann* by E. T. A. Hoffmann and Klingsor's summoning of Kundry in *Parsifal*.

116 TO ROBERT FREUND
in German

Berlin 22.4.1912

Today I am departing for Italy and shall give instructions that my vocal score be sent to you.

A few minutes ago I read your kind letter:– your opinions have always been a guiding line to me and this time too, they will cause me to think things over.

By the prelude to Act 3 I presume you mean the whole scene at the Froschteich.

What then follows (in the same act) is completely in the hands of Leonhard, who on the evening of the première[1] sang either erratically or not at all. – The postlude is supposed to fall naturally into two parts; half of it light-hearted comedy, the other, concluding half mystic and remote.

10 Busoni in Hamburg, May 1912, at the time of the world première of *Die Brautwahl*

11 Busoni in Warsaw, December 1912 (cf. letter No. 134)

The desired style of production, as I had initially visualized it, was to be unrealistic; it should have been more refined, *deceptive*, more like a picture book or puppet play. The technical facilities of the old theatre in Hamburg were inadequate for such hocus-pocus. For Leonhard I had imagined a figure rather like that of Liszt in his fifties. Noble, amicably ironical, superior.

More than half of what the orchestra played was wrong: (the score is actually clean, individual and seamless: solidly constructed).

The work occupied me for *six whole summers*: the first half of the composition was completed before the Elegies, the rest before the Berceuse élégiaque. Since then I have learnt much and also changed again.

I made a special point of enunciation and inflexion; not only that each character should have his own manner of speaking, but that this should also be modified according to the mood and temperament of the moment, while also affording a sense of melody. –

Since Wagner and Verdi, I don't believe that any so comprehensive a combination of character, sonority, form and melody has been achieved with such relative originality: but I must admit that I myself have learnt my lesson from it, which can hopefully be applied to a succeeding work – also that nothing is perfect.

I am sorry that I was unable to talk to you while still in Hamburg; but thank you for coming. I shall not forget it.

[1]The world première of *Die Brautwahl* had taken place on 13 April 1912 (not 12 April, as is generally stated).

117 TO EGON PETRI
in German

Florence 3.5.1912

Yesterday evening, passing through Bologna, we saw a theatre piece acted by Italian Masks. The
Arlecchino
cut a most impressive figure; he was personified by an actor who endowed him with a tinge of monumentality. Nowhere the low comedy of the Germans (into which – for example – my Thusman also lapsed). When Arlecchino entered as Captain, with an altogether false name, wearing leather knee-boots and a red cloak which stood up at the back like a cock's feathers – due to the angle of his sword – he became exactly like one of Callot's figures in Hoffmann's 'Prinzessin Brambilla'.

═══

The ancient town of Bergamo, where Anzoletti's Aesculapian brother has his abode, made an unusual impression on me. – Its gloomy, legendary walls contrasted with the utter springtime grace of Pistoia, where we stopped today, breakfasted, had a stroll and enjoyed 7 unknown friezes of della Robbia which surround the façade of the Ospedale.

Yesterday, today and tomorrow as well are free days! – Until now the journey has been quite strenuous, on top of which it 'deluged', as one so quaintly says here. Only today does it look like 'the first of May' and Florence offers a bright prospect.

Every street-corner here curbs back the forward impulse of my thoughts by several centuries. In a country which still has to arrive at the present, it is difficult to concentrate on the future.

(Incidentally, the phrase 'to look to the future' is impossible and short-sighted; it would be better to say: to drag oneself out of the past.)

4 Maggio

My holiday reading of late has consisted of a few recent Italian novelists, good writers and observers, not lacking in humour and lively enough but . . . restricted to a circle of slight, almost trivial occurrences. I also read 'L'oiseau bleu' (Maeterlinck), a spectacular play for children, with philosophy. Its most beautiful moment: as the two children, at midnight in the church-yard, fearfully await the dead, the graves open and blossoming shrubs (instead of what was expected) rise out of them. 'Light' comes on the scene and tells the little ones: 'There are no dead.'

Yesterday evening I purchased a wonderful, absolutely clean mezzotint based on a marvellous picture by Reynolds . . . for 20 Francs!

=====

This is the first letter I am writing on this journey. I hope it still reaches you at home. From the 6th to the 9th I shall be in Rome, on the 11th in Florence, on the 12th in Bologna (Hôtel d'Italie) – should you feel the epistolary urge.

There remains to report that I have made the acquaintance of a few splendid Italian women who have raised my opinion of their sex in this country; that Boito kissed me, that I have tasted amply of 'the noble wine'.

Nevertheless, I have been thirsting for my *own* work, for which I cannot find the necessary concentration here: but I feel it concentrating itself.

118 TO EGON PETRI
in German

Rome 8.5.1912

A German railway inspector, visiting here, commented that the Italian railway has a different timetable every day; a state of affairs which would (so he says) render a German official helpless; while here greater speed of thought and alert presence of mind always manage to restore some semblance of order. –

This characterizes the difference graphically. –

– Rome, springtime and a jubilant reception.

119 TO EGON PETRI
in German

Basle 15.5.1912

[. . .] I left Italy yesterday. The little concert tour passed off with verve and sparkle; although it did nothing to add to the incomplete picture of myself which my home country evidently retains.

I remain the distinguished 'concertista', which is incidentally the fourth grade down the ranks of practising musicians; and the order is:

composer,
  singer,
    conductor,
      instrumentalist.

There is no hope of my ever attaining the second grade. –

However this order originates in theatre terminology, in its function of leading musical institution. Accordingly, the singer's rank is the
second highest.

But even the maintenance of this leading establishment is uncertain.

For every theatre is annually confronted with the question whether it can run a 'season'. The vocal ensemble, indeed even an orchestra has to be built up anew every time. Who makes the decisions? One of the two powerful publishers, a rich musical amateur (who thrills at the smell of grease-paint) and (at secondary level) an 'impresario' and a conductor. A work is often chosen for the sake of a singer. The public, too, is fickle and lets the 'Scala' down (with increasing frequency).

At the present time, Puccini is the sole Italian opera composer with an international reputation: – and his countrymen do not like him at all. – Strauss is performed once and then vanishes – never to be seen again, it would appear.

The same with Pelleas und Melisande. There is a strong lobby against Verdi, but he still stands, like the Bismarck [statue] in Hamburg. Everyone gapes at mention of the word 'Falstaff', but nobody wants to hear it. Four of the Master's operas still survive: Trovatore, Traviata, Aida, Rigoletto. (Which is not so stupid!)

On the other hand, an epidemic has begun to spread; the continual return of second-rate German conductors with 'classical' symphony concerts.

The Italians are becoming 'educated' and hence tedious, like women when they make serious conversation. – Toscanini, that fine fellow, spends his winters in the north, his summers in the south – – of America. If he were to stay at home, which he d . . . d well ought to do, he would be hampered at every turn; this is unfortunately a typical characteristic of the Italians and of their cramped cities, the inheritance of a history abounding in treachery. –

Is Italy about to begin anew, or has it finally ground to a halt? – The élite is indeed blessed with superior intelligence and culture, but the percentage of stupidity (degli imbecilli), negligence and ignorance is horrifying. On top of this comes the Americanization of the business and sport world, from which the optimists promise themselves a new upsurge. A confused ideal of 'smart business man' and 'lawn tennis parties' obscures the image of the typical Italian; the 'Carreras'[1] type is on the increase; a nephew of Anzoletti's, actually a medic, is a professional athlete; – what has happened to the visual arts, this country's legitimate heritage?

And now the war, of all things, and colonialist mania!

Does this put you in the picture?

I have done my best.

======

[. . .] I found a little 'court circle' in every town. I visited and 'played' Bergamo, Milan, Turin, Ferrara, Rome, Bologna, altogether nine concerts. I have actually only earned 'half' of it, but the journey afforded diverse pleasures; there was often excellent wine and I am bringing a few lovely things home with me. (Including the score of Falstaff.)

[1]Busoni's Italian agent (further unidentified).

120 TO ROBERT FREUND
in German

[Berlin] 19.5.1912

Arriving back 'home' from Italy today, I had the great joy of reading your letter.

Your endorsement of my belief in my work raised my spirits again, for I have once more (for the umpteenth time) had to run the gauntlet.

On the other hand: if the likes of Schiller or Verdi were obliged to revise their dramas 'for the theatre', it is nothing to be ashamed of if this need arises in the case of Die Brautwahl.

You are justified in complaining about Mahler's mistakes. On my journey I had the opportunity to discuss the opera with one of his real pupils, Bodanzky.[1] He is going to perform it and will submit his suggestions for the revision. –

Although you know the piano reduction, you haven't yet seen the orchestral score! The latter is truly clean and seamless. Bodanzky gave me the impression that he will bring out the best in it. What do *you* think of him and Mannheim? [. . .]

My attention has often turned to the 'illustre magicien'[2] but I have become uncertain as to the viability of the libretto; – when one is under fire from *all* sides! . . .

Instead I have formulated a new idea (not unlike it), sketched it out and entrusted it to a talented poet (Vollmoeller).[3]

And yet – the first scene (which he sent me today) has already given me cause to doubt the validity of the principle of an outsider writing the text for a composer. (Incidentally, he himself advised me against it, for he is very intelligent.)

I shall pass on your appreciation to *P–e–t–r–i*. He is still in London. He will certainly be very glad, for until now he has only been criticized for his good, extensive work.

This is the disadvantage of being a beginner: one's works are only checked through for errors, whereas standard works are lovingly studied merely for the sake of their subtleties (or indeed in search of new ones).

[1]Arthur Bodanzky, 1877–1939, Austrian conductor. He left Mannheim in 1915 to become Principal Conductor at the Metropolitan Opera, New York.
[2]i.e. *Der mächtige Zauberer*.
[3]Carl Vollmoeller, 1878–1948, poet and playwright. He had adapted Gozzi's *Turandot* for Max Reinhardt's production in 1911, which used Busoni's incidental music. The work in question here is *Das Geheimnis*, based on a story by Villiers de l'Isle-Adam.

121 TO EDWARD J. DENT
in Italian

Berlin 20.5.1912

On returning home from Italy today I found three exquisite volumes of Marlowe awaiting me, which are certainly your splendid gift. They will spur me to occupy myself with (and perhaps to bring to a conclusion) the problem of Faust, which will probably be the material for my chief work. In the meantime my thoughts are turning to another opera, on which I am planning to start work this summer.

Bodanzky, a distinguished pupil of Mahler, has promised me to perform 'Die Brautwahl' in the theatre at Mannheim. He wants some alterations in the action, which I shall endeavour to carry out.

I very much hope for a more homogeneous performance of my score, in which I invested so much hard work and loving care. I also hope to see you in London, where I shall be at the beginning of June, and I shall be very happy to meet you there.

In Italy I had the chance to see a comedy of '*Masks*' which made a great impression on me and in which an 'Arlecchino' played his role in a style which verged on the monumental. I was also present at an excellent performance of the Matrimonio segreto, by which I was *charmé*.

I22   TO IRMA BEKH
in German

Berlin 26.7.1912

But of course magnetism exists! It's just that we take too little trouble to develop the possibility. Had we done so, then telegrams and telephones would be superfluous. Read 'La maison du bonheur' in Villiers de l'Isle-Adams's 'Derniers contes', there you will find out more about it and derive great intellectual pleasure. [. . .]

I23   TO HUGO LEICHTENTRITT
in German

Berlin 6.8.1912

I return the score of the
Symphonia
into the hands of its creator – as requested – while congratulating you on the completion of a work so auspiciously begun. –

It was an unfortunate coincidence that I was dining out the very day you visited me. (My friend *Middelschulte* from Chicago came with me to the Petris.)

In the last few days I have finished a concert suite from the Brautwahl music, a second sonatina,[1] a reduced version of the Fantasia contrappuntistica[2] (with an entirely new prelude) and the completion of the Figaro fantasy.[3] Then I have at last received my new libretto, which is distracting me from all other composing projects. All that remains is the revision of my 1st opera for Mannheim. In the meantime I am taking a scant week off to relax. – [. . .]

---

[1]The *Sonatina seconda*, completed on 8 July 1912.
[2]The *Edizione minore* of the *Fantasia Contrappuntistica*, completed on 20 July 1912.
[3]Franz Liszt, Fantasie über zwei Motive von W. A. Mozarts *Die Hochzeit des Figaro*. Completed from the almost finished original manuscript by Busoni. Dated 11 July 1912.

124 TO EGON PETRI
in German

Paris 13.8.1912

I wrote these few lines while still in Cologne – from where I sent you a detailed letter.

Here I have met Widor, Vollmoeller, d'Annunzio. Shall tell you more in a few days.

[On a page of note paper from the Dom Hotel, Cologne:]

Psychology of pitch

I was passing Café Bauer in the Hohe Strasse and heard the *Oberon* overture being played within. As I passed out of earshot, the last 16 bars or so were still lacking. – Two hours later, at the same place, I heard the last 16 bars of the *Freischütz* overture. 'Tiens,' I said to myself, 'they're still playing the Oberon overture.' *And because I thought it was that work, I heard it in D major.*

125 TO EGON PETRI [postcard]
in German

Berlin 30.8.1912

To deprive you of a small stabbing weapon – I am today able to announce the arrival of the missing volume of Flaubert. But I am also happy to administer the balsam for the wound. The very rare first complete edition of E. A. Poe consists of 3 volumes and I have only the first two. Had I found all three of them, I would possess none – for the price would have deterred me. – Br. & H.'s engravers have thrown up their hands in despair at the distribution of the accidentals (Sonatina [seconda]). It will evidently be necessary to add an explanatory note. – We want to perform the entire Froschteich scene in my concerts; Birrenkoven has agreed.[1] – Tomorrow I shall be receiving the vocal score of the latest operatic phenomenon: '*Der ferne Klang*'.[2]

This is the bulletin for 30 August 1912.

[1]Willi Birrenkoven, the tenor who sang Thusman at the world première of *Die Brautwahl*. The scene was performed at the Blüthner Saal on 28 December 1912 with Julius Lieban and Nils G. Svanfeldt (but without Birrenkoven) in a concert conducted by Busoni.
[2]On 22 August 1912 Busoni had written to Emil Hertzka, director of Universal Edition, asking for a vocal score of Schreker's opera. He evidently intended to perform a scene from it in one of his Blüthner Saal concerts.

126 TO HUGO LEICHTENTRITT
in German

Berlin 4.9.1912

I thought the enclosed catalogue might be of interest and am taking the liberty of giving it to you. I must admit to finding myself on unexplored territory here, and of the many wonderful names only a few are familiar to me – and those only from my school days. (Arcadelt, Lasso, Cyprian de Rore, Willaert . . .) I note that Messer Salinas is asking the highest price; no doubt because of the first edition?

I could well consult Fétis to find a prop to support my shaky knowledge – but I might just as well catch up on my Chinese history! Man is built entirely forwards, to walk and look ahead; he looks (and has to look) to his children and not to his parents. *We learn from our children.* As you have none, as yet, your task is different.

Perhaps you could arrange for a library to purchase the items which seem valuable to you.

NB The maid inadvertently threw the pages away. They have been salvaged but spoiled. Please excuse.

127 TO HUGO LEICHTENTRITT
in German

Berlin 6.9.1912

I found your letter very interesting: I should like to write a fugue on its theme. Perhaps detailed knowledge of the past does not 'hinder' – but does it help? You, at any rate, have dedicated a very large part of your life to it; to your satisfaction – as you say – which is the decisive factor. The value one sets on such historical art must increase or decrease proportionately to the degree with which one occupies oneself with it. Where others look upon it as a landscape, you draw up an ordnance survey map; and every cross on the road becomes significant.

As I myself take great pleasure in making and reading catalogues, I can understand yours; but I have never associated this occupation with furthering one's understanding of literature. – But every organism is different and each of us can only speak for his own – and even then he can be mistaken. –

I have the greatest trust in your single-mindedness and am delighted to hear that you have completed your symphony. My sincerest congratulations.

As a bibliophile I was enchanted by the beautiful copy of 'Chinesische Zeiten';[1] I shall study its contents conscientiously, meanwhile I thank you for the magnificent gift.

[1]Hugo Leichtentritt, *Chinesisch-deutsche Jahres- und Tageszeiten* (Goethe), op. 4. Song cycle. Published Leipzig, 1912, by Hofmeister. The presentation copy mentioned here is preserved in the Deutsche Staatsbibliothek, Berlin.

128 TO EGON PETRI
in German

Berlin 7.9.1912

Mannheim seems to be reaching a decision, in 2 days I hope to have the vocal score and orchestral scores at home; and I ask you to consider whether you are able and willing to undertake the job.[1]

My cold is better, my taste buds are in action again.

As for the subject of seeing ghosts, this is a phenomenon which one cannot readily shrug off.

Assuming the Omnipresence of Time (which is harder to disprove than to postulate), it should be possible for a particularly qualified person, at a particularly clairvoyant moment, to perceive an individual from 'other' times: naturally not as a ghost, but in whichever way the moment affects the individual.

If that seems amateurish to you, I would add that none of us has any deeper knowledge of the subject.

One of the few really well-written articles in 'Meyer['s Konversationslexikon]' deals with

‹ o c c u l t i s m ›

with great seriousness: it is worth reading. I very well understand your scientifically empirical method, but an a priori hypothesis could also show the way. – Both approaches have always existed. –

Forgive this reference to yesterday's not very satisfactory conversation. Thank you nevertheless for your pleasant company.

[1]i.e. of marking in cuts and alterations.

129 TO EGON PETRI
in German

Berlin 14.9.1912

It has been on my mind for some time and now I want to put it to you in writing. Br. & H. have for several years been promising a *Complete Edition* of *my Bach transcriptions*. It has foundered on their (Br. & H.) parsimony, as they would have to acquire the '*Wohltemperierte Clavier*' [Part I] (as well as some other works) from other publishers. To produce such a Complete Edition, a preliminary revision of the works would be necessary.

To be on the safe side – and with a particular view to the possibility of the plan being carried out without my honoured presence – I would like to pass the following information on to you for safe keeping.

The Complete Edition embraces *all* Bach transcriptions published by Br. & H. + the Well-t. Clav., the Fugue in E♭ and the Chromatic fantasy. As supplement to the Well-t. Clav. are added:

1) the two substituted fugues from Part 1;

2) the Versio minore of the fugue from The Art of Fugue;

3) the fugue from the Chromatic fantasy, as an example of my manner of interpretation;

4) the Fuga figurata (last part) from 'An die Jugend', for the D major fugue;

1) 2) and 3) form the 5th, 6th and 7th *appendices*; 4) an interpolated *composition study*. –

The organ fugue in E♭ needs some polishing.

The *6 pieces* are to be incorporated according to their categories.

The forewords to the Chromatic fantasy and the Toccatas are to be omitted. In the introduction to the Well-tempered Clavier, the footnote on Mendelssohn's advocacy is to be cut.

The transcriptions cover the period from 1891 to around 1903, only the original version of the organ fugue in D major originates from my Leipzig period. – Well. –

====

(Today I looked over the Variations and Fugue on a Prelude of Chopin: *they are not worth saving!*)

====

Because Part II of the Well-tempered Clavier is to be edited from an entirely different standpoint from that of Part I, and is to concern itself with the profundities of polyphony, the roots of melody and the innermost workings of compositional mechanisms – because its relationship to its predecessor must needs resemble that between Faust, Part II and Part I – because it could possibly happen that the good principles of Part I should come to be designated as evil in Part II – as in Die Zauberflöte – : I scarcely believe that anyone other than myself could perform this task; not due to any lack of insight, energy or knowledge, but as the outcome of the reversal of the guiding transcription idea.

Words to this effect could serve as an introduction to the Complete Edition; – however, I may still possibly hold this 2nd Part in reserve for my old age as a sort of testament.

Pardon these outbursts, they are an indication of my trust in you.

130 TO EDITH ANDREAE
in German

London 30.9.1912

Just got here! This arrival never fails to stimulate. The difference between the city in which one lives and the one which one regularly visits is like that between a 'marriage' and a 'liaison'; – especially in the case of a place like London, which one never quite finishes exploring, one's expectation of the unforeseen in familiar surroundings is newly exciting every time.

I have always envied *Dickens* in that he was able to link the scrutiny of this city with his profession, to connect the study of a metropolis with artistic activity; two notions which appeal to me.

Consider that everything which occurs here *simultaneously* in one minute could never be recounted by even the most prolific of writers in a lifetime! It would take *at least* 7 million sentences! (Quite a statistic.) [. . .]

Wells has published a new book: 'Marriage'.

131 TO EGON PETRI
in German

London 6.10.1912

[. . .] I have received a detailed document from Kestenberg, an autobiography and self-portrait with illuminating sidelights on the 'work' of the 'comrades'.[1]

I replied in detail and have tried for Toronto. This city has the same relationship to Montreal as Glasgow to Edinburgh: the one industrial, the other cultural. (Perhaps 'industry' is the culture of our time.) I wonder if he would like it there.

– Strindberg's 'Dance of death' made a strong impression upon me, I wrote at greater length to Gerda about it.[2]

This week has been very strenuous; (if only I could rid myself once more of a feeling of 'shame' at playing in public!), it seems to me that my playing has changed again. At the first concert I observed myself and collected criticisms. Something is still lacking! –

My [2nd] violin sonata is beginning to please people. (Kreisler[3] for example): I find it atrophied. It has a few well-felt moments – respectable craftsmanship.

Life grows shorter, one falls ever shorter of one's goals——how inhuman the task! Enfin, if only one could appreciate this——! [. . .]

I have bought the 2nd Edn. (expanded, in 3 vols.) of Boswell–Johnson for 10/–. The first costs almost 100 Marks.

[1]Leo Kestenberg was at that time a Communist.

[2]The letter, written the same day, is published in *Letters to his Wife*, but has somehow found its way into 1920!

[3]Fritz Kreisler played Busoni's 2nd Violin Sonata in Liverpool, with the composer at the piano, on 4 October 1912. The programme also included Busoni's (first) Sonatina and *Fantasia nach J.S. Bach* for piano, followed by three of Kreisler's compositions for violin and piano (which Busoni did not accompany). The concert then ended with César Franck's Violin Sonata in A, for which Busoni had bought the music in London the day before the journey. The entire programme was repeated in Edinburgh on 5 October.

132 TO EGON PETRI
in German

London 8.10.1912

<u>Life *can* be beautiful sometimes</u> – it was yesterday, today it is not! God *knows* why and I have a *hunch* myself.

Generally speaking, it really is not, and the pleasant moments are interruptions – (even then dampened by lurking anxieties) – whose logical reaction is a return to the prevailing state.

But we consider life in general as something beautiful and convince ourselves that the many rough patches are due to an ill star which must be overcome. So it becomes a matter of continually overcoming.

The third sonatina seems to have the character of a butterfly (hoping straight away for the best) – at any rate it is undergoing a metamorphosis, has for the moment assumed the form of a caterpillar, is feeding on smuggled half-hours and crawling up the trunk of the orchestra-tree.[1] (You don't care for these exhaustive metaphors, but I had already started out ——)

Yesterday was a recital in Bedford, present were: Miss Bruce, [Rosamond] Ley, Mr and Mrs Creighton, Backhaus[2] and Peters, the piano tuner. The two latter recognized each other as Saxons. 'Ich bin ooch aus Leipzig' (said Backhaus); 'aus welcher Stråsse sind Sie —— ?'[3] – Now I have to leave for Eastbourne.

[1]The work in question did indeed become an orchestral piece, the *Nocturne symphonique*, op. 43.

[2]Geo Albert Backhaus, concert agent.

[3]'I come from Leipzig too.' 'Which street do you come from?' (Saxon dialect).

133 TO EGON PETRI
in German

Helsinki 26.10.1912
(= 8.11.1912 new style)

The journey from London via Berlin and Moscow to Helsinki is a reasonable prospect when its crowning object is a performance of the [Beethoven] op. 111 sonata and other pieces. One is bringing culture to countries far off the beaten track and feels like a missionary. Now I can view the matter from a more commanding position and have no need to be in awe of Russia, as I used to be; so much so, that I have lived with memories of it for 20 years. Some things have also perhaps been improved. In the interim came the revolution and the streets of Moscow have been asphalted.

The aged faces of former acquaintances are frightful, merciless, worse than rust and verdigris, while those to whom they belong are unaware of it, enter with a triumphant smile of acquired familiarity, and there is a tacit agreement to act as if nothing had happened.

Women who have aged even find a courage they never possessed in their youth, re-establish affections nipped in the bud, speak out that which was on the tip of their tongue 20 years ago, plant the kiss for which they had pursed their lips 20 years before! And I, who cannot bear to look back! Who would like to look upon each new day as a beginning!

Fortunately the public considers me as a '*débutant*'; in certain circumstances this can be agreeable. [. . .]

In Russia a violinist is promoting himself; he plays, in a moonscape setting – on the violin! – the celebrated sonata in C♯ minor. – Violon à lumière.

134 TO IRMA BEKH
in German

Moscow 16.11.1912

It isn't exactly that I have been short of time – one can always find a spare half-hour – but to write a letter one requires inspiration and this is difficult during precisely *the* half-hour that is free. This daily projected letter has a fellow sufferer: the manuscript of my new piece,[1] which has made no progress at all for two weeks. – You can scarcely imagine how this has been preying on my mind. Repeatedly I took up the completed pages between overnight journeys and rehearsals, between business meetings and calls; but a mind already weary is not so flexible, and I am happy to have retained enough critical clarity to prevent me writing down any old nonsense.

By now I have missed too much correspondence to append a detailed report for you. It would be over-long and yet full of gaps.

Let it suffice to say that I have had a relatively good time; and – if I were a virtuoso – I would be proud and content, for in that capacity – everything I could wish for has been successful.

Yesterday – at last! – I also felt a fresh breeze on my MS, the pages seemed to ripple and there was a springtime rustling amongst them. – How often has one thus been deceived!

But let us trust and delight in such deception until such time as the contrary is proved.

Soon I shall be coming to Berlin, but only for a few days! A greeting from you could still reach me in Warsaw (Hotel Bristol) and would be heartily welcome. –

I embrace you, dear Bekirma.

[1]The *Nocturne symphonique*, op. 43.

135 TO H. W. DRABER
in German

London 21.1.1913

[. . .] I have heard Mahler's 7th symphony, fragments of Wagner (whom I always find more agreeable in concert) and S. Saëns's Rouet d'Omphale. The latter gave me the greatest pleasure, but was admittedly the best performed.

St. Saëns (and Rimsky K.) also contributed to the Turandot music (because mine was insufficient) – which was played in Varieté style by a 20-piece orchestra. The success was great!! The newspapers are captivated. Fascinating! How should one defend oneself?

Certainly, I have now learned a little about composing, but have not yet learned composer's conduct. This would afford a new course of study – and yet I have to catch up on so many other things —— !

Now my dear Draber, Traber, Draper, Trapper – I am beginning to understand, it is dawning on me, late, in the twilight of my life – that, as one cannot form the world according to one's own ideas, one has to form oneself – in accordance with the world. Which is also what most people zealously do and are right in doing, in which they are all wrong.

====

Could one not bring it home to the critics that there are *no dissonances*?
    That the concept of
                    cacophony is no longer valid?
Please, I beg you, do try. In the B[erliner] Z[eitung]. Then we would make more rapid progress. I am full of optimism. And with this and the kindest regards I remain,
                    Yours incurably,
                    F.B.
                    Professor at the highest school.

136 TO H. W. DRABER
in German

London 24.1.1913

Your letter differs from my Concerto in that the 'Pezzo serioso' is the weakest.

What if I do *not* pay Roeder?[1] When I am owed money, the most brilliant solicitors fail (as in the case of Hanson and Harmonie, for example), but vice versa: any scoundrel is allowed to make me pay through the nose.[2] Oh culture! One should view the question of creditor and debtor in the following light – so long as one has the effrontery to blare out the word culture – : he who can prove that he can least afford to part with the money should be protected. The creditor is generally the richer. No, I am no dreamer, the rule that $2 \times 2 = 4$ penetrates even my understanding: but the $2 \times 2 = 4$ men are unable to understand me.

Incidentally, this same Roeder has a small supply of vocal scores in stock. He must have about 80 of them.

Our letters have crossed; for yours many thanks [danke ich Ihnen herzlich]. À propos 'herzlich': the man in Vienna is called *Hertzka*. I wonder if he, like other publishers, has 'ka Hertz'?[3] I believe: Tempora mutantur sed nos non mutamur, et nunc, et in saecula saeculorum.

Amen.

---

[1] C. G. Roeder, Leipzig firm of music engravers and printers. Busoni was in debt to them, due to problems with Harmonie Verlag over *Die Brautwahl*, to the tune of 10,000 Marks.
[2] Orig. das Gehirn aus der Nase herausziehen = to pull my brains out through the nose.
[3] Viennese dialect for 'kein Herz' = no heart.

137 TO SIR ALEXANDER MACKENZIE
in English

London 29.1.1913

Dear Master,

I had such a curious experience this morning at the Philh. Society rehearsal that I feel it my *duty* to refer it to you. The R. Ph. S. did me the honour to *invite* me to conduct one of my works, which honour I did not ask for but accepted thankfully.

After being intimated to arrive strictly and punctually at Queen's Hall before the beginning of the rehearsal, I was there at half past nine, an early hour for a man which has been ill for seven days.

It was quarter to twelve as I was allowed to begin with my piece, which is

long and difficult and uncommon in style, so that I was not able to reach the
end of the Fantasia and the rehearsal closed in a fragmentary way.

Presently I expressed my doubts to Mr Wallace[1] as to the possibility of a
performance under these conditions and Mr Wallace had the goodness to
assure me that my work was not worth rehearsing nor performing at all.

I doubt whether it is the intention of the Philharmonic Society that
composers should be invited by this historic institution only for the result of
being criticized by its secretary. And with the certainty that the facts will not
meet with your approbation I take the liberty of referring them to you.[2]

I remain, Sir Alexander,
     always your sincere admirer and obedient
         Ferruccio Busoni.

[1]William Wallace, 1860–1940, author and composer.
[2]The fracas to which Busoni here refers centred round the projected performance
of the so-called *Sinfonia Contrappuntistica* (orchestrated by Frederick Stock) for
the Royal Philharmonic Society. The details of the event are to be found on pp.
199–200 of Edward J. Dent's *Ferruccio Busoni: a Biography*, Oxford, 1933.

138 TO EGON PETRI
in German

Kassel 25.2.1913

Your comment about the two types of opening in Chopin's Etudes suggests to
me a certain analogy with the months of the year, which consist of either 30
or 31 days.

I found another in the E minor étude, op. 25 no. 5, which brings me to
dub it:
                    'Mazeppa on a rocking-horse'.
Take a closer look at it and see if I am right (in jest).

This brings me to the great Mazeppa again. Don't you think that the
climax of the theme in the major key (2/4) is not quite successful?

I think the following realization would come closer to the intended effect:

My recent run of bad luck persists. I specially came here to conduct the

Brautwahl Suite and – it has been cancelled!* Allegedly due to insufficient rehearsal time – but, I imagine, because of a mild shock at the first read-through.

What an overestimation! I am not so great as to be able to say, with Liszt: I can wait. I consider that my art belongs altogether to its time. Those who think otherwise are simply 'behind'. [. . .]

*The joke of it all is that I was asked to play two pieces more 'as compensation'. Did you ever . . .!

[1]Original version of the passage:

139 TO H. W. DRABER
in German

Bologna 18.4.1913

This morning, fairly shattered by the strong emotions of yesterday evening, I would nevertheless not wish to delay in sending you a report. The town council here has officially offered me the directorship of the Conservatoire, the press and the public have availed themselves of my concert visit to demonstrate their sympathy in articles and personal tributes, to express a unanimous desire to have me as their musical director.

What I have often dreamed of, a position of high authority in Italy, is thus offered to me.

With a few strokes I could transform Bologna as a city of music into the focal point of the country and even perhaps thus raise it to a higher standing in Europe. Concerts, orchestras and liberties, too, are being conceded, many doors are opening to me——

And yet I am painfully undecided, indeed I initially turned down the whole idea.

B. is small, constricted and animated intellectually only by a small circle of men, otherwise silent and dead, with an architectural style which is not vital, indeed rather uncongenial.

In the long run, even an exceptional post with many rights and far-reaching concessions would remain subject to the town council. To settle here would be an essential condition. Heine's battle with the fleas 'die mit Gestank fechten'[1] would become quite animated and consume half one's energy.

And my beautiful big wide world, in which I feel so much at home, would recede into the distance, would become a foreign land.

But the Italians have accepted me entirely as a compatriot – at last – while Berlin would always consider me a foreigner and scoff at my Beethoven playing, for it has – (again with Heine) – 'niederträchtig schlechte Treppen'[2] and this climbing up and down stairs gives me cramp in the legs and in the soul.

This is how things stand and, as yet, I know nothing.

3 fifths of the 8 concerts in Milan[3] have been accomplished. This affair, too, is a fine demonstration, organized and carried out with the greatest noblesse.

Frau Marga (Weigert),[4] who was present yesterday, will be able to give you an eye-witness account.

I have a sensation of warmth and of a certain sadness, but many good presentiments.

---

[1]'whose rapier is their stench'; freely adapted from Heine, *Atta Troll. Ein Sommernachstraum*, Caput XI, l. 79.

[2]'villainous rotten stairways'; Heine, ibid., Caput XII, l. 12. The rest of the sentence is a continuation of the quotation.

[3]This cycle of eight recitals at the Conservatorio Verdi in Milan (described by Busoni as his 'Octomeron') was the most extensive event of the kind he was ever to present. After an initial programme of Bach transcriptions, followed by Beethoven's 'Waldstein' and op. 111 sonatas (7.4.1913), there followed a full evening of Beethoven (11.4.), two evenings of Chopin (14.4 and 19.4.), two evenings of Liszt, with transcriptions (21.4.) and original compositions (5.5.), an evening of Brahms, Franck, Alkan and Schumann (9.5.) and finally a concert devoted to Busoni's own compositions, including the world première of the *Sonatina seconda* (12.5., see letter no. 143).

[4]Marga Weigert, ?–?, piano pupil of Busoni at Weimar.

140 TO EGON PETRI
in German

Milan 20.4.1913

[. . .] Here there is much work, much emotion, much pleasure, which is constantly reducing me to the mental and physical state of 'the morning after'. On the 17th I was the centre of unprecedented demonstrations in Bologna, the rumour of my being appointed Director of the Conservatoire having been leaked around the town. Yesterday, the 19th, was the fourth concert of the Octomeron, already tomorrow the fifth is to take place. Then off to Rome and Naples.

To answer the Bologna question poses some problems. Theoretically, everything I ever dreamed of for myself in Italy is available here; but, in practice and seen from close up, the matter seems rather more suspect.

I have so many plans for the coming season that I don't know what I should do! (Geheimrat von Hase[1] would say: 'vigorously promote' the Bach Edition.) – But now I have conquered Italy and am being unconditionally recognized not only as a true compatriot but perhaps even as the leading musician. Could I fail to acknowledge and exploit the situation? Would that be the correct course of action? Thus the idea of settling in Italy, [even] without an appointment, seems to be a clear, almost moral obligation.

The composer [in me] has rested too long, here too an urgent inner voice is summoning me to unilateral action and will hear nothing of postponement. I feel very tired, almost exhausted, unnecessarily so. But that will soon return to normal.

If my letter should strike you as being too serious and heavy-handed, you can see why. I send you my fondest greetings and regret that the rumour blared out by Mrs Fama-Koelliker – that you were here – is unfounded.

Truth, says A. France, is inferior to falsehood; firstly because it is one against many, secondly because it is inflexible. –

Unfortunately I have had to drop the idea of your playing my Concerto here (an orchestral concert is being planned as a concluding tribute). [. . .] I have babbled on for a page and ruined the form of this letter, *because* I lack mastery in this field.

[1] Oskar von Hase, 1846–1921, director of Breitkopf und Härtel from 1888 until his death.

141 TO EGON PETRI [postcard]
in German

Naples 28.4.1913

Having had a taste of Rome and of your dear mother-in-law, we are now enjoying the Bay of Naples. This time I am looking at Italy with open eyes and it bewilders me. As does your dear mother-in-law.

142 TO EGON PETRI
in German

Milan 3.5.1913

On the first of May of this year I made an agreement with the mayor, the town clerk and the member of parliament for Bologna, whereby I have been nominated Director of their Conservatoire for life, for my part I am entering into a trial year and reserving the right to resign at any time after the termination of this year.

I wanted to try it, if only because I would have reproached myself for not trying; and then because I, as life's connoisseur, wanted a taste of this new situation; also because this incident coincides with a moment of indecision with regard to the future, which is thus brought to an end; finally, because I have my reasons for wishing to draw closer to Italy again.

These reasons are entirely of an artistic nature; my significance, if I have any, requires a national background in order to make itself felt; – also I am planning a major Italian work, for which I need the atmosphere.

I shall be retaining my apartment in Berlin and my friends there will scarcely detect any alteration in my way of life; only that my absence from home, instead of taking me to Russia or England, shall bring me to Italy.

On 2 May I received 14 telegrams from Bologna, from the city council, the Conservatoire, all the papers, even from strangers, expressing wild enthusiasm at my acceptance.

One cannot entirely disregard such a demonstration of solidarity nor underestimate the unanimous wish of an entire city. But also the rest of Italy is resounding with a welcoming fanfare which is for the moment very well in tune. – Bologna is the spiritual heart of the country, its institute bears the oldest and most worthy of names. Even *Mozart* studied here and I shall be working in the same building in which this young prodigy went to school. A fine house! Originally a monastery, it has the appearance of an opulent historical palace, elegantly tasteful and thrillingly atmospheric! Here I shall be the Master and actually have to do nothing which is not my personal wish.

I shall not have to be bothered with managerial and administrative duties, nor shall I be expected to give tuition. – For this eventuality, my fee is to be raised to an unprecedented figure; which is nevertheless *very* modest and merely honorary, but a formal exception which is intended to lend my position the appropriate gravity.

The students' tuition is financed by the city, they themselves pay nothing and the school is a non-profit-making institution.

You see, it has its fine and noble aspects. The most attractive of these is that one has material at one's disposal and a free hand to form it according to one's own intentions.

Perhaps Bologna will one day attain a European reputation as a musical centre.

My suggestions are being readily accepted and the city council will take care of everything. There is an orchestra and a theatre. The former is my first object for improvement.

What do you think of me, my Egon, my Benjamin, my Eckermann; are you shaking your head in disbelief, are you beginning to doubt the durability of good, do you 'not agree' or do you 'not see why not'?

I hope you will play in B. (a city cast architecturally in *one* mould, unique), and that you will see 'my' Liceo and the heroic landscape surrounding it, which is powerful and serene, as a hero should be, and that you are content.

========

This time Naples made an excessive and fantastic impression on me; Rome improves at every visit. Your dear mother-in-law was very kind to us; the previous time I had rather let fly at her, which I regretted, without entirely being able to suppress the pleasure this gave me.

(A telegram from Papa Serato has just been delivered.)

Fried is conducting 2 concerts at 'La Scala', Birnbaum is about to arrive for the same purpose.

Now I must do some work.———

Consider this letter as a page of a diary . . .

(You can show it to anybody you wish.)

143 TO EGON PETRI
in German

Milan 13.5.1913

Remarkable evening yesterday; after the 2nd Sonatina something like an uproar arose at the back of the hall, Condottiere Marinetti[1] engaged in fisticuffs with some of the rebels, from the artists' room I heard squabbling voices and one very loud one which repeatedly bellowed 'Fuori'![2] – But all ended with roses and bouquets and a *cenacolo* attended by distinguished men and beautiful women.

An attractive crowd indeed, and memorable.

Toscanini, Bossi,[3] the Conservatoire directors from Milan, Parma and Naples, the mayor of Bologna (who once received a letter from Wagner), the Futurists Marinetti and Boccioni, Borelli, the composer Sinigaglia,[4] guests from Venice, Parma and Bologna – as well as 'our' circle: Birnbaum, Ley, Bruce, Madame Blumer from Strasburg; also Borgatti, Italy's Wagnerian heldentenor, who presented me with nothing less than a golden laurel wreath; – all of these, as well as Carreras with his entire clan, were present, and many others.

Had you not – sadly! – been absent, you would perhaps have enjoyed yourself and found it a memorable occasion. (You would have found me 'the same' but yet, thanks to new developments, also changed.) [. . .]

[1] F. T. Marinetti, 1876–1944, leader of the Futurist movement.
[2] 'Get out.'
[3] Enrico Bossi, 1861–1925, organist and composer.
[4] Leone Sinigaglia, 1868–1944, composer and collector of Italian folk-music.

144 TO EGON PETRI
in German

Mannheim 22.5.1913

[. . .] Here you would experience more of an 'Auswahl'[1] than a 'Brautwahl'; for out of the cut passages one could assemble a perfectly respectable opera. Once again Leonhard is not quite right and Thusman, as before, makes his own effect. On stage things generally look better than in Hamburg; but the orchestra is incomparably superior, presenting an opportunity to judge the values of the score, a great consolation to me in somewhat discouraging circumstances.

No matter how much one thinks one has seen of the world, it still has its curious aspects.

For example: for quite some time now it has been my cruel, inescapable fate to have been born and brought up, and quite possibly also to have to take my leave, with *Wagner*. How fortunate was a Carl Maria von Weber or even the young Verdi!

Is it all conviction? Is there not a tacit agreement amongst thousands who stand and fall only with him, to adhere to Wagner alone? It seems astonishing that a little, contemptible Saxon, with boring music and some strokes of genius, could call an international society of this magnitude into being. One is reminded of that rather restricted Jewish rabbi from Nazareth, who had to suffer for the sake of the extension of the ecumenical power of Rome, and who filled the bill so perfectly.[2]

At any rate, my personal situation is as follows. To shorten the end of Die Brautwahl, Bodanzky cuts 8 bars of *Presto* and, on the same day, invites me to an uncut performance of Tristan. Can you imagine how persuasive that sounds? (Or am I getting nervous?)

Sometimes I could break down. –

[1]Selection.
[2]This letter was written on the 100th anniversary of the birth of Richard Wagner.

145 TO EGON PETRI
in German

Berlin 4.6.1913

I am having increasing difficulty in understanding the ways of the world (like everything with which one begins to make deeper acquaintance).

Backhaus – who owes *me* money – has filed a suit against me!!

The art of living consists of following one's own goals and delighting in the passing moment. If only I were as capable of the latter as you are. I am glad you are enjoying yourself and only regret your delay in returning home; for time is on the wane and there remain only uncertainties.

The *Mannheim* reviews of Die Brautwahl were disgusting, but some of those from elsewhere were first-rate. For instance the 'Kölnische Zeitung'.[1] (But how does Mitta come to know about it?) – I believe that, for a definitive decision on the fate of the opera (one way or the other), a *third* production would be necessary. A little more polishing – already in M. it made a lively impression, almost too full of brief episodes. No, it is not boring, and this time I have emerged from the ordeal entirely *convinced*. [. . .]

Wolf-Ferrari, Caruso, Leoncavallo, these are famous names: a concept with a persuasive effect. As I am personally acquainted with success *and* failure, I have no respect for the former and the latter comes as no disappointment.

But I am becoming more serious and hope that I shall still have time to attain that final, superior serenity.

---

[1] The first night of *Die Brautwahl* in Mannheim was on 24 May 1913. The following review was published on 31 May 1913 in the *Kölnische Zeitung*:
    . . . The work is accredited with 'artistic appeal'. The word artistic has of late been as much misused as its counterpart, kitsch: that which one cannot define is looked upon as artistic . . . Un-artistically speaking, *Die Brautwahl* has a highly fascinating individuality which, however, addresses itself primarily to the listener's cultural intellect, not his feelings, and is in fact founded on Busoni's astonishing mastery in manipulating the elements of this art, hence, some would say, on his great artistic ability . . . The question as to whether the work is viable must be answered, even after this performance, in the negative, because it suppresses the listener's desire for beauty and warmth too far in favour of an interesting ugliness. But it constitutes a valuable contribution to the enrichment of modern means of expression, for which purpose one may boldly consider it to be a handbook worth exploiting.

146 TO EGON PETRI
in German

Berlin 9.6.1913

In the last few days – after my experiences with the Mannheim production and before I forget my impressions of it – I have made a *Theatre Edition* of the vocal score of Die Brautwahl, intended to establish a text which should be definitive for further performances. (Further performances? Nous verrons.)

On Thursday there's a conference about contracts, publishers, engravers, lawyers, magicians, Jews, Ma(h)ler-hotheads[1] (actually Bodanzky is the only one of these).——

The [review in the] 'Kölnische [Zeitung]' was by Neitzel.[2]

Now I have finally come clear with this work and can take your advice to start on a new one.

I would really like to write a one-act opera which could be 'on the spot' by the autumn, but the text! Vollmoeller has botched one up for me but it could still be saved and I shall look to this at once. One-acters are harder than three-acters, and comedies rarely as good as tragedies.

I have read Wilde's 'Florentine [Tragedy]', which is based on a joke and, incidentally, eschews music, mine at least.[3]

Do you know 'Die Frau am Fenster' by Hofmannsthal? I believe she is strangled by her 'mari'. These triangular[4] dramas are basically all the same – but they have the virtue of using perennial themes. In comedies the husband is foolish and cuckolded, in tragedies he is dangerous and 'makes a weapon of his horns'. (Wilde indeed admires him as a *bull*), he stabs, and shoots, strangles him or her or both of them. (How aptly Daumier illustrated this in his theatre picture!)[5] In opera there are more stabbings than in spoken drama. As a child I played 'opera' in the mirror and I know that I always drew my sword and, at the end, fell dead myself. [. . .]

The one-acter will be followed by something on a large scale.

Mannheim has taught me two things: it has *convinced* me of Die Brautwahl and also of the current impossibility of imagining music except for the theatre.

(This will pass.)

I have attempted to get rid of *Basle*. Either the affair must be called off entirely or I shall be persuaded to keep my promise after all or – more probably – I shall be sued. (Everyone who owes me money is wanting to take me to court. Hanson, Harmonie Verlag, Backhaus. Möchte sie doch der Cerberus . . .!)[6] – But I would like to keep free of commitments and, furthermore, at the beginning of October comes Bologna . . .

Thank you for your letter and goodbye. Regards to the Surbitone-poets.[7] (What do you think of this expression for composers in the style of Reger: 'Teutone-poets'?)[8]

---

[1]Orig. Ma(h)ler-Wütrich = painter-hothead, i.e. Edmund Lehsen in *Die Brautwahl*, *or* hot-headed Mahlerian.

[2]Dr Otto Neitzel, 1852–1920, pianist and critic. Wrote for the *Kölnische Zeitung* from 1887.

[3]*Eine florentinische Tragödie* was set to music in 1916 by Alexander von Zemlinsky.

[4]Orig. Drei-Ecktigen – pun on Dreieck = triangle *and* dreiaktig = in three acts.

[5]Honoré Daumier: *Murder in the Theatre*. A drawing published in *Le Charivari* in 1864.

[6]'May Cerberus [take] them . . .' quotation from *Die Brautwahl*.

[7]Petri was at that time living in Surbiton.

[8]Orig. Teu-töner, as opposed to Neutöner = modern composers.

147 TO EGON PETRI
in German

Berlin 19.6.1913

By the time you arrive I may already have departed. What a great pity you could not be here 3 days earlier!

On 17 June, a Tuesday, I enjoyed the great privilege of receiving the
Pierrot lunaire
ensemble in my house and of hearing a complete and wellnigh perfect performance of the cycle. A small audience was present, including Mengelberg, Schnabel, Serato; Schoenberg conducted, Steuermann and Kindler[1] were amongst the performers, also an excellent young Hungarian violinist.[2]

What a level of taste and ability these young people have attained in comparison with the youth of my younger days! – It was an ideal musical afternoon; a highly ingenious new work, a perfect ensemble, afterwards stimulating exchange of ideas, tea and cigarettes and charming, intelligent women. This is the way in which art should be presented – and no other. – Schoenberg's Pierrot lunaire cycle is a work that stands alone and one hopes it will remain so. In it one finds masterful passages and some moments of genius. As if a large musical mechanism had been assembled from crumbled ingredients, and as if some of these ingredients have been put to uses other than those for which they were originally designed. It is unforgivable that the poems have not remained in their original French, which certainly comes closer to the 'esprit' of their content. – This longing for the native hills of Bergamo doesn't 'sound' in German.

It would have to be proved genealogically that Pierrot is a native of Bergamo. He is probably a borrowed Italian masque figure (Arlecchino comes from Bergamo) who was transformed by French comedy (Molière?). Pierrot's costume is reminiscent of the Italian Bajazzo or Pagliacco (man of straw) who is, however, neither a masque nor theatre character but a carnival figure. – The form of Pierrot lunaire is very satisfactory. It consists of three times seven poems, hence three movements. The number and sequence of these poems seems – chemin faisant – to have been established and thought out first. Everything came together during the process of composition. Although all are grotesque, one can describe the three parts as respectively lyric, tragic and humorous (according to their prevailing characteristics). – Between some of the songs, short linking passages seem to have been added *later*, struck me as 'seams'. In the second part a complete instrumental Intermezzo (without text) is inserted, a three-part paraphrase of an earlier flute monologue (which is, by the way, descended from the 'traurige Weise' in Tristan). –

The rhythmically and melodically modulated declamation often sounds affected; in certain places, however, almost like a new instrument, charming and expressive. – The heredity of this medium – often genuinely, sometimes only seemingly *new* – could be established. I received a similar impression when I first heard Berlioz's song 'Ma belle amie est morte' (from 'Les Nuits d'Eté') for the *first* time. – I wanted to jot down these few sentences, so allow me to address the jottings to you.

In occasionally writing you a 'feuilleton' and considering you as the dust-jacket of my diary, my intentions are as friendly as ever, and indeed more confidential.

For me it was most refreshing.

[1]Hans Kindler, 1892–1949, cellist and conductor. Busoni dedicated an arrangement of Bach's Chromatic Fantasy and Fugue for cello and piano to him.
[2]Jakob Maliniak.

148 TO EDITH ANDREAE[1]
in German

Berlin 22.7.1913

The moon has its halo, the comet its tail and Saturn its rings: grant this wretched moon-cadaver thy pallid splendour and shine before thy devoted dotard in his dismal antechamber.

Should this honour be granted during the morning hours, said chamber shall be vacant and thou shalt be received with most grateful cordiality by
Thy Ferruccio Busoni.

[1] One presumes that Frau Andreae was one of the 'charming, intelligent women' present at the performance of *Pierrot lunaire* mentioned in the previous letter. This brief invitation to morning coffee, couched in 'moon-drunk' language is clearly intended as good-natured mockery of the verses of Otto Erich Hartleben which Busoni had found so lacking in 'esprit'.

149 TO EDITH ANDREAE
in German

Berlin 5.8.1913

It is just as well that you were the first to write for, to my shame, I had entirely forgotten your address! –

In the summer one's friends become associated with the most unlikely and complicated place names, which do not fit at all with the image one retains of them.

A place like the one in which you are staying can be attractive (as a painting): but soon one has scrutinized all the visitors, one meets the same people at all hours of the day and if no single person has any particular fascination, the 'affair' becomes a hopeless case. This is what makes the metropolis infinitely preferable to any seaside town; public places preferable to private circles. –

I finally grasped what this means when Sobernheim[1] recently took us off to a restaurant at a race-course. Soon I had singled out *one* good-looking girl (as there was none more attractive), spotted three acquaintances whom I would have preferred to avoid and about a hundred different apparitions, and – I longed for the Potsdamer Platz with its constant variety! [. . .]

I am beginning to get absorbed in the Bologna business; already countless letters from young people have arrived, to say nothing of the official communications. Had I already been informed, when you last called, that the symphony concerts (which I had suggested) have been approved, and that I have a 90-piece orchestra at my disposal? [. . .]

[At the head of the letter:] I had previously written a long letter in Italian and I fear that my German style has not benefited from it.

[1] Curt Sobernheim (see p. 424).

150 TO EGON PETRI
in German

Geneva 20.9.1913

Should you not yet have done so, I would ask you to read Schopenhauer's short essay on creative writing and style[1] and, if possible, also rub Draber's nose in it, for which D's nose lends itself particularly well.

Lichtenberg,[2] had he known it, would most certainly have written an article with great wit and relish on the inverse proportion of the length of a nose to 'flair'.

S's essay contains almost nothing which we have not discussed and which I have not mentioned to you on occasion; but he expresses everything precisely, powerfully and with humorous ferocity, underlines many points and sets everything out cohesively.

Thus, for example, his superb idea of substituting the word 'piece-worker' for 'journalist', and his suggestion that critics should employ the singularis humilitatis (thus, for example, 'meine erbärmliche Lumpazität')[3] instead of the pluralis majestatis!

However, although the idea transpires from his every word, I have found no mention in S. of the following distinction, namely that there are three kinds of good style:

 – that of precise expression,
 – that of beautiful sound and rhythm,
 – that of elevated thought and refined feeling.

Examples of the first kind: Schopenhauer himself, Balzac, Flaubert
       of the second kind: English poetry
       of the third kind: some utterances of Beethoven, to whom the use of
language was of secondary importance.

A Dante makes use of all three forms, which is the difference between him
and Hans Heinz Ewers,[4] who makes use of none.

Precision goes hand in hand with conciseness, for he who chooses the
appropriate word has no need of superfluities. Nor of repetition; which does
not apply to Schopenhauer as, for the sake of utmost clarity, he cites his
maxims time and time again.

His pamphlet could well be applied, and with considerable usefulness, to
music making. Many things in it would, without alteration, be relevant to the
new subject. It is a pity that such a book does not exist: this is probably so
because authors indeed possess the ability to write about literature, while
musicians lack the literary talent.

I have been considering something of this kind and would like to express
some views, which could be noteworthy, under the heading 'Themes and
melodies'; maybe one day I shall be able to incorporate all this in the 2nd part
of the Well-tempered Clavier, which would ultimately be the most appropriate
place. –

========

Gerda often says to me, 'Your letters are essays', and I myself once wrote to
K.:[5] 'If you have some magazine articles ready, please address the manuscript to me.'

And someone else drew a distinction between my 'literary' and 'personal'
correspondence.

But, in a letter, 'personal' matters cannot be separated from creative
writing. [. . .]

---

[1]'Über Schriftstellerei und Stil', ch. XXIII of Schopenhauer's *Vereinzelte, jedoch
systematisch geordnete Gedanken über vierlerlei Gegenstände*, 2 vols., Berlin, 1851.
[2]Georg Christoph Lichtenberg, 1742–1799, master of the aphorism.
[3]= approx. 'my wretched skulduggery'.
[4]Hans Heinz Ewers, 1871–1943, German writer. Busoni expresses distaste for his
literary style on more than one occasion, yet it was thanks largely to Ewers's efforts
that so many copies or originals of Busoni's letters were collected for posterity after
the composer's death.
[5]Name obliterated.

151 TO EGON PETRI
in German

Bologna 16.10.1913

Is the public entirely wrong? Although it should have detected in Lucia the less vulgar of the two! The first theme is, on the other hand, more closely related to 'Santa Lucia'.

Now I would dearly love to know what the encore was. Maybe 'La Traviata'?

Should I edit these pieces as an appendix to the Paganini–Liszt Variations? [. . .]

'And what does one do when evening approaches?' A volume of stories and anecdotes 'from provincial town life' – the first complication: when it rains. The second: when it's a Sunday. The third: when the only decent person is out of town.

For the time being my chief concern has been to reform the water closets and pissoirs, and I have detected (after many unsuccessful experiments) a
Monte pulciano
which is not a mountain bringing forth fleas[3] but rather a sparkling red wine which costs 80 Pfennigs a litre. Thus I am working on matters of hygiene and literature. (Egon).[4]

Mountains which bring forth fleas are rarer than those which bring mice into the world; Italy is the land which coined the phrase 'parturiunt montes'.

As a counterpart to your 'pigheads' and 'chicken hearts'[5] we have excellent *Schweinshaxe* here, called zampino,[6] and I have also been active in this field. –

Only water, trees and women are lacking in B., in exchange we have stone umbrellas which endure for centuries.[7] Also: dignity – dust – stamped paper – elections – Wagnerians – and countless monastery buildings which have been converted into: music schools, an art museum, an orthopaedic hospital, a riding school, an artillery magazine and other such profane things. – (vide Encyclopaedia.)

My parenthesis leads me to England and the poem about Clifton Bingham was entirely to my taste. But why Bingham? Let us say: English lyric verse.

(This partial 'vision' and then utter blindness is remarkable!)
    This is one of those letters.
    I dedicate it to you as a sign of reconciliation. [. . .]

[1]Brahms *Paganini Variations*.
[2]Donizetti–Liszt *Reminiscences de Lucia di Lammermoor*. It appears that Petri had juxtaposed these two works in a recital.
[3]Pulce (Italian) = flea. The play on words continues by alluding to Horace's famous line 'Parturiunt montes nascietur ridiculus mus' = The mountains labour and bring forth a ridiculous mouse.
[4]i.e. As Egon would say.
[5]Orig. Ochsenbein and Hasenfuß (terms of abuse).
[6]Pig's trotter.
[7]i.e. the stone arcades of the buildings in Bologna.

152 TO EGON PETRI
in German

St Petersburg 28.11.1913

I hope you had a pleasant time in Holland. Did you hear of Wijsman's death while you were there? His mother-in-law informed us of it today. *I* fear that it was suicide, and there one stands, once again, confronted by a final cadence, dumbfounded and also a little grazed by the blow oneself.

Backhaus has disappeared, W. is no more; what then was the meaning of the animated intermezzo of the last two years? –

Did I not say so repeatedly?

I was ill when I arrived here, had to miss a rehearsal and was obliged to get out of bed for the concert, at which I played my Skyscraper Concerto. A frightful strain, with influenza and a single rehearsal on the same day. The St Petersburger Zeitung expresses its thanks to me with the words: 'If only Herr B. had not won the Rubinstein Prize for *composition*! Then he would have stuck to his Bach transcriptions.' – What for? –

Another paper (to digress) speaks of *your* victory in the case against Paderewski. (In Warsaw, allegedly, nobody has mentioned it.)

While watching a piece of coal glimmering in the fire, I observed – as everyone has – how the flame (following a vein) would go out in one place and ignite in another, always on the move, constantly dying and reviving. – Thus, I said to myself, does culture expire and awaken in the world; one need only imagine a period of 5,000 years between one epoch and the next and one already senses that one's momentary irritations are to an extent transcendental. – Perhaps, as A. France once said, our entire planetary system is nothing but a pimple on a microscopic insect. ('Everything is pus.') [. . .]

– Groups of 'Malays' stroll around the city like figures out of Turandot. It has already turned very cold, the day is tremendously short.

I had to let myself go a little, but please forgive my strained tone.

153 TO EGON PETRI
in German

Paris 18.1.1914

Five times I had already come to the end of the slow movement of the Redskins;[1] four times I had to scalp it, but hope that I've found the solution today. A miracle!! Considering that, between times, one has to learn a Trio by Pfitzner,[2] to travel and memorize, and that the composer, cast to and fro in constantly changing surroundings, is unable to find any peace of mind.

Ley and the Creightons are here and still full of their Petronian impressions from London.

Petronius is the patron saint of Bologna and Petrus is the stone on which the church of a certain man (who had until then only worked in wood) was founded. Thus, when you come to Italy there will be a Trinity, which will however sound not unlike one of Schoenberg's triads.

Szanto[3] has announced 3 piano recitals with ambitious programmes (spread over four months) and in which the above-mentioned Schoenberg appears, as well as Ravel, Bartók and——Busoni; for in the past 3 years Szanto has come just one Elegy further.

The orchestra of the Conservatoire (with which I shall be playing 2 hours from now) is made up entirely of 'premiers prix du Conservatoire', is uniquely perfect and would be even more so if it had ever had a conductor.

But generally they have the respective professor of harmony or some such.

[1] Red Indian Fantasy, op. 44, for piano and orchestra.
[2] Pfitzner's Trio in F, op. 8, which Busoni had performed on 12 January 1914. Pfitzner himself conducted Busoni's Piano Concerto, with the composer as soloist, in Strasburg on 8 January 1913.
[3] Theodor Szanto, 1877–1934, Hungarian pianist and composer. Pupil of Busoni in Berlin.

154 TO HUGO LEICHTENTRITT
in German

Berlin 25.2.1914

From the collector's point of view, the enclosed score is
'unique'.
You can follow the process of rewriting, in comparison with the score of the opera, from the hand-written passages and the alteration of the page-numbering. –

Brautwahl Suite, 5 pieces[1]
1. *Spukhaftes* [Ghostly music]

concentrates chiefly on the whirling dance which Leonhard
summons up and forces on Thusman.

2. *Lyrisches* [Lyric music]

is based on the following poem by Fouqué:

> Ein Flüstern, Rauschen, Klingen,
> geht durch den Frühlingshain,
> fängt wie auf Liebesschwingen
> Geist, Sinn und Leben ein.

> Säng ich es nach, was leise
> solch' stille Leben spricht,
> so schien' aus meiner Weise
> das ew'ge Liebeslicht.[2]

3. *Mystiches* [Mystical music]

encompasses the more solemn, magic moments of the action.

4. *Hebräisches* [Hebrew music]

A chiaroscuro portrait of *Manasse*. His orthodoxy and diabolism.

5. *Heiteres* [Cheerful music]

drawn chiefly from the introduction and the close (the fire-
conjuring) of the 1st act.

[in the margin]

I and II, IV and V follow *attacca*, the IIIrd, the mystical music, stands
separately between them.

======

Chronology:
  – 1st sonatina
  – Berceuse élégiaque
  – 2nd sonatina
  – Nocturne symphonique

======

Takes the 'polyphonic harmony' of the Berceuse a step further, strives to
dissolve massed orchestral sound into individual elements, does without
trumpets and trombones.

Indian Fantasy

the most recent work.

Draws on themes of the North American redskins; sets out primarily to be a
piano piece; then to create a balance and mutual cooperation between the two
elements (piano and orchestra). Consists of three sections without a break: a
Fantasy (orchestral introduction, prolonged piano solo without orchestra,
reprise of the orchestral introduction and short set of variations); a *Canzone*
formed out of two songs; and a *Finale* based on three genuine motifs and one
original one. The first of the genuine ones appears previously in the Fantasy.
The last of the three is characterized by continually changing $\frac{3}{4}$ and $\frac{4}{4}$ time.

The third movements, uninterruptedly animated, finishes without the customary coda (which heralds the close), like a vanishing phantom.

The most frequently used scale in the Fantasy is the pentatonic one, which corresponds to the black keys of the piano, but the Hungarian gypsy scale also appears. Scotch snap (♫.). No programme. But poetic simulations, such as the melancholy of the race; a glimpse of the Mississippi caught in passing; a hint of warlike proceedings; exotic colouring.

Orchestration of the N[octurne] S[ymphonique]:

   3 flutes, 2 clarinets, 1 bass clarinet, 1 oboe, 1 cor anglais, 2 bassoons, 1 contra-bassoon, 3 horns, harp, celesta, timpani, percussion, strings. –

[1]This letter served as material for programme notes which Leichtentritt wrote for a concert in the Beethoven Saal, Berlin, on 12 March 1914.

[2]   A whispered springtime singing
Runs rustling through the grove,
My heart and soul, a-winging,
To thoughts of love remove.

I'll sing the strain hereafter,
This song of life so fine,
Until with heavenly laughter
Eternal love may shine.

155 TO EGON PETRI
in German

Bologna 13.4.1914

I have just written to Frau Kathi, your mother and my friend, but my heart is so full of concern for you that I can find no words.[1]

Perhaps it would be possible if I were to see you.

——Maybe it would be beneficial if you were to pack *at once* and come here;[2] the spring weather is magical, the surroundings would be new to you and you would find friendship and stimulation.

Come!

I shall await your telegram.

[1]Henri Petri had died on 7 April 1914.
[2]Egon Petri was anyway due in Bologna for concert engagements between 22 April and 10 May.

156 TO H. W. DRABER
in German

Bologna 13.6.1914

[. . .] Of unperformed operas by living composers I would like to single out
Ravel's 'L'Heure espagnole'. In second place also Dukas's 'Ariane et Barbe-
bleue'. These are valuable and uncommon scores, e.g. which could not be
said of the 'Ferner Schreck'.[1] In Berlin the 'brilliant' mediocrities have an
immediate triumph. German families still readily marvel at the coloured extra
supplements in the Gartenlaube. Example: Hugo Wolff [sic]; Or: Die Jagd
nach dem Glück (I have forgotten the name of the artist);[2] or: Jörn Uhl.[3] Or:
Dr Wüllner.[4]——

I have just 'discovered', for my Bach Edition, *four duets* (for piano) by the
great Cantor! These are delicacies! – And despite all researching and kowtow-
ing[5] on the subject of Bach, these duets are never played! Not even by me
But I am actually only a gourmet (not a 'connoisseur') and have to find my
own way in matters of taste.——

Yes, what could I, after Schlesinger and Draber, reveal on the subject?!
Were I to suggest a *Theatre of Novelties*, I would, for lack of novelties – like
B. Shaw – have to advocate my own works. Of the ones you mention, only
Boris Godunov cries out for performance and *yet it is so exquisite that it does
not suffer from remaining unperformed.*

Consider, on the other hand, the gentleman who has neither arms, legs nor
face! What would remain of *his* score if it were not *played*?!

My dear H.W., one has to give children lemonade and not some decolourized
and disembodied Château-Margaux. And when the lemonade is *fizzy*, then –
well, it just fizzes.

I have taken pains to write clearly, but perhaps I have been unsuccessful. –
I hope to be in Berlin at the end of the month.

Yesterday I sent off the programme books from Bologna. The tour [with
Petri] was a success. The Brautwahl Suite was very intelligently assessed. [. . .]

[1] = the distant fright, i.e. Schreker's *Der ferne Klang*.
[2] Rudolph Henneberg painted this popular allegorical picture *c.* 1860.
[3] Gustav Frenssen, *Jörn Uhl*, Berlin, 1901. The tragic story of a farmer's son.
[4] Dr Ludwig Wüllner, 1858–1938, actor and reciter, later concert singer and violinist.
[5] Orig. Auf dem Popo-Rutschen = sliding on one's backside.

157 TO EGON PETRI
in German

Berlin 1.7.1914

I have just attempted to speak to you on the telephone, but you were asleep. (Sleeping at night: fate, sleeping during the day: sin.)

Like this you will rust and come no further . . .

It was the following that was bothering me: I am making no headway with the '*Italian Concerto*'. I am at a loss; I don't know what to say about it. Are you at all partial to the work and have you, perhaps through your teaching, reached any conclusions? In short: have you gathered any 'notes' about it? In which case, should you be so inclined, I would leave the Concerto to you. –

On the other hand I have worked well at the *Chromatische Fuge* and – (I believe) – excellently at the *Abreise Capriccio*. – (A delightful little piece.)

VI

1914 – 1915
The Great War (1)

158 DIARY[1]
in German

With a readiness that had been feared, all signs already now point to the first musical fruits of the violent events, announced by a certain patriotic oracle of the arts with a jangling German name.[2] With a decisive gesture he hurls the meagre package of foreign culture back across the frontiers at a time when these are in the process of being shifted.

The jangler thrusts these shreds and tatters at the feet of the French and the 'Orientals'; and how fortunate it is that the English have no music of their own to speak of, for they would have had it thrown in their faces.

In his self-righteous fury, sincerely believing that the art of the future 'will attain strength and purpose on the battlefield' – (an outcome, incidentally, which he visualizes only for the Germans and Austrians) – the jangler unexpectedly turns his weapon on one of his kinsmen, striking the Austrian Schoenberg with as much force as if he were Japanese at least.

Thus   'Daß der Blinderzürnte
              Statt des Sünders, unversehens,
              einen ganz Unschuld'gen traf,
              den Schlemihl ben Zuri Schadday'[3]

as Hitzig tells Heine.

The jangler, his lunge miscarried, proves however, through his inadequate representation of foreign music, that he has no idea of it; namely by declaring that the Germans cannot be misled by its 'prowess' and hence that the 'influence', so disdainfully sent packing, in actual fact does not exist; for the simple reason that art possesses other qualities than mere prowess, which are entirely necesssary in order to withstand this influence.

Finally the jangler, by formulating a sentence such as the following: 'In this, the greatest of wars, which has been kindling for centuries', shows that he has just as deficient a knowledge of his own language as of those foreign idioms which he rejects. No, the war was 'kindled' only six weeks ago; but an alien such as I quickly comes to understand such language, even if it is foreign to him and clumsily expressed; the jangler actually means: 'In this, the greatest of wars to have been kindled in centuries'.

[1] Busoni grouped this and the succeeding diary entries together under the heading 'Notizen aus der "grossen Zeit"' (Notes from 'Momentous times').

[2] Dr Ferdinand Scherber, Viennese editor of *Signale für die musikalische Welt*, who had published an article entitled 'Krieg und Kunst' in the issue for 9.9.1914.

[3] Heine, *Romanzero*, Book Three, Hebräische Melodien, 'Jehuda ben Halevy', 4, v.50:

> That in his blind hatred,
> Unintending, not the culprit
> Did he strike, but a good man,
> Old Shlemihl ben Zuri Shadday.

159 TO JELLA OPPENHEIMER
in German

Berlin 11.9.1914

[. . .] All in all one can at present sense a brightening of the atmosphere – (so God willing, not just for a day). My work, which had ground to a dejected halt, is beginning to progress again, even if sluggishly and in short bursts. The architect of the house in which a custom-designed apartment is to be incorporated for me has come along with plans. My publishers are not entirely idle and I shall even have to go through with my American tour!

I shall set out in a different frame of mind to that in which I signed the contract; I am taking my children with me and there remains the uneasy question: in what state shall I find the country I am leaving? Who will be missing? When shall I be able to travel my straight path again?

How, finally, will Europe manage to return to health (and how long will it take)? I fear we shall no longer experience the new zenith. [. . .]

160 TO CURT SOBERNHEIM
in German

Berlin 16.9.1914 [postmark]

The arguments *for* my trip to America (under the altered circumstances of these 'momentous times') are,

    firstly: *the country is at peace,*
    secondly: *there is a commercial interest;*
  against my trip to A. speak
    firstly: *the uncertainty of the voyage,*
    secondly: *the fact*
that neither their orchestras nor conductors are at full strength!
    thirdly: *that Hanson has disappeared.*[1]
What do you advise?

I am truly undecided. I can find enough to do and to earn in A. even without Hanson (I often told you how unnecessary and tiresome he is!). –

What scares me is the journey and the idea of abandoning everything here without anybody to manage my affairs; for I would certainly take all my people with me.

But waiting for special editions of the newspapers is also fruitless and the valiant Germans are not noted for their imprudence. Otherwise I could have made pleasant and profitable use of *this very time* to make plans for the future and for peace-time with publishers, architects and other contractors; but all courage is being vented on the field of honour.

The thought of actually being *obliged* to send a MS to a publisher makes my hair stand on end! The celebrated musical patrician F.B. would then not even expect 25 Marks. –

The situation is more promising in the 'grosser Freiheitsstall'[2] across the ocean. – But also not enticing on that account.

Therefore I would again ask you for advice.

[1]Hanson had not 'disappeared'. On the contrary, he published a letter on 23 November 1914 in the *New York Musical Courier* explaining that, although postal or telegraphic communication with Germany was almost impossible, there was no reason to assume that Busoni would disappoint his public by not fulfilling his American commitments.
[2]'Great freedom sty' (Heine). See footnote to letter no. 175.

161 TO EMILIO ANZOLETTI
in German

Berlin 17.9.1914

A few days ago I wrote to Bologna, asking for *one year's leave of absence:* I don't yet know whether I shall go to America – everything is uncertain. For me this war is downright tragic. At present one should be 15 or 70, but not 50, as I almost am; it amounts to amputating a man's two sound legs without anaesthetic. If Italy is spared, it will have a great cultural responsibility on its shoulders: to fulfil everything which the other countries will have to neglect – during the coming 10 years.——

A letter from Bologna informs me that there has again been talk of building a new concert-hall – discussions were interrupted by the outbreak of war but have been resumed. [. . .]

162 DIARY
in German

27.9.1914

Yesterday I heard that the consumptive baker's apprentice Gorki has also donned his armour. – He must be incensed, this one can well understand, at a nation that loudly applauded his 'Lower depths'. – I would not say the same of the works of Maeterlinck, in his case there must be some profound reason why he – *despite* his successes in Germany – has assumed so hostile an attitude. – One resents the fact that d'Annunzio has proclaimed the brotherhood of Italy and France: but is he not right in principle? – (He is absolutely right.) –

– I am often reminded of Jules Verne's 'Une idée du docteur Ox'.

Now that Belgium has been stormed, Reims attacked and the composer A. Magnard executed by firing squad,[1] the system and intention of this kind of 'defensive' have become entirely clear to me. Prussia, having taken the bull by the horns, will have to achieve its object at all costs. One cannot expect, let alone demand, 'humanity' or 'aesthetics'; but there remains the modest wish that these flags should not be hoisted. –

The Germans have ascribed to Beethoven German attributes which he does not possess. Therefore I believe that the Germans are now at the furthest remove from a just assessment of Beethoven.

29.9.1914

I have been sick for 3 days now and for the 3rd time this year. Only full-scale moral refreshment could cure me completely, but where is this to spring from? Wherever I look, I see the same things. Covetousness from above, stupidity from below, between them great blood-lust – bestiality let loose; and one says to oneself: I have been thoroughly hoodwinked, and for a long time. At present I no longer feel the strength to build altars; to be architect, priest and congregation for myself and in one person.

2.10.1914

I used to say: there exist in the world, all in all, either *incipient* or *moribund* cultures. Only the diminutive area between London and Rome, between Paris and Moscow can credit itself with a culture which is florescent and vigorous, mature yet still youthful (I used to say). I declare this opinion to be one of the greatest mistakes I ever made. – The readiness with which all people between London and Rome, between Paris and Moscow, were able to relapse into primitive bestiality proves that the culture ascribed to them was a crude illusion.

I advertised a recital of Bach for charitable purposes[2] and today received a card (on this subject) from Herr August Ludwig,[3] in which he advises me 'to keep my bowdlerizations to myself'. – August Spanuth, reeking of patriotism and other such worthy things, describes the executed composer Magnard as a 'treacherous murderer'. – (Germans with the name of 'August' have this particular vein of noblesse.) –

At the close of his war-series, Goya says: the truth is dead; the overall outcome of the horror he depicts. (Also an expression of the feeling that one no longer knows what is right and what is true.)

A musician in Amsterdam, Diepenbrock,[4] has published an insulting anti-war article, in particular anti-German. The honourable August takes him to task for it in his paper. – Diepenbrock enumerates the 'virtues' which the Germans themselves consider as their own: German loyalty, German honesty, German seriousness, German assiduity, German thoroughness, German soulfulness [Gemüt]. These are attributes of gold with the weight of lead. Soulfulness: they can talk!

8.10.1914

One must be very patient, also *with oneself.* – I am dreading my 50th birthday, which is something of a funeral, also my 'collected works', which are a bundle of misery.

Yesterday there was an orchestral rehearsal with Cottlow[5] – the 'Philharmonic' actually played Beethoven most perfunctorily of all; on the other hand they are brilliant in Tchaikovsky and Wagner.——

At first people hurl abuse at a new artist, then they exaggerate their good opinion of him, then a new, younger generation reacts against him and by the 3rd generation he has already become a classic and not worth disputing – and who benefits from all this?

No news bulletin concurs with another any more – things happening under our very eyes – and yet one is supposed to have faith in the accuracy of history!

Yesterday it was reported: the task of reconstruction would not begin for 6 years. I shall be 54. That would still be possible! Speriamo!

9.10.1914

The agonizing question now is whether, when and how to set out for America. – The venom of the 'situation' only gradually permeated my spirits, so that I was able to remain immune for the whole month of August. But in September it began to make its effect and prostrated me. Yet it would seem that I could still recover from it; I am beginning to 'disengage' from the affair; I am no longer getting involved and am little more than an observer; I am turning in on myself and contemplating matters which cannot be settled with guns but also cannot be destroyed by them. But to have come this far, one first had to penetrate the jungle. –

To experience something of this kind, even at my age, is not without value, and the fact that I am bearing up to it so well is a good sign. –

The apartment in the Bendler Strasse could be a great consolation to me. – One is constantly expending too much energy on inessentials! –

Something cheering happened two days ago. Benni showed me his detailed oil sketch for a picture: the Comrades. It was something almost exceptional. The picture is fascinating and remains quite aloof. Absolutely pure idealism achieved with absolutely realistic means. The 'happy man' and the 'unhappy man' are equally detached and isolated. –

10.10.1914

Today Herr W[ilhelm] Kl[atte][6] wrote that he was distracted from the lovely accompaniment to the Beethoven concerto two days ago by the soloist. Actually this pleased me greatly! – Today *Antwerp* 'fell'. What do they actually intend to do with Belgium? Hand it back a little damaged? – Today is my 'Bach recital', which is causing me some headache.[7] –

[1]Albéric Magnard, 1865–1914, distinguished French composer. He was allegedly executed as a sniper on 3 September 1914 by German troops. In fact his house at Baron near Senlis was set on fire by the invading *Bosch* soldiers and he perished in the flames. Busoni had been personally acquainted with Magnard, whose Symphony no. 3 featured in one of Busoni's concerts of contemporary music on 12 January 1905 in Berlin.
[2]This concert, originally scheduled for 5 October, was postponed to 10 October. See footnote 7 below.
[3]August Ludwig, 1865–1946, editor of the *Neue Berliner Musikzeitung* from 1894 to 1903, then freelance critic. He wrote a completion of Schubert's 'Unfinished' Symphony.
[4]Alphons Diepenbrock, 1862–1921, Dutch composer and philologist.
[5]Augusta Cottlow, 1878–1954, American pianist and pupil of Busoni. An unpublished *Etude en forme d'Adagio d'une Sonate*, written in the 1890s, is dedicated to her (it contains the main theme of the Piano Concerto's *Pezzo serioso*).
[6]Wilhelm Klatte, 1870–1930, critic of the *Berliner Lokal-Anzeiger* from 1897.
[7]This concert for the *Verband konzertierender Künstler Deutschlands* was given 'in aid of needy artists' and included the world premières of three completely new Bach transcriptions, the Capriccio über die Abreise des vielgeliebten Bruders, dated July 1914, the Praeludium, Fuga und Allegro in Eb [BWV 998], and the Goldberg Variations, dated 'in wartime, August 1914'.

163 TO EGON PETRI
in German

Berlin 8.11.1914

I am gradually preparing my edition of the Well-tempered Clavier, part two. Therefore I would ask you to return the opening pages (which are in your safe-keeping); although (or because) I consider them unusable, in the light of my more fully developed plan. [. . .]

164 DIARY
in German

2.1.1915

New Year 1915! And the war has made little progress, there is no sign of an approaching peace. Just as at the beginning!

On the third day of Christmas I completed the text of

Dr F[aust]

which came to me uninterruptedly and unhesitatingly, like a revelation. I have thus taken possession of the stage and broken with the traditions of opera.

If the work evolves as it should, it will offer as much to the layman as to the connoisseur. What a gift!

America, today, 3 days before departure, still undecided.

165 TO EDITH ANDREAE
in German

Berlin 3.1.1915

I have had to make the hasty decision to depart this evening, sooner than expected. – Although nothing could come of our meeting, I shall look upon the sentiments which moved you to your kind invitation as a fine pledge of your faithful friendship towards me. I hope that this crisis will be overcome and that, as soon as it has been weathered, I shall be able to plan my life more to my inclination and according to my duty to myself.

Then I would be able to enjoy a settled and productive existence, which would moreover enable me to find time for my friends.

In the last few days I still succeeded in completing to my greatest satisfaction a drama for music, of whose inception you already knew.[1]

This is an intimate message, intended to show that I confide in you more than in others.

[1]The libretto for the opening scenes of *Doktor Faust* had been written as long ago as September 1910, in Basle. The last two scenes (Zweites Bild and Letztes Bild) were then written in December 1914; the spoken prologue was added in 1915 in America.

166 TO EGON PETRI
in German

SS *Rotterdam* 10.1.1915
Holland–America Line
Hoboken 20.1.1915 [postmark]

We had to make a forced stop in *Zurich*, later in *Genoa* and *Naples* and now we are approaching *Gibraltar*, from where I hope this letter will reach you. We were obliged, moreover, to interrupt the voyage for two hours whilst – in the middle of the night – a torpedo boat held us up and took away two passengers. – The days in Italy were dazzling, Genoa shone with truly regal splendour.

On board – the refuse of the war! Mamma Cottlow as retired barmaid. – A few good books are helping me through the first days, subsequently I hope to resume work.

Of the books, one by Wells, which I read in French, inspired me: La découverte de l'avenir,[1] no longer a 'Utopia' but a systematic 'anticipation' of what is to come, of what has to come.

Of my projects, *three* have been inaugurated: the general outline of the Well-tempered Clavier II, a 'grotesque' in one act[2] and a music-drama in five tableaux. I have brought the material for these three with me: otherwise not one sheet of music! These plans sustain me in the face of the uncertainties of the immediate future.

Yes! – For when shall we meet again?

This aimlessness, after ten years of systematic progress, at the height of my powers, is the hardest blow!

The children are a great consolation to me. They are growing up to be fine and good-natured. It is as if Benni had been purified, he has become cheerful and congenial. –

I can tell you nothing further. Send us news of yourself if you feel so inclined or if anything worth telling should occur.

Address everything to *Br. & H.* New York.

Kindest greetings to Kestenberg, Draber, Rita,[3] Sobernheim.

---

[1]H. G. Wells *The Discovery of the Future*, a discourse delivered to the Royal Institution on 24 January 1902, London, 1902.

[2]*Arlecchino*, of which Busoni had written the libretto in the summer and autumn of 1914. In November and early December of that year he had also composed a substantial portion of the score.

[3]Rita Bötticher, Busoni's secretary.

167 TO EGON PETRI
in German

SS *Rotterdam* 19.1.1915
Holland–America Line
Hoboken 20.1.1915 [postmark]

Seventeen days have passed since I left B[erlin] and I am still aboard this storm-tossed crate. But tomorrow, at the latest, the land of 'Freedom' should hove into sight.

No news has reached us here except of a severe earthquake in Italy.[1] – But the voyage was pleasant and warm, as we were sailing almost entirely in the latitude of Gibraltar, only recently did we set a course slightly further North.

If fate guides me well, from the moment of my return I should closely follow one straight path. Meanwhile I have succeeded in completing the main outline of the first volume of the W.Cl. II.

Reports from Switzerland and Italy of the principal events of the time differed from that which we had been led to believe in B[erlin] to the point of utter confusion.

What then are we going to hear in 3 weeks!?

On board ship I met a young painter who had lived in the Dutch East Indies for 1½ years and who, like Gauguin and Stevenson, had grown unaccustomed to European tastes.

I have been reading a biography of this Stevenson (by Balfour)[2] which, due to a certain mildness and blandness of tone, makes a truly nauseating impression. Only an 'essayist' can write with such lack of temperament. The book's saving grace is that it includes lengthy quotations from R.L.S.'s own autobiographical writings.

I was very interested in an edition of *Faust* which includes all the scraps of paper on which notes and initial sketches for the work were jotted down.[3] Altogether over 500 pages! Many things 'missed the mark' but in this unique work every word counts.

My art seems to be becoming ever harder for me and the Ideal (perhaps fortunately) absolutely unattainable.

Even if this is nothing new, it is a truth on which one must personally have burned one's fingers before one will acknowledge it.

But with burned fingers one cannot play the piano, and thus I shall have to pass over the concert in Boston on the 21st. Everything passes. In your thoughts do not pass over

Your
F.B.

[1] The earthquake, with its epicentre in the Abruzzi, occurred on 14 January 1915. The town of Avezzano was totally destroyed, an estimated 12,000 were killed and 20,000 injured.

[2]Sir Graham Balfour, *The Life of Robert Louis Stevenson*, 2 vols., London, 1901.
[3]Probably Erich Schmidt's so-called 'Sophienausgabe' of Goethe's works, Weimar, 1887–8, vols. 14–15. The sketches and notes are traditionally called 'Paralipomena'.

168 TO EGON PETRI
in German

New York[1] 31.1.1915

'Correspondence' may need a 'counterweight' but, in writing to you, I am playing my game of chess alone and calculating my opponent's moves.

Why do I repeatedly do so, while knowing that many others would react faster and more feelingly to my letters?

It could be that my letters have too impersonal an effect, like a chronicle; and the recipient hence feels he is not directly involved!

Yet this explains the effect, but scarcely the cause, of my writing to one and the same person. – I sent you two long letters from on board ship and the same vessel took them back to Europe.

I posted the letters in full view of the giant buildings of the N.Y. waterfront. The morning was made magical by a light fog and that haze which I describe as sun-particles. The boys were excited; for each one of us this arrival is in its way confusing and stimulating. I too was moved by the spectacle and the ideas which one associates with it, – but, by the time we had reached the centre of town, my heart had sunk as far below zero as it had been above it – and so it has remained until now, the twelfth day. – Today is 31 January. The month has passed irretrievably and fruitlessly!

I can usually console myself with new initiatives, but this time I am unable to make plans, since their fulfilment relies on third parties, namely the politicians. –

The weather has been different every day, this is one of the city's peculiarities; today there is thick snow.

My friend Rothwell[2] has been relieved of his post as conductor in St Paul, Minnesota. The orchestra was financed by a railway company which made use of it to inform the cities on its line that St Paul was a cultural centre worth visiting. But evidently St Francis found a readier audience amongst the birds than St Paul amongst the cities of Minnesota, for the orchestra, being deemed an unprofitable undertaking, has been disbanded. To the great joy of the neighbouring, rival city of Minneapolis, which is now proclaiming its orchestra as the cultural figurehead of the entire state and sending it out and about.

Their conductor is a German who (when he wears a hat) has a head of long, thick hair, but is bald when he takes his hat off, wears gold-rimmed glasses and likes to be photographed in tails. Incidentally his name is Oberhoffer.[3]

Rothwell is a pupil of Mahler and has all the typical attributes of his fellow students. His place is somewhere between Brecher and Bodanzky. The other fellow, on the contrary, is a musical-director type. – However, they are all 'making' their way (as I previously described), thus enabling me to play La Campanella wherever they are operating. The piece is so popular that Hanson recently said 'Campanella' when he meant a church-tower, which is a campanile. – Church-music, then. –

Madame Sans-gêne is a new opera[4] in which one of the characters is Napoleon. A tricky business for the singer, as he is unable to sing with his arms folded and is left with the alternatives of either remaining silent or giving the game away.

Yesterday I heard Fidelio and was moved by the music. What a pity that the singers are such a distraction in opera performances. And one has to listen to them! The public goes to the opera because of the singers, not the music. But yesterday the audience listened with much concentration and the greatest success was the Leonora overture [no. 3]. This piece is a wonder. – I learned something new. – Now I must get changed for the afternoon concert; I am playing at 3 o'clock with Stransky.[5]

====

Now it's over. Amongst those present were the pianists: [Josef] Hofmann, [Harold] Bauer, [Karl] Friedberg, Percy Grainger, [Rafael] Joseffy; [. . .] – all very kind. –

The ice is thawing, but not in my heart. –

Even *with* a war, Europe is preferable. – I send you my very warmest greetings, also to Kestenberg! –

Your friend in exile,
F.B.

[1]Busoni had rented a house at 264 Riverside Drive.
[2]Walter Henry Rothwell, 1872–1927, English conductor. Before going to St Paul he had worked in Hamburg. From 1919 he was orchestra director in Los Angeles.
[3]Emil Oberhoffer, 1867–1933, was chief conductor at Minneapolis from 1905 to 1922. He had been an assistant of the celebrated conductor Anton Seidl.
[4]Opera by Umberto Giordano (after Sardou and Moreau). Busoni must have seen the world première at the Metropolitan Opera, New York, on 25 January 1915.
[5]Busoni played the Liszt Eb Concerto at Carnegie Hall.

169 TO EMILE BLANCHET
in French

New York 17.3.1915

[. . .] You cannot imagine what an effect – at this time and in this country – well-reflected words (and well-expressed reflections), dictated by friendship (which counts above all) are capable of producing on an exile. Your letter was sympathetic on this account.

No, nobody is neutral. And America is completely lacking in character. The masses are hostile to the Germans, while the government coldly calculates its European connections.

As for my countrymen, may God guide them! I fear they are wicked and terribly opportunistic.[1]

Do not reproach yourself in the least about your scanty productivity. Circumstances are weighing on all of us and the disorientation of our thoughts is beyond our control. You complain about your fellow men, yet it is they who have conjured up the present situation, which you describe as 'l'ambiance'.

[Isidor] Philipp[2] and I have found ourselves in agreement on a certain analogy which exists between Saint-Saëns and A. France. Since you admire the latter, I take it you also like the former. His skill lies in having the good sense not to involve himself in problems beyond his technical ability. And to climb a precipice of thought with an elegant gesture. 'A sweet and terrible look' – 'a tragic and exquisite story' – that leaves plenty of room for interpretation without stating anything precisely.

I don't know the articles on Strauss in 'L'Intransigeant': but, whatever they are like, they should accredit the paper with a certain historical significance – thanks to the situation.

You quote, in this context, a phrase borrowed from my edition of Bach. I am in the process of finishing the *second part* of the [Well-tempered] Clavier, having previously edited the Goldberg variations. This completes my work on this master, which is to be published, God willing, in six volumes.

Your recital must be taking place any day now and I hope that your little accident will prevent nothing. Your études arouse my artistic curiosity. And I await your Passacaglia. I am unable to compensate you for it from here, but would like to draw your attention to my *Fantasy on themes of the Redskins* for piano and orchestra, the score of which is published by Breitkopf (Indianische Fantasie).

Finally I am trying to work, but it eludes me. However, I have some compelling plans.

[1]Italy was negotiating a treaty with Britain, France and Russia, despite a triple-entente with Germany and Austria. Finally war was declared on Austro-Hungary on 23 May 1915.
[2]See p. 428.

170 TO EGON PETRI
in German

Chicago 29.3.1915

A New York journalist said to me in all seriousness: there are three great organizations in world history: the Catholic church, the German army and the American Oil-Trust Company.

– In San Francisco, Kreisler and Sembrich gave a concert together; *she* sang some song, 'Down the sweet river' or whatever, and he played Dvořák's Humoresque with a mute, to go with it. (Which pieces don't go with each other——?)

Yesterday I heard a hotel orchestra of the better sort playing Liszt's 2nd Rhapsody. A cadenza is frequently interpolated before the final stretta. On this occasion it was the cadenza from *Grieg's piano concerto*. [. . .] – All this should give you a thumbnail sketch of American culture. –

A letter of yours arrived, in which one read of your satisfaction with Dutchmen and boar-hunting. I am amazed that you are still able to take pleasure in such details. All my life I have made the error of looking upon pleasant moments as temporary distractions and I have not fully apprehended them. And at the present time, indeed . . . every little pleasure is akin to the picture-books in a dentist's waiting-room. –

– Three days ago I was in Kansas City, where our old friend Georgine N[elson][1] is living . . . as a prostitute. Poor G! She came to my concert, the manager having extracted a promise from her that she would remain sober. – She was an outrageous sight! With peroxided blond hair and bloated, coarse features, coated with make-up – and I fear this is not yet the end of the story. – This is what happens when the world is based entirely on false principles. Not a single thing is in order; and in later history books our epoch will be recorded as the bad end of the Middle Ages.

The fact that art still survives at all is proof of its prodigiousness; indeed, every effort has been made to stifle it. –

This state of affairs is masterfully depicted by H. G. W[ells] in his 'In the days of the comet'.[2] This prophetical book was published as early as 1906; maybe you already know it – ? –

Conan Doyle has concocted a new Sherlock Holmes story, 'The valley of fear'[3] – one has to admit the author's adroitness. – In New Y. I found the first edition of W. Irving's 'Tales of a traveller',[4] a beautiful book, inwardly and outwardly; but one in which the spirit of America already begins to prevail over its English origins. – This is the book in which the original idea for [Auber's] 'Fra Diavolo' is to be found.

– Middelschulte (whose family in Westphalia has been hard hit by the war) has transcribed Bach's Chaconne for strings and organ. – The work is inadequate for such large forces and sounds thinner than on the piano. – The gentlemen of the violins occasionally obtruded when they lit upon the celebrated passages from the David and Joachim interpretations.

There are about 20 famous and distinguished pianists at present in New York. Hofmann, Bauer, Godowsky, Ornstein, Hambourg, Gabrilowitsch, Ganz, Sapirstein, Jonás, P. Grainger, Schelling,[5] Joseffy, H[arold] Foyer, Stojowsky, Gruenberg, A[driano] Ariani, A[urelio] Giorni;[6] – the American reaction: nobody wants to hear them. As soon as anything becomes easily accessible here, its value falls.

There is no question of productive work: when someone has a pistol pointed at him, if any thought enters his head at all, then it is of rescue. But the 2nd part of the W. Clav. is more or less finished. It was all I could manage between playing and travelling.

– Blanchet wrote me a finely worded letter, brilliant, stylish and sensitive. In Lausanne, too, many people are hanging around.

It's deplorable how people are seeking out little islands to save themselves from the great flood. – That would be doing *this* country too great an honour. [. . .]

[1]Georgine Nelson studied the piano with Busoni in Vienna.
[2]H. G. Wells, *In the Days of the Comet and other stories*, London, 1906.
[3]Sir Arthur Conan Doyle, *The Valley of Fear*, London, 1915.
[4]Washington Irving, *Tales of a Traveller*, 2 vols., London, 1824.
[5]See footnote to letter no. 189.
[6]Others were Arthur Friedheim, Leonard Borwick and Richard Epstein.

171 TO EGON PETRI
in German

New York 12.4.1915

For the time being I have finished with my concerts and the 2nd Well-t. Clavier; an orchestral piece is under way,[1] intended to conclude the series of '*studies*' for my new style which began with the 'Elegies'. Thus prepared, I hope for a work with the same relationship to Die Brautwahl as that of my 2nd sonatina to my pre-elegiac piano pieces. –

My fastidiousness led me to seek counsel in Bach=*Riemann*, which has been most amusing. When he 'climbs the mountain' (against which Don Quixote warns the boy who explains the puppet-play), he trips over himself constantly. In the B♭ minor fugue he discusses the possibilities which Bach left unexploited, proving them with the following example:

A theoretical rose with many a thorn and exuding a questionable perfume! He comes no further than this; and did you know that the possibilities of this theme are almost as inexhaustible as chess? – I have made a thorough study of them.[2]

I have also completed my 49th year; but this brings me slighter benefits and hence less joy. – The 'address' which I received from Berlin[3] temporarily succeeded in reviving this vanishing joy. I was sincerely delighted at the good intentions and thank you, too, for your contribution.

– What now? – How long shall I have to pursue this joyless existence? – It is very hard. –

The 'saison' is drawing to a close, soon the opera will be at an end, the symphony concerts finished. – I would have liked to take care of the *engraving* of the W-Cl. *here*; it would be an enjoyable task, but it is so difficult to communicate with Leipzig!

It will be all the more pleasant and eventful at home. Let us hope so!

[1]The *Rondò arlecchinesco*, op. 46.
[2]Busoni produced a whole page of possible combinations of this theme, indicating some twenty not exploited by Bach.
[3]Several friends in Berlin had sent a message of good-will to mark Busoni's 49th birthday, cf. Schoenberg's letter to Busoni, Appendix no. 33.

172 TO HARRIET LANIER
in English

New York 4.5.1915

[. . .] I have received the Granados. 'Goyescas' is the work of a distinguished amateur. Although I would be able to prove my opinion, I abstain from becoming tiring to you with extended arguments. I am sorry to be in opposition with you, but I cannot alter my impression – and in matters musical I am bound to speak honestly. Nevertheless I have to thank you for sending the book to me.

Scriabin's death – alas! – has been repeatedly confirmed and I have to accept the fact.[1] He was most admirable in regard to the fact that he never felt satisfied with his achievements.

It is a rare quality in men and an exception in Russian composers. –

To return to Granados (I have to say something more to justify myself) I direct your attention to the fact that the French composers – since Bizet – have been very busily interested in Spanish folk-music. Lalo, Saint-Saëns, Debussy, Ravel, Chabrier have written Boleros, Fandangos, Habaneras in the rhythms and the atmosphere of Spain – and the remarkable thing is that the Spanish composers follow the French (instead [of] obeying their own nature) in their national efforts.

So did a man named Albéniz, who wrote a series of piano pieces entitled 'Iberia'. He, as well as G., does not possess the sense of proportion between the harmless popular tunes and an overburdened setting; not to speak of their prolixity. For orchestral music the French remain the master on this little subject; as for piano music, *Liszt* has resolved and exhausted the problem in his transcriptions (rather re-creations) of many Hungarian, Russian, Spanish popular melodies. –

About your extremely kind intentions towards myself and a plan for the autumn campaign I will take the liberty of writing you a special letter.

I am intent on the composition of a score (of a lesser orchestral piece) which is intended as a 'study' to the one-act play with Arlecchino as the central figure.

The summer may bring the realization of the entire work. –

Mr Hanson is still offering me in California, but I think it will result in nothing; – as I am seriously debating within myself my near departure to Europe, the failure is welcome to my plans. – [. . .]

[1]Scriabin had died on 27 April 1915.

173 TO HARRIET LANIER
in English

New York 17.5.1915

[. . .] After what you have written in defence of the Castilian composer I almost regret my sudden sincerity, although I cannot alter my impression. The facts in the case of Señor Granados, which you kindly relate, are circumstances '*attenuantes*' and to be considered for the love of justice. I have been told that G. has written an entire play, with scenes taken from Goya's pictures. The idea is happy, but its realization would require the biting, fantastic and superlatively *human* mind and soul of the painter-philosopher, which are not far from the spirit of Cervantes. –

[I] myself once thought of a *pantomime*, introducing on the stage some of Beardsley's drawings.[1] But this task would be incomparably more simple and easy!

I spent today half an hour with Mr R. Schirmer, who told me that he had made an extensive contract with Granados. I hope that it will result in favour of Señor G., though I do not believe in publishers' contracts for the benefit of composers.

To Mr Schirmer I proposed some matters in common apropos my one-act comedy, on which subject he expressed himself so obviously reserved that I withdrew the argument. – The idea that led me was to have a definite purpose to sustain my summer's work, if I should be compelled to spend this time in America.

But this (and other disappointments) have taught me to remain firm in my resolution of abandoning your country.

I have, of course, postponed my departure to a more favourable instant, which I calculate to be not too far in the future; but the departure, when it occurs, will be *final*.

This resolution I regret on account of two or three blessed persons, of whom you are – perhaps – the most precious to me; but you will understand, as you seem to understand everything through your refined instinct and your genuine feeling.

How sad I am about the wrongs of the world! Of them I will not see the ending. – [. . .]

---

[1]*Der Tanz vom Leben und vom Tode*, a scenario written in 1913 for Maud Allan. The manuscript is preserved in the Deutsche Staatsbibliothek, Berlin.

174 TO HARRIET LANIER
in English

New York 6.6.1915

Yes, I have to remain here indefinitely, on account of the awakened heroism of my sympathetic countrymen. The way leading back to my home is cut off and peace-making is postponed.

It is not comforting. – But your letter was, and so was the arrival of the books. For both I thank you most heartily.

(I do not know whether you would prefer a letter in *French*, in which I could display a little higher ability. But I thought it correct to respond to the language in which you address me.)

Of the three arts represented at the exhibition, the architecture appears to me to be the more successful. The motives seem to be taken chiefly from Spain, which accounts for a certain fantastic richness of their effect. One meets several old friends, but this may not weaken the beautiful impression. – Your sincere enthusiasm proves that the arrangement deserves the admiration of people of taste. I am very happy about the way you enjoy it. Just as I can understand your love for your country, your unhappiness over its mistakes; as I feel very much alike towards Italy.

S., the publisher, used to be a very good friend to me and always treated me kindly and tactfully. I found him changed (not only in connection with me), *hardened*, more matter of fact than ever and ent-nobled (is that the word?), deprived of the noblesse which he formerly possessed. – *S.*, the piano man, never had it and there is no disappointment. And, apropos *S.*, I have to tell you that I was invited by Mrs Untermeyer to play at Graystone on the 25th of May for the 'Poetry Society' (I believe), where I had an excellent Steinway at my command, which helped me very much. The afternoon was a complete success as for the social and spiritual element assembled, the hospitality and the beauty of the site.

It is possible that I will be active in the autumn season. Meanwhile I try everything to keep the wheel of my mind rolling; I have three or four smaller matters in hand and will – when I have done them – presumably take up the one-act comedy, in spite of the absence of any chance for a practical result. –

Your kind offer to introduce me to some 'Metropolitan' people I have considered and I felt grateful for your delicate thought. I am extremely shy to expose myself to examinations, well-meant advice and (possibly) refusals. So I do not know whether I ought to accept this way. [. . .]

Now: 214 Riverside Drive.

175 TO FREDERICK STOCK
in German

New York 8.6.1915

'Uns ist ein Kind geboren'![1] Today, 8 June, the *Rondeau harlequinesque* has been completed. Exultate!

I am glad it bears your name,[2] for it is my most mature score (heaven knows, meanwhile, what it will sound like). With this modest homage I would like to repay part of my debt of gratitude and prove how highly I estimate you.

Tell me, what does your orchestra do during the summer? Is it dissolved – (in the heat) – or does it stimulate indolent females at some spa? – Is it occupied in San Francisco (even if one cannot 'detract'[3] from it) or does it rehearse at close quarters? –

A letter of mine – addressed to Orchestra Hall – went unanswered.

Now an enticing summer stands before me and I can enjoy the prospect of freedom —— if I go down to the harbour. – For how can one rhyme:
Country of liberty and
Prohibition State?
Independence – and Morality?
Equality and upper 400?
(Incidentally, are these 400 numbered?) – Even Heine's abusive words of
    'dem grossen Freiheitsstall
    und den grossen Gleichheitsflegeln'[4]
are no longer true. – But I must nevertheless be thankful that I am at peace and in good health (God willing!) – [. . .]

[1]'Unto us a child is born'.
[2]The *Rondò arlecchinesco* is dedicated to Stock.
[3]Orig. auszustellen. Untranslatable pun.
[4]Heine, *Romanzero*, Book Two, Lamentationen. 'Jetzt wohin?'
    Manchmal kommt mir in den Sinn
    Nach Amerika zu segeln,
    Nach dem grossen Freiheitsstall,
    Der bewohnt von Gleichheitsflegeln. –

slightly freely:
> Sometimes it occurs to me
> That America's the sequel,
> That the spacious freedom sty
> Beckons, where all swine are equal. –

176 TO EGON PETRI
in German

New York 16.6.1915

In answer to the opening pages of your letter I am taking the liberty of quoting a few lines (perhaps unknown to you) from [Goethe's] *sketches for 'Faust'*; firstly because they are worth communicating; also because I could not express myself better (or indeed as well):
> 'Auch diesmal imponiert mir nicht
> Die tiefe Wut, mit der du gern zerstörtest,
> ....
> So höre denn, wenn du es niemals hörtest:
> Die Menschheit hat ein fein Gehör,
> Ein reines Wort erreget schöne Taten.
> Der Mensch fühlt sein Bedürfnis nur zu sehr
> Und lässt sich gern im Ernste raten.
> Mit dieser Aussicht trenn ich mich von dir,
> Bin bald, und triumphierend, wieder hier.'[1]

Just as I had to omit the third line, which would have credited you with 'a tiger's eye' (this strikes me as not only inappropriate but also impolite), so should I also have cut the final couplet on grounds of not being 'ad situationem'. – (Quotations become unsatisfactory when applied, because they are reduced to comparisons.) For there is unfortunately no question of 'soon returning' nor, moreover, 'the hero of the day'.

Belated greetings on entering your 35th year, from which I expect other gains than an increased aversion to 'speaking your mind'. You have such talent and facility that the bringing of your abilities to fruition lies in your hands alone.

Meanwhile I have completed my orchestral work to my satisfaction and now I can tell you its title: it is to be called *Rondò arlecchinesco*.

Another gap has been filled: I have found the <u>complete</u> First Edition of Poe, which extends to all of *four* volumes.

Yesterday I finished a libretto (for Gruenberg).[2] He is delighted with it and I find it charming, concise and colourful. An Indian legend in which the heroic figures of two lovers are etched against a grotesque background. (Thus similar to Turandot.) – Gruenberg is at present a close friend, plays excellently and is most understanding; which, in his case, is a sign of continuing development. – [. . .]

– I shall not trouble you with my grievances about the U.S.A., which I could substantiate 100 times over. I find it regrettable that you cannot be here, but would scarcely wish it upon *you* (although you would find your bearings better than I).

– Zadora's post has been given to *R. Ganz*.[3] He was also offered the position in Geneva (left vacant after Stavenhagen's death),[4] but this is now being taken over by *da Motta*!!

In the autumn, *Bodanzky* is coming to the 'Metropolitan'. Frau [Elisabeth] Schumann ('*Albertine*' in the Hamburg Brautwahl) has been here and will be returning. Hambourg (not the city) is concertizing in London. Ley and Bruce sent their kindest sentiments: the latter would have liked to hear from you. –

The Well-tempered Clavier is being engraved here. –

We are in good health, thank heaven, and together! –

Unfortunately I have heard nothing from Sobernheim since *1 April*; no doubt he is waiting until he has satisfactory news.

(Today is 16 June.)

---

[1]Lines addressed by Faust to Mephistopheles and intended for Act I of *Faust* Part II:

And even now, what could I care
For that great rage with which you would destroy us,
[Your tiger's eye, your energetic air.]
So listen well, lest further you annoy us:
Attentive is the human ear,
The merest word incites audacious action.
Occasion all too often does appear
For man's grave deeds of satisfaction.
With this intention I now go my way,
Shall soon return, the hero of the day.

[2]*Die Götterbraut*, set to music by Louis T. Gruenberg as *The Bride of the Gods*.

[3]Rudolf Ganz, 1877–1972, Swiss-born pianist and conductor. Pupil of Busoni; Director, Chicago Musical College from 1923 to 1954.

[4]Bernhard Stavenhagen, 1862–1914, German conductor and pianist. He had occupied the post in Geneva since 1907.

177 TO EDITH ANDREAE
in German

New York 23.6.1915

Your kind letter and the news of the demise of Herr Rathenau[1] arrived simultaneously in N.Y. today. Therefore I shall lose no time to tell you how very close I feel to you at this moment! – Actually I should be thankful that my nearest and dearest are in good health and close to me.

But I cannot overcome a feeling of missing something which is irretrievable.

And your description of the glories of Berlin makes my detested exile intolerable to me.

Work–? Yes, I am keeping myself occupied all the time and beginning to detest even that (although I cannot desist from it). You can scarcely imagine how limited and limiting this country is. Every stimulus, beauty or humanity has to be created from inside oneself, which is the cause of facetious exasperation; and what emerges is something grey, not unrelated to 'theory', lifeless and unmotivated. – But it is useless to bother you with comparisons which can give you no idea of the true state of affairs; just as here, in the war reportage, the highest figures make the greatest impact, while failing to conjure up in the imagination of the insatiable newspaper readers any real picture of the war.

I have not dared set to work on the 'opera' (which shall not become an opera) for fear that a false start would destroy my last moral foothold.

I write and write – words and music – and read a lot; but without any real interest.

When one is no longer *master of one's own freedom of movement*, life has no further value. No matter whether it is the result of sickness, old age, imprisonment or – the glorious matters of the present time. – (As you know, I have always sacrificed chances of earning more money in exchange for my personal freedom – gladly!) –

Your kind letter brought consolation and intensified my longing. Every letter from one who is dear to me and who – knows me has this effect. – (I shall never be 'known' here.) – I have not yet reached the age for resignation and am no longer so young that I can afford to miss opportunities. – I shall never overcome this criminal amputation from my life. – And when we meet again, I shall be older.

Now I am seriously considering coming to Switzerland via Italy. (I would give 100 United States for one corner of old Europe.)

If this comes to pass, I shall bring some things with me (though no 'treasures', as you say so categorically). – A Rondò arlecchinesco for orchestra and a major work on the Well-tempered Clavier, as well as a few slighter things.[2] A harmonium with ⅓ tones. – If the humour in the *Rondò* manifests itself at all, it will have a heart-rending effect. –

Of course we shall remain friends, because it could never be otherwise.

In Switzerland a friend would be able to visit me now and then!!

Farewell and thank you.

---

[1]Edith Andreae's father, Emil Rathenau, the founder of the AEG concern, had died on 20 June 1915.

[2]There were two piano works, the *Indian Diary* and the Sonatina ad usum infantis, and a transcription for cello and piano of Beethoven's *Adelaïde*.

178 TO HARRIET LANIER
in French

New York 2.7.1915

I have not written to you for a long time; meanwhile I have had to pass through diverse emotional states whose reflection I did not wish to appear in my letter.

All these phases have resulted in a feeling of placid resignation, sad rather than painful.

My 'affaires' have been transferred from the hands of my impresario to those of Messrs Steinway. But the latter, who are very indecisive and afraid of imaginary 'rights' of which H[anson] might avail himself, have done nothing and are still awaiting the return of H., who has been away for nearly three months. Thus they have missed the opportune moment for fixing engagements – and now I find myself unable to return to my 'home' and ignored by the concert societies here; in fact *out of work* (except for that which I continually find for myself). It's like a bad dream; and when comes the awakening?

Mr Stokowski has had the courtesy to invite me to conduct one of my works in Philadelphia. But he has no vacancies for a soloist. The same goes for Chicago. *Hanson* owes me a good deal of money. – And the war!!

– However, I have been working and have completed several 'minor works', with which I am content. –

Do you still think that there is any possibility of one of your nice projects for the Society of the Friends of Music? –

Are you still enjoying California? Are you happy and in good health?

I feel so lonely and isolated, and your news brought me much cheer.

Please forgive this tiresome letter.

179 TO HARRIET LANIER
in French

New York 18.7.1915

Not only do I have faith in telepathy, but I have also always believed that children should be properly initiated and educated in this direction: it is a gift *inherent* to mankind, but in a primitive, undeveloped state. Elevated to its utmost strength and potential, it would render 'supplementary' inventions, such as the telephone and all other material means of communciation, *superfluous*. All *prevarication* would be in vain; our goal would be *prescience*, which is nothing more than *inverted memory*. Thus I am not surprised that a person of such sensitivity as yourself should possess the key to it; but we are as yet unable to count upon the reliability and precision of these rare telepathic inspirations.

In the last hour of sleep in the morning I have often *seen* the precise position of the 'hands' on my watch. They have always pointed to the exact moment of my awakening, and I could ascertain [this] afterwards.

This is *one* form of telepathy. – Now that I have paraphrased the introduction to your letter I must begin mine afresh by thanking you for having written so generously – generous with your space and with your heart.

I am still not certain what I am going to do. To remain sheltered here is painful to me and I feel it unworthy to be a cowardly refugee, waiting for peace to be declared. I am a European and (God be praised) much more of a social animal than a professional virtuoso.

Today I have just read that I have been accused of failing to appear in *Rome*, where I was expected. They are perfectly justified, there is no excuse. It is forgivable to cancel in peacetime, when one can be replaced with ease; it is almost inexcusable in time of war, when a nation (*one's own* nation) is undergoing hard times, which could be eased even by my slender talents. It is understandable that none of the German or Austrian artists go to Rome (and sad that this is made impossible for them), but an Italian! –

– On the other hand, a Berlin newspaper has accused me (also in public) of having been seen at the Metropolitan in the company of *M. Saint-Saëns*! That is preposterous. Just think that this significant event was transmitted by cable! –

So the Germans and the Italians are equally up in arms about me: – at least they agree on something. [. . .]

The arrangement with Steinways need not change either your or my plans. Therefore I am available for the *Friends of Music*. You write, '*it was practically decided that*' but in fact it had only been decided 'theoretically' – I am very glad to hear that the Society wishes to make use of me.

One orchestral concert costs as much as *two* solo piano recitals (or perhaps more). Thus it is not for me to make (or even suggest) the choice. This will depend on the amount you are able to spend – and of your preferred interest in the one or the other form. If you think it would be interesting to get to know me as composer and conductor, an orchestral evening would be 'highly welcome' to me; but if you would prefer to hear me play the piano, I could make up *one* or *several* 'style' programmes, and almost think that you would suffer no financial loss by presenting them to the public. My fee (since you ask!!) has been between [$]600 and 1,200 per concert. – [. . .]

If you are intending to mount a performance of Mahler's *Eighth*, it will be necessary to concentrate all your forces on this important and beautiful enterprise and I shall *quite* understand if you are obliged to withdraw from all other projects in favour of the principal item.

All that you have written of your stay [in California] has given me great pleasure: I am very happy that you are enjoying it so much and that your health permits you to do so. – It is a long wait until September to see you again, but I have learned to resign myself. –

180 To the *Vossische Zeitung*[1]
in German

New York July 1915

An American contract, already signed in peacetime, forced me to *leave Germany* at the moment when many nascent hopes seemed to be reaching maturity but also at a time when the country was striving in a unified direction, due to essential issues.

In a nation with which I have shared so much in the course of the last 20 years, this great activation compelled and continues to compel my sympathy.

Therefore nothing would have stopped me returning to Germany, were it not that recent events had in fact prevented me from doing so; were it not that events and obstacles are today still in force. I would no longer remain in a country which is not *the country of my choice*, would not be spending the best years of my life inactively and far away, at a time when the profusion of stimuli bore promise of new youthfulness.

I have attempted – with personal success – to remain an independent artist, dedicated to my specific goals, with the notion that it was my allotted and not unworthy task to devote myself to serious peacetime duties, and in the belief that music, above all, has the least in common with worldly enterprises.

It has come to my ears through rumours and the reports of friends that I have nevertheless been thrust into the field of *political issues*. And I fully understand that, due to my nationality, these reports are bound to be sharply accentuated. This I truly regret, while at the same time understanding that – at a time like the present – an open confession is called for.

Should you wish to receive confirmation of what you must long have already known, then I shall be happy unreservedly to declare that I hold the *culture of Germany* in high esteem and that the attitude of your countrymen compels me fully to confirm my opinion.

Your staunch sense of honour would never permit this acknowledgement of German virtues to lead to the renunciation of my own nationality; that I remain a human being and artist, and am willing and able to acknowledge and respect human beings and artists wherever I might believe myself to have perceived them, can only increase the significance of my regard for Germany and substantiate the sincerity of my statement.

[1]This letter was published in the *Vossische Zeitung*, Berlin, on 20 August 1915.

181 TO HARRIET LANIER
in English

New York 6.8.1915

If anything is troubling a resolution which makes me feel like a new man – it is the thought of leaving this country without having seen you again. –

But my decision is firm and I expect to sail on the 28th of this month, to reach Italy and to settle down in Switzerland temporarily. –

It is not the fault of your country that I seem not to be fit for it, nor is it mine.

This has been my fifth visit to America and will remain most probably the last (if not a highly honourable amendation should be offered to me by the artistic element of the States); – every one of the five visits has proved a disappointment, and every time I have returned with renewed faith and with hopeful anticipations. – I tried to give my best, but they refused it and asked for the average. The result was (and could not be otherwise) unsatisfactory to both parts. – The experience with your society remains a single exception, to be remembered gratefully, and the receptions at Chicago and Philadelphia were dignified.

I know the U.S. since 1891, when I first came to Boston and lived there (and afterwards in N.Y.) an uninterrupted period of *three years*. – 1894 I was able to sail back to Europe, this date marking the beginning of my life and development. – All my achievements and hardest labours during a lifetime do not prove of any value to the American managers and to the public of this country.

They who heard me or approached me have appreciated me (I am thankful to them) – but the echo of my efforts remains confined to this handful of people. I am not young enough to represent a new sensation, nor to force a new way, which would be not a new direction of life for me but merely the repetition of what I have already amply done. – This would be a wrong experiment at my age, when the time imperiously calls me to achieve what is left for me to fulfil.

Besides, I have tried (through much of thought and of *suffering*) to perfect[1] my human and philosophical views on life and mankind, on morals and beliefs, and find myself here not understood, suppressed and forcibly drawn back to points which were happily surmounted and dismissed. – This is an attitude of your citizens which one does not realize or notice when one is only an occasional visitor,* flying through the country driven by the force of a contract; but which one begins to feel heavily lasting upon him when he lives under your laws, which are nominally free but are interpreted with cruel narrowness and merciless severity. –

Finally the eternal argument of money and 'paying' and financial success (which also belongs to the series of surmounted and dismissed points in *my conviction*) depresses me; as this argument is pointed out to you at every step and every trifle, and it assumes the character of madness. The despotism of money is in no way better than the 'terror' of militarism; the latter is confined to a *class* of people, the former is general.

To me money is a mean (the French call it 'les moyens') and not an aim. Moreover the worthiest things, as art and philosophy, love and nature, good taste and inner satisfaction are independent from it. – (I do not underrate the importance of industry, though I am not much convinced of the necessity of

mechanical inventions), but I have a disgust against the tendency of producing quickly, cheaply and in great masses. It results in the destroying of
individuality, which is (or was?) one of the most precious qualities among
men and – things too. – It is possible that society will overcome (with time) all
these miseries – and others – but as I will be no witness to the change – it
interests me only abstractedly and distantly.

– Now this letter has become abstract and distant enough, and I have to
find the way back to you. – This is not easy for me, though[2] I always return
with pleasure to your sympathetic and noble personality. – Your splendid
letter of July 30th affirms it again and completely.

I have to repeat what I said at the beginning and could almost regret to
have known you for the bitter consciousness of missing your return and your
vicinity. – I owe you very, very much and thank you for all your interest and
kindness from the deepest of my heart.

*1891 I was too young to observe –

[1]Orig. perfectionate.
[2]Orig. who.

182 TO EDWARD J. DENT
in Italian

New York 12.8.1915

I cannot express the pleasure I derived from your letter, nor the changing
emotions which its contents engendered in me, or rather which beset me
while reading it. What you have written has found me in my isolation, the
sense of culture which emanates from it and the important events to which it
alludes have had much influence on my spirits, alienating me and drawing me
nearer, bringing me cheer and grief by turn.

Above all, I thank you for remembering me, troubled as you are by sad
events. Your funeral elegy on the demise of poor Browne[1] (of whom I have
precise and most sympathetic memories) – with its unexpected modulation in
the coda – ('si muore, ma si vive') reminds me of the beautiful verses for the
chorus in Part Two of Faust, on the death of Euphorion. It is said that they
contain an allusion to the figure of Lord Byron and this presents an analogy
with your ill-fated friend:

Doch erfrischet neue Lieder
Steht nicht länger tief gebeugt:
Denn der Boden zeugt sie wieder,
Wie von je er sie gezeugt.[2]

Conscientious reading of this work has been one of the various occupations
I have been obliged to create for myself during the course of this summer, in

order to make myself capable of withstanding the sufferings of exile. [. . .]

I was happy to find myself in agreement with you once again in your estimation of Mozart's libretti. Not tiring of translating them, you are producing excellent opera and with it are contributing to the sustenance of the masterpieces of music's Raphael, even in old England.

For the rest, I hope to be able to follow your progress from a little closer, having decided to return home, and I am reckoning on taking a boat for Europe towards the end of this month.

Your work on the Seicento interests me greatly, all the more so for the egoistic reason that I expect to find in it the information which I lack on this subject. – I have asked Schirmer's permission to read your article on the piano in modern music[3] from the proofs, and hope that I shall be able to do so before departing. – Initially, the Musical Quarterly created a dignified enough impression, no longer carried over into the last number, which featured a piece of humbug by Percy Grainger.[4]

Benni is in the country and showing no sign of any talent for becoming a millionaire. – We are well, thank heaven, and all send our affectionate regards.

[1]Denis Browne had died in action in Turkey on 4 June 1915, shortly after the funeral of his friend Rupert Brooke.
[2]   But new songs shall still elate him,
    Bow no longer and deplore!
    For the soil shall generate them,
    As it hath done heretofore. (Translated Bayard Taylor, 1870)
[3]Edward J. Dent, 'The pianoforte and its influence on modern music' *Musical Quarterly*, vol. II, April 1916, pp. 271–94.
[4]Percy Grainger, 'The impress of personality in unwritten music' *Musical Quarterly*, vol. I, July 1915, pp. 416–35. With respect to Busoni, this is a perfectly serious 'anti-art' essay on folk-music and its influence on contemporary composers.

183 TO HUGO LEICHTENTRITT
in German

New York 15.8.1915

At this very moment – it is three o'clock on Sunday afternoon, 15 August and I have just finished revising the complete first proofs of the Well-tempered Clavier, Part II. All of seven months have passed since I began work on this project aboard the SS 'Rotterdam' and since that 15 January it has occupied me practically every day, with the exception of the month of May, during which time the finished MS waited its turn at the engravers'. The engraving process took 2½ months, with three engravers working at it. Thus the volume represents the work of 4 men over a period of six months.

For my part I did my best, taking into account the limitations I had set myself. The edition is 'preponderamente contrappuntistica' and I have tried, as Schopenhauer would say, to project my clarity on to Bach's profundity.

I believe I have thereby completed my life's work on Bach!

Sunday! And in Berlin it is now between 9 and 10 o'clock in the evening. – I see you turning the corner of the Nollendorfplatz and regret (how deeply) that I am unable to encounter you.

That I cannot do so is partly to blame on this 'blessed' Bach, which I didn't want to leave unfinished here. Because of it I missed 'the' moment for my return.

All the more welcome as compensation for the missed encounter was the arrival of your letter on the banks of the Hudson River, which are lined with picturesque stone blocks (taller than they are broad).

(If I compare the globe to a human head, its expression is situated in the face of Europe, while this side represents the bald pate and protruding ears.)

– My warmest thanks for your excellent letter. – At the same time I received one from Mr Dent in Cambridge.

Without wishing to indulge in further comparisons, both letters had the following in common: they came from friends, brought a whiff of culture with them, both mentioned articles for Schirmer's Musical Quarterly and were written by music historians. – Your article[1] has not yet been announced; the issues are prepared six months in advance and the editors still have old material available.

I read from the galley proofs an article of Dent's on the influence of the piano on modern music.[2] It is very fine and stimulating.

My dear Doctor, I now come to the specific points of your letter. – My early works on your desk! I blush. My development as a composer went in stages; it was sharply intersected by ten years of assiduous piano studies: these lasted from my 25th to 35th year. –

There is just as little talk of my remaining in America as, I fear, of a return[3] to Berlin. By giving me friendly encouragement to do so, on 11 July, you have thrown a light on the situation which I would otherwise not have perceived.

In the meantime I have written to the *Vossische Zeitung*.[4] – You must have heard about it.

I congratulate the composer in you who has successfully given birth to a quintet.

In the case of your 'slowly advancing' violin concerto I was moved (quite absurdly) to recollections of Lipinsky's *Concerto militaire*,[5] all the more so as there was so much talk of an 'attack' and of other military *terminis technicis* in conjunction with your developing work. – But the violin is no particularly belligerent weapon and the Fiddle family with Auntie Viola, Uncle Tschello and the grumpy old grandfather suggests something out of Iffland rather than anything sonorous, and forms a touching portrait group.

But if one considers Beethoven's 'op. 130s', then one discovers soul and culture of the purest sort in the family. – Due to this attractive aspect, we return repeatedly to the 'gentlemen' of instruments, namely the strings; as if to some desirably refined circle of friends.

Create something pure, warm and vibrant, and may I soon have the pleasure of being able to hear what you have written!

[1] Hugo Leichtentritt, 'Ferruccio Busoni as a composer' *Musical Quarterly*, vol. III, Jan. 1917, pp. 69–97. The alterations and additions requested by Busoni in letter no. 190 were all incorporated.
[2] See footnote to letter no. 182.
[3] Orig. Einzug, which suggests a triumphal entry.
[4] Letter no. 180.
[5] Karol Lipinski, 1790–1860. The 'Military' Concerto in e. op. 24, was his most popular work.

184 TO HARRIET LANIER
in French and English

New York 18.8.1915

In troubling your conscience with unjustified doubts about the attitude of your Society towards me you are being much too sensitive. It has done incomparably more, '*plus et mieux*', than any of the others. If it continues to operate on the same basis on which it has set out – artistically speaking – it could even succeed in doing good things and improving the situation of the public in questions of art and artists.

Even admitting that the artist really needs a public (in the same way that strings need a resonance), the public to whom he will address himself in his imagination will always be a small circle of intimate and chosen people, with whom he has mutual intellectual interests, whose capacity, culture and inclinations are in sympathy with his own intentions and aspirations. For instance, the 'Salle Erard', in which Liszt gained his historical reputation, held no more than 250 persons. The audience was composed of people who knew one another, belonging to the best society, whether by birth or talent – amongst them were: Heine, George Sand, Meyerbeer, Rossini, Victor Hugo, Delacroix, Berlioz and still others in no way their inferiors.

Now appears the businessman – he sees in the prestige of the artist means of coining money. He says to himself that this man, who can convince the best minds and reap their admiration, will create a furore among the masses, less critical and well informed. And here appears the great misunderstanding in the world, since it is absolutely necessary for one to have the highest ideals to be able to appreciate the highest things.

=====

The artist should therefore receive money to be able to avoid popularity, since it is only in a relative isolation that he can continue to aim at higher things. The circle of intellectual and homogeneous friends is sufficient for him and it is in the support of their friendship and their intelligence that he finds his satisfaction and the needed encouragement. This is the direction which the 'Society of the Friends of Music' should follow. The artist must be helped and cannot do without a quiet existence, but he should not seek to become a millionaire, not even rich, for that would be more fatal than useful to his activity.[1]

(Here once again, instead of a letter, is an article for a magazine!)

But here is also the reason why America seems so undesirable to me. In order to make money I have to prostitute myself; in order to find satisfaction in modest, sympathetic artistic surroundings, *any cultural centre* (including New York) would do: with the difference that here I would have to start *all over again* (and at an age when one does not make débuts), whereas in Europe it is a question of *rounding myself off*.

═══

Your confession with regard to the matinée at the Ritz-Carlton (which I have just read, *after* having written mine) is like a positive answer to my reflections. You complain about the lack of money. But I assure you that a true artist will not ask for any, if he is certain of gaining other, better things: – I myself would always be happy to play for you, on no other condition than that it should give you pleasure.

On the subject of your programmes. Mr Arnold Schoenberg (a very advanced and unusual composer) has a work 'PIERROT LUNAIRE', which comprises 21 short poems (very brief), rhythmically declaimed to the accompaniment of 7 instruments. – He performed this work in my house in Berlin after *29 rehearsals* and it was perfect and unforgettable. (Fourteen persons were present.) This would be an interesting piece for your Society to perform and I would like to draw your attention to the fact that *one of the performers* (who took part in the 29 rehearsals) is now in Stokowski's orchestra in Philadelphia: he is the principal cellist, Mr Hans Kindler. He is very intelligent (a young man of 23 years) and would be capable of directing (to lead, not to conduct) an authentic performance. – Another man, my former pupil Mr Gruenberg (a very gifted pianist and composer), is in New York; he too has played with Schoenberg.[3] – S.'s composition lasts *one hour*, which is sufficient for an afternoon performance. Kindler and Gruenberg are friends.

═══

I have written in reply to a gracious letter from Mrs Kahn, explaining some points and details concerning my opera. If I leave it unfinished for the time being, then it is for two reasons: to start with, I read my libretto through for the first time in 6 months and was a little anxious about the rather philosophical, biting tone of my 'Arlecchino', who is an important character 'and a grim friend of disagreeable truths'. The action, which is very rapid and unusual, leaves the audience 'at a loss'. It would represent a failure combined with astonishment. The opera is also intended to represent a sort of parody of music-theatre. The conventional situations are there (the cuckolded husband, rivalry between two men, a tragi-comic duel, the '*woman*', honour, a ridiculous *tenor*): but all this – *the sum of my opinions* – performed in three-quarters of an hour in an unaccustomed form and with 'alienated' music, seems to me to be neither the thing for *Commendatore G.C.*[2] nor for a public which does not know me (vide the beginning of this letter). – The second reason is the fact that I am impatient to start work on a different subject (whose libretto is *finished*), which is going to be my principal work. (This summer I have written another libretto, for my friend Gruenberg: – part comical, part heroic, based on an Indian legend.)

Enough of myself.

=====

Madam, I find that it would be unfair to leave this country without seeing you again. – My long letters have been a small proof of my complete confidence in you; my sympathy towards your very noble personality has not wavered. [. . .]

I repeat that your valued friendship and consideration have been an ample recompense for many unpleasant things; and I have the fortune of taking back happy memories and a priceless acquisition with me. [. . .]

Madam Gerda, who is quite devoted to you, sends you her best wishes and kindest regards.

[1]The English translation of paragraphs 2–4 of this letter, which is evidently by Busoni himself, is dated 19.8.1915.
[2]Giulio Gatti-Casazza, 1869–1940, director of the Metropolitan Opera, New York from 1908 to 1935.
[3]See footnote no. 1 on p. 415.

Early in September 1915 Busoni set sail for Italy with his wife and younger son, Raffaello. Benvenuto Busoni, who was born in Boston and had the right to American citizenship, remained in New York. It was Busoni's intention to obtain residence permits for Italy, where he hoped to obtain a permanent teaching post, preferably in Rome.

12 Ferruccio and Gerda Busoni, Berlin, December 1914. At this time Busoni was working on his operas *Arlecchino* and *Doktor Faust*

13 and 14 (on facing page) Two photographic portraits of Busoni in Zurich, 1916, by Michael Schwarzkopf

15 Busoni in London, autumn 1919. The picture was taken at West Wing, Regent's Park, the home of the dancer Maud Allan, where Busoni also met G.B.Shaw

VII

1915 – 1918
The Great War (2)

185 TO ISIDOR PHILIPP
in French

Milan 19.9.1915

I have had to tear myself away from America, which was destroying me; the journey was pleasant, but I arrived here sick. (The reaction had finally to break out; and yet it is mild enough and not particularly enduring.) They wanted to appoint me professor of piano in Rome – that would have been 'el final de Norma', as the Spaniards say.

At the moment I am considering going to Switzerland and remaining there for a while, primarily so as to see certain items to the press, for which everything is ready.

I shall be giving some concerts in Rome and perhaps elsewhere. I would like (when I feel restored and free) to come to Paris – incognito. I really have no plans. I am insufficiently aware of the situation to be able to make any. (And anyway, one is not master of one's own decisions.)

(I have now been waiting a week for my passport, so as to leave Italy!)

I am sure that everything will follow its natural course. [. . .]

186 TO JELLA OPPENHEIMER
in German

Lausanne[1] 27.9.1915

I sent you two letters from New York, where I had taken refuge at the turn of the year. An insurmountable restlessness, insuperable aversion drove me away and – despite everything – back to Europe. These lines are intended to inform you of my arrival on Swiss territory. We took the route via Italy on an Italian boat. I was captivated by the magical landscape of the Mediterranean from Gibraltar to Genoa. We sailed between Sardinia and Corsica and docked in Naples: without lights and with lifeboats at the ready. Totally exhausted, I disembarked and for almost two weeks lay sick and helpless in Milan. Here I am now convalescing: regaining strength to take decisions.

At present, however, I can determine but little, as little as anyone else. How much is being neglected! Meanwhile I am trying to do what I am able, and in New York I completed a few things which are not entirely futile! For: what, if not art, can survive all wars?

I have heard nothing from you and ask urgently for news; (preferably to *Basle*, c/o *Gebrüder Hug*). I hope to hear soon and call down blessings on your head.

[1]In Lausanne Busoni was a guest of Emile Blanchet.

187 TO ARRIGO SERATO
in Italian

Zurich 7.10.1915

I am very sorry to have been unable to see you before your departure, which Gerda tells me will be final. I still feel unwell and would not risk the arduousness of a journey so horribly complicated by the nauseating transit conditions. This applies to an appointment I had provisionally made with Count San Martino[1] for 7, 8 or 9 October in Milan (Hotel Cavour). But a discussion with the vice-president, Count Blumenstihl,[2] has already made me suspect that Count San Martino was thinking of me as *piano professor* in Rome, and no more. I immediately declared that I was scarcely interested in such a post. Then there was talk of one or two concerts at the Augusteum, which I promised to accept. I gave Count Blumenstihl to understand that an invitation as conductor would be most welcome.

Now everything is silent.

But the question has not been resolved, and I am dependent on Count San Martino's formal invitation, while still knowing nothing of the promised concerts, whose dates and programmes have yet to be arranged. I hope I have described the situation clearly.

Therefore I would ask you first of all to present my apologies to the Count and ask him to make up his mind as soon as possible.

Here I have had a splendid reception and, no sooner had I arrived, than I received a wide range of offers as pianist, composer and conductor in Zurich and elsewhere. Before accepting, I would like to be certain about Rome, so as to avoid compromising my position there any further. So please ask the Count to be patient and to inform me as quickly as possible of his intentions concerning myself.

The question of renting a house, etc., here or elsewhere, depends largely on the Count's plans; but it does not suit me to have to wait much longer. You will understand that I would not go to Rome in a subordinate capacity and that it would be a sin to suppress my artistic abilities, which are now at the height of their development.

See if you can meet the Count in Milan, and send me a telegram without delay.

Yesterday evening, the violinist Carl Flesch[3] played the Brahms concerto, which brought back memories of our performance at Bologna! Dear Arrigo, what a difference! Well, I hope you attain the recognition you deserve; and I hope that I can be with you and remain close to you! But life is cut off, and by the time I see the world called to reason again (after the present confusion), I shall be an old man.

That half-hour in Iselle[4] was more revealing to me than all I had read in the papers in a year! That moment of humiliation clearly demonstrated the disavowal of law and order, of all rights and all human relations, it was socially unjust, brutal and vile.

Here, thank God, the atmosphere of war is absent and yesterday after the concert, in company, X. was alone in standing up for his 'obligations to the Fatherland'.

I have suggested that you should be invited to Basle; they will probably write to you and I shall conduct. I would be delighted to see you here.

[1]Count Enrico San Martino di Valperga, 1863–1947, Italian musicologist. From 1895 until his death he was president of the Accademia di Santa Cecilia in Rome.
[2]Count Paolo Blumenstihl, ? – ?, vice-president of the Accademia di Santa Cecilia.
[3]As a good colleague, Serato had omitted this name in his Italian edition of the letters.
[4]Frontier town on the route from Milan to Lausanne.

188 TO JELLA OPPENHEIMER
in German

Zurich 8.10.1915

I sent you a distress call from Lausanne and now, in Zurich, I have received – on the rebound from America – your letter of 14 August. It is a great comfort to me. For six months I had heard no news of you! *Here* 'the spirit' may not be 'lifted', but at least 'the view is free'.[1] It is the first country I have found in which there is an attitude of incomprehension towards the war and concern only for matters of internal security. You say I had set no narrow bounds to my home country: but in fact the outcome (as I have come to realize here) is that I have no home at all. Thus I have a double burden to carry, but many people have far graver difficulties; a consideration which affords painful solace!

Destiny, which also likes to be bountiful, did indeed grant me a few things which cannot be confiscated at borders: I safely brought back a respectable little pile of works with me, and a few good plans into the bargain, which should soon come to fruition.

A home is all that I lack.

I have had an extremely warm welcome here and found people of whom one had scarcely suspected it, to be *friends*; so much so that my homelessness is mitigated in a country on which I had set no great hopes. I also look forward to visits from older and more dependable friends: I go so far as to presume that you yourself could well appear here some day!

Thus I shall wait out the end of the affair and then emerge anew – assuming it will not be too late by then. I am glad you were able to enjoy the company of Hofmannsthal and Wassermann. How I missed such society in America! I am very happy that their thoughts were with me. Shortly before receiving your letter, I had asked after the works of these authors in the book stores. Unfortunately a renewed contact in book form was not possible.

Is it not comforting that one can exchange news more rapidly? My old soul, which had almost wasted away in America, is vibrating in me just as in old times. Let us consider the present moment as a new, this time indeed definitive, beginning.

[1]Goethe, *Faust*, Part II. 11989:
Hier ist die Aussicht frei,
Der Geist erhoben.

189 TO EGON PETRI
in German

Zurich 31.10.1915
Scheuchzer Str. 36!

[. . .] Szanto is living in Lausanne, where I – having only just arrived – came across him. (Every word a dissimulation, every question a pitfall. – Why?) – D'Albert is in Zurich. Stravinsky is also in Lausanne. On the other hand, the two Swiss property owners, Paderewski and Schelling,[1] are in America. Not only these two but also Gabrilowitsch,[2] [Rudolf] Ganz and [Josef] Hofmann have American wives. Schelling has thus become a multi-millionaire and has difficulty in bringing his personality in line with his standing. – An American book begins with the following characteristic passage: – 'Until then I had only thought of making money; without knowing what I would do with it later –'. This goes for the entire nation. –

In America I 'made' other things, and of all these I am particularly fond of the Rondò arlecchinesco for orchestra and a Sonatina ad usum infantis, which I warmly recommend to you. –

Breitkopfs tell me that the proofs of 4 volumes of my Bach Edition are ready. (Together with the two volumes of the Well-tempered Clavier there will be *six*.) Thus I have completed a capital undertaking. (By which I don't mean: capitalist.)[3]

[1]Ernest Schelling, 1876–1939, American-born piano virtuoso, pupil of Leschetitzky and Paderewski.

[2]Ossip Gabrilowitsch, 1878–1936, Russian pianist. His wife was Clara Clemens, the daughter of Mark Twain.
[3]Busoni makes a pun on Kapitel = chapter and Kapital = capital.

190 TO HUGO LEICHTENTRITT
in German

Zurich 12–13.11.1915
(midnight)

Having read the 38 pages you have devoted to me, I must thank you most kindly for the loving care with which you have compiled them and so adroitly put them across to the reader. Coming from a musicologist of your standing, I regard it as a historical honour.

Much as I value the publication of this article in America, I consider it almost more essential that so significant an exposé of my aims (and of my attempts to realize them) should be circulated in German. Breitkopf & Härtel who, thanks to their trust in me and despite every difficulty, have printed and published my works splendidly and fearlessly all along (and who have recently proved themselves to be personally the most reliable of friends), would certainly be grateful to you for the accolade to their activities which your book represents, and gladly accept it for publication.

═══

I am enclosing a few private annotations to your article but leave it to you *whether* you wish to make use of them. – Is the copy you sent me the only one? –

Meanwhile the MSS of six new 'items' are on their way to Br. & H.

═══

to Chopin variations

1) The 7 piano études [opp. 16 and 17], dedicated to Johannes Brahms himself, also date from this period. Their precursors were the *24 Preludes* [op. 37, composed in 1881], which I cannot entirely disclaim. – 'The most extended and most ambitious work' was however actually the cantata '*Il Sabato del Villaggio*', a setting by the 'sixteen-year-old' of a poem by Leopardi for soloists, chorus and orchestra, performed (in 1883?)[1] at the Teatro Comunale, Bologna. (A score of 300 pages.) It is unpublished.

to Turandot   stage works

2) I began work on the sketches for my first attempted opera in *Frohnleiten*** and finished them in Leipzig (around 1889), '*das versunkene Dorf*' to which the librettist Frida Schanz imparted the less characteristic title 'Sigune'. (The idea came from Baumbach's Sommermärchen.) At the age of 18 I had already had a stimulating exchange of letters with J. V. Widmann[2] in Berne****

on the subject of librettos. A. Wildbrandt recommended him to me. We discussed the dramatization of Keller's 'A village Romeo and Juliet'.★★★ – Gottfried Keller was asked about it himself and replied that this short story 'ran after him like a trimmed poodle'. – Widmann had various reservations and suggested 'El niño de la bola' by Alarcon in its place. In this play the lovers never get the chance to talk to each other. Because of this (and because of the demanded fee of 1,000 Marks, which I simply couldn't afford), the plan came to nothing.[3]

to Resumé

You should mention my *boundless* admiration for Mozart, also that part of me which can be traced back to him. – My initially instinctive, later rationalized rejection of Wagner, whose influence has afflicted me, of all my contemporaries, the least.

═══

During my year's study in Graz (with Mayer) I visited the seminary, where at the same time I was instructed in church-music. At that time I wrote a six-part a capella mass.[4]——

═══

NB The *2nd quartet* deserves more than a passing reference.

Merikanto[5] + Melartin[6] are *not* to be mentioned.

★Village in Styria.
★★The librettist of 'The taming of the shrew'.[7]
★★★Later taken up by Delius.

[1]The performance of *Il Sabato del Villaggio* took place on 22 March 1883.
[2]Johann Viktor Widmann, 1842–1911, Moravian-born writer.
[3]Widmann sold his libretto to Busoni's fellow Mayer-student, Heuberger, whose opera *Manuel Venegas*, composed in 1888, was first performed at Leipzig on 27 March 1889. Further suggestions for opera libretti which Widmann made to Busoni included a Cervantes *entremes*, *La ilustre fregona*, Byron's *Sardanapalus*, Firdosi's *Fall of Siyavush* and Grillparzer's *Traum ein Leben* and *Jüdin von Toledo*. On 18 October 1884 Widmann wrote to Gottfried Keller as follows:
    I have something amusing to tell you. A young musician in Vienna, Ferruccio Busoni, who is said to be a very talented artist and can pride himself on the esteem of Brahms, has suggested that I might write an opera libretto for him based on your novella 'A Village Romeo and Juliet' (!). He set great hopes on the particular effectiveness of the Black Fiddler. I replied, of course, that a theatre adaptation would have to sacrifice just such profound and beautiful moments . . .
Keller's reaction, in a letter to Widmann dated Zurich, 9 November 1884, was indeed:

I am grateful to you for not agreeing to a versification of my fateful village tale, which follows me through my life like a trimmed poodle.

[4]Missa in honorem Beatae Mariae Virginis, Graz, 1880. The manuscript is preserved in the Deutsche Staatsbibliothek, Berlin.

[5]Oscari Merikanto, 1868–1924, Finnish composer.

[6]Erkki Melartin, 1875–1937, Finnish composer. Director of the Musikinstitut, Helsinki, from 1911 to 1922. He and Merikanto were piano pupils of Busoni at Helsinki.

[7]*Der Widerspenstigen Zähmung*, opera by Hermann Götz (1874).

191 TO EGON PETRI
in German

Zurich 6.12.1915

At the same time as your kind letter I received one from Leipzig with the footnotes to the Bach Suites, which I am supposed to check for the Italian translation. – Is that fair? (Without access to the music and without musical examples I am denied even the pleasure of following your train of thought.)

At present we have the '*Föhn*' here, a southerly wind which has raised the December temperature to 15°: so much so that one can scarcely bear to wear winter clothes. The day before it started we had already suffered 11° below zero.

These extremes are as ill-suited to the Swiss temperament as their high mountains; of these, Spitteler[1] says that, if the Swiss had made them, they would have turned out considerably flatter.

In the midst of this temperature change (the only sort one experiences), I have once again made a thorough study of the score of 'Die Zauberflöte'. While remaining an admirable work, it is – as a whole – inferior to other things by Mozart.

It surpasses earlier works in three passages – in the overture, in the sonority of the 3 boys' first entrance and in the mysticism of the two armed men – otherwise the melodies are indifferent and less noble than one expects from him, and the construction is all but sketchy. The tragic Queen of the Night, who suddenly begins to gaggle, reminds me of Poe's 'The system of Prof. Tarr and Dr Fether'. But the supremely simple solutions to certain problems are once again astonishing.

I personally find the Latin virtue of creating an art of cool serenity, with a preference for the extrovert, most refreshing. Indeed it was Beethoven alone who navigated music into stormy waters, who subjected it to the puckered brow which was his nature, but which, perhaps, should have remained 'his' lonely path. – Why so angry? one would often like to ask, especially in the 2nd period!

Following on from these observations, my delight at the plan to perform the 'Indian [Fantasy]' seems paltry and wellnigh impertinent. But then, nothing is perfect (with the exception of Figaro), and even my little piece has its justification in that it offers something which is not to be found elsewhere. –

– The second part of 'The Trojans'! The vocal score is a desert, and one needs a telescope to locate the oases. Here we have an important work which – stripped of its orchestration – has really nothing to offer except bare patches! –

These opinions may be governed to a certain extent by my present mood.

But I have arrived at the point where I can scarcely continue to restrain my impatience at the futility of life's course. – I have experienced such fallow periods too often in my life and always, disastrously, at decisive turning points.

Switzerland, sadly, is not unlike America; there is more refinement but, on the other hand, less scope.

I once quoted a passage from Goethe's *paralipomena* to Faust with regard to America:

'Bestünde [nur die] Weisheit mit der Jugend
Und Republiken ohne Tugend,
[So wär die Welt dem höchsten Ziele nah.]²

Unfortunately the first line does not apply to Switzerland at all – but the second, on the other hand, does in full measure! –

Indeed, I heartily dislike republics in general, as well as the qualities which go with them (especially when they take the form of a national institution).

In a monarchy the principle of sovereignty dominates at every step on the social ladder, and every individual is able to become the head of his respective group.

In a republic, on the contrary, everybody has equal status (in principle and in practice).

The following clause is said to be included in the Swiss penal code:

'Men under the age of 20 may not be seduced by maidservants' – what is this supposed to mean? (One could just as well say: mountains under 6,000 feet may not be brought into the city.) –

But I have gabbled on as if I were an immature youth (under 20) or rapidly on the way to becoming senile. – Excuse this inundation: the flowing waters have to run off somewhere, preferably into that clear and familiar reservoir which preserves the same relationship to them as you do to your

faithful

F.B.

---

¹Carl Spitteler, 1845–1924, Swiss author.
²Lines originally intended for Mephistopheles in the 'Walpurgis night' scene from Goethe's *Faust* Part I:

If only youth could learn to be judicious
    And federalities malicious,
The world would soon achieve its highest aim.

192 TO EGON PETRI
in German

Zurich 20.12.1915

In all humility I am sending you the first proofs of my new sonatina[1] as a Christmas greeting. – In its simplicity and earnestness it is a true Christmas piece. (First page, last line, last bar, left hand, the third semiquaver should be E♮.) – Together with the Rondò arlecchinesco it is my favourite piece of the past year. What a year! – My most fervent wish is: that the future should never bring anything like it.

From your centre of stability[2] you can scarcely appreciate what it is like to be tossed and turned about.

To miss every old pleasure, to interrupt every promising enterprise. And yet things have turned out relatively tolerable.

[1]Sonatina ad usum infantis.
[2]Petri had settled in the Polish town of Zakopane.

193 TO EGON PETRI [postcard]
in German

Zurich 26.12.1915

I sent you [two] letters, cards and the sonatina proofs, as well as the suggested plan for a piano recital. – Please write a brief acknowledgement.

[1] *(grimly)*
I wish you a happy year,
I wish you a better year,
Of bloodshed and warfare clear;
Perhaps even peace is near!

Your loving friend F.B.

194 TO EDITH ANDREAE
in German

Zurich 31.12.1915

Now a whole year has passed, which I have spent, without interruption, far away from you and Berlin. – And even if this has meant nothing more than giving up a favourite pastime, that would be enough. But it means more than that. – I hope that the year has brought you nothing of this upheaval, and trust that it will always remain so. – Sadly I have for a long time heard nothing of your fate; this can have no connection with the bleak experiences of sea-sickness which I mentioned. Consider that I suffered severely from the after-effects of that condition in my own unfortunate childhood.

I have been able to observe in my own life that situations repeat themselves symmetrically, and just as I made my ascent in the 70's, so shall I make my descent during the coming 20's. –

New Year's Eve in 'purified' Berlin would still be more agreeable than in this paragon of a city, or in dreadful New York or dirty Bologna, or wherever else I have sacrificed my existence. – Must it go on like this? – It is a matter of making new decisions. –

In the meantime my 'working' year has also been rounded off and only yesterday I added the last note to an orchestral work[1] which still belongs to 1915.

Meanwhile progress has also been made in the composition of a one-act opera. While sketching the piece, I had [Max] Reinhardt in mind. It calls for a speaking role and provocative production. More than 45 orchestral players would be superfluous and therefore I envisage the 'Deutsches Theater' as the appropriate milieu for it. – Should I make enquiries in this direction for the coming autumn? But here we are once again confronted by unknown and unpredictable factors. – That's how things are at present. All is well with me physically and financially, thank goodness, and my mind is active.

[1]*Gesang vom Reigen der Geister*, op. 47, for small orchestra.

195 TO EGON PETRI
in German

Zurich 7.1.1916

Your high dudgeon was amusing, on the whole I entirely agree with you and, curiously enough, my musical greeting – on the postcard – was also pitched in no mild key. – I trust that my little musical joke (which is borrowed from the one-acter on which I am at present working, only with different words)[1] arrived safely.

I am very happy that you derived some pleasure from my little gift.

Joking and pleasure[2] aside, our lives are to be pervaded once again by earnestness, in the familiar form of the . . . Bach Edition.

But I bring relatively assuring news.

I have surveyed the master-plan and ascertained (somewhat arbitrarily . . .) that, of the more substantial compositions, only the following still need to be edited:

– 2 Suites, 1 Partita,
– 5 Toccatas,
– Fantasy and fugue in A minor.

Let us divide these nine items between us: this means that I (with my constantly increasing commitments) shall have to take the smaller half: 3 Toccatas and the Fantasy and fugue. The latter has inspired me to a special contrapuntal study; this is why I should like to do it. – I have refused all the other odds and ends, temporarily thrust them into the background. – Let us promise to finish by the end of the summer. Do you agree?

[1]The music is to be found in the last 'movement' of *Arlecchino*.
[2]Orig. Gefälligkeit und Scherzen. Allusion to Blondchen's aria in Act II of *Die Entführung aus dem Serail*.

196 TO HUGO LEICHTENTRITT
in German

Zurich 9.1.1915 [sic = 1916]

[. . .] Although the facts you put forward in your 'Ben Akiba'[1] essay are thought-provoking and nicely observed, I must contradict your statement that all that has been renews itself with new significance, and
'a man stands differently on the selfsame side of the river
before and after he has crossed it'
– as I once wrote of the naïvety which Liszt later re-assumed.——

In particular, I cannot agree with your concept of 'wrong' notes: have you not realized the painstaking measurements with which a Schoenberg writes down an interval? (– my efforts are, at least, no slighter –). Any other note would grieve him. It is just as impossible for sounds to be 'wrong' in music as it is for stones, plants or formations in a forest. We just have to learn to discern harmony away from the text-book.[2] – Our goal is this highest state, which shall however be founded on polyphony (also comparable to the forest). Or do you consider the baroque garden to be more beautiful and correct? The clipped hedge?

Perhaps your historical objectivity makes it less easy for you to reach a decision.

Apart from this unvarnished truth, I found your study valuable and stimulating. – I would like humbly to indicate how sincerely I value your investigations and how grateful I am to you for your friendly efforts on my behalf. Therefore I would ask you kindly to accept the dedication of my next theoretical work on music. It will be a study of the 'contrapuntal Urmotif', occasioned by a transcription of Bach's Fantasy and fugue in A minor.[3]

[1]Ben Joseph Akiba, celebrated Talmudist and allegedly author of the cabbalistic book *Jezirah*. He was executed by the Romans, according to tradition, at the age of 120, in AD 132. (The article by Leichtentritt is unfortunately not traceable.)
[2]Orig. Harmonielehre.
[3]Fantasy and Fugue in a [BWV 904]. Busoni's analytical edition was published in 1917 together with the Canonic Variations and Fugue from the *Musical Offering*.

197 TO EDITH ANDREAE
in German

[Zurich] 10.1.1916

[. . .] I was almost beginning to fear for you . . . and the unexpected arrival of golden Veronika[1] put me into a completely human frame of mind – because it signifies something wonderful for you and because I adore children – and 'yet', in my heart of hearts, I am opposed to all-too-nuptial bonds. – That's what I call a start to a New Year!

The letter in which I told you about my work cannot yet have arrived. I too announced the birth of a child (a sonatina for a child, which itself has the air of a child) and I recommended the little piece to you as friend and – mother.

I have in fact achieved a good deal: a round half-dozen smaller and more sizeable things. And in my last letter I asked your advice about the one-acter which I am at present working on. But first you must regain your full strength and you will have enough with looking after yourself and your fourth symphony.

My heart – I wrote to you of the symmetrical situations in my life – is in a state of adolescence again: bashful and full of longing and lacking practical impact. –

A lovely person, a genuine, pure, big-hearted creature from America's far-West came very close to me for three days. That happened while still in New York.

This is a land of exclusively masculine society . . . Letters from long-trusted female friends are therefore all the more welcome, which is why I sincerely hope for a continuation during the year which has, in this respect, begun so promisingly.

[1]Edith Andreae's daughter Veronika was born on 11 December 1915.

198 TO HUGO LEICHTENTRITT
in German

Zurich 13.1.1916

I have just received your splendid letter, while the last one I sent you should meanwhile have arrived. In it I took the liberty of carping at your pro modu contrario chronology and at the idea of 'wrong' notes. I was subsequently nonplussed at the news you sent me of the microtones which have been produced in physics laboratories, because I have struggled in vain for years to render thirds of tones audible. But I did succeed in New York, where an old Italian organ builder (and connoisseur of Dante) fashioned reeds for me which were retuned accordingly, and which I have with me in my workbox. – I beg to protest at your confusing third-tones with *quarter*-tones, and would like to claim for myself the sole right of having worked out the theory of a system of thirds of tones in two rows, separated from each other by a semitone! [. . .]

Thirds of tones give rise in fact to new *harmonic* principles, while quarter-tones find their origins in semitones. That seems to me the most substantial difference.——

What you told me about *Henderson*[1] is typical of the American tone, which is evidently only a whole-tone and dispenses with any cultivated divisions! Rather than being surprised, I am in fact delighted to receive confirmation of everything I experienced and which got its dues from me over there.

(Their bragging lack of respect became unbearable.)

The prospect of the projected book for Breitkopfs, for which I am to provide the subject matter, fills me with delight!

Hans Huber has done the same good deed here, in the most condensed of forms.

What you confide to me, intimissime, of your own activities, also deserves congratulation. If I may make so bold as to express an opinion, it is this: you should precede your major dramatic work with one of more limited means, by way of trial run.

PS So-called *biographies* of yours truly have been impending from two quarters. Let them prattle. However, it would in that case be desirable that a genuine book should hold its weight against them. Therefore I would like to express the desire that you produce the more authentic work which seems to be needed, by expanding and bringing up to date your basic outline (F.B. ein Lebensbild). I would be glad to provide you with information and materials.

---

[1]William J. Henderson, 1855–1937, New York music critic.

199 TO EGON PETRI
in German

Zurich 7.3.1916

I have just (i.e. yesterday evening) returned from Rome. It was a most
successful week with (admittedly) no less than 9 rehearsals and 4 concerts, all
in 8 days, but it was nevertheless artistic, cordial and fruitful. The Rondò
arlecchinesco had a surprising effect, positive and pliant. –[1]

– It is extraordinary how circles, whose centres are far apart, can be
tangential! An impression verging on deep emotion was made on me by a
marionette performance at a newly founded 'Teatro dei piccoli', organized
with great understanding. They staged a comic opera in two acts which
Rossini wrote at the age of 20[2] (a miracle of expressiveness!) – The production
was astonishing. The singing (executed by invisible voices) was perfect. – I
felt as if liberated – at last! – from those pompous gods whom I have all my
life been unable to avoid. I rediscovered – cum grano [salis] – *my* theatre and
the theatre.

This was something of an experience, and well-timed for the completion of
my one-act opera. – (They want to put on Turandot with my music. In Italy
the marionettes will popularize Die Zauberflöte for the first time. Is the
world turning over on to its right side? Just as in mechanics, only excessive
momentum will cause such a reversal.) –

I had a wonderful reception, respectful and affectionate. An attractive
circle of intelligent youngsters was formed straight away. The people are by
nature very quick of understanding. As, for instance, the orchestra, which
took in all the novelties and surprises immediately; complied and performed
correctly. – Well, I am grateful. – [. . .]

[1] Busoni had conducted two orchestral concerts, on March 3 (Santa Cecilia) and 5
(Augusteum), the second of which included the world première of the *Rondò
arlecchinesco*. See also letter no. 206.
[2] *L'occasione fa il ladro*, first performed in 1812.

200 TO EGON PETRI
in German

Zurich 28.3.1916

[. . .] Strindberg's *Dreamplay* (a piece which I have been 'proclaiming' since
its first publication) is said to have been produced in Berlin with thrilling
effect. – This play is yet another step forward in the evolution of theatre. On
the other hand, to prevent the balance rising too rapidly on the side of
knowledge, H. H. Ewers has collaborated with d'Albert to put a libretto into
the world of the kind which the critics describe as 'a stroke of inspiration'.

A blind lady loves a monster, Jesus restores her sight and she falls round the neck of the first handsome man she sees, convinced that he is her lover. The monster kills him and she expresses her loathing for her murderous lover. Thereupon she voluntarily blinds herself again, goes off with the monster and, at the end, a shepherd walks across the stage with a new-born lamb in his arms.[1]

'Thanks to the meaningful and theatrically effective libretto' etc. – is the reaction of the critics.

Well, my one-acter means to scourge these things a little; it is an opera which itself turns against opera. –

The last news I had from you was of your departure for Zacopane (is that the name?): I imagine you will have returned happy from this interesting part of the world.

The 2nd part of the Well-t. Clavier is now finished, as well as the Red Indian pieces.

[1]*Die toten Augen*, text by Marc Henry and H. H. Ewers, music by Eugen d'Albert, was first produced in Dresden on 5 March 1916. There was a production in Zurich, which opened on 15 February 1917, but it seems unlikely that Busoni would have seen it. Some years previously he had already coined the nickname 'd'Alberich' for this composer.

201 TO ARRIGO SERATO
in Italian

Zurich 1.5.1916

You need not worry: I think I have fully understood the situation, while the concerts committee, too, has not the slightest doubt as to your good intentions and innocence in the affair.[1] However, we found ourselves in a somewhat awkward and embarrassing situation at the last moment, and were disappointed that you could not be with us.

The blame lies entirely with the god of war, his hostility to artists and his preference for trumpets instead of violins! As, before your letter had arrived, I received one from Ricordi, in which there is no mention of a contract, I need to clarify the situation before sending a reply. In his letter, the Commendatore[2] makes me the (trivial) offer of collaborating on editions of classical works.

It is sad to reach the age of 50 (after all my endeavours and many successes) and find myself receiving the *first offer* from the house of Ricordi, and then in so disheartening a form.

You will understand that I cannot dedicate the sixth and last decade of my life to making instructive editions for Italy's leading publisher!

I am all the more surprised and baffled by the passage in your letter which indicates a different attitude to that which I find in the letter from the publishers themselves. Please do not confuse the issue, for your lack of precision could lead me to send an inappropriate reply.

[1]Serato had been unable to obtain a passport and was obliged to cancel two concerts in Zurich, on 17 and 18 April, in which he was to have played the Dvořák Violin Concerto. He was replaced by Fritz Reitz, principal cellist of the Tonhalle Orchestra, who played Haydn's Cello Concerto in D.
[2]i.e. Tito Ricordi.

202 TO JOSE VIANNA DA MOTTA
in German

Zurich 2.5.1916

Since your letter has already been lying on my desk for several days, while I have only just returned 'home' from St Gallen,[1] I shall reply at once. In all good will, I cannot at present tell you what I shall be doing on 21 June: I am confronted by new, inevitable decisions, whose nature, however, still seems vague; because I alone cannot decide, but am dependent on factors beyond my control. For 12 years I had been accustomed to seeing my way clearly before me and determining it myself; my present situation, caused by this derangement of my way of life, has become almost intolerable.

Moreover – to speak of more concrete matters – I have become most disaffected towards teaching the piano: I find it embarrassing to observe others wandering along the same road (with greater or lesser difficulty) as I continuously travelled and have now finally left behind me; to have to listen to something for 20 minutes, when I have already adjudged it from the first 10 bars – does this strike you as unnatural? Above all, I have a sense of 'begrudging time', which I cannot better explain than with Balzac's 'La peau de chagrin'. Does that strike you as artificial? [. . .]

[1]Busoni had played a recital of Bach, Beethoven (op. 111), Chopin and Liszt in St Gallen on 1 May 1916.

203 TO HARRIET LANIER
in French

Zurich 9.5.1916

[. . .] You are well informed about my activities here, where I have been given a regal welcome. I would have sent you press cuttings to keep you up to date, but experience has proved that the censors forbid this form of correspondence and I have had to abandon it. – A brief letter of thanks for the great honour which the Society of the Friends of Music wished to accord me seems not to have arrived. Permit me to repeat my feelings of gratitude and to ask you to pass them on to your worthy committee.

I am very proud of the triumph scored by Stokowski with the composition of Mahler.[1] No doubt you have occupied yourself intensively with Goethe's text, the last scene of whose 'Faust' serves as the basis for the second movement of the symphony. In Goethe the whole is directed *vertically* towards the summit; in Mahler the movement is *horizontal*; not so much a superimposition as a lateral series of episodes. This would be my one criticism of the composer.

You have not written at all about Granados, whose unexpected death has been announced in the press.[2] Did he fulfil the high hopes which you placed in his work?

I am delighted to hear of Bodanzky's success. He is a gifted musician and dependable friend. Is he remaining in New York next year? I am working on the one-act opera which I had begun to think over during my stay in New York and will soon be finished. Bodanzky has graciously accepted the dedication.

My plans are still nebulous, the situation incomprehensible. But I have had invitations from *every country*, just as I received messages of respect and greeting from every country on 1 April, the day on which I celebrated my fiftieth birthday. – So time is running out; I must calculate how much is left for me. [. . .]

Mrs Busoni sends all her love.

[1]Stokowski had conducted the American première of Mahler's Symphony No. 8 on 2 March 1916 in Philadelphia.
[2]Granados drowned in the English Channel on 24 March 1916, when the *Sussex* was torpedoed by a German submarine.

204 TO EGON PETRI
in German

Zurich 13.5.1916

It is always I who have 'the good grace' to attempt a resumption of contact. Sometimes I scarcely have the confidence – it almost looks as if you may not desire it, at least not strongly. If I am doing you an injustice here, then I have already been punished and – gladdened for it. Nevertheless, today I have a good excuse: to thank you for your birthday telegram. Even if 1½ months have meanwhile elapsed, consider that I have been so busy that I was able – sadly – only to reply to the very fewest greetings for 1 April! – The most touching of these was printed in grandiose style and framed, '*from his publishers Br. & H.*' – But other kind words from worthy and illustrious people arrived as well – least of all, however, from musicians.

The piano recitals[1] are turning out even more magnificently than expected. At the last one all the annexes and the stage itself were crowded, about 2,000 people were present. The subscription concerts were rounded off with the 'Eroica', I would say: in a dignified manner.[2] [. . .]

I hope you will have received my nine items from Br. & H. Well-t. Clav. II has now been published.

My one-acter is more or less finished.

A composer called Granados, who was invited to New York last season with a great flourish, *drowned* in the English Channel on his return. Fate often acts so prudently. This uncommonly slow-witted man had advanced through this N.Y. episode beyond his possible zenith. From then on he would have experienced nothing but disappointment (which he had already been for N.Y.), and fate intervened at the right moment.

Whether this opinion also applies to the demise of *Reger*[3] remains for the moment uncertain. But here too I sense the logic of the situation. Nevertheless, both events have affected and shaken me – and, despite all the organized horrors, we are still not insensitive to those of nature. They have a genuine impact in contrast to the artificiality of the others. –

This last chapter must also include the news that Serato was unable to come to Zurich. Kept waiting until the last minute, he had to cancel two days before [the concert].

Under these circumstances I don't know what to do next. – At the end of the month I shall be travelling south. The painter Boccioni, who has become something of a genius, wants to paint my portrait. It will be the first time I do anything of the sort with conviction. – Szanto has returned to Switzerland intact. Blanchet is hard at work. Lochbrunner[4] has become a very dear friend. I shall remain here for the rest of the summer to complete my score. And you? –

[1]Busoni gave four recitals in the Tonhalle, Zurich, on 23 March (Bach), 6 April (Beethoven), 13 April (Chopin) and 27 April (Liszt). For these concerts he also wrote his own – sometimes provocative – programme notes.

[2]Busoni had conducted the 'Eroica' Symphony at the Tonhalle, Zurich, on 17 and 18 April 1916.

[3]Reger died on 11 May 1916.

[4]Ernst Lochbrunner, 1874–1923, Swiss pianist. Pupil of Diémer and d'Albert, later of Busoni in Berlin.

205 TO HUGO LEICHTENTRITT
in German

Zurich 16.5.1916

Fräulein Bötticher tells me that you have been dedicating the intervening time to me and have finished your book about yours truly.[1] For the moment, accept my sincerest thanks.

This book, which marks my 50th birthday, represents the best and most significant celebration of it. – I also hear with interest that you wish to take up my suggestion and are planning a one-act opera, intended to forge a link between chamber music and music-drama. As to the latter term, I am, as usual, going too far in putting it on paper. I am diligently going through the scores of Mozart's operas once again and they give me the impression of being more youthful than Parsifal. They are more theatrical, more dramatic even, to say nothing of their superior quickwittedness.

But should you be seeking an object to compare and contrast with the lightness of Wolfgang Amadeus – for the preparatory studies I presume you are making – then consider, from the standpoint of an *opera composer*, the 2nd part of Goethe's Faust. As opera plot it combines Mozart and Wagner and surpasses them both.

Numerous remarks of Goethe's indicate that he had conceived the work as an opera and that, for example, he required two actresses for the role of Helena, one to recite and one to sing. Goethe himself had Mozart in mind – or more generally a composer born in Germany and educated in Southern Europe – or vice versa. (Hence: Wolf-Ferrari).

Strangely enough, such a man has now been discovered, only he has no talent. Ricordi sent me a 'Faust' trilogy of his, and he calls himself Brüggman.[2]

He is an Italian, probably of Flemish extraction, and studied in Germany.

He has made the Italian adaptation of Goethe himself and it is most praiseworthy. But the music is helpless and one cannot but be amazed that he contrives to fill 3 [sic] evenings with it. – Taking a lead from these news and views, I would like to suggest that you write a historical-aesthetical study of the various *Faust-compositions*. The literature is more plentiful than you might perhaps think. I have counted between 35 and 40 works of this kind – not counting the single songs –. An attempt at such a book is to be found in the little series which was published under the aegis of R. Strauss.[3] But it is not exhaustive. – I fear that my writer's zeal will have exhausted *you* and so – to show mercy – I shall close.[4]

Doubtless you know Byron's 'Sardanapalus'. – As a young man I considered it as the text for an opera.

[1]Hugo Leichtentritt, *Ferruccio Busoni*, Leipzig, 1916.
[2]Actually Alfred Brüggemann, 1873–1944, born in Aachen, a pupil of Humperdinck. In Germany he is remembered for his translations of Italian operas. His *Faust* cycle consists of *Der Doktor Faust, Gretchen, Faust und Helena* and *Fausts Verklärung*.
[3]'*Die Musik*', *Sammlung illustrierter Einzeldarstellungen herausgegeben von Richard Strauss*, Berlin, 1904–1919. No. 21 of this series is: James Simon, *Faust in der Musik*.
[4]Orig. abriegeln = lock up.

206 TO ARRIGO SERATO
in Italian

Zurich 22.5.1916

Curious: every time I have attempted a reconciliation with Italy, I have experienced brutal rejection.

Only two days ago I received the 'Tribuna' review of the concert which I conducted at the Augusteum.[1] It reveals little sympathy; and even if I were to console myself with the article's manifest ignorance, this would not suffice to erase the writer's evidently spiteful intentions.

Pity. Such abuse is unjustified.

Tomorrow I am obliged to give another concert in Zurich. Then, in all likelihood, I shall make my way to the home of the Marchese Casanova in Pallanza, in order to meet Boccioni.

If the sun is not too hot, I might possibly travel on as far as Bergamo.

Do you think there would be any chance of seeing you there? I hope so.

[1]The concert, on 5 March 1916, consisted of Liszt's 'Les Préludes', Busoni's *Rondò arlecchinesco* and Beethoven's 'Eroica' Symphony. The review in *La Tribuna*, dated 6.3.1916, sharply criticized Busoni's conducting, particularly his performance of the 'Eroica', an opinion shared by Toscanini, who was present at the concert. The reviewer (A.G.) also found little to praise in the *Rondò arlecchinesco*, writing, 'If the Rondò in question had been composed by one of our younger musicians: Casella, Tommasini, Gui, etc., it would have met with tumultuous disapproval.' However, the second paragraph of this long review begins as follows:

The minor shortcomings of great men. Busoni is without doubt a great musician and has the right to his shortcomings. But we would consider ourselves cowardly, were we to encourage him to proceed with the new [conducting] career he has chosen for himself. Let him not be won over by false admirers, foolish flatterers or bogus friends: we say with all sincerity that we admire him as an exceptional artist, as a true glory of our country.

207 TO ARRIGO SERATO
in Italian

S. Remigio, Pallanza 10.6.1916

[. . .] Outside rages a primordial storm. In this weather the isolation is complete. Before one's eyes is the blessed lake, inexorable, unchanging, with always the same hills and those little bays and gulfs and the eternal vaporetto plying to and fro . . . I shall not be able to endure it for long; especially as I have brought no work with me. And further away the war, this war without any purpose and without any result, apart from that of having brought me into the most unpleasant of situations!

You can imagine how welcome your letter was! Mail! I don't know when it was that I last saw such a thing! Boccioni (I have come here for his sake) unfortunately started my portrait *in the open* and, with this particularly cold and unpleasant weather, his work is making no progress.

I would be glad to go to Rome and make a fresh attempt to explain my art to the Italians; they would realize too late (for me) that their leading contemporary musician had passed unnoticed. I tell you this in confidence, as anyone else would laugh behind my back at hearing me say such things.[1] Meanwhile, I myself am progressing further and have already planned a large-scale, all-embracing project, upon which I shall embark without delay as soon as I have finished the little one-act opera;[2] I hope to have achieved this by September. Invitations are pouring in from all sides, from England and from Spain, but what should I decide?

Your comments on La Tribuna have comforted me. The pianists' conference in Milan took place without me; I am sorry to have missed the luncheon at Cova, but am otherwise content. [. . .]

[1]'Busoni was right. He has never been understood, nor valued as a composer; nobody could perceive in him the founder figure of contemporary music.' (Footnote by Serato.)
[2]During his stay at Pallanza, Busoni wrote the first musical sketches for *Doktor Faust*.

208 TO HUGO LEICHTENTRITT
in German

Zurich 24.6.1916

After an absence of a month, I returned home yesterday, 23 June 1916, to find your postcard (under a heap of mail piled up two foot high); but, contrary to the message it contains, only the *5th* quire of your book!

So I would ask you for the remaining sections. – In the country mansion I was visiting I found the original manuscript of a first version of Liszt's Totentanz, which includes an Intermezzo – based on the liturgical *De Profundis*. The 'Futurist' Boccioni completed a magnificent portrait of me. I sketched out a piece for 2 pianos.[1]

Now, however, I am resuming work on the score of my one-act opera
Arlecchino
in order to complete it. I am all the more in a hurry to do so, as I want immediately to set about my 'official standard work', a play with music in 5 scenes or acts, in which everything for which I have all the while been preparing myself with experiment and observation should finally be embodied.

Thus I have extensive plans, which explains why I must remain brief today.

[1]Improvisation über das Bachsche Chorallied 'Wie wohl ist mir, o Freund der Seele, wenn ich in deiner Liebe ruh', for two pianos. It is dedicated to Busoni's host in Pallanza, the Marchese Silvio della Valle di Casanova.

209 TO IRMA BEKH
in German

Zurich 25.6.1916

[. . .] I am glad for Benni's sake that you are travelling to America, for he complains of being lonely: what you yourself will find there, apart perhaps from him, I cannot judge. When that wonderful man Christopher visited it for the first time, the country had some beauty and abundance; I find the sort of dough which the Anglo-Saxons, since the commencement of their independence, have kneaded from this manna to be repugnant. The fact that a swarm of desperate, starving criminals on the run found refuge there was the cause of an ardent desire for prosperity and of an insolence in those who had escaped the law, of parvenus amongst those who had made money and of a general lack of education; and all this had a semblance of decency forced upon it, thanks to the aridity and narrow-mindedness of the surviving Puritans: like closed shutters, barring the light from a house in which all manner of things carry on in the dark. – The dubious and yet childish part which the United States has been playing in the past year demonstrates most clearly that mixture of insatiable urge for business and of surviving prejudice, which is typical of these people.

Democracy, which Heine compares to
– 'einem grossen Freiheitsstalle
    mit den grossen Gleichheitsflegeln',[1]
was followed by the aristocracy of millionaires, universal ten-penny transport was succeeded by private automobiles. A hunt for the '*unique*' replaced the former equality and uniformity, which now survives amongst the middle classes and characterizes the American bourgeoisie. They all wear the same clothes, do the same things at the same time, read the same paper, live in identical houses, are moral, lacking in instinct and entirely impersonal; while being merciless towards anyone who may think and act differently. – On the whole, the women come off better than the men; this would be a study in itself, but too long and too infuriating for me to go into here.

Finally I should add that, where a woman perhaps has the best of it, an artist definitely has the worst, above all if he should have a sense of humanity. While remaining tolerable for a brief visitor, it is fatal for most settlers. But these are mostly mediocrities. Striving for wealth and social (hm!) advancement devours all seriousness or idealism. – I, who spent altogether the best part of 5 years of my life there, take this view of America. – What you will think of it, going as you are with expectations altogether different from mine, cannot be predicted. In that country, an independent, educated girl who behaves sensibly is esteemed very highly. So one may hope that you will be fortunate. – That I wish this for you, you already know. I embrace you and bless you on your way.

[1]See footnote to letter no. 175.

210 TO HUGO LEICHTENTRITT
in German

Zurich 27.6.1916

I take it back! Quires 2–4 have arrived and the diligent intelligence of which they bear witness obliges me to express my grateful admiration. I have found nothing which needs changing. (Page 67 should read: final piece, no. *8*, instead of 7; likewise: 'for these *eight* pieces', instead of 'seven'.)

You end with the Nocturne symphonique which, together with the 2nd sonatina, creates a genre which does not 'lack a comprehensive system' – as you write – but is founded on a system which arises *out of the structure and content of the piece itself* and which, in a third or any subsequent essay of this kind, *will always have to create its own system anew.*

A third essay of this kind is to be found in the '*Gesang vom Reigen der Geister*' (for strings and 6 wind instruments), which has just been engraved by Br. & H. – The publishers would be happy to let you have a score, also of the 'Rondò arlecchinesco',[1] which likewise has just been engraved. – I must tell you about the latter. Be patient, for I have to go back a long way.

More than 2 years ago, the figure of Harlequin, as played by an Italian actor, made a most thrilling theatrical impression on me. I resolved to create a brief stage work about this character and in the autumn of 1914 I wrote the text. – The war and long journeys interrupted the plan. The following summer I had almost made up my mind to abandon it and I preserved its essence, using some of the sketches to embody its idea and feeling – condensed – in an orchestral piece.

The comment of a Berlin critic with regard to my *Nocturne*, that 'my harmonic system was only suitable for slow and muted compositions', stimulated me to apply this system to an animated, noisy piece.

Thus arose the Rondò arlecchinesco,[2] and it has already proved itself in 2 performances. This success caused me to recall my original plan, and now I have also set the *libretto* to music and the orchestral score is well on the way.

If you find all this worth mentioning, then I would ask you to incorporate it – or at least allude to it – in your little book.

[1] and [2] Orig. 'Harlekins Reigen', the German title devised for the work by Breitkopf und Härtel.

211 TO EDITH ANDREAE
in German

[Zurich July 1916]

Industry rather than insolence is the cause of my silence. – I write for about 6 hours a day and the remaining time I reflect on the following day's 6 hours. In this way I have, in the shortest of time, filled up 200 pages of my one-acter with dots and dashes; just about 4 fifths of the whole thing. [. . .]

On my desk are now lying the proofs of the new edition of my little music aesthetic. This time it is to appear in the 'Inselbücherei', a series (bound in brightly patterned paper) which only includes select shorter writings and with which you will certainly be acquainted. *R. M. Rilke* recommended my little book to the publishers on his own initiative.

While I was away I missed a visit by Moissi.[1] Subsequently I spoke to him on the telephone in Arosa, where he is receiving official medical care. It was quite a peculiar sensation for me actually to hear his own, unmistakable voice. His attitude towards me is pleasant and kind-hearted.

It is no secret that my one-act opera is called 'Arlecchino' or 'The Windows' – a 'theatrical capriccio'. It is what one used in olden times to call an 'intermezzo', a genre in which Cervantes made eight monumentally comic essays. It also signifies an intermezzo in my creativity and the transition to a more vigorous onslaught. [. . .]

Almost everything was ready for a production by Reinhardt – but circumstances are becoming noticeably more difficult. And here we happily arrive at 'that' subject on which I would prefer to remain silent, rather than talk too much. Thus it is time to end this letter.

[1] Alexander Moissi, 1879–1935, distinguished actor and for many years a leading member of Max Reinhardt's ensemble at the Deutsches Theater, Berlin. Of Albanian-Jewish origin, he spent his childhood – like Busoni – in Trieste. Busoni created the title role in *Arlecchino* for him.

212 TO HUGO LEICHTENTRITT
in German

Zurich 10.8.1916

As my biographer, you will not be indifferent to the news that, on 7 August, I completed my one-act opera 'Arlecchino' (238 pages of handwritten score).

It turned out to my satisfaction; this is my present opinion and what I also hope for the future. Only on stage will one be able to judge its scenic
'values'
(a word which I hate).[1] [. . .] Now for a short breathing space! Much has been neglected due to exclusive concentration on one piece.

A letter which arrived today from my 'first publishers'[2] informs me that the plates of the 24 Preludes (amongst others) are to be *melted down*. Sic transit juventus! – But they also speak in passing of a new edition (which could only be done as a revision;[3] although, as the work of a 15-year-old, the original is not insignificant).

How brief seems the cycle of life!

[1]Orig. Werte. Busoni continues: 'a word which I hate, especially without an *h*', for he still preferred the old-fashioned spelling, Werthe.
[2]Lucca, Milan, published these Preludes *c*. 1882. The firm was taken over by Ricordi in 1888.
[3]A new edition was published posthumously by Ricordi in 1927, edited by Gino Tagliapietra.

213 TO EGON PETRI
in German

Zurich 11.8.1916

I am taking 3 days' holiday – or perhaps more! On the 8th I finished the score of 'Arlecchino'; the work was accomplished quickly and relatively easily (it took me no more than 4 months for the whole thing), but it was as if I were holding a thread in my fingers on which endless little knots had to be untangled. Minor problems occurred over and over again, and each one – once solved – led to further problems. Never before have I been so clearly conscious of the 'horror vacui' provoked in me by *each* empty page – I was constantly obliged to find a way to begin it, to fill it: it was a fortunate occasion when the first bar was inferred from the preceding music!

And yet, every evening I looked forward to the following morning and now . . . my little friends have deserted me, and due to their absence, the house of my soul seems empty. – I am anxious to see how they will spring out of the pages of the score and take their place on stage; as Hoffmann so beautifully tells the tale of the hobgoblin-folios of Prosperus Alpenus.[1] At present they are squashed flat under the binder's press like common hand-coloured figurines. – I believe the piece lasts about 50 minutes, a jest, a scene, an 'intermezzo' – in its own right and also in my creative life. [. . .]

Well, now I must 'get on with' our A.B.C. (Arrangement of Bach's Compositions) and let us hope that *its* conclusion will coincide with the peace (also as a comfort to us) – for at present both these things seem to be as remote as the invention of perpetual motion. – I have sketched out and almost completed an introductory fantasy for the variations for 2 pianos.[2] [. . .]

[Here] you will find an exquisite (ex-qui-si-te) 'Neuenburger' and a splendid young St Bernard,[3] the former to be tippled, the latter to be fondled.

[1]Actually Prosper Alpanus, a reference to Chapter V of E. T. A. Hoffmann's *Klein Zaches*.
[2]i.e. Improvisation on 'Wie wohl ist mir'.
[3]This was Giotto Bernardone, to give him his full name.

214 TO EGON PETRI
in German

Zurich 26.8.1916

Your letter gladdened me, all the more so as, when it arrived, I was much in
need of comforting. You know that I spent the whole of June with the painter
Boccioni and that he produced a magnificent portrait of me. – Then he was
'called up' and — died, after a fall from his horse. I am consumed with
bitterness. I am trying with all my might to sustain myself with work. Having
completed the one-acter on 8 Aug., I wrote an interesting study of a Fant. &
fugue in A minor by Bach. Now I have taken up the idea of the variations
from the [2nd] violin sonata and have nearly finished them. The piece turned
out to be a complete transformation of the original; the idea of placing the
theme at the very central point of the variations strikes me as novel. – How I
should like to try it through with you! Could this, in the end, provide the
motive for a 2-piano recital? (Which could be repeated in Basle.) Think it
over.

I can write no more, this fresh wound is aching too intensely.

215 TO JOSÉ VIANNA DA MOTTA
in German

Zurich 6.9.1916

[. . .] What a pity that Br. & H. only passed on my criticisms of the Liszt
Edition and not my praise. For I was moved to the greatest respect for your
conscientiousness! I was (justifiably) carping at the translator's zeal, and this
was actually directed at the publishers themselves. – 'Album' is not a diary,
the Germans have the word Journal. Apart from which, *Album* is universally
understood. Furthermore, the title is a part of the composition itself and the
translation is a transcription! Taking the matter to its logical conclusion, as
'Venedig und Neapel' has been substituted for Venezia e Napoli, one would
also have to write Franz Mehl [or Frank Flour] instead of Franz Liszt. How
would this sound: Wiener Abende (instead of Soirées de Vienne) or indeed:
Gesellschaftsabende in Wien.[1] – Well really!! [. . .]

In the Liszt Museum, when it was still under Obrist's[2] direction, I
discovered some printers' proofs with neither name nor title. The content
corresponded partly to that of V[enezia] e N[apoli]. From the initials T.H. at
the bottom of the plates, I deduced the name Tobias Haslinger. Initially
uncertain, I asked about them at Schlesingers (the successors to T.H.), who
at first denied any knowledge of the matter. I was persistent enough to oblige
them to search more thoroughly and the plates of these proofs turned up in
Lienau's[3] cellar. Although I immediately suggested that they should be
published under my auspices, Lienau could not be persuaded to risk the cost
of the title page and the paper. But he had an impression of them made for

my collection, with a hand-written note to the effect that this print was intended exclusively for my own private use. – I am the only person to have played the *four* pieces in public, once complete, once only two of them.

– Bach–Busoni –

Would you not like to purchase the beautiful Complete Edition? For nearly everything has been slightly altered in it, as for example in the Chorale preludes which I dedicated to you, of which I have made a 2nd version.

(I would have to buy the things myself in order to send them to you.)

The war has again inflicted great pain on me. You can read about it in the enclosed newspaper cutting.[4]

[1] = society evenings in Vienna.

[2] Dr Aloys Obrist, 1867–1919, curator of the Liszt Museum in Weimar from 1901 to 1907, subsequently conductor at Stuttgart.

[3] The firm of Robert Lienau took over Schlesinger in 1864 and Haslinger in 1875.

[4] Busoni published an article in the *Neue Zürcher Zeitung* on 31 August 1916, entitled 'Der Kriegsfall Boccioni'. A copy of it was enclosed with this letter.

216 TO EDITH ANDREAE
in German

Zurich 8.9.1916

In your kind and spirited letter you write: your friendship with me is stranger than any other; with the added flourish: 'à qui la faute?'

But has it never occurred to you that you *too* could – at least partly – be to blame? – No, there is no question of 'hatred', but sometimes you provoke me, not so much personally as because I see in you, without thereby denying you your own individuality, the symbol for a whole class of people. But it is precisely this, the fact that so utterly individual a person nevertheless bears the imprint of her class, that stimulates my aggression.

Oh yes, the Catholic aristocracy! Here you are indeed reaching high. – Did you know that, in my first years of adolescence, I overcame only with difficulty the desire to take holy orders? And I would certainly have made it to become a bishop. And such a bishop has a palace, a park, a library, a gallery, a cellar, a crook, a flock . . . and, I believe, many, many women.

And I have often said: a human being seems to me to resemble a clown who comes into the arena wearing seven robes, which he then proceeds to remove one by one. This dream of episcopal bliss also counts amongst my discarded robes.

217 TO HANS HUBER
in German

Zurich 16.9.1916

Warmest greetings to you, dear master, in Locarno, through which I passed
at the end of June after taking my leave of Boccioni. Bitter memories well up
in me and various communications from Italy (to which, for all I care, you
can give the glad eye from Locarno) have constantly torn the wound open
afresh. The world accepts all too readily such great, horrifying or extraordinary events (and yet is thrown into confusion by the greatest platitudes).
The docilité stupide with which people nowadays accept everything formerly
of concern only to those professionally interested in the 'noble' art of war
astonishes me more than the deeds they accomplish. This fine organization of
universal militarism (I was informed that we are indebted to the Swiss for it)
is an admirable system of stifling the individual. A sword, a Bible, an
umbrella (as if a drop of water were just as unhealthy as a gun-shot) and the
jolly flashing of bayonets, just as I had the historical joy of witnessing here on
1 August,[1] as well as a few well-tuned male-voice choruses – I am most
susceptible to such a display of culture. – I have not worked for three days
and, as you will have noticed, this does not suit me at all. The wise deed of
my Fatherland[2] has isolated me completely and also financially restricted me.
(This in passing, but nevertheless palpable.) In order to sustain myself, I
must create something with my 10 fingers. If the Conservatoire in Basle sets
out on an enterprise which would appear to afford some satisfaction (it does
me credit), then it should also be prepared to contribute something towards
it, and resolve to bridge the gap in the proposed fee out of its own funds.
Such concerts cost me more time and energy than a normal engagement, for
which I receive the same amount.[3] (Do you find this odious of me?)
Incidentally, the Conservatoire hall is a little small for such an undertaking. I
myself have no intention of advertising my concerts.

The work dedicated to you[4] has gone straight to the publishers. It blinded
me to certain events for a few days. I am now embarking, I hope, on my
'chief work'. God be with you.

[1] 1 August is Federation Day in Switzerland. The *Neue Zürcher Zeitung* for 2 August
1916 contains the following report for central Zurich:
> The Zurich Municipal Military Society had . . . invited its members to a
> Federation party in the Drahtschmidli gardens and over one thousand comrades at
> arms rallied to the call. The Zurich municipal band Concordia's participation, in
> which a selection of Swiss songs provoked particular enthusiasm, contributed
> greatly to the success of the celebrations.

[2] Italy had declared war on Germany in August 1916.
[3] Busoni had been invited to give a series of recitals, illustrating the history of piano
music, for the Conservatoire in Basle. See also letters nos. 220 and 226.
[4] Kanonische Variationen und Fuge, for piano, from Bach's *Musical Offering*. The
foreword is dated September 1916.

218 TO EGON PETRI
in German

Zurich 17.9.1916

Unfortunately I have had no news from you, nor have you replied to my little suggestion. You constantly forget, thanks to your triumphs in Zakopane (no malice intended), that the greatest store is set in these times upon any friendly comment. Especially when – as I told you in my letter and with my article – I had just lost a friend myself. – But your hesitation is also deleterious from a purely commercial point of view. The Tonhalle here – despite my good experiences – is a real 'Trust', which looks on everything it does not itself organize as being opposed to its plans. Therefore, if one has no desire to be fobbed off with the glib reply that the hall is already booked, one cannot apply soon enough.

A fine autograph copy of the piece for 2 pianos, ready for the printers, has already been sent off. – I took advantage of the resultant compositional ebb-tide to bring ashore the solutions to all the canons from the
Musical Offering.
I have arranged them as a set of piano variations, for which the Fuga Canonica in epidiapente serves as finale. – The result is a rather strict school-book. – (Have also sent off the Toccatas.)[1]

And now the 'Saison' begins, the 'third' autumn——the mists begin to thicken. –

[1]Bach's Toccatas in e, g and G, BWV 914, 915 and 916, transcribed for piano. The foreword is dated August 1916.

219 TO JELLA OPPENHEIMER
in German

Zurich 19.9.1916

[. . .] I read a report of Hofmannsthal's 'Frau ohne Schatten', which leads me to expect fine things of it. The story fascinated me. – Unfortunately he (H) had to decline an invitation to assist me, too, as librettist. Hence I have to resort to self-help. I completed the Faust libretto at Christmas 1914. I am satisfied with, and completely convinced of it. I hope to set about the musical side in the near future. Meanwhile I have written many things. On 8 August I completed the score of an 'Arlecchino' in one act. Numerous piano pieces, orchestral works and Bach studies are entwined around this small, singular work, which I wrote half as parody, half as confession, from the heart. – A few days ago Breitkopf & Härtel published a biography of yours truly, from the pen of the esteemed music historian Dr Leichtentritt. And in a few more days the 'Inselbücherei' is publishing a new, enlarged edition of my little 'Aesthetic'. [. . .]

I cannot subdue my feelings about Boccioni. Apart from the fact that I loved him, he was at last, after a lengthy interval, an Italian painter of historical significance. And he felt he was only at the outset! – Enough. – [. . .]

220 TO HANS HUBER
in German

Zurich 25.9.1916

carissimo e veneratissimo, I consider it unforgivable of myself that my letter 'piqued' you. You deserve letters of the kind which generate warmth, as yours do (infallibilmente)! 'Allein die Schuld liegt nicht an mir'[1]; everywhere I see too much unpleasantness and wickedness manifesting itself, and it is only my offended loving-kindness, my violated sense of justice, which causes me to become or appear unpleasant and wicked myself. Shooting in war and account-books in peace are things which irritate me. I avoid them, ignore them as long as possible (most successfully when I am really absorbed in my work), but when I am brought in contact with them, I find it difficult to maintain a benevolent air. The affair of the bayonets on the evening of 1 August in Zurich was and remains repellent, and has destroyed much of my so far sympathetic impression of the Swiss. Since then, I see Switzerland in a different light. This hypersensitivity, as you call it, can be explained by the beginning of my third year of exile; since the Italians' declaration of war on Germany things have become even more entangled for me. Everything I have developed artistically and financially over 20 years will quite possibly collapse; and this is happening to me at an age when a new beginning demands a moral effort antipathetic to the insights I have gained. In plain language: one no longer finds it worthwhile. Happily, I can see the first light of a new working day which, if it fulfils its promise, will be a beautiful day and should last 2 to 3 years. Or, in more popular tone: I am occupying my thoughts with the realization of my 'chief work'.

Now you will read my last letter more indulgently, will be more readily forgiving. Reluctantly, ever more reluctantly do I sit myself down at the piano to practise (I have not yet stirred for the 1st subscription concert here).[2] La prospettiva of a representative cycle of four concerts in Basle, in itself attractive, confronts your listless friend with a considerable task of strumming, which will steal much time from his 'first light'. Hence my stern fascination with the question of the fee, even if, strictly speaking, no connection exists between dispensing a portion of life and collecting a thousand Franc note. Will your treasurer understand that? Hopeless. Perhaps, however, the well-to-do music-lovers on the committee. – Remain my friend, for you understand everything.

¹Actually 'ist nicht an mir' (but the blame rests not with me'), words of Pamina in the first Finale of *Die Zauberflöte*).
²On 2 and 3 October Busoni was to play Beethoven's 4th Piano Concerto, Bach–Liszt Variations on 'Weinen, Klagen, Sorgen, Zagen' and Bach – Busoni Chaconne.

221 TO JOSÉ VIANNA DA MOTTA
in German

Zurich 6.10.1916

Thank you for kindly letting me have the Sp[anish] Rh[apsody]. I myself possess 2 or 3 complete sets of orchestral material, which I purchased (but in Berlin). Hence, in this case, I am scarcely an interceptor of royalties. – Forbidden? Killing people is also forbidden. And never – before or after the outbreak of war – have I spoken untruthfully or acted illegally. – On the other hand, I have myself been the object of several transgressions and I count the little affair in Geneva¹ amongst these. My opinion of it, in brief, is:

Merde!

Or, at greater length: 1) Herr M.K. is probably Maurice Kufferath,² a man who has founded his entire existence, spiritually and financially, on *Wagner*. 2) Whenever there may have been anything positive to report, the J[ournal] de G[enève] has never bothered about me. 3) It has lied intentionally and falsely accused me, or acted in a criminally incorrect and misleading manner. 4) After all the self-improvement which I have rigorously practiced (particularly in the past 15 years), my greatest achievement has been my integrity of character. I find it repulsive that someone should lay their filthy hands on it. 5) Who has the right – under such irrefutable circumstances – to demand an 'alibi' of me, as if I were a defendant and they my incorruptible judges?

While thanking you for your friendly intervention, I would stress that it is less a case here of *my* having to justify myself than of the paper being put to shame. Nevertheless, I repeat: thank you. [. . .]

¹The *Journal de Genève* published an article in which it was alleged that Busoni had given a concert at Brussels for the German army.
²Maurice Kufferath, 1852–1919, Belgian musicologist. From 1900 he had been joint director of the Théâtre de la Monnaie, Brussels.

222 TO JOSÉ VIANNA DA MOTTA
in German

Zurich 9.10.1916

Accept my unreserved thanks for your truly kind letter. The 'ifs' and 'buts' are connected with the fact that I had sent a reply to the 'J.d.G.' and would have found it important to see the authentic text in print. But, thanks to the editors'

'Rectification'

it has been rendered null and void. – For this 'amendment' still contains inaccuracies or, in plain speaking, lies. (I cannot avoid using that awful word.) 'Bien que M Busoni eût refusé son concours', for instance, is incorrect. For I never received an offer. And finally: how does Herr Kufferath (for *now*, as has been substantiated, it *is* he) come to meddle in matters of no artistic consequence with regard to myself, while he nevertheless purports to be an *art* critic and moreover (this too I cannot suppress) has been a brainless Wagnerian all his life, a parasite of those tedious spear-waving gods of Bayreuth, without whom he would have remained a nobody. I have chosen frankness as my guiding principle, not because it offers me the best prospects (God only knows) but because it maintains an honest standpoint.

This is an opinion closely related to my contempt for the Wahnfried system. In a final analysis it is nothing but lack of intelligence, short-sightedness and confusion of the relationship between our heaping up of 'worldly goods' (?) and our brief, uncertain existence; – a miscarriage of our true mission in life.

If everyone realized this, there would be no war.

This is why I find it wretched to see how people, who pass over my works in silence, wish to besmirch me as a

personnage de parti.

May God enlighten them.

223 TO JOSÉ VIANNA DA MOTTA
in German

[Zurich] 20.10.1916

What is this Rondo of yours?

On my honour, an op. 4 of Liszt with such a title is new to me. – If it is a French edition, then it precedes the Etudes, op. 6.

Otherwise two works exist as opus 4 (Allegri de Concert?), in oblong format, published by Hofmeister (?). (I have not considered the matter for a long time and my memory could be deceiving me,[1] but the collector's urge in me has been aroused.)

The fragment of Wagner's letter to Bülow causes something to shine through which looks very much like the system of a bogus banker.★

(W. to Bülow: 'Of course, since I became acquainted with Liszt, my harmonies have changed entirely. But does one have to make that known to the public straight away?')

But W. changed after getting to know L. not only in his harmonies but also in the style of his themes and decorations. Things like the Forest Murmurs and Magic Fire Music are quite clearly Lisztian piano études, and the Ride of the Valkyries is such a shamelessly cheap imitation of the form and content of 'Mazeppa' that I was staggered when I heard this piece of kitsch again at the beginning of the year:[2] staggered that the moving spirit of the work, aped by this almost parodistic imitation, was constantly rejected and despised. – And I coined the following aphorism: Liszt was the foundation stone of all modern tonal edifices and, as foundation stone, he lies deep below the surface and remains invisible.

*The Brussels branch of the bogus bank (in the Journal de Genève) has acted with as much ingenuity as benevolence, and their deed has been made known and provoked unfavourable comment about me in Italy.

[1]Two works of Liszt comprise his op. 4, an Allegro di bravura and a Rondo di bravura, both composed in 1824. This nomenclature was evidently the source of confusion.
[2]Volkmar Andreae had conducted the work in the Tonhalle, Zurich, on 7 and 8 February 1916. Busoni himself had conducted Wotan's Farewell and the Magic Fire Music from *Die Walküre* at Tonhalle concerts on 13 and 14 March 1916.

224 TO EGON PETRI
in German

Zurich 9.11.1916 [postmark]

No, to my great anguish I have *not* received your letter about M. Reger, which is a real disappointment. For you would have helped me let off steam about that certain Merger (contrapuntal inversion in his style)[1] of feelings with which he pervades my musician's heart. Pity. [. . .]

Something must be lacking in H. Mann (perhaps in his perspective, attention to detail or proportions; who can say?), for I have difficulty in reading him, most certainly not because he is above my head.

There is much talk of Max Brod's 'Tyho Brahe'(?),[2] the subject of which is said to be the relationship of the teacher to his pupil (Kepler).

– The important question as to which piece should be coupled with the hour-long '*Arlecchino*' so as to fill an evening in the theatre, my resultant increasing difficulties[3] and the desire to establish such a programme in a durably valid form have led me to the hasty decision to form an opera in 2 acts out of the material and substance of Turandot. For a few weeks now I have been hard at work on this delightful task, writing the libretto and music for a Turandot opera. I am re-writing the text completely and independently, and bringing it closer in tone to a pantomime or stage play. It is more arduous a task than I had initially assumed, but is coming easily to me.

The *mask*-figures common to both pieces serve to link them (although they otherwise contrast completely with each other).

This will lead to my next (chief) work, whose libretto is already finished.

The day before yesterday was my 1st piano recital.[4] The 6 Preludes from the Well-tempered Clavier made a good effect.

[1]Orig. M. Erger (= Ärger = anger). Reger himself once signed a receipt for a particularly scanty concert fee as 'Rex Mager' (= Rex Meagre).
[2]Max Brod, *Tycho Brahes Weg zu Gott*, Leipzig, 1916. The philosophical questions discussed in this novel are in fact very close to Busoni's own ideas.
[3]The Stadt-Theater in Zurich was unwilling to accept the work for performance, as it required a companion piece.
[4]A recital at the Tonhalle, Zurich on 7 November 1916. The programme featured Beethoven's Sonata in E, op. 109, Weber's Sonata no. 1 in C and four Schubert–Liszt transcriptions. An introductory group of Bach and Bach–Busoni included the following Preludes from the 'Well-Tempered Clavier': A♭ (Book II), C♯ (Book I), b♭ (I), F♯ (I), f♯ (II), D(II).

225 TO EGON PETRI
in German

Zurich 23.12.1916

[. . .] 'Practice' is gradually becoming an insurmountable obstacle to me. Nevertheless, I plough the deeply furrowed field further, as you can see from the enclosed programme book.

The Turandot opera is going smoothly and swiftly – however, it is doubtful whether I shall be finished on time.

I frequently spend my quiet evenings at home, reading.

Thus it was inevitable that 'Das grüne Gesicht'[1] should come my way. What 'cheap rubbish'! And at the same time so carelessly written that one fails once again to understand how the entire German press could raise its voice in acclaim. In the midst of mystical hocus-pocus one comes across sentences such as: 'A fact of this ilk speaks volumes.' (!) – Here is a direct quotation:

'You don't know how much more different it is returning home, *when* one has *long* been absent, than when one has always stayed put.'

The following is very fine:

'Green is no true colour as such, although you can see it.'

You find things of this kind on every page. – (This would have been of little consequence, were it not that it constantly obtrudes——.)

(mit frommen Ingrimm)

es ist ein Hang in den Men-schen, die an-ge-bor-ne Gü - te zu ver-ber-gen!

(says my Abbé in Arlecchino.)
What a great pity *that* it must be so; but it *is* so and will never change.

[1]Gustav Meyrinck, *Das grüne Gesicht*, Leipzig, 1916.
[2](*with devout rage*) 'It is but human demeanour to hide one's quintessential loving kindness.'

226 TO HANS HUBER
in German

Zurich 16.1.1917

Your kind words were a fine reward.[1] Your trust is an incentive to me: although I have only earned half of it, this half, which I retain for myself, cannot be unequally distributed between the creative and the reproductive artist in me. For these two are one and the same or, at the most, the former is the extension of the latter. But while the virtuoso in me still abides by older habits, I believe that I have, as composer, stripped myself of all superficiality and 'inevitability' in the practice of my profession. Where the performer has, after all, to reach a compromise between his own originality and that of his programme, the composer is free of such binding agreements. If he nevertheless appears to be less conspicuous, this is because he is not carried by the force of the object (Bach or Beethoven), but stands alone and must make his own effect. But that which is unique to my interpretations must be just as much so in my compositions; in the one case overrated, in the other still inadequate, simply because less well known. Finally, the same personality, the same standards, the same feeling still obtain and make themselves apparent in a man beyond his profession. So much so that I could never believe a coarse man would be a gentle artist, a wicked person could create something elevated or intimate, a trickster could produce something sincere. This also all applies to one's level of self-criticism, of logical thinking and of temperament. Please forgive me for taking the liberty of analysing the praises lavished upon me by a friend and master, but who would understand it better than you, and you will also appreciate that I occasionally feel the need to voice my feelings. I thank you with all my heart.

[1]On 12 January 1917 Busoni had given the first of a cycle of four recitals at the Stadtkasino, Basle, a programme of Bach, Beethoven, Weber and Schubert–Liszt.

227 TO JOSÉ VIANNA DA MOTTA
in German

[Zurich] January 1917

[. . .] If matters with the 'Liszt Commission' were different, and had they been different from the outset, I would still be involved in it. The story of the Complete Edition is quite interesting, because I forced the issue at a time when everyone was opposed to it. *Eleven* of the thirteen publishers of original Liszt editions had already promised me – as editor – the works they owned. In the face of this fait accompli, the Liszt Foundation capitulated and took the whole thing over. I wrote and received some 100 letters, drew up the plan, became their 'public servant' and finally handed in my resignation. This – in a nutshell – is the authentic story.

I surmise that the Mephisto Walz is by R.F.; for I knew that it was written down by a pupil and that the accompanying work (Der nächtliche Zug) bears the name R.F. in print.[1] For this reason I had the impudence to make a new arrangement of it.

By 'Albumblatt' I meant the Valse mélancolique; now I also recall the dashing little waltz in Ab (?) of the same name . . . I must insist that each of the three Caprices-Valses (not Valses-Caprices) had an earlier version, indeed the one on Lucia e Parisina had two. The Valse de Bravours was first published as *op.* 6 and the Valse mélancolique (considerably altered), which was also published separately, was written in the same period; – only the third originally bore the title Valse a capriccio, which was later applied to all three.

If you publish the sketches and earlier versions in direct association with the final versions (which I think is right), then you have contradicted yourself in the case of the Harmonies poétiques.

The title Post Galopp was not my invention: I read it on the manuscript.[2] The piece *is* complete, but very erratically written down, and until one has found one's bearings in the MS, it appears to be fragmentary.★

I have sometimes played the passage from the Paganini Etudes[3] with the right hand in thirds. – I didn't want to destroy the alternating pattern.

The cut in the coda applies of course to the *first* 5 bars.

C'est tout pour le moment.[4]

★Therefore do not rely on the copy.

[1]'R.F.' could be Robert Freund, but it seems curious, if this is the case, that Busoni did not verify the question with him directly.
[2]The piece is published in the Liszt Society edition as 'Galop (?1841)', Searle no. 218.
[3]Paganini Etude no. 2 (pencilled annotation by da Motta).
[4]da Motta's work on the Breitkopf und Härtel projected Complete Edition of Liszt led to an extensive correspondence with Busoni in this style.

228 TO ROBERT FREUND
in German

Zurich 5.2.1917

[. . .] A strong gust of wind has blown in from Germany. R. Strauss visited Switzerland,[1] accompanied by people from Vienna and Mannheim. R.S. appeared just like the ostrich[2] from which he takes his name, partly in brilliant plumage, partly – bald; the largest of his species, yet not aggressive in appearance; the only vertebrate bird that doesn't fly; exotic yet without humour; in a word: an ostrich and not an eagle. But we all need to make allowances, and this one individual has remained in the forefront for quite some time.

The Basle concerts are over[3] and have brought much joy to me and my audiences.

I was and still am intermittently working at my nearly complete *opera*, 'Turandot'.

It is gratifying to hear that my little book has also been well received [in Hungary].

Strangely enough, nobody has yet taken any notice of Part II of the Well-tempered Clavier, which includes discussion of some things for which I found neither the space nor the occasion in the Aesthetic.

[1]Strauss conducted a programme of his own works at the Tonhalle, Zurich, on 29 and 30 January 1917. The programme was:
   Also sprach Zarathustra
   Burleske. op. 17 (soloist, Vera Schapira)
   Don Quixote
[2]Straussvogel (or Strauss) = ostrich.
[3]The four concerts had taken place on 12, 17 and 26 January, and 2 February. The two latter concerts were entirely devoted to Liszt.

229 TO JOSE VIANNA DA MOTTA
in German

[Zurich] 21.3.1917

[. . .] Your opinion of the Improvisation [on 'Wie wohl ist mir'] pleased me immensely. Which of the pieces listed on the back page do you *not* know? And which of them would you like to know? The Goldberg Variations have now been published separately in a (cheap) four-language edition. –

The Lisbon idea seems to be promising, worthy and appropriate for you.[1]

It is not easy to suggest a composition teacher. But, should an opportunity present itself, I would like to draw your attention to my 25-year-old assistant *Philipp Jarnach*. A Spaniard by birth, educated in France, German in outlook, he has a very rapid mind and great clarity in understanding and planning. He has helped me, prepared the vocal scores of both operas, which he is also going to rehearse with the singers; as, at my instigation, he has been engaged by the Zurich Stadt-Theater. A string quartet and a violin sonata of his have been played,[2] an orchestral work is on the programme for the next symphony concert.[3] – He is also very fond of 'theory' and often elucidates my own works to me. He speaks perfect French and cultivated German. – Voilà Philipp! (Is a skilful pianist.)

Why don't they consider Emile Blanchet in Geneva? He is the most interesting Swiss piano connoisseur.

I must have *absolute* rest for a while, and therefore your visit would be most opportune.

[1]da Motta had been invited to Lisbon as director of the Conservatoire and conductor of the symphony orchestra.
[2]Jarnach's Violin Sonata, op. 9, was played at the Tonhalle, kleine Saal, by Lidus Klein and the composer on 16 November 1916. A performance of his String Quartet no. 1 is untraceable.
[3]On 26 and 27 March 1917 Jarnach conducted his Zwei Orchesterstücke at the Tonhalle.

230 TO JOSÉ VIANNA DA MOTTA
in German

Zurich 13.4.1917

Thank you for taking so lively an interest in my libretti.

To save you a disappointment, I would like to assure you 'vorneweg'[1] (as they say in Leipzig) that I have *refrained* from so-called 'orchestral jokes' (in the Straussian sense, for instance). I have been at pains to write as comely and durable a score as possible. For music remains what it is, untouched by the coincidences of life, even if sometimes, depending on the situation to which it is applied, it *can* in certain cases make a comic effect. – (The text, moreover, has a certain element of seriousness: – particularly the disregard for the tragedies of life.) The hotch-potch of German and Italian is intended as a parody, indeed the Italian translation will have to *dispense* with this piquancy! – The general objection that natives of Bergamo are speaking German here could be applied to every opera:* to Schiller's Don Carlos and Maria Stuart, Shakespeare's Othello and Merchant of Venice. – Is it not clear in my Arlecchino that I am poking fun at 'theatre' itself? If not, then this is indeed *my* fault and a greater one than you mention.

I needed to write these introductory words and almost fear that I should have had something of the sort published.

It now looks fairly certain that the first performance could be scheduled for the first week of May: you are of course very welcome to attend the *dress rehearsal*.

*which plays somewhere else.

[1] = in advance.

231 TO JOSÉ VIANNA DA MOTTA
in German

[Zurich] 15.4.1917

My letter was not intended as a *reproach* but rather as self-justification.

Diverse people, as I have already been able to observe, react diversely to my Arlecchino. – There would be less dissension if they were to take the first four lines of the rhymed introduction to heart,[1] and the two last lines.[2]

At any rate, thank you for your thorough assessment of my bagatelle, of this not dramatic but 'theatrical' capriccio.

The two works are united by the title 'La nuova Commedia dell'arte', which refers to the reintroduction of the Italian mask figures into the action.

To have quoted 'Dante' in translation would have been even more improbable and less striking; but the Italian aria is an illustration of the 'operatic tenor', who strains his lungs only in this style. Of course the manner is humorous. But Arlecchino's words are just as seriously intended as, on a monumental scale, those of 'Don Quixote', and the scene with the windows and the inquisitive, apathetic faces is not exactly amusing and unfortunately quite true.

Naturally the music remains the main thing, for this is my standpoint with regard to opera.

[1] 'The play's not meant for gods and not for minors,
   Its message is for adult heart and mind,
   Its words not à la lettre, but combiners
   Of hidden things, where he who seeks will find.'
[2] 'In mirrors does the little world diminish,
   And living truths as metaphor do finish.'

232 TO HANS REINHART
in German

Zurich 15.4.1917

Sincerest thanks for your kind words about my two theatrical bagatelles.

Your essay on Wagner–Uehli[1] is clearly constructed and thought out and, as far as this goes, deserves my respect!

But I am no more a Wagnerian than I am a Christian, and I feel that the time may have come to do away with both of these terms – or at least to leave them in peace and not mess them around.

Wagner's gods leave me cold and I consider 'Tannhäuser' – with the exception of the overture – to be a weak, sometimes even vulgar work; – while Wagner's *scores* are a guiding light and instruction to musicians, Wagner *on the stage* is – in my own (entirely personal) opinion – a composer for non-musicians, fundamentally untruthful and actually boring.

Here you will have to make certain allowances: particularly my Latin origin and the general adherence to his school of thought throughout my life, which weighed heavily on me.

I cannot understand how a nation which is blessed with 'Faust' and 'Nathan [der Weise]' (and even Hebbel's 'Nibelungen') can take Wagner seriously as a poet and subsequently read so much into him. In my (still personal) opinion, Uehli has arrived a little too late and is meddling – in the hope that he might find a resonance – with our 'progress forwards and backwards'.

On the 19th I am playing a more significant programme here.[2] [. . .]

[1]Ernst Uehli, *Die Geburt der Individualität aus dem Mythos. Erlebnis Richard Wagners als Künstler*, Munich, 1916–17. Hans Reinhart had reviewed the book for *Individualität*, a short-lived anthroposophical journal.
[2]This was a recital given for the *Gegenseitige Unterkunftskasse jüdischer Studierende* at the Tonhalle, Zurich, the principal items of which were Beethoven's 'Waldstein' Sonata and the complete 'Italie' from Liszt's *Années de pèlerinage*, including 'Venezia e Napoli'.

233 TO HANS REINHART
in German

[Zurich] 17.4.1917

If someone commits themselves to the Wagner cause with so much heart and soul as you do, then one can only bow out respectfully. However, I would warn you against prematurely considering oneself fully developed. Life is boundless and cannot completely be grasped by any one person. Every new day is one experience which cannot be shared with – the dead – and already therein, we are at an advantage over them.

I hope to have the pleasure of 'Der Schatten'[1] before too long.

[1]See letter no. 336.

234 TO EMILE BLANCHET
in French

Zurich 13.5.1917

I am sorry to hear that you are ill, although your 'nevertheless pretty strong' reassured me a little. Your continued absence from Z[urich] – justified (eloquently) by your convictions – is no less regrettable . . . for all of us, and particularly so for me. – Tutto il mondo è paese,[1] one finds fault everywhere and also – if one so wishes – good things. Every nation considered 'en masse' is unsympathetic (yes, every one of them), yet each country produces its chosen few.

For this one (chief) reason, it would seem sad to *change* one's nationality, as it could never be proved that any particular one were, as a whole, preferable to any other. For this reason I have *not* assumed Swiss nationality: to which you can 'give the lie' in Paris; (should any significance be attached to it). It is enough to have been born with one's nationality imprinted on one's body . . .

You see that the little truths of my Arlecchino represent my beliefs . . .! Its theatrical début, incidentally, was very successful;[2] there is a further performance this evening and again on Tuesday or Wednesday.

I wish you good luck for the new life in Paris upon which you are embarking, and a splendid follow-through in your artistic existence. Embrace master Philipp[3] for me – embrace everybody –.

'Diesen Kuss der ganzen Welt.'[4]

Finally the warmest embrace for you.

[1]'All the world's a village', Goldoni, *La vedova scaltra*, Act I scene 1.
[2]The world premières of *Turandot* and *Arlecchino* had taken place at the Stadt-Theater, Zurich, on 11 May 1917.
[4]i.e. Isidor Philipp.
[4]Taking his cue from the French 'tout le monde', Busoni quotes Schiller's 'Ode to Joy'.

235 TO JOSÉ VIANNA DA MOTTA
in German

[Zurich] 29.5.1917

[. . .] 2 days ago I began to write out a 'major' edition of Liszt's Fantasy on Don Giovanni. It is a real pleasure to be able to talk of L. and Mozart at one and the same time.

On the other hand, I had to restrain my bitterness in order to refute certain statements of *Hans Pfitzner*; he has slandered me and my Aesthetic with a stab in the back, entitled 'Futuristengefahr'.[1] – You should be receiving the pamphlet and my reply to it in a few days. – Germany is always turning out lesser Martin Luthers, men who seem, in the people's eye, bold reformers but who are basically quarrelsome, rigid sectarians. – You can make up your own mind about the business.

[1]*The Danger of Futurism*. Pfitzner published his attack on Busoni's *Outline of a New Aesthetic of Music* in the *Süddeutsche Monatshefte*, May 1917. Busoni's reply, an open letter to Pfitzner in the *Vossische Zeitung*, was published early the following month (and later reprinted in *Von der Einheit der Musik*).

236 TO HANS HUBER
in German

Zurich 4.6.1917

It was so good of you to demonstrate your sympathy even on this insignificant occasion. I could well have replied in quite different tones to our Herr Doktor of the Munich Festwoche[1] (which will bring us no 'Neueste Nachrichten'),[2] but had I wished to make a rude assault, I would have had to become abusive, which in turn would have implied *his* victory. He is entirely unjustified in his argument that, in criticizing the catchwords 'musikalisch' and 'tief', it had been my intention to instruct and educate the Germans. The situation is quite the reverse. It is I who, since my childhood and even as a mature man, have continually been receiving instruction, and any copyist, any provincial beer-drinker could and did assert his superiority over me and intimidate me with those two words. I experienced a similar fate with the vogue-word 'Gefühl', and they succeeded in labelling me as a man 'of intellect but no soul'. No, they could not win an unconditional victory, you are right. Now you will better understand my revolt against Suter's canonization of Reger; I had nothing against Suter and scarcely anything against Reger: I was opposing a principle which I had hoped that the Swiss were sufficiently un-German not to support. With all respect to the greatest of the Germans, the mediocre ones feed on their catchwords and say, with herd instinct, 'wir'. 'Wir halten durch'[3] is the latest.

The fourth performance of my pieces took place on 31 May with excellent success. Now I am working at a major, critical-instructive edition of Liszt's Fantasy on 'Don Giovanni', in which I refute several ideas. I expect to come and hear your symphony in Basle[4] and look forward to both music and company. The concert is on Saturday, isn't it? [. . .]

[1]Allusion to the Pfitzner Festival in Munich, 11 to 18 June 1917, which included performances of *Der arme Heinrich* and *Die Rose vom Liebesgarten* as well as the world première of *Palestrina* on 12 June.
[2]Pun on *Münchener Neueste Nachrichten* = Munich latest news, a daily paper.

³'We shall hold out.'
⁴A performance of Huber's Symphony no. 7 in d, which took place on 9 June 1917 (cf. letter no. 242).

237 TO JOSÉ VIANNA DA MOTTA
in German

[Zurich] 20.6.1917

[. . .] Apart from Paul Bekker, the 'Signale' and the 'Wiener Tageblatt' have spoken out *against* Pf[itzner] – I enclose a review of his opera. – I have written and sent off an extended foreword to my major edition of the Don Giovanni Fantasy. – Let me know when you are leaving – I can hardly bear it. When you have gone, there will be nobody apart from Hans Huber with whom I can discuss music intelligently. This is not only a musical question but also a matter of human loyalty and fellowship. – Petri is becoming increasingly distant, geographically too. (I can do nothing about his pedalling; but I think, even if it is wrong to write such pedal markings down, in practice one could well make use of them.) Jarnach is faced with having to make a decision. – While I would be loath to lose him, this would be insufficient reason to block his path.

Altogether, the thought of spending yet another winter here dismays me a little. I had summoned up my composure and energy with a certain approximate maximum duration in mind, and this has been stretched still further. Now even these reserves are beginning to dwindle. For me personally, Switzerland has practically nothing left to offer.

Therefore it is in new work that I am seeking diversion from irksome and futile thoughts. I have begun to have ideas for my 'chief work' and want to have accomplished it by the autumn (or Christmas) of 1918. By that time I shall be no more than 52 and can still hope for a cheerful coda to life.

In the end I shall visit you in Portugal at some point! If this were possible 'without playing the piano', I could enjoy pleasant (unclouded) times.

238 TO PHILIPP JARNACH
in German

[Zurich] 20.6.1917

[. . .] Despite your ingenious arguments, I would warn you against wishing to set a

'Weltanschauung'

to music, in the sense that the commentators on Pfitzner mean it. To be quite honest, I have never fully comprehended the concept, and I see even less how music can express it.

'The Barbarians' (says my Abbate in the original version of Arlecchino) 'are the nation of music and philosophy.' – But when you jumble the two together, the result is that grey art which, as music, fails to satisfy the musicians and, as philosophy, does not come up to the expectations of the philosophers (while the reverse is true).

To live for and to love humanity, which was Beethoven's chosen goal, fulfils the ethical requirements of the notes: 'Trance' as contrast to
'Existential norm'.
This is even further removed from the essence of our art: for is music not in itself dreamlike and only tangible through its actual sound? – [. . .]

239 TO PHILIPP JARNACH
in German

[Zurich] 21.6.1917

'Das Wandbild'[1]

I have drawn up the first rough sketch for a scenario and have come to two important conclusions:

1) The first scene – *for the sake of a palpable distinction between the real and the unreal* – should not play in the Chinese temple but, for instance, in an antique shop in a modern city. For this, I had a milieu in mind such as that of Balzac's 'La peau de chagrin'. The priest should be the antique dealer, the young people Parisian students viewing the curiosities.

2) *The unreal* should chiefly be represented by
'Pantomime'.
Perhaps *only this section with music*; the prelude and postlude spoken.

Thus we could come a good deal closer to the possibility of – and indeed the justification for – creating a dramatized version.

I have already sketched a synopsis on three pages of this size; so drawn up that one could translate it into theatrical terms without any particular technical difficulties. But it is not yet sufficiently polished to give you to read.

In the meantime you could write and tell me what you think of my efforts, or call in person.

[1]On 19 June 1917 Jarnach gave Busoni a copy of Martin Buber's *Chinesische Geister- und Liebesgeschichten* (Frankfurt, 1911), suggesting that one of these brief Chinese stories could serve as source material for an opera. Busoni set to work at once and completed *Das Wandbild*, a scene and a pantomime, on 27 June. Jarnach abandoned the project after composing the Prelude and first scene. The work was eventually set to music by Othmar Schoeck.

240 TO EGON PETRI
in German

Zurich 5.7.1917

[. . .] You are – sans comparaison – just like my beloved St Bernard dog, who will never offer a paw on demand but affords all the more pleasure when he gives one of his own free will.

Your plans, like everything you do and think, are clear and well organized. Yes, I was on the right track when I translated Zakopane as 'sack of bread' (sacco – pane) – and I hope you get the butter as well.

It was a relief to read that you derive some satisfaction, in retrospect, from the Bach Edition (this, too, was one of the predictions in my 'Fantasie sur le Prophète).

Following on from this Fantasie sur le Prophète, I am able to announce that I have committed the long-intended 'major' edition of the *Fantasy on Don Giovanni* to paper (and the post has conveyed it to Leipzig). [. . .] – It consists of a detailed foreword, dual musical texts (vertically aligned) and 30 footnotes. It is being published as the *first instructive* edition of Liszt, and hence assumes the significance – for us pianists – of the 'classicalization' of Liszt's pianistic style.

I have sketched out the synopsis of a 30-minute mime for my friend and pupil Jarnach (with whom you would certainly get on well).

This (as well as a few additions and improvements to both of the operas) is all that I, in my relatively exhausted state, have achieved since 31 May; the day on which my operas received their 4th performance, one of improved standards and greater effect. – (I have not seen the Signale review of it). –

Now I am slowly approaching the work which I consider to be my future 'masterpiece'.

I have only to attend to one further 'volume' of the Bach Edition, which is rather unexciting but must nevertheless be done (?). (The collection of 25 makes a fine impression.)

Otherwise I am demoralized and somewhat impatient and I yearn for change, for a great, definitive scheme, for freedom of movement, for the great cities, for clarity and finality. I am scarred all over by the countless amputations of my deeds, wishes and hopes. Now perhaps you will have come to understand how unjust that letter of yours to me in America really was! – I am banking on a new impulse in my work, so that I shall need to look neither right nor left.

241 TO PHILIPP JARNACH
in German

[Zurich] 16.7.1917

I would like to acknowledge receipt of the manuscript of 'Das Wandbild', which followed your letter. – I am delighted that you were just as pleased with the libretto after having read it through several times. Let us call the piece:

'A Scene and a Pantomime'

You already have the opening bars of it? The ice has been broken! – For the religious chant I would recommend you to have a look at old Oriental melodies. Something of this kind – even if one does not use it note for note – always helps to get things started. The chorus of girls would perhaps have to begin and end dispersedly, becoming more concentrated towards the middle. – Now (already two days ago) you had 30 of the 50 pages of the Ritterspiel[1] on paper, today there will be 35. Today is 16 July. Thus: du courage, et toujours en avant.

Nikisch and d'Albert have now also raised their low- and high-pitched voices against me.

---

[1] Jarnach's 'Prolog zu einem Ritterspiel' was first performed on 1 and 3 December 1918 in the Tonhalle, Zurich, conducted by Volkmar Andreae.

242 TO EGON PETRI
in German

Zurich 10.8.1917

[. . .] This time there has been no halt to the flood of Zurich 'appearances'. Once the Stadt-Theater had closed its doors (the last performance, on 31 May, was devoted to my operas), *Reinhardt* moved in to make a guest appearance[1] and he was followed by the Viennese operetta, led by the 'original' composers in persona.[2] A 'major' Swiss art exhibition[3] remained open throughout the summer; there was an associated exhibition of the works of *Hodler*, about 450 pictures.[4] This was the first Swiss art manifestation which created any sort of impression and revealed a splendid fellow. – Meanwhile the Stadt-Theater has resumed work and is performing, as first novelty of the season, H. Huber's 'Belinda and the monster'.[5] In June there was a festival of Swiss composers in Basle, at which Huber's 7th (new) symphony sounded vigorous and brilliant. He is now working at an 'eighth': Mors et vitae, with texts taken from the Bible.

Finally, this summer we also experienced the world première of 'Morgen' by Hans Ganz (a brother of Mr Ganz in New York).[6]

[. . .] Apart from working a little at the Bach Edition, I have written out the score of the orchestral introduction to my new stage work[7] and sketched out the scenic introduction itself. Now I am to transform myself into a pianist again, bringing on a fit of nausea, as in the case of Dr Jekyll. (Only that opinions differ as to which part of me is Mr Hyde.)

Insel Verlag has written to say that the polemic against my little 'Aesthetic' has had a

'very profitable effect'
and the little book is now going into its second impression.

[. . .] Alice Landolt, Rita [Bötticher], Prof. Ludwig Gurlitt,[8] my particularly valued friend Ludwig Rubiner, Wedekind and many kind, celebrated people are gathered here. At the present moment Z. is a prominent city. Nevertheless——!

[P.S.] da Motta has returned to his home country.

[1]The Deutsches Theater, Berlin, played Hauptmann's *Rose Bernd*, Strindberg's *Ghost Sonata*, Kotzebue's *Die deutschen Kleinstädter* and Büchner's *Dantons Tod* between 9 and 16 June 1917.
[2]The Theater an der Wien performed operettas by Léhar, Leo Fall, Oskar Straus, Oskar Nedbal, Heuberger and Johann Strauss between 5 and 29 July 1917. The works of the first four above-mentioned were conducted by their respective composers.
[3]13th Swiss Art Exhibition, with contributions from all over Switzerland, which ran until 31 July.
[4]Ferdinand Hodler, 1853–1918, Swiss painter noted for his monumental symbolic realism.
[5]Hans Huber, *Die schöne Belinda*, first performed in Berne in 1916. The Zurich production opened on 11 November 1917.
[6]Hans Ganz, *Der Morgen*, tragedy in 4 acts. The world première, as the final event in the guest appearance of the Deutsches Theater, took place on 26 June 1917.
[7]The Symphonia of *Doktor Faust*. Busoni's manuscript full score is dated Friday 13 July 1917.
[8]Ludwig Gurlitt, 1855–1931, distinguished German pedagogue and educational reformer.

243 TO JELLA OPPENHEIMER
in German

Zurich September 1917

I feel compelled to write to you; without having withdrawn from society, I sense that I am becoming progressively more isolated. It is noteworthy that very many of the men who took refuge here have remained aloof, have not fraternized with each other. Nevertheless I know that there are individual and estimable personalities amongst them, who remain isolated. I do not have many pleasures. I am attempting to maintain my cherished contact with the young, but numbers have to be limited; I have abstained from wine, I enjoy it no longer and yet I miss it. I love to rummage in old book-stores – but by now I know every one of them, and the dealers are receiving no new deliveries from abroad.

I now yearn for travel, which used to cause me so much suffering; but only to great countries and cities. This yearning cannot be stilled. Of my old ways, I most sorely miss my library – where I found something to occupy me every day – and my evening strolls in the hurly-burly of the great city.

There remains nothing but to work incessantly, which I find indispensable, but would be even more pleasurable and productive with the aid of all the above-mentioned – presently unavailable – forms of inspiration. This is my personal standpoint. I know that other good (and better) spirits require different working conditions: of all these, I have never felt or experienced the need for 'loneliness'; although this in particular is often associated with being a genius (which I am not).

I am tired of waiting, and the approach of another autumn is humiliating me. I had quite nicely completed the round of my Zurich activities – and now I find it sickening to have to set the wheel in motion once again.

My *'work'* is now under way – but I am no monk, who constantly contemplates the same tree through the window of his cell – and writes and writes. Nevertheless, I am glad to have this companion – the growing opera – with which I can occupy myself daily while it continually takes shape under my hands.

1 October

The above lines must be one month old. [. . .]

In the meantime, the *first scene* of my stage work has been completed in fair copy. Now there is a return to the 'Clavier' (i.e. the W. Cl.) The operas are also to be revived here in November; as well as this I have promoted 3 concerts of my own works during the same period.[1] [. . .]

[1] In the event, only one such recital took place (see letter no. 246), on 6 November 1917 at the Tonhalle, Zurich, in which Busoni played nos. 1, 2 and 4 of the Elegies, the first Sonatina and the Sonatina ad usum infantis, the *Fantasia Contrappuntistica*, *Indian Diary*, Zwei Tanzstücke and the *Fourth Ballet-Scene*, op. 33a.

244 TO EGON PETRI
in German

Zurich 5.10.1917

[. . .] A letter, which I wrote quite some time ago and in which I asked you to be so kind as to send me the alterations in my second Elegy, remains unanswered.[1] – Today, in meteorological reckoning, is the first day of autumn, following a month of uninterruptedly brilliant weather. One has to interpret this as gradually leading to a new spring. For a whole year, likewise, I had enjoyed good health, until two weeks ago (when I had a violent attack of influenza). I am still recovering from it.

Despite this – and other hindrances – I have been working hard. Above all, the score of the first scene of my new stage work is complete![2] – I have embarked on a *study*-work for piano, which will in time be finished off.[3] – I arranged the little Albumleaf, which you liked, for piano solo.[4]

– I still have expectations for my life and art; but the catchword is: courage, keep your head held high; swallow your own bitter pill: – and this is something which I am only now really learning, and it is this which comes to all of us. [. . .]

[1]The letter was dated 11.7.1917.
[2]Vorspiel I of *Doktor Faust* (one cannot help noticing that Busoni *never* mentions the title of the work at this stage) was completed on 29 September 1917.
[3]The *Klavierübung*, first published in five books, which appeared between 1918 and 1922. Book I is dated 10 October 1917.
[4]Albumblatt for flute and piano (dated 1916), which is also to be found in the opera *Turandot*, where it serves as Altoum's second aria.

245 TO VOLKMAR ANDREAE
in German

[Zurich] 7.10.1917

I shall have several matters to discuss in the Tonhalle tomorrow, including the programmes, and it will become clear whether I can perform a Mozart concerto, and also which one.

Dr Giesker, whose letter I enclose, is actually right, and the work in C minor is one of my personal favourites.[1]

And Mozart is altogether terra incognita; for how much is known and played of all his 650 works? While not a single bar of Dr Johannes, for example, is overlooked, whether for clarinet or – contrabassoon!

If I can find the time (which I shall soon know) to study the C minor concerto and compose cadenzas for it, then I shall be happy to do both these things.[2]

[1]Busoni had made his concerto début with this work, at the age of 9, in Trieste.
[2]The cadenzas were written in 1918 and Busoni took the concerto back into his repertoire as from 1919, when he first played it in St Gallen.

246 TO EGON PETRI
in German

Zurich 20.11.1917

[. . .] Your odyssey over dry land drew a wry smile from me; your comments about the experiences in Berlin provoked a less cheerful reaction. I am quite furious about the aggravating tone of the critics there, but would be just as unwilling to surrender – under the same circumstances – as ever; (there is, moreover, nowhere to throw the sponge) – were you, however, at last to make a public appearance as a *composer*, your piano playing would henceforth be held above reproach.

Meanwhile you have found another outlet for your creativity and this too is fine and gratifying. – The German papers are treating me no better: that Teutonic genius H. Pf[itzner] is never mentioned without an accompanying passing shot at me:

'und der Schuljung auf der Schulbank
lernt zugleich die beiden Namen'[1]

as Heine sings so grimly – (sans comparaison) – of Christoval and the impertinent Cortez.—

Meanwhile my intended trilogy of concerts has been reduced to a single recital of original works.[2] (The first of this kind on my part).[3] The success was exceptional. [. . .]

In the meantime: the circle narrows continually, inspiration must repeatedly be drawn from one's own vital parts; just as if one had to gnaw at one's own arm for want of other nourishment. – On the other hand, a crowd of distinguished people is once again assembled here, making Zurich a centre of unaccustomed character and interest. – On the 24th there is to be a perform-ance of 'Palestrina'.[4] Whole hordes of people have been granted travel permits for a purpose such as *this* . . . The affair seems to have been particularly well organized. And once again I shall involuntarily be given a part to play . . . Vitzli-putzli! –[5]

Three passages in your letter had been carefully scored out by the censor. – I suppose it is about time to wish you a happy Christmas – ?[6]

[1]Heine, *Romanzero*, Book One, Historien, 'Vitzliputzli', 1, v.3. Actually:
Und der Schulbub auf der Schulbank
Lernt auswendig beide Namen –
(And the schoolboy at the school-bench
Memorizes both the surnames –)
[2]cf. footnote to letter no. 243 (recital on 6 November 1917).
[3]i.e. in Zurich. Busoni had given recitals of his own pianoforte works in Basle (1910) and Milan (1913), to mention only the two most prominent.
[4]There were two performances of the original Munich production of Pfitzner's *Palestrina* at the Stadt-Theater, Zurich, on 23 and 24 November 1917 (also performances in Basle and Berne). The tour had been organized by the propaganda department of the German Foreign Ministry, led by Harry Graf Kessler.
[5]Reference to the Heine poem quoted above. Vitzli-putzli, 'Mexico's blood-thirsty God of War' eventually emigrates to Europe and works in league with the Devil.
[6]Petri's previous letter to Busoni had taken a month to arrive.

247 TO EGON PETRI
in German

Zurich 1.3.1918

Your letter of 18 February arrived only yesterday. I opened and read it with great joy and thanks – even if it also disquieted me. Your activities are now manifold; you are making yourself useful and giving pleasure to many. Should I, as an old, honest friend, conceal something from you? At the risk of your misunderstanding me, let it be spoken: in your letter I find a lack of opposition and of suffering, of an idealized sense of purpose. Nowhere does one find a comment on art or life; but I refuse to consider this opinion as final, as you yourself have – instinctively – drawn my attention to the deceptive nature of this one letter.

You really shouldn't bear such a grudge about the 'Bach Edition'. It is winning you – as far as I can ascertain from here – a great reputation and does more to make your name than a concert in Lodz, for instance, even with its excellent (and long-deserved) newspaper reports.

The only literary experience you mention (after a lengthy period of time) is L. Franck's [sic] book.[1] I admit: he is a fine person, the author I mean; but his book? I have an aversion to this new species of literary fruit, produced by factory workers turned artist. – And these anti-war orisons irritate me no less than the jingoistic ones: the inversion of a theme is still an imitation of it, and the beginning of a sunrise has a fatal similarity to the end of a sunset.

I was delighted to hear of your mother's visit and of the high spirits of your dear family. What is the name of the youngest child? And what sex? Could you forget to mention such important news!!

Benni has been called up but not yet exempted. I can tell you no more about it, for it would strain the calm elegance of my epistolary style. – Our esteemed colleague Ernest Schelling is established in Berne as a 'Captain' (cf. Arlecchino) and military attaché. – Here there are many men of letters, including Werfel (yet another German poet): all of them are people with a sense of purpose and great culture. (Franck is also amongst them.) In Berne (at my concert) I was able to see high-ranking people, from countries hostile to each other, sitting side by side.

---

[1]Leonhard Frank, 'Der Mensch ist gut', in *Die Weissen Blätter*, Zurich, 1916, subsequently published in book form, Zurich and Leipzig, 1917. Described by the author as a 'radical, directly effective manifesto against the spirit of war', the book was immediately banned in Germany.

248 TO HUGO LEICHTENTRITT
in German

Zurich 31.3.1918

Today, on this 1,918th Easter Sunday, your splendid letter arrived. Much of it interested me in that it referred to dear old Berlin. – The musical news was no longer unfamiliar to me. Now everyone is tossing the word Futurism around. It is being used to cover everything that one cannot otherwise categorize. The word is self-contradictory. Fundamentally it has to do with bewilderment – the briefest manifestation of sensibility – and should be called: Momentarism. Judging from your description, Schnabel's experiment[1] belongs to this category. – Those who dedicate themselves to and give themselves up to Futurism are throwing out all past achievements and thus impoverishing themselves. The main point is: we must enrich, we must refine our means of expression; not build castles in the air but rather on solid ground, on powerful foundations.

Those works which are compiled exclusively from new experiments must be considered as *studies* and should be further utilized for the real work, which reaches out in all directions. I have prepared myself in this way and accordingly, in the last few 'conscious' years, it has been my ambition to carry out this plan. – Thus, when I publicly proclaim this confession, people will be disappointed; but meanwhile our narrow-minded Dr Hans's[2] catchword continues to have its effect, and I am unable to play a C major chord without having people fall into paroxysms of Futurist hysteria!

In the meantime I continue to work and, once again, some things have been finished. – I have had scanty news from my son, but nothing directly disturbing (although quite absurd in the situation it creates for him.)

[1] A reference either to Arthur Schnabel's String Quartet No. 1 (composed in 1918, published in 1927) or to his hour-long Sonata for solo violin, the first movement of which was published in 1920 in *Melos*.
[2] i.e. Hans Pfitzner.

249 TO VOLKMAR ANDREAE
in German

[Zurich] 3.4.1918

I have written a brief concerto for clarinet and small orchestra[1] (6 wind instruments) for your excellent Allegra,[2] and have the following request: would it be possible and would you be prepared to give me half an hour with the orchestra in the last week of April in order to play the little work through?

It would be important for me to hear the work before it is printed. [. . .]

[1]Concertino for clarinet and small orchestra, op. 48.
[2]Edmondo Allegra, ? – ?, principal clarinettist of the Tonhalle Orchestra and dedicatee of several original works and arrangements by Busoni. On 28 September 1918 he played in the world première of Stravinsky's *Histoire du soldat* in Lausanne.

250 TO HANS HUBER
in German

Zurich 9.4.1918

[. . .] I looked up my Paul,[1] which I happen to have here, and read that Strindberg refers to a play unknown to me, 'Das Band', which he intended as an opera, in which context he mentions my name.[2] Adolf Paul is a former pupil of mine from Helsinki in 1889, older than his teacher, and in Berlin he attached himself to Strindberg. I myself never met Strindberg in person, sadly, perhaps just as well. A. Paul is Swedish, not Finnish. With the 'schoolboy' Sibelius[3] and the Jaernefelt brothers[4] we formed a lively coenaculum. We called ourselves the Leskovites, after my Newfoundland dog Lesko. In my eyes, Strindberg has already been through three phases: at first he disgusted me, then he fired me with enthusiasm and now I am beginning to sense his weaknesses more painfully. But with his unique Dreamplay and the chamber-plays he gave theatre after Schiller and Ibsen a new physiognomy, which I could not say of anyone else. – I find his lingering on and penetrating into 'les petites misères' of everyday life, and a certain artistic carelessness in his form and feeling, disagreeable (the latter is said to be less evident in the original Swedish). As with Voltaire and Heine, I detect in him a great longing for love, goodness and beauty, and inward rage at eternally finding these qualities lacking in human beings. [. . .]

[1]Adolf Paul, *Strindberg-Erinnerungen und Briefe*, Munich, 1914.
[2]In a letter dated 21.6.1894, Strindberg suggests that Paul should make a libretto for Sibelius, suggesting *Das Band*. In his next letter, dated 25.6.1894, he writes: 'What do you think of Das Band as an opera? Busoni can read it in French at – ? – Unter den Linden!'
[3]Sibelius was in fact four months older than Busoni.
[4]Armas Jaernefelt, 1869–1958, composer and conductor, and his youngest brother, Eero, who also studied music.

251 TO GERTRUD DRABER
in German

Zurich 21.5.1918

[. . .] I did not quite understand why Hermann,[1] as an artist, should come to me with the essay by A. Paul: unless it was that he was submitting it to me as a wartime curiosity. Paul is 'badly brought up' in the German language; but I thought that life had taught him greater firmness and conviction. Enough! To be an artist one needs character, and then more character and (only in *third* place) talent! – Goodness knows, I would have composed E. T. A. Hoffmann's 'Der goldne Topf' if I had not already done his 'Brautwahl'. There is, moreover, so much music in Hoffmann's text itself that the introduction of audible sounds would have been bound to be disturbing. Where music of supernatural effect is described, actual music can never be its equal. Apart from which it would afford too slight a contrast within the opera itself. (I don't know if I have expressed this clearly.) It is – a comparison I once drew – as if one were to feed hens on eggs. [. . .]

I hear almost nothing from Petri: – which is nevertheless more of a comfort than hearing depressing news.

[1]i.e. H. W. Draber.

252 TO HANS HUBER
in German

Zurich 30.5.1918

Due to a misunderstanding which can indirectly be blamed on the war, the Klavierübung is being published without the intended preface.[1] By no means did I wish to devise possibly curious but unplayable piano figurations. The unfortunate pupil would blame his own lack of ability, run amok and sprain his fingers. For this reason, the transposable examples should only be taken so far as to avoid unnatural hand-positions. Therefore you will find nothing particularly striking, while on the other hand everything in the book, particularly the fingerings, is drawn from my experience. I am planning at least four such volumes (the second is already in preparation), so as to achieve a complete entity, but fear I shall not attain the universality desired of this study-work. The Fantasy on Don Giovanni is, I believe, the first attempt to present an analytical edition of Liszt. I have taken the greatest pains to write down everything observed during years of study, not a single note has been overlooked. The German translations are my own, they correspond more closely than their predecessors to the original and to Mozart's intervals and rhythms. It seems to me that this exceptionally difficult pianistic problem has been solved almost effortlessly, or am I mistaken? In the coming days will follow a Sonatina in diem nativitatis Christi,[2] a little Christmas piece, and therewith you have the entire harvest for 1917. Please accept all this with grace and, if possible, with joy.

The 8th and last performance of my operum theatrali[cum] took place on the 24th. The concerto for clarinet and orchestra was rehearsed on the 10th. These events wound up my 'season'. The summer calls for the completion of several works in progress, meanwhile I am relaxing until 1 June into a pleasant holiday spirit, brought about by the weather and the natural pause in my work, but not supported by any other circumstances. For it is as if I were standing at the mouth of a long, dark passageway, which I am supposed to enter, but which leads I know not where. Does it lead back to the light? A grave moment! Before this holiday is over, the answer to this question will have emerged. For what is your opinion of a further extension of my sojourn in Switzerland? It would occur at that moment in my life, after the development section, where the basic tonality should be re-established. But a new motif in the coda? Counts as an exception, as my old teacher Rémy used to say. [. . .]

[1] The preface was eventually published with Book 3 of the *Klavierübung* ('Lo Staccato') and was dated July 1920.
[2] Sonatina in diem nativitatis Christi MCMXVII, completed on 22 December 1917 and dedicated to Benvenuto Busoni.

253 TO H. W. DRABER
in German

[Zurich] 1.6.1918

At last I enjoyed once again the pleasure of hearing from you. Some weeks ago I had the opportunity of replying to Frau Gertrud. On your instructions, she sent a dubious creation of Adolf Paul's, in which the 'principal characters', personally known to me, were of interest and alone enabled me to read it. – Today you tell me – also through the no longer unusual medium of a feuilleton – about Carl Hauptmann. How fortunate, how enviable he is!

To be able to wander along in the spring-fever of his 60 years and pluck masterpieces from right and left! – (But not to wake up or to test oneself:—— that would be dangerous.)

Here too, I know someone to whom everything falls from heaven – sometimes nothing but rain – sometimes rain mixed with ammonia . . . according to the climate of his creative disposition.[1] The Goldne Topf is not filled with such fluid: I had implied this in my letter to Frau Gertrud. Why should you not attempt your scenario? (My only fear is that the story itself has too many musical motifs . . . as does Klein Zaches . . . it would mean feeding hens on eggs – the error of the 'Meistersinger' – of the 'Sängerkrieg'[2] – and, raised to its highest power: the error of all those opera libretti which introduce a composer's life-story on stage.) —— Schumann sinks into the depths of insanity, composes Clara Wieck who rises out of a trap as the 'Träumerei'; curtain. In Act Two they play piano duets (because neither of them can play a piece on their own), and from the nostalgia of this four-handed Romanticism arises the first glee-club chorus of Goethe's Faust. Each of the four hands plays one part of this male-voice quartet . . . and so it goes on until we come to our contemporary, Dr Hans! –

Heaven forbid that you should think me malicious! Rather consider how good-natured I remain in my outbursts; the times, the times must be taken into account! [. . .]

My great work is maturing. Thus – now that the express train of life has been transformed into a hand-cart, thanks to the providential goodness and perspicacity of fate, we are filled with grateful admiration to see that one wheel still manages to turn. –

Our guardian angels are vigilant. Your letter has all the colours of the chemical bath in a pretty mottled pattern, green, yellow and cerise. Almost like end-papers. Do you know my Albumleaf for *flute*? – Do you hear anything of Petri? [. . .]

[1]This is probably intended as a slur on Pfitzner (cf. the end of the paragraph).
[2]i.e. *Tannhäuser*.

254 TO HUGO LEICHTENTRITT
in German

Zurich 21.9.1918

Thank you for your kind and informative letter. I was particularly cheered by the news of yourself you included and I hope that the 'Sicilian' will make his way to Darmstadt and prove himself there![1] – Have you introduced any new material into your 'Formenlehre', or is the book appearing unaltered?[2] I would have liked to discuss this with you. I am becoming increasingly convinced that musical forms feel the *need* to be moulded adjustably, according to content and motif; just as a building, according to its given purpose and terrain.

Schopenhauer, I recall, writes somewhere that a dog's head is elongated and therefore beautiful because its body is also formed horizontally. – A *text book* on form implies for me only a *history* of form, an enumeration of available examples and prototypes. – A warning should be printed at the bottom of every page: just as this master here found a form for his idea, so should you seek the only one for your idea. – What do you think of this point of view?

I have only very personal news. I am working, thank goodness, with good results. Three days ago I was able to count the 1,500th bar of my new stage-score. That means about half of the whole work. The way I write, however, this makes no guarantee for the second half, as I make no use of leitmotifs and always have to stand anew before closed doors, which only inspiration can open. But I feel quite optimistic about completing it.

[1]Hugo Leichtentritt's comic opera, *Der Sizilianer*. It was not performed at Darmstadt; the world première took place on 28 May 1920 at Freiburg.

[2]Hugo Leichtentritt, *Formenlehre*, Leipzig, 1911. He was at work on a revised edition, which was published in 1920.

255 TO OTTO KLEMPERER
in German

Zurich 26.9.1918

Your letter of the 21st was a pleasing complement to our recent agreeable chat; but the favourable outcome for my operas came as a surprise and was on that account no less welcome.[1] My warmest thanks and my blessing for the enterprise. – [. . .] Meanwhile my next work is making good progress and is thus half way to becoming my 'latest'. – Here – as is so often the case – a Mozart score will provide a new stimulus; therefore I am particularly indebted to you for kindly sending me 'Così fan Tutte' (So kann's nur Einer')[2]. –

Judging by your description of his artistic abilities, Herr Clemens[3] will certainly be suitable for 'Arlecchino'. The character should combine *impudence* with a lithe *gracefulness*. It is – incidentally – no 'buffo' role; rather (as you said) a 'buffone', i.e. 'fool'; but this, however, in the Shakespearean sense. – I am pleased to hear that the 'mutes' prove effective in 'Der Freischütz'. I once called for sordini at the close of the overture to 'A Midsummer Night's Dream'; they imparted an effective weightlessness to the distant echo.

May you take further pleasure in a constantly new approach to our beautiful musical heritage. The works you mentioned are also my favourites.

Thus we are perfectly in agreement with each other.

[1]Klemperer had arranged to perform *Turandot* and *Arlecchino* at Cologne, where he had recently been appointed First Conductor. The first night took place on 26 January 1919.

[2]'Only one can do it', play on the German translation of *Così fan tutte* = So machen's Alle. From *Conversations with Klemperer*, compiled and edited by Peter Heyworth, London, 1973: 'Before 1914, *Così fan tutte* was almost unknown. When I saw Busoni in Zurich in 1918, I discovered to my amazement that he didn't know the work at all. I sent him a score and he wrote that he had "lapped up the music".' Clearly, Busoni did not express himself in these terms; nevertheless there are some echoes of *Così* in the score of the opera *Doktor Faust*.

[3]Hans Clemens, 1890–1958, buffo tenor. Began his career at Cologne in 1912; from 1930 he sang at the Metropolitan Opera, New York.

VIII

1918 – 1920
Zurich in Peacetime

TO MARCHESE DI CASANOVA
in German

Zurich 3.11.1918

I read your letter with sympathy and I respect your convictions.

However, you know how little I care for Wagner and his <u>World Champion,</u> the young Siegfried.

I have never understood the meaning of Hebbel's Siegfried, whose superiority over his comrades lies in his being able to throw the heaviest stone the furthest.

Indeed I have difficulty in understanding 'sport'. Rules and fouls – man as adversary to man – I find such things distressing. And I would even question the penal system, which does nothing to prevent crime and does more to hinder people's independence than to protect them.

At the risk of your smiling at my 'Olympian naïvety', I would go so far as to state that Germany, as a democratic state, will flourish anew. Not as in the United States, ignorantly familiar, respectably religious, persecutors of the Negroes and exterminators of the Indians. Not as in Switzerland, limited to petty cantonal horizons – Germany will give the word to those select, cultivated minds who have until now had to remain silent.

Even the Germans should no longer be rallied and then forced to their knees by flying colours and glittering helmets, they will demonstrate their greatness in other ways.

To live in such hope should strengthen and revive the spirit of every Germanophile – amongst whose ranks I do not unconditionally number.

257 TO VOLKMAR ANDREAE
in German

Zurich 1.1.1919

[. . .] The little gift dedicated to you[1] is all but ready; indeed I intend to have the piece ready for the rehearsal on the 14th. But I would like to warn you in advance that the somewhat unusual scoring calls for the following: 3 flutes, one oboe and *two* English horns, 3 trombones and a contra-bassoon; harp and celesta, 3 timpani, tamtam and bass drum.——The normal strings.——

I would like to pair the Sarabande with a related work, the as yet unperformed 'Gesang vom Reigen der Geister', a sort of chorale prelude on a Red Indian theme. These two short works, both entirely *un*-brilliant and contemplative, represent my most individual style. The score of the Reigen calls for solo flute, oboe, clarinet, trumpet, trombone, timpani and a bassoon. One could attempt to use solo strings as well. That would make a
'Duodecimet'!
Meanwhile I have been appointed President of the Republic of San Marino. My seat of government is in the Scheuchzerstrasse: electrical cables connected to the piano keys transmit commands to my kingdom by finger-tip control. My maiden speech was the Intermezzo of Mascagni: – I shall gradually begin to sound an individual note as well. But first the people must be diatonically prepared.

[1]*Sarabande* for orchestra, op. 51.

258   TO HUGO LEICHTENTRITT
in German

Zurich 5.1.1919

Your kind New Year's letter, which I have just received this morning, brought me good cheer, far more on account of the writer than of what he has written. In fact he himself sounds cheerless; and with a heavy heart I must acknowledge the causes and effects of his mood. At least it arrived here *without censorship*! That, at least, eases matters somewhat. – You have ideas and plans: the Formenlehre, a violin sonata, an opera, the Klagelieder. – That gives you enough to work on for a long time. – I still have my reservations about the Formenlehre which – I believe – I have already mentioned to you.

If only you could give your book a title such as: 'A handbook of musical forms up to the beginning of the XXth century' – then I would understand such a work. I consider it erroneous as a composition text-book. The older I grow, the better I learn to differentiate between strengths and weaknesses; but I also come to see more clearly that good cannot come of repeating that which is already extant and concluded! That it is, in fact, impossible to repeat anything. How do you want to set about it? – It is certainly your intention to open your violin sonata with a movement which doesn't remind one of anything familiar. And so things must go on, with the same independence. –

I am also coming more and more to think that music must impart to us a beautiful game.[1] We have Beethoven to thank for having introduced bad temper into music. – That might sometimes be appropriate for him, but it is essential that we come away from this attitude. This is how I feel *today*, but please do not confuse 'beauty' with frivolity. (Let us not forget Mozart.)

Therefore, at a time when I am intensively battling my way through to a reaction of this kind, I cannot welcome your project for the Jeremiah-Lieder as a godsend. There is no need to depict the coda to the war as a satyr play, if one is not so inclined; but . . . does one really have to relate one's work to the war at all?! Do you perceive in the works of the Renaissance anything whatsoever of the many terrible things which occurred while they were being written? Such things happened at a later date, when the events had become legendary and could be artistically manipulated by deployment of forms. – Moreover, people are in need of cheer and encouragement, they must regain their confidence. This can be achieved, if not through religion, then through the arts; and of the arts, music. – These comments are entirely impersonal and not intended to dissuade you from doing what you feel or see to be necessary. On the contrary: I congratulate you on the profusion of your plans, rejoice at your creative urge. But: such productivity must put you yourself in a *good mood*, and that is how your works should sound.

——I have something of a harmless superstition which causes me to write a short piece at the turn of every year. This year was no exception and I wrote a Sarabande for small orchestra. It belongs to the series of the Berceuse [élégiaque], the Nocturne [symphonique] and the Reigen der Geister, which I shall call Elegies for orchestra. – My old contract with Br. & H. has expired. I would like to see a catalogue raisonnée of those of my works which are published in Leipzig being written and published. I have mentally been designating you for this task and passed on the idea to Br. & H. – It would be good to publish at Easter. – What do you think? [. . .]

Let us wish for constancy and clarity, in and around us.

[1]Orig. schönes Spiel.

259 TO HANS HUBER
in German

[undated][1]

I generally begin my working day by writing letters, and your kind postcard affords me the welcome opportunity of addressing my morning thoughts to you. [. . .] Is your information about my so-called great success based on Bekker's letter in the Frankfurter Zeitung? I was not very pleased with it, it teems with incorrect assumptions and conclusions and claps me only too benevolently on the shoulder. It would not cause me to revise my opinion of critics. Enough that it has made a favourable impression on the public, as I have been more or less able to observe. My two little operas are intermezzi in the theatre and also in my creative life, they should not be understood as a final achievement. My next work, whose poem can be read in last October's issue of Die Weissen Blätter, should assume other proportions. Unfortunately

I possess no spare copy of it, otherwise I would have taken the liberty of dedicating one to you. – Apropos dedications: the second book of the Klavierübung is engraved and ready for printing, a third has been inaugurated. A fifth sonatina on a small theme of Bach has also been completed.[2] My new score has already passed its 1600th bar.

Have you already seen the programme for the Tonhalle concerts?[3] There have already been complaints, requests and rectifications concerning the sequence, nobody is entirely satisfied with the choice. For the first 4 concerts I have consciously excluded living composers, the 5th concert is a sort of extra programme; Saint-Saëns, at the age of 85, no longer counts as contemporary. Did you know that the repertoire extends to about 500 playable piano concertos? Only a few days ago I heard of two by a pianist called Zimmermann[4] who, in his day, was greatly admired in Paris and was also Alkan's teacher.

And while on the subject of new musical acquaintances, I would cite, from the last few months, above all the score of Mozart's Idomeneo. This work, written at the age of 24, surprised and astonished me. Absolutely youthful in its virility and maturity, an abundance of original ideas, orchestration (with 4 horns and 3 trombones) which is phenomenal for its time and even today still amazing. Those of us born in the middle of the 19th century have been incorrectly educated: it would have been shameful not to know a work of Beethoven's but no discredit to ignore a masterpiece of Mozart's. Now I am turning progressively away from the former's sulky seriousness and perceiving more and more the great seriousness of the latter, which is actually superior, behind its serenity. At a time when much is changing, the symbolic and legally enforced cult of Beethoven should be restrained within its fair limits. Are you angry with me?

[1]The letter in the *Frankfurter Zeitung*, mentioned in the first paragraph of this letter, which was a review of *Turandot* and *Arlecchino* at Cologne, dates this letter around the end of January or the beginning of February 1919.

[2]Sonatina brevis. In Signo Joannis Sebastiani Magni. The work was completed on 19 August 1918 and dedicated to Philipp Jarnach.

[3]A series of concerts illustrating the history of the piano concerto; 25 February 1919: Bach in d, Mozart in c K.491, Hummel in b op. 89; 11 March: Beethoven no. 1 in C, Mozart in A K.488, Beethoven no. 5 in Eb ('Emperor'); 25 March: Schumann in a, Mendelssohn in g op. 25, Weber *Konzertstück*, Saint-Saëns no. 5 in F; 8 April: Brahms no. 1 in d, Liszt no. 2 in A, Rubinstein no. 5 in Eb; 29 April: Liszt *Totentanz* (original version), Busoni Concerto. The conductor was Volkmar Andreae.

[4]Pierre Joseph Guillaume Zimmermann, 1785–1853, a pupil of Boieldieu and Cherubini and friend of Fétis. Gounod was his son-in-law, his pupils included Bizet, César Franck and Ambroise Thomas.

260 TO VOLKMAR ANDREAE
in German

Zurich 1.2.1919

[. . .] The suite from the music for Idomeneo[1] is to be performed in St Gallen on 6 February. As for the *Gavotte*, I was uncertain for a while whether or not to insert a piece in F or G major between the two movements in D major. Both were unsuitable and the 'Opferhandlung'[2] emerged triumphant. Perhaps a second concert suite could also be arranged from the Idomeneo music. – The *Cortège*[3] has advanced as far as its 'Stretta', which will occupy me for a few more days. The score calls for *two* harps. If the second one presents difficulties, we can find an expedient. But a 2nd harp should also be useful at the close of Strauss's Don Juan. This Don Giovanni, who is almost senile in Gräner,[4] sadly begins to show his age in the Strauss. Nevertheless I shall look forward to hearing it again under your vigorous direction.

It seems a matter of course to me that your name should also adorn the Cortège. I hope you agree.

[1]In 1918 Busoni made a three-movement concert suite from *Idomeneo*, which he dedicated to Othmar Schoeck.
[2]'Ritual sacrifice'. From Act III of *Idomeneo*.
[3]*Cortège*, op. 51, for orchestra. The companion piece to the *Sarabande*.
[4]*Don Juans letztes Abenteuer*, opera by Paul Graener (sic), first performed at Leipzig on 11 June 1914.

261 TO HUGO LEICHTENTRITT
in German

Zurich 27.2.1919

[. . .] So you too have now come to recognize that 'greed, stupidity and wickedness' are the moving forces in the whole of world history! (Which is why I have all my life been apathetic if not hostile to reading history books.)
Fortunately you are also able to find an 'isolator' in work and you deserve to be congratulated for this achievement (which has reaped a rich harvest). – Bravissimo. – Since your last reports, the Formenlehre is beginning to arouse my interest. The day before yesterday I played the first in a cycle of piano concertos, which is to consist of 5 concerts. (I. Bach, Mozart, Hummel.) – In the Adagio of the Bach concerto I again spotted a form which is unique to him, is to be found in several instances in the Book II Preludes of the Well-tempered Clavier and which has never since been employed nor – I believe – taught. It generally consists of the quadruple (this time sextuple) reiteration of an 8–12 bar formula which appears harmonically and melodically modified

at each appearance, but which runs through without a middle-section or development. – If you have not yet incorporated it in your Formenlehre, then permit me to draw your attention to it. – Examples in the W. Cl. II are the Preludes in F – F♯ – A♭ (and A) – which I expounded – I believe – accordingly.

The chief object of this letter was to mention this.

262 TO H. W. DRABER
in German

Zurich 9.4.1919

[. . .] Your letter has helped me to attain a certain perspective, but not enough to draw a conclusion. – I consider two things important for further progress in music. First of all: many experiments have been made in this young century; now, from all our achievements – older and newer – it is time to form something *durable* again. This is my own goal. *Accomplished creation* and the *joy* of making music must come into their own once more. There has been too much brooding and melancholy and subjectivity. Also unnecessary noise. Uncommon things – says Schopenhauer – should be expressed with common words, and not vice versa. Hence: Mozart and Goethe. –

Secondly: one should everywhere avoid (but not necessarily disavow) *narrow-minded*, bourgeois nationalism (provinciality).

For this the moment, particularly in Germany, is inopportune. – For the rest, each person should try his best on his own behalf, without relying on groups or communities; then everything would be more genuine and honest. These lines have not been written fortuitously and improvised on the spur of the moment as an answer to your letter, but are the matured outcome of personal reflection. – In Berlin they would in the end be disappointed with me. I have grown tired of everything unpremeditated! –

Now I must thank you for so kindly remembering my birthday – (the enclosed news-cutting[1] tells you how it was celebrated here) – and the news of Richard Strauss's willingness. – I hope to have Doktor Faust ready by 1920–21. Do you know the libretto?

---

[1]Enclosed was a cutting from the *Neue Zürcher Zeitung* for 4.4.1919, a review of the Tonhalle concert on 1 April which included performances of Busoni's Violin Concerto, the Concert Suite from *Idomeneo* and the world première of the *Sarabande und Cortège*, op. 51.

263 TO VOLKMAR ANDREAE
in German

[Zurich] 11.4.1919

Is this coincidence or self-recollection?:

Brahms Concerto no. 1 Andante[1]

Brahms Concerto no. 2 Andante

[1]Busoni had performed the Brahms Concerto no. 1 in d with Volkmar Andreae at the Tonhalle, Zurich, on 8 April.

264 TO HANS HUBER
in German

Zurich 13.4.1919[1]

I do not doubt that it was a matter of intuition with Liszt. Incidentally, he used liturgical chant as a poet, not as a researcher. When I visited d'Annunzio in Paris, he was working on his drama La Pisanella;[2] on a shelf stood a whole little library of books about the history of Cyprus, the island on which the play is enacted. In three of these books, just one page was marked with a paper strip. A characteristic phrase on one of these pages sufficed for him to grasp enough of the atmosphere of the country and period for his purposes, he never read the rest. – An antithesis: in Geneva lives Professor M., art master at the Academy. In his own student days there, he was directed to paint a picture of a watchmaker's workshop for his final examination. Whereupon M. disappeared for nine months, and only the registry retained any record of the business. However, at the end of the year, M. reappeared with a portfolio bulging with sketches, several hundred sheets, on which the minutest components of a clock had been individually studied and copied. He never painted the picture. – I believe that Liszt rather worked like d'Annunzio. Why do you marvel at this particular facet of him, that of Gregorian chant?[3] Did he not take possession of everything from Bach to Bellini, from Schubert and Weber to Wagner, did he not adapt the folk-melodies of every land in the appropriate spirit? Why should he stop at

Gregor? After all, he remained a Catholic, and Rome was his dwelling place. – [. . .]

[1]Busoni's dating of this letter, '13.A.19', led Edgar Refardt, the Swiss editor of the letters to Hans Huber, to ascribe it (and the following letter) to August instead of April.
[2]Gabriele d'Annunzio, *La Pisanella ou la mort parfumée*, a lyric drama. First performed in Paris, 12 July 1913.
[3]Huber was at work on his oratorio *Mors et vitae* and, for this purpose, had been studying Liszt's *Christus*.

265 TO HANS HUBER
in German

Zurich 22.4.1919[1]

How nice of you to think of me on Easter Sunday, actually it is my birthday, for in 1866 1 April fell on Domenica di Pasqua, a highly flexible birthday, which this year has made me all of three weeks younger. Although it concerns me directly, I have never entirely understood the method of calculation, which evidently shifts the day around quite irregularly. – Wolfrum[2] is in the Engadine. He sent me the proofs of a foreword to Liszt's sacred works[3] and, as this discusses in detail the question about Liszt which was recently on your mind, I have asked Wolfrum to send you the essay in Vitznau. You will certainly find it interesting, if unsurprising . . .

[1]See footnote to previous letter.
[2]Philipp Wolfrum, 1854–1919, conductor and musicologist. From 1907 he was Generalmusikdirektor in Heidelberg. He died on 8 May 1919.
[3]Vol. III of the incomplete Liszt Edition, Breitkopf und Härtel.

266 TO HANS HUBER
in German

Zurich 31.5.1919

In Basle there was an uncut performance of the St Matthew Passion, a work whose content is in places monumental, but whose form is a frieze, indeed an elongated frieze, not even a ring, almost like a wall-paper pattern with the design: chorus, recitative, chorale, aria. In this frieze, the aria is the crippling, desanctifying moment, the pedantic bigot's passing comment, and indeed, so offensive is the disharmony between these texts and that of the Gospel, that I am amazed at the absence of any protest against them. The arias themselves also follow a fixed pattern. Consider the process: each aria opens with an introduction, usually with some fortuitously chosen solo instrument; the first four bars of this introduction are often fine inspirations, but they are extended and spun out sequentially through the circle of fifths. The content of the aria as a whole is thus already exhausted at the very outset. Now the voice enters, generally in the manner of the inner part in a keyboard fugue: the variants are astonishingly diversified but in fact lacking in proportion, giving the sense of a development ad infinitum. As I see it, a complete performance of the Passion without the arias would have a striking effect, a dramatic saga with great expressive power and a theatrical heartbeat. For such a version, the chorus involved in the action would have to be separated from the one which prays the chorales, visually too: the Testament and the Congregation. What do you think of the idea?[1]

Your unqualified appreciation of my little Klavierübung pieces has rendered me confused yet grateful for so much intense sympathy. Now I shall continue gladly. My concern for your state of health was painfully stirred by the news of your sufferings at Vitznau. I presume that you have been restored to good health; it seems to me that you long for the South, physically and spiritually. Were it not for the Italians, or were they otherwise disposed, I would invite you to move to Rome with me, so that we could produce a few good works and enjoy much beauty together. But now, with neither Man proposing nor God disposing (if they call *that* proposing and disposing, then so much the worse), one has no option but to crawl back into one's own house like a snail.

---

[1]In 1921 Busoni published an 'Outline for a scenic performance of the St Matthew Passion', reprinted in his book *Von der Einheit der Musik*.

267 TO ALICJA SIMON
in German

[Zurich] 20.7.1919

[. . .] I failed to thank you for [. . .] the little Keller book. Please forgive me and permit me now to thank you kindly. – In return, I would like to tell you a little about my mother, who as a girl was much admired for her looks and her piano playing, and is believed to have been born in 1833 (for a long time we thought it was 1835) in Trieste. There she studied the piano with *Lickl*[1] (an Austrian) and composition with *Ricci*[2] (a Neapolitan, who wrote the opera 'Crispino e la Comare',[3] which is my *first* memory of the theatre). Her father, who was born in Lubljana, was of Bavarian extraction; his father was a gilder and painter; we possess a life-size Madonna in pastel colours by him. My grandfather was a great man and an original, of whom one could tell many a tale. His name was Josef Weiss, that of his daughter (my mother) was Anna. She had one brother and one sister. Her brother, who showed great promise as a painter, became mentally disturbed at the age of 20 and lived until his

48th year in an asylum. The sister died an early death of consumption. Her two daughters still live in Trieste (fit as fiddles).[4] – I enclose the beginning of the song which my mother wrote. I find it very high-spirited and quite Italianate. More another time.

[1]Aegidius Karl Lickl, 1803–1864, Viennese pianist and composer. He settled in Trieste in 1831 as musical director.
[2]Federico Ricci, 1809–1877, composer of nineteen operas. He was a pupil of his brother, Luigi, and of Bellini.
[3]*Crispino e la comare*, with a libretto by Piave, was first performed in Venice in 1850. Written jointly by Federico and Luigi Ricci.
[4]Their names were Ersilia and Carolina Grusovin.

268 TO VOLKMAR ANDREAE
in German

[Zurich] 10.8.1919

I was very pleased to read your card, from which it transpires that you are satisfied and that the concert performance of Faust is in principle a fait accompli. If only I had 'accompli' my part of the score, I would already be with you! – But I am nearing my goal and my feet have been lent little Mercurial wings by the imminence of the journey abroad, speeding things along. (This is my nature: the quieter things are, the less creative I feel.)

Even if only as a document, I should like to record the fact that the performance, which at present is only theoretical, would last about 1¼ hours. The programme would include: Vorspiel I and II, the intermezzo and a study for the last scene; all in all four items. The score calls for 5 horns and 2 harps, a *virtuoso organist*, trumpets and horns off-stage, bells. – A reciter. – A thunder machine. – A large chorus.
Singers: *in Vorspiel I*
                Faust – baritone
                Wagner – bass
                3 students (small parts)
      in Vorspiel II
                Faust
                Mephistopheles (high tenor)
                Six separate spirit voices
                3 solo womens' voices (invisible)
      in the Intermezzo
                Gretchen's brother (tenor-baritone)
                Faust
                Mephistopheles
                Lieutenant (tenor, small part)

Sketch for the final scene (Serenade)
  Wagner
  Mephistopheles ([off-stage] voice)
  Students (chorus and solo voices)

I visualized Milner[1] for the role of Faust, he is co-operative and has a resonant voice. The vox diabolica is a problem – and the organist? – The bells will be ready.[2] – (Thank heavens we don't need a prima donna.)

How does all this work out in practice?

I have written to Cosomati[3] about the publication of a libretto for the concert programme.

[1]Dr Augustus Milner, 1884–?, American baritone. He was a member of the Zurich Stadt-Theater ensemble from 1915 until 1920 and sang in the world première of *Arlecchino*.
[2]Busoni had ordered three bells, inscribed with the names of Gerda, Benvenuto and Raffaello, from a bell foundry in Aarau. They were intended for the closing pages of Vorspiel II.
[3]Ettore Cosomati, 1873–1960, Neapolitan painter who later settled in London. He produced some fine designs for *Doktor Faust* which were, however, never used in a stage production.

269 TO EGON PETRI
in German

Zurich 7.9.1919

[. . .] Your letter took 13 days to get here, just as long or even longer than one from America: therefore I shall answer it straight away, especially as I shall be leaving in 11 days for a sojourn of several months in England. This will be my first attempt to fly, after 4 years of immobility.

As for Switzerland, I shall support you in everything you wish to undertake. Write to Dr Volkmar Andreae immediately. – I always regretted that, at the time when R. Freund left Zurich, you were not here to take over from him. Instead, a man was hastily assigned to the post, who is most estimable and reliable, but . . . . .

It is now 3 weeks since our friend 'Theodor'[1] turned up. He appears to want to settle here. You can picture the rest yourself.——In a word, you would have found everything here that you have in Zakop. and more besides. Everybody of renown has passed through; many 'stranded' people had settled here, interesting people too. Amongst them were Lenin . . . . . . R. Rolland, Paderewski . . . . Recently Rilke and Wassermann paid me a call.

Meanwhile life here has been treating me increasingly kindly; my work, influence and reputation have been developing constantly, culminating in my being appointed Doctor hon.c. by the University of Zurich on 30 July. – 2 fragments from Doktor Faust have already been performed;[2] they signify my greatest success as a composer. About half the entire score is finished. – Benni is at last making his way from New York to France, free and healthy, having gone through trying times and been separated from us for 4 years: – separated in every sense, except our inner inseparability. –

[. . .] You were right to turn down Vienna. –

(I still don't know what my final decision will be.)

[1]Presumably Theodor Szanto.
[2]i.e. *Sarabande und Cortège*, op. 51.

270 TO EDITH ANDREAE
in German

Zurich 17.9.1919

[. . .] Two salient points have now been clarified: *tomorrow* I am leaving on my first new European expedition, to England; and my son Benni has, after four years, at last arrived in Europe! –

Further decisions about my future are undefined, even for me; but I hope to find enlightenment and orientation from the impressions and observations with which I shall be consciously confronting myself. In my heart of hearts I am strongly attracted to the idea of Berlin, the only place – except for Italy – which finally comes into question: if I do not opt to remain in Switzerland, to which – despite my many obligations to this country – I am the least inclined. (In the end I have been awarded an honorary *doctorate* here.)

The decisive factors are neither ambition nor financial considerations. But *the* convincing offer has not yet been made; it would have to be definitive and guarantee sufficient artistic scope. – Intimations of such things have come to my ears from various sources, but nothing conclusive.

Thus your letter is a warmly gratifying human document, which did me good and for which I thank you sincerely (it will help tilt the balance of my decision), but it alone does not yet motivate me to act on your kind appeal.

If you – and my 'countless admirers' – still expect anything from me and place so much trust in me (which I am immodest enough to believe), then you should find me the opportunity to give you what I can, in living conditions of relative tranquillity. – I thirst for this, have need of it, deserve it. And time is pressing. – My Doktor Faust is maturing. – I have many things in mind; and other things, too, would come to fruition, given the chance and the suitable conditions. –

If you see anything in this which could interest you, then think things over a while. You see how seriously I have taken your letter.

271 TO VOLKMAR ANDREAE
in German

London 26.9.1919

This letter will find you in the midst of rehearsals for your symphony; musical life begins sooner in Zurich than in London, for here nothing has opened yet and, when it does, there will be little of interest. Superficial high spirits and disquieting agitation beneath the surface – incurable sorrow on the part of a third, smaller group – serve to ensure that nothing gets done or is taken seriously: except for difficulties with passports and customs regulations. Otherwise Heine, and you yourself in Ratcliff,[1] have described the scene so vividly that the words retain their validity even today.

Thus one gathers that London has not changed – outwardly, at least: – Paris, on the other hand, has in certain matters changed beyond recognition. – There it is like a company on board a pleasure boat tossed by a storm. At any moment the mast might break, but the people continue to dance around it. Compared with this, the so-called general strike in L.[2] is like a cheerful peace celebration.

Only the bread is incomparably better in Paris; I had forgotten what it is to eat good bread, and heartily enjoyed the delicious white loaves! – I seem to have forgotten many other things, unfortunately, including: enjoying myself unreservedly. – But perhaps this, too, will return, and at Christmas you will find a smiling cosmopolitan, in whom however you will always be able to recognize your

truly grateful friend
F. Busoni.

[1]*Ratcliff*, opera by Volkmar Andreae adapted from the play by Heine. First produced at Duisburg on 25 May 1914.
[2]There was a railwaymen's strike in England, which lasted nine days.

272 TO PHILIPP JARNACH
in French

London 5.10.1919

How sorry I am that you are not here! Not for you, but for me. Just as I have seen nothing new, so you too would see almost nothing new, but would help me tolerate this absence of novelty.

You can scarcely imagine how everything has deteriorated here, as in Paris; how base and mean the world has become – or (more likely), how these qualities have become apparent, have risen to the surface – the masks have fallen.

Everywhere the outlook is indifferent and narrow-minded; in the end: the only concern is for security and sustenance, just as in prehistoric times. I have the good fortune to be living in the middle of Regent's Park, where Maud Allan[1] has offered me the pleasure of her generous hospitality. But it is solitary and monotonous so far from the centre. The dawn is always charming, the view over the majestic trees, turned to gold by the autumn sun, is heart-warming. – But the evenings are wretched; they vanish into dark silence during interminable hours; at such times there is an air of inactivity; just as if it were a play by Maeterlinck. –

Outside, far away, everyday life has an intensity I had forgotten: a huge sum of tiny existences. –

A book by A. France is offering me pleasant diversion, amusing and thought-provoking by turn. It is a selection of old feuilletons, published in four volumes with the title: La Vie littéraire.

France is magnificent when he attacks Zola; more agreeable when he is content gently to philosophize. –

As neighbours here we have a colony of *blind war-veterans*, which I find more repellent than moving. – They are admired! – (How despicable.)

There is nothing to report about music. It is altogether poverty-stricken and second-rate.

The strike is oppressive.

I repeat: how sorry I am that you are not here. I am afraid of forgetting myself – one cannot listen to oneself. The 'elements' of our conversations in Switzerland are unknown here. I believe they think I have deteriorated. –

---

[1]Maud Allan, 1883–1956, celebrated dancer. She was a piano pupil of Busoni at Weimar in 1900. Busoni was often her guest at West Wing, Regent's Park.

273 TO VOLKMAR ANDREAE
in German

London 6.10.1919

I neither expect nor ask for a reply to my chatty letters, but beg your leave to send one now and then. – Today's is prompted by my having been informed of your Tonhalle programmes, which I read with an interest necessitated by my relationship to Zurich. On the whole you are making better music than the Londoners. – I see that your popular concerts, which were planned as international events, have become quite the opposite. The white cross shines on its red background! – It shines indeed on 3 and 4 November, and I shall be truly sorry to miss your symphony.[1] [. . .] On 2 February the Bach family is resplendent. – (A few days ago I purchased here a history of music by the Englishman Hawkins, in 5 volumes, from the 18th century. I was stunned to read how little was known of J. S. Bach at that time: he is only briefly mentioned, and then chiefly as an organist.) Then there is a rush of more recent composers: Tchaikovsky, Mahler, Hausegger, early R. Strauss, the problematic introduction to Tannhäuser – here nevertheless outdone by Leonore No. III. Then however comes Schoeck's 'Ratcliff'[2] – a printers' error. – [. . .]

[1]This was the world première of Volkmar Andreae's Symphony in C, op. 31.
[2]Othmar Schoeck: Eine Ratcliff-Ouvertüre for large orchestra, composed and first performed in 1908. It is unpublished.

274 TO VOLKMAR ANDREAE
in German

London 14.10.1919

You entirely misunderstood my remark about *Leonore No. III*! Certainly, I expressed myself most clumsily. What I meant was: these more recent composers (Tchaikovsky, Mahler etc.) are still surpassed by Leonore No. III, outdone, overshadowed. – Is that now clear? (I really am not demoralized.) I admire this work unreservedly. (As well as the Mass and the sonata [op.] 106.)

On the other hand, I still insist – despite your historical and biographical note – that the *'Ratcliff Overture by Schoeck'* is a misprint. I wrote this last word quite consciously. I could give several reasons for so doing; but to write them down would require an inordinate amount of space and finally result in further misunderstandings. – [. . .]

What a pity that I shall be unable to hear Berlioz's Faust! I really am sorry. For this is a work with *talent*. Don't laugh. I mean it quite seriously. – The same also goes – to a lesser extent – for Sibelius's 1st symphony. –

I never cease to be astonished that the Swiss have so entirely neglected their most celebrated musician – Joachim Raff. – A Swiss explained that this was so because Raff is dead. 'You see,' said the Swiss, 'Raff is dead, which means that he can't perform our works. So there is no point.' I swear to you that a Swiss expressed this to me in these very words, and that this is no malicious composition of my own invention. – For, truly, at present I cannot even compose malignities. In fact I am playing the piano and as I have, so to speak, got into my stride, I shall be happy to do the same in Zurich on 27 January.

275 TO VOLKMAR ANDREAE
in German

London 21.10.1919

I had not been expecting your reply: I regret having repeated myself with regard to Raff. Would dearly like to perform his *Giga con Variazioni*;[1] a work which used to please me. (Not out of spite, for on the whole I share your point of view.)

I can say, with some satisfaction, that my London recital was surprisingly successful.[2] The beginning was quite moving: I had to rise from my seat three times before I was able to begin. – I am only mentioning this because this little bright spot contrasts so strongly with the general musical mist with which I am surrounded and in which I have to grope! (Oh yes.)

Szanto would never 'swear' about somebody. He would say, with an indulgent shake of the head, 'What a shame about this fellow Andreae, he is so kind and talented . . . . .' (and break off with a gesture of hopelessness). – At least, this is how he *used* to behave when I was a closer friend of his. It is possible that he has improved, for he too has had a full taste of life – and so I am unable to say anything further about him, particularly in writing, than – that he caused me considerable grievance at the time. (But perhaps he too has suffered.)——

I would ask you to treat even this, however, as 'confidential'.

I am very sorry not to have been present at the presentation of the works of Schoeck and Brun.[3] On the whole, however, I dislike hearing the scores of new works played through on the piano. It is *more* but also *less* fruitful than is *actually* the case. One is deceived and, as a member of the audience, personally captive and not free. I feel so strongly about this that I could not even bring myself to perform my own works in this way. – But this is neither here nor there. I would have given anything to have heard Liszt, when he performed *Gretchen* from the Faust symphony to his intimate circle. – I also have the best artistic recollections of the afternoon devoted to your new symphony. – And with joy I recall the performance of *Ein Heldenleben* by Strauss himself in Berlin,[4] with R. Freund and myself as sole spectators. But I reject the so-called 'improvisation' which usually creeps in and takes control on such occasions. – I hope I have not expressed myself contrary to my intentions again, as I recently did in the case of the Leonore overture! Yes, even a language is an instrument that is difficult to play and, if one has no full command of it, one must handle it with the greatest of care.——

In the last few days I have been writing cadenzas for Mozart's C major concerto [K.467]. Today I have already begun to think out a plan by which the concerto in E♭ major [K.482] could bring forth similar fruit. – In March I shall be giving six concerts in Paris, two of them with the Orchestre du Conservatoire, a third, dedicated to my own orchestral works, with the Association des anciens Elèves; the whole project is solemn and dignified, partly supported by the Ministry. – Two days ago I was in *Edinburgh*, which was as impressive as ever. I was reminded of Ratcliff again and – of the misprint, hence also of you.

[1]From the Suite no. 4 in d for piano, op. 91.

[2]The recital took place at the Wigmore Hall on 15 October 1919. Busoni played the Prelude and Fugue in C from Book I of *The Well-tempered Clavier* and an abridged version of Bach's Goldberg Variations, Beethoven's 'Hammerklavier' Sonata and a Liszt group, which ended with the *Don Juan* Fantasy.

[3]Fritz Brun, 1878–1959, Swiss composer.

[4]This took place on 29 December 1898, as can be deduced from a letter which Richard Strauss wrote to his parents on the same day:

> Dinner with a well-to-do American lady, Mrs Codman, where Robert Freund from Zurich, the pianist, is currently staying; . . . Pauline [Strauss] sang, Busoni and Freund played etc. The two latter joined me today for a stag lunch, as Pauline has been confined to bed since yesterday . . . 'Heldenleben' will be receiving its [first] performance in Frankfurt . . . on 3 March.

276 TO ALICJA SIMON
in German

London 22.10.1919
On a 'yellow' foggy morning.

Your letter of the 8th in Italian, for which I thank you kindly, is lying in front of me on the table. [. . .]

'Malanno' means a calamity or misfortune or even 'une mauvaise dance', but not 'Katzenjammer',[1] for which there is no word in Italian. [. . .] One still occasionally becomes aware of this hung-over feeling, but it is *occasionally* also absent. Its causes are generally *external*, at times when I have absolutely no desire for it, for instance as a result of the 'Melba Concerts' or the benevolent notions of my bear-trainer, generally called an impresario, who then takes on the function of pink elephant.

I actually paid £3 for the Hawkins,[2] i.e. 75 Francs; on the other hand I got an Italian edition of Virgil (Traduzione d'Annibal Caro) in two volumes,[3] imperial folio, as good as new and with large, beautiful engravings, for just £*1*. – Yesterday I found – next door to Queen's Hall – an even older English book about music – do you know it? – It's called:

A Treatise / of / Musick / speculative – physical – historical /

By Alexander Malcolm / Edinburgh / Printed for the

Author 1721. (15 shillings).[4]

'Musick is a Science of *Sounds* whose *End* is *Pleasure*'
[. . .] I have difficulty in imagining the pleasures of English *musick* in 1721, but the principle seems to me to be correct. I said (in my book): the aim of music is the reproduction of human feelings through the medium of notes, according to artistic principles.

On the 15th I attempted to play according to these guide-lines, and it would seem that my playing had just such an effect. This review (Daily Mail) is one of the strongest that has ever been written about me; therefore I am enclosing it.[5]

[1]= hangover.

[2]Sir John Hawkins, *A General History of the Science and Practice of Music*, 5 vols., London, 1776. Busoni bought a copy of the First Edition. (See letter no. 273.)

[3]Busoni bought a luxury edition printed in Rome 1819 for the Duchess of Devonshire.

[4]Alexander Malcolm, 1685–1763, scientist, clergyman and musician. His *Treatise* runs to 608 pages, with musical examples. Hawkins praised it as 'one of the most valuable treatises on the subject of theoretical and practical music to be found in any of the modern languages.'

[5]R.C. (Richard Cappel) wrote in the *Daily Mail* on 16 October 1919:

[Busoni is] far and away the greatest musical executant now with us; a commanding figure – more, a well-nigh awful one; a maker of music that is tremendous and statuesque; a steely and terrible power that regularly cowes you as you listen, leaving you almost too humbled to admire.

277 TO ALICJA SIMON
in German

London 28.10.1919

[. . .] I have completed a concert-edition (with some licence) of the Rondo-Finale from Mozart's E♭ concerto [K. 482].[1] As it now stands, it is a brilliant piece (<u>little science and much pleasure</u>).

This work gave me the rare pleasure of observing how a '<u>climax</u>' was gradually built up from a piece which I had originally disparaged. At first I considered it too light-weight a counterpart to the sublime minor-key Adagio. But now I have come to admire the instinct with which the listener is drawn back out of those depths. It had gaps in it (evidently passages which had not been worked out); a cadenza was called for; two transitions were completely missing; the piano writing could bear a few (discreet) amendments; the theme returns six times in exactly the same guise: I took the liberty of introducing three variants. – In this way I enjoyed 3 stimulating mornings. – Now I am thinking of other things again.

Maybe you, too, will think of me again.

[1]The cadenza for this Finale is dated 26 October; on 29 October Busoni then composed a cadenza for the first movement. The score of the entire Finale, which was published in 1922, is dated 'London – Zurich, December 1919'.

278 TO VOLKMAR ANDREAE
in German

London 19.11.1919

[. . .] The word 'hostility', which you use in connection with the reviews of your symphony, leaves me in the dark about their actual nature. 'Hostility' suggests an inimical *intent*, which I can scarcely assume in the case of Isler[1] – not towards you! The likes of Gysi,[2] however, seem to be born 'enemies' of *art*: – at best, due to a misinterpreted love of it – due to a lack of capacity for loving altogether. But, there again, not because of any personal hostility towards yourself. – One can but assume that your work has had the effect of initially arousing opposition and alarming such gentlemen: an excellent indication of the work's value and individuality. – I shall not forget to mention your name to [Henry] Wood. Bodanzky in New York asked me if I knew of any 'significant new works'; I sidestepped the question by asking him in return whether he and his public had already devoured all the 'old' ones. – But you should send him some of your own new material: address Metropolitan Opera House, N.Y. Bodanzky is one of the finest conductors and his orchestra is superb. – From Milan (directly) the news that Toscanini had been nominated – as an electoral candidate. *Cortot* is head of the artistic police (sic) in the French Foreign Ministry. My pupil Kestenberg secretary to the Minister of Culture in Berlin. Ernest Schelling – if he is still alive – a Major and military attaché; Paderewski President of a Poland which the political doctors had previously declared a hopeless case; d'Annunzio a Condottiere – . . . . . . How insignificant my silent activity appears to me, how historically unclear my outlook has become! This latter criticism does not apply to Paul Bekker, who shows a clear grasp of everything in his latest short book, 'Neue Musik',[3] where he finds a pigeon-hole for each and every thing produced by way of combinations of notes in the last 25 years. – A mixture of knowledge and miscalculated perspective, which makes the book – written altogether without affectation – worth reading. – He too distinguishes between Germanic and Latin characteristics, and lists the latter in first place. One could describe the two (without exhausting the question) as *subjective* and *objective*. If this description rings true, then Brun's symphony[4] is, of course, *subjective*. But if you are of the opinion that we Latins appear amateurish by comparison, then I think you are wrong. Finding the simple solution to entangled knots is proof rather of the hand of a *master*. A straight line is the most difficult to draw, simplicity the final achievement. –

With this eternally valid platitude, I take my leave of you for today.

[1]Ernst Isler, 1879–1944, editor of the *Schweizer Musik-Zeitung* from 1910 to 1927.
[2]Dr Fritz Gysi, 1888–1967, Swiss art and music critic.
[3]Paul Bekker, *Neue Musik*, Stuttgart-Berlin, 1919.
[4]Fritz Brun's Symphony no. 3 in d was first performed at the Tonhalle, Zurich, on 15 December 1919.

279 TO EMIL HERTZKA
in German

London 20.11.1919

Having been on good terms with *van Dieren*[1] for years, and well aware of his versatile talent, I have today been requested – by a third party – to draw your attention to his piano pieces.[2] – Despite the intervening six years or more, I can recall the book. At the time, the pieces struck me as bold and stimulating; to what extent they would still have this effect on me is something I could not say with any certainty. It is certain that van Dieren – a more recent work of whose I recently read through with satisfaction and admiration – is a man from whom much can still be expected, and who is worthy of your attention.

I shall take advantage of this rare opportunity to ask kindly after yourself, your edition and your city: I know you have been admirably active, which is always – and particularly under the present circumstances – to be highly valued. – What is Schoenberg doing? And what have you published?

How gladly I would have liked to come into closer contact with you. Perhaps the propitious moment will still come – I have grown accustomed to delays!

[1]Bernard van Dieren, 1884–1936, Dutch composer who had been closely in touch with Busoni in Berlin before the First World War. In 1919 he settled in London and subsequently adopted British nationality.
[2]6 Skizzen for piano, op. 4a, composed in 1911. Universal Edition, Vienna, published them in 1921.

280 TO ALICJA SIMON
in German

London 28.11.1919

[. . .] That which seems to you to surpass the spoken Othello in the sung version may well be the more concise diction and the correct Verdian accentuation, which actors seldom achieve. One could in this case find an argument in defence of opera: justly set words can never sound wrongly stressed; while, in a play, anything can be spoken incorrectly.

– Do you know so little of me that you really think so-called 'concert triumphs' would make me lose my head? – Oh Alicja! [. . .]

I was surprised this morning by a letter from Shaw. He attended the *symphony concert* last Saturday[1] and wrote about it quite spontaneously. His letter contains kind and apt comments. [. . .] – Long live Intelligence. She is the mother of Beauty and Goodness. (Outline of a new mythology.) [. . .]

Yesterday evening, on the way home, my chauffeur 'stopped dead'* half way and refused to drive any further. We had halted in the *thickest of fogs*. I had to find my way home, a stretch of about a mile, in this fog. That's not easy in Regent's Park.

This was not without its charm; – and now I know what it is to be blind (10 monosyllabic words!!)

*Just in front of the [Royal] Academy of Music, what's more!

[1]Concert on 22 November 1919 at the Queen's Hall. Henry Wood conducted the British première of the *Sarabande und Cortège*, op. 51.

281 TO PHILIPP JARNACH
in German

London 1.12.1919

Have you ever had any further thoughts about 'our' Aesthetic of orchestration? Note anything down which occurs to you (or strikes you while listening or reading). – I have made a slightly free arrangement of the Finale of a concerto in Eb by Mozart (as 'Rondo Concertante') – a light-weight but eminently playable piece; it will certainly become a favourite of the 'Concours de piano' – and have used the opportunity to make a closer study of the orchestration. One of Mozart's secrets lies in his use of each instrument in its most natural register – for example in the doublings of a Tutti, where he assigns greater importance to this than to equal strength in every octave. Thus each instrument is able to give its fullest sonority.

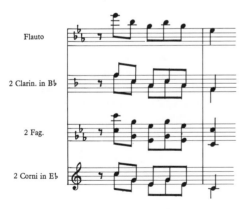

Here the top octave is *single*, the next *doubled*, the third *trebled*, the last *single*. And yet this is the best way; contrary to the teaching of Wagner: he assigns three unison voices to each octave, which is illusory, inasmuch as different instruments produce varying intensity on different notes; an oboe in its lowest register sounds disproportionately loud, a high bassoon weaker. In studying Mozart I am constantly finding confirmation of my theory that a *limited* number and choice of instruments *compels* new possibilities; in that the *routine of full scoring* becomes literally impossible. Besides – just as Flaubert once taught his pupil Maupassant how to reduce a two-page descriptive passage to a single sentence – one should bring composition pupils to reduce a 30-stave score to 18 (or even less). (The same applies – by analogy – to long development sections, modulations and transitions – things in which Wagner lost all sense of proportion.) [. . .] We could find much to discuss on this subject, and I hope we shall soon do so.

I am delighted and gratified that you wish to play my Improvisation on 10 Dec (by which time I shall unfortunately not yet have returned), with Lochbrunner.[1]

'Who is Jarnach?' is the question everyone asks who sees the vocal scores.[2] Well, it will take a while, but then they shall know . . .

New composers: Bernard van Dieren
                         Kaikhosru Sorabji (Indian)[3]

---

[1]Two-piano recital in the Tonhalle, kleine Saal, Zurich, in which Philipp Jarnach and Ernst Lochbrunner played Busoni's Improvisation on 'Wie wohl ist mir' and works by Reger, Mozart, Schumann and Saint-Saëns.

[2]i.e. of *Turandot* and *Arlecchino*.

[3]The 27-year-old Kaikhosru Sorabji played Busoni his Piano Sonata no. 2 (which he also dedicated to him) in the last week of November 1919. Busoni wrote the following letter of recommendation (in French), which is preserved in the Rowe Music Library, Cambridge:

Mr Kaikhusru [sic] Sorabji
    had the goodness to play me a sonata of his own composition on the piano.
    – Judging from an initial impression – surprising enough, incidentally – Mr K.S.'s talent manifests itself in the harmonic and ornamental complexity of his sonorities, which seem to come to him naturally, easily and in a generous vein.
    Here is a realm of liberty, even if still disordered and exuberant. The music is written conscientiously and is unaware of its irregularities – chiefly of proportion – : but it departs, not without a certain effect, from 'traditions' and breaks through to a zenith which is no longer purely *European*, and is capable of producing exotic vegetation. (Not in the sense of our charming Oriental dances, for example)!
    Above all: a budding talent of an altogether novel variety, which gives us cause to think and hope——

In a letter to Gerda, dated 25.11.1919, Busoni described the sonata as '. . . ugly music: a jungle with many a weed and bramble, but exotic and lush. –'

282 TO PHILIPP JARNACH
in German

London 2.12.1919

I trust I am not being importunate or verbose, which would be a sign of old age (it must be so, for old people think they still have so much to say and not much time to say it)——

– I wanted to write the following as a supplement to yesterday's letter: I made use of my free time yesterday to do my friend Maud the favour of looking through an unpublished score of Debussy's, which he constructed, prepared, tailored and compiled at Maud's commission.[1] Maud needed more freedom of motion (i.e. 'time') than the composition permitted, and I took it upon myself to edit the work.[2] – Whereby I came to see that Debussy's style of orchestration is, in a final analysis, a continuation of Wagner's, instead of being – as he thought – a counter-reaction to it. I admit that my thoughts turned to your (Ph. J's) scores, and hence today's letter.

It is – I believe – a matter of historical fact which one can already formulate 'at this juncture', that music from the death of Wagner (1883?) until at least 1923 will simply be described as *post-Wagnerian* or *neo-Wagnerian*, Stravinsky and Schoenberg not excepted, just as Tintoretto and Tiepolo still belong to the world of Titian.

– Here it is a question of seeking out older sources again, so that one alone does not conceal that which is less well known.

– I am making no post-war proclamation when I sincerely believe that the moment has arrived to shake off 19th-century Germany. And do not be shocked if I mention – in this sense only – Beethoven in the same breath as Wagner.

All this is not meant 'nationalistically' but is viewed purely from an artistic standpoint. By 'old sources' I mean:

Palestrina – Mozart – Berlioz
line   form sonority

The distinction between classical and romantic then disappears of its own accord: the two together – like Helena and Faust – should procreate a Euphorion strong enough not to perish in his adolescence. We must smooth the path for this genius to come (one always does come). And this we can do with insight and sense of purpose. – After all, this is not the first time I have said such a thing, nor does it come as a surprise – and I believe I have noticed that Germans under 30 are dimly beginning to sense something of the same sort: they would like to break free from – or if possible transcend – themselves.

In his poetry, Goethe succeeded in achieving that which the Germans need in their music. This was possible because poetry is so much older an art than music.

To return to the Debussy score, its 'security mania'* (with underlinings and doublings) and, above all, its perpetually illustrative style are still entirely Wagnerian. Debussy and Richard Strauss have raised the register (la 'Tessitura') of the orchestra – where Wagner characteristically writes low-pitched music.

They would have composed the opening of Rheingold four octaves higher. But they would be equally attuned to the idea of a monotonously 'flowing' motion.

Wagner – just like these two later composers – would not have been able to resist the 'Trial by fire and water' in Die Zauberflöte. The waterfall in the Alpine symphony is the counterpart to the Magic Fire Music. Mozart alone does what is necessary. – This is what distinguishes Die Zauberflöte from Idomeneo. – One could describe Idomeneo as wellnigh Wagnerian: *the idea alone is not yet sufficient* – it is superficially decorated.

How much is still to be done! And how self-evident this will later appear! – 'From Mozart I learned how to express significant things in an unstrenuous and entertaining manner', Bernard Shaw told me. – He also wrote to me: 'If we do not make up our minds to cultivate a vulgar appetite for diatonic melodies, we shall refine ourselves into "nothingness"!' – (These last words do not follow quite logically from the previous sentence.)

– But will you be able to distil the essence of all these words and sanction them?

I believe you will.

– Apropos 'sanctioning': do you think it fair *that I am not permitted to set my 'Wandbild' to music*?! (I have received repeated warnings to this effect from Zurich.)

In a situation like this – I think – the hairs of justice stand on end . . .

I have any number of new ideas in my head (beneath my ruffled hair) and hope to be able to work in the holidays.

★I would argue as follows against security mania: assuming you consider one voice to be under-scored – let this voice play *wrong notes* and you will soon see that it can be heard . . .

[1]The ballet *Khamma*, composed 1911–12 and orchestrated by Charles Koechlin in 1913. It was not performed until 15 November 1924, and then as a concert piece.
[2]Busoni was apparently unaware that the orchestration of *Khamma* was not by Debussy. Maud Allan's copy of the orchestral score, long considered lost, was found amongst her posthumous papers and is now at the library of the University of British Columbia, Vancouver. (Information kindly supplied by Mr Felix Cherniavsky.)

283 TO EMIL HERTZKA
in German

Zurich 5.1.1920

[. . .] Thank you for your kind interest in van Dieren. While you were deliberating over his case he hovered between life and death, with a disquieting tendency to the latter. A Carnival piece for a group of solo instruments (a small orchestra),[1] which he dedicated to me as something of a last will and testament, gives proof of his development. – At the same time I became the dedicatee of a piano sonata (from the pen of a 20-year-old [!] Indian, Kahushru Sorobdji [sic]) with tropical ornamentation, luxuriant foliage, absorbing. Here in Zurich lives a young man with a fine mind, Philipp Jarnach, from whom I expect the greatest things, as he is already doing well. – All in all, one can say: that which was exceptional, startling and forbidding 20 years ago has today become the norm. I therefore consider this era and schooling to be concluded, hence surmounted. – It seems to me that our next object is, with the aid of all the acquired techniques, to create a *Young Classicality*.[2] I myself am working in this direction and still have many plans. (But how should our 'approach' be brought about? I can think of nothing better.)

– The text of Schoenberg's oratorio has not yet arrived.[3] I was interested to have your news of him. The M.Bl. des Anbruch[4] promise excellently. It was refreshing to hear of your manifold activities (expressed in such an ideal way). I congratulate and thank you.

[1]*Carnival Overture*, op. 7, for 16 instruments. 'The entire work is filled with Latin gaiety and exuberance,' wrote Cecil Gray in 1927. Today the work is virtually forgotten. (Information kindly supplied by Mr Denis ApIvor.)
[2]Orig. Junge Klassizität.
[3]*Die Jakobsleiter*, cf. Appendix, letter no. 36.
[4]*Musikblätter des Anbruch*, a new music journal published in collaboration with Universal Edition. The first issue appeared in November 1919.

284 TO PHILIPP JARNACH
in French

Paris 4.3.1920

[. . .] I am staying in a princely apartment* just opposite the Arc de Triomphe and it is precisely time for black coffee after lunch. By a stroke of luck, I have been given some German cigars from Alsace. My recitals are 'ausverkauft' (here one says 'hired' instead of 'sold out').[1] All this sounds fine, don't you think? – The truth of the matter is that my schedule is so tight that it is scarcely manageable.[2] In addition to the enclosed programmes come two Sunday concerts with the Société des concerts du Conservatoire and an extra recital on 26 March; all in three weeks! – I can see no end to it.

On my last evening in Zurich I visited the marionette theatre, where they performed the old play of Faust.[3] It spoiled my departure, because it left me full of impressions and ideas. At this performance, which I followed as if it were a model for my own, it was touching occasionally to come across lines which appear in my libretto; I was satisfied to ascertain that my judgement had been sound in the question of what to retain or eliminate from the old 'Puppenspiel' in forming my own personal version.

But I should have remained at home and engrossed myself in my work, spurred on as I was by what I had seen and heard. It came as no surprise to me at all, as if I were often taking part in the action myself; so much of the text was immediately familiar, which proved how conscientiously I had studied it.

The commitments awaiting me here will be a fatal distraction from this promisingly productive frame of mind. This is causing me to become impatient and leaves me with no 'Musse' (leisure) to enjoy myself. – I have heard no news of your compositions for a long time. You are at present in the midst of an artistic crisis, and I would suggest that you write *short* pieces and polish them until they are perfect; in their *formal proportions, modulations* and *sonority*—— All these things are not yet accomplished in your major scores: – it is a question of your not having applied a system by degrees, despite your eminently systematic mind. Perhaps you have no desire for my spontaneous advice? But I would like you to feel assured of my continuing interest and would not wish to make an impression of indifference towards you. –

This evening I have my first concert[4] and am obliged to bid you farewell.

*Address: Villa majestic.

[1]Orig. 'loué' and 'vendu'.
[2]Busoni's schedule in Paris: recitals on 4, 12, 19, 26 and 27 March, orchestral concerts on 24 March (conducting a programme of original works), and 14 and 21 March (solo appearances); an extra appearance with orchestra was also arranged for 2 April; on 22 March six young French pianists gave a concert of Busoni's music at the Salle Erard.
[3]The Marionetten Theater Münchener Künstler performed the puppet play of *Faust* at the Kunstgewerbemuseum, Zurich, in March 1920. Busoni would have seen the performance on 2 March.
[4]A recital of Liszt at the Conservatoire.

285 TO PHILIPP JARNACH
in German

Paris 10.3.1920

[. . .] I wrote to you from the hotel. Now I am the guest of the proprietor[1] in his private home. *What* I wrote to you came impulsively and I committed it to paper straight away. It was more a general reflection than a personal gesture. I hope you did not find it immodest of me.

Art has so many ends that one has, from time to time, to be reminded of *those* which stand in opposition to one's own centres of activity and investigation. The same goes for all of us. Therefore you should not take my comments – which I wrote down also to reinforce my own thoughts – as being dogmatic.

After the sanatorium existence of Zurich, Paris has a liberating effect. It is like a homecoming for me (as I wrote to Andreae) to find life on the grand scale again; so familiar and so sorely missed. Here one is not assessed according to one's age or how much one spends, whether one is seen in the company of a lady or climbing into an automobile. I was brought up to appreciate the grand style and could never be persuaded that it is reprehensible, as the Zurichers would like to have it. Altogether, I was brought up never to show whether I was rich or poor (I was poor and was considered rich). This counting of every penny, of one's fortune, in public and private life, is most injurious. In Switzerland it is customary and indeed officially sanctioned.

My first concert, which followed my last letter to you, was vibrant and moving. I shall never forget it. Not as a virtuoso but as a human being, I sensed this tremendous devotion from a public that scarcely knew me, in a spoilt and hardened capital city, as something quite phenomenal.

The applause continued all evening, from the end of one item to the beginning of the next: during each piece the most religious silence.

All my concerts are sold out and two additional recitals (26 and 27) have already been arranged.

The weather, unnaturally hot until 4 days ago, has suddenly broken, causing me to catch a bad cold. –

So I am sitting at home (I have two whole floors at my disposal on the Avenue du Bois de Boulogne) and keeping myself occupied in various ways. As a gesture of thanks to my host I am trying to construct a brief *Carmen Fantasy*, an interesting pastime. – But in the depths of my consciousness lurks a feeling of impatience; I see 'la peau de chagrin' shrinking up quite pointlessly; it is my desire to make an end to this state of affairs which – as has been the case almost all my life – prevents one living for the moment.

[1]Leonhard Tauber, whose home was at 48 Rue Ville-Juste.

286 TO PHILIPP JARNACH
in German

Paris 22.3.1920

[. . .] Today I have my first free afternoon since arriving here: there was an orchestral rehearsal until midday. The orchestra was very co-operative (they presented me with a silver medal), and when it is co-operative, it is one of the most wonderful of instruments. They read the 'Cortège' so well (despite the appallingly written parts) that, the second time through, it was already technically perfect and evoked precisely the right *atmosphere*. Things were hovering and bounding through the bushes of the garden at Parma. –

What strange people they are.

While it is difficult to keep them interested, armed as they are with a disdainful indifference, the moment one has gained their attention, they are capable of the greatest achievements and are quick of understanding.

Occasionally one comes across people who are profoundly serious, widely knowledgeable, highly sensitive.* Thus, I have made the 'conquest' of a certain Professeur Emmanuel[1] who, while possessing all these qualities, makes not the slightest show of them. – I also met a man called Paul Léon[2] (Directeur des beaux arts), whose facial expression is unforgettable. – What has the 19th century achieved? – It has spoiled people, this one can understand. – On the other hand, mediocrities of the murkiest kind – almost as if by agreement – stand out: moreover, the system whereby one has to fish for every single person and win them over is disastrous and unhealthy.**

But one thing is slowly changing. – Even a minor composer like myself is received seriously*** – I am not saying that this gives any grounds for hope for any particular section. (Rather the contrary.)

The little Carmen fantasy (*Sonatina super Carmen*) is finished. – It is 12 pages long, with five themes and four short sections. – Bizet is not yet out of copyright here (not until 50 years after his death), moreover one has to reckon with the *librettists*, who only died later. It is all very well for Choudens.[3] As only 30 years apply in Germany, I have found myself once again on the horns of a legal dilemma. – For here they assert that the Germans have no right to treat Carmen as a 'free' work; meanwhile Bizet's works are being printed over there in every shape and form.

The only person who no longer benefits (nor *benefited*) from all this is poor old Bizet himself!

Sometimes one has to admit (but only between ourselves) that the Bolshevists are right.[4]

The golden light of these spring days has had an irresistible magic. The South vibrates in the air. And yet the indifferent faces of everybody one meets contrast unpleasantly with these palmy days. Truly: one could scarcely find less agreeable people anywhere. You see that I retain my impartiality, even if I myself am experiencing only the very best and most cordial treatment! Suddenly there is a great craze for Liszt!! (Even six years ago, I was the first person who *dared* to give a Liszt recital at the *Conservatoire*.)[5] They are clamouring for Liszt recitals. And they really are spelling his name 'Liszt' and no longer 'Listz' (or: Litz), as one finds in the dedication of Balzac (La duchesse de Langeais).

I heard a delightful saying of Gounod's: Beethoven c'est le plus grand, mais Mozart est unique. –

I have been thinking about the successors, the 'school' of Mozart. There are only few disciples, but they are masters. The most significant are Cherubini, Rossini and Mendelssohn.

Then came the fatal popularization of the 'Ninth' symphony, confusing the issues and bringing forth no fruit. The followers of Wagner signify an unbroken regression. But where do we go from here? To Young Classicality, but not 'back', this is the 'poodle's core'.[6]

The quotation is appropriate only as a transition to Faust. I hope for work, for a resumption and rapid progress. Will the puppet-play be running in Z. at Easter? I would hope so. But even without it . . . . . .

For I have my last appearance here on 2 April (my 9th) and expect to be home on Easter Sunday.

'Home'? – the word invokes all the problems awaiting me; and this time I shall ignore them.

25.3.1920
Postscript

The morning after my compositions' concert, which was one of the most wonderful evenings of my life. In the old hall of the Conservatoire, where once the likes of Berlioz or Bizet were to be seen, an initially very concentrated then increasingly enthusiastic crowd (it was completely full) listened and applauded with the finest understanding and greatest warmth. The end of the concert was indescribable, people stood up and shouted. The orchestra performed miracles, particularly in the Sarabande und Cortège. Allegra played very well,[7] even if confused by the many impressions of the journey. [. . .]

I was happy the whole day yesterday, already in expectation, and very inspired and full of ideas. Thus I go my way, strengthened.

*Just think of Littré . . .![8]
**I have been bombarded with piano music.
***See postscript.

[1]Maurice Emmanuel, 1862–1938, musicologist and composer. From 1909 to 1936 he was Professor of music history at the Paris Conservatoire.
[2]Paul Léon, 1874–1952, author of books on the fine arts. He subsequently became 'Directeur général'.
[3]The original publishers of Bizet's *Carmen*.
[4]In Benvenuto Busoni's transcript of this letter, this and the preceding paragraph are inserted later, evidently due to confusion in the original pagination.
[5]In January 1914 Busoni had devoted two separate halves of recitals at the Salle Erard to Liszt; there is, however, no record of an earlier complete Liszt recital in Paris.
[6]'Des Pudels Kern' (Goethe, *Faust*, Part I, 1323).
[7]Edmondo Allegra had opened the programme with the Clarinet Concertino, op. 48 (substituted for the *Comedy Overture*); then followed the *Sarabande und Cortège*,

op. 51. In the second half Philippe Gaubert conducted Busoni's Piano Concerto
with the composer as soloist.
[8]Emile Littré, 1801–1861, philosopher, lexicographer and politician. Author of a
Dictionnaire de la langue française.

287 TO GISELLA SELDEN-GOTH
in German

Zurich 14.5.1920

Your 'torrent
regenerates, its
content also stimulates.'

not to be	'ich eile wie der Bach
used	der sich vom Felsen stürzt;
for the	über Bergeskämme
public reading!	durch die Felder sprudelnd,
	hin, bis zum Ozean.'[1]

Thus sings the (revised) third Spirit in my Doktor Faust. I also enclose some
other alterations. Particularly during the process of composition – the text
becomes misaligned in some places: the poet has to yield to the composer,
who, in return, must come to his aid; and this is one of the reasons why I am
my own librettist. I intend to write a preface to Dr Faust, which seems to me
to be indispensable. But I cannot give it to you nor finish it in time. The
poet's 'octaves' to the audience explain how the story attracted me, but how I
was intimidated by Goethe's monument, how I hence availed myself of the
puppet-play.

I follow the puppet-play – (I saw a performance of it here two months ago)
– fairly literally in the two prologues and the Parma scene. The Intermezzo is
my own invention. – However, I take the Duchess as the point of departure
for my own thought-process, hence diverging from the puppet-play. – 'The
Child' becomes a symbol that causes and permits an almost reconciliatory
solution, transcending the framework of the play. – Born of the merest whim,
this creature is the starting point for the spiritual survival of the individual, of
'the Will', as F. finally describes himself. I have no philosophical intention:
the argument emanated purely as poetry. By allotting Mephisto the role of
night-watchman, I eliminated Casperle (he plays this part in the puppet-
play), whom I had originally envisaged. The scene with the students in the
tavern is entirely my own invention. The vision of Helena occurs in this
milieu in the folk-legend too; I make her appear as the unattainable Ideal,
conjured up for Faust by Meph. so as to distract him from the significance,
the meaning attached to the Child. The conciseness was demanded by the
music, for music flows on average three times more slowly than the spoken
word. The fragmentariness of the text is also intentional, as it permits the
music to fill out the gaps. A drama that is complete in itself *has no need of*

music. I wrote the libretto in six days during the first Christmas of the war, as if in a fever; before abandoning a world which collapsed after me. – The mystical ending, however, was written here, much later, as a result of Rubiner's criticism. – The score is still in progress; I am working with enforced interruptions and with almost too great a sense of responsibility. The extant portions seem to me to be successful. Soon I must return to England – for practical reasons – then, as has now been decided, comes my departure from Zurich: all this by way of continuous mild distraction . . . . .

Today I have written a twelve-page newspaper article and am exhausted. The coming event honours and delights me greatly: pass on my warmest greetings to Prof. Devrient.[2]

---

[1]   I hasten like a stream
      cascading through the rocks;
      over hill and dale,
      I gush ever onward
      into the ocean.
Gisella Selden-Goth had organized a public reading of the libretto of *Doktor Faust* in the Goethe-Haus, Weimar, for 20 May 1920. This alteration, and indeed most of the comments in the remainder of the letter, were intended to assist her in preparing a programme note.
[2]Heinrich Devrient, 1868–1927, actor. Grandson of the celebrated Ludwig Devrient, friend of E. T. A. Hoffmann.

288 TO PHILIPP JARNACH
in German

[Zurich] 16.5.1920

Typical: in *Finland* I occupied myself with Finnish folk-songs, in *America* I worked on Redskin themes and recently, in *Paris*, I made an arrangement of Carmen: –. Only in Switzerland have I written nothing Swiss.

I still find that the finest Swiss symphony is the overture to William Tell.
Have you read the manifesto by the new director of the Berlin Hochschule – Schreker – in the B[erliner] T[ageblatt]?
One comes across such phrases as:
  'Schmerz und Sehnen, Glück und Leid'[1]
and it finishes with:
  'Seid umschlungen Millionen'.[2]
I remarked that this appeal could only make its effect as a chorus in four-part harmony.
What kind of a figure would I cut in this apparently hidebound atmosphere?

How I would fume! Adieu, douce philosophie; – one must swim with the tide.

Finally: what do you think of the word 'Futu-purism? I coined it myself, as my own label.

[1]'Pain and longing, joy and sorrow.'
[2]From Schiller's 'Ode to Joy' (in the translation by Natalia MacFarren): 'O ye millions, I embrace ye.'

289 TO HUGO LEICHTENTRITT
in German

Zurich 25.5.1920

I know: it is too long since I last wrote to you, but – what can one do – the struggle of proposing man

against disposing God

has at present become almost hopeless. There was also too much to do: I have been sitting in a spider's web of correspondence. 'On the side' I have been working day after day and sometimes also in the evenings, which I had given up in Berlin.

Apart from the composition of

Doktor Faust

I have written several lesser pieces: only yesterday the final pages of the score for a *Divertimento for flute and orchestra*. More significant composers have also been prompted to this kind of 'special literature', through personal contact with instrumentalists. One is also influenced by one's milieu: my visit to Paris caused me to carry out an old plan for a *Fantasia da Camera on Carmen*. The fact that my friends Lochbrunner and Jarnach are giving 2-piano recitals brought forth a *Duettino Concertante* on themes of Mozart.[1] – I have a good half-dozen such things stored away.

But the uncertainty of my fate has been giving me a complete and utter headache: a fiendish game was being played, in which I was offered all kinds of tempting things and was at the same time being warned not to accept them. Reports from the countries which came into question varied like the weather in Zurich, of which I am now sick and tired and – of which I must continue being sick and tired. I am still waiting for several decisive items of news. Then I shall pull myself together for the decision to which I am inwardly already clearly committed. – Now and then I have managed to compose myself in the face of all these entanglements and to feel in the mood for writing friendly letters. That your turn should come so late is un-intentional. [. . .]

[1]The manuscript of this free arrangement of the Finale of Mozart's Piano Concerto in F, K. 459, is dated 'D[iem] Nativitatis 1919'.

290 TO PHILIPP JARNACH
in German

[Zurich] 7.6.1920

[. . .] The (deplorable) vocal score of Berlioz's The Trojans made and makes a propitious impression. What inspiration! Emmanuel by no means said everything that is to be said. He (Berlioz) is the only composer who always works towards inventiveness. Every page reveals something new and surprising. I do not know the orchestral score of this second part. It must be an 'object lesson'. – I possess part one: a dramatic poem. What is the explanation for the persistent deafness of the French to such a man? It is tragic. – While they raise Wagner, who is in every sense alien to them, on to a pedestal. – I have found *one* solution: Berlioz's music is, above all, *chaste*. – In the last fifty years, music has had to be *erotic*: whether Tristan or operetta. Wagner's music is sexual, inactively erotic, thus: *lascivious*. This also explains why his inordinate duration is tolerated. *Potency acts swiftly*. Eroticism is protracted. I have been obsessed with this theme since my exchange of letters with Bekker; forgive me for expounding it here. God willing, I shall find time to write about it in detail. –

291 TO VOLKMAR ANDREAE
in German

London 23.6.1920

[. . .] Yesterday evening I made my 'début' here with an uncommonly successful orchestral concert: the Brautwahl suite, the Indian Fantasy and Liszt's Faust symphony. The programme was chosen to comply with the organizer's wish to make my acquaintance as composer, pianist and conductor;[1] planning it – in such a way that it should remain clear and not appear fragmentary – was a little difficult. Bernard Shaw was in the audience at Queen's Hall. The London Symphony Orchestra, which I had at my disposal, is really excellent. Virtuosic and quick on the uptake. Moreover it has preserved the good manners one used to value before the war, and to which a return will have to be made, as with several other things.——London has also improved its appearance a little, if not entirely. At this bright and sunny time of year, the city is bewitching; although I take singular pleasure in the mystery of the fog.

– I can see that my years in Zurich have not failed to influence my reputation abroad: my standing in the world of music has – without any intervention on my part – risen noticeably; just as a work can mature inside a person without his consciously thinking about it. – I am all the more grateful to your country for the calm surroundings which made this possible. But now this chapter, too, is finished, and it is a matter of solemnly and sadly taking my leave. Therefore the purpose of my return in July will be the taking of all necessary steps in this direction. The parting will not be easy, but my sense of form tells me that this section should not outstay its time. – Thus, although I had had no such intention when I began this letter, I find myself taking my leave. But I am certain of seeing you and talking to you often in the meantime.

[1]The conductor of the Indian Fantasy was Julius Harrison, Busoni was the soloist. As we learn from the review of this concert in *The Times*, the Indian Fantasy was encored in its entirety.

292 TO ARRIGO SERATO
in Italian

London 27.6.1920

[. . .] The hostility towards me in Italy is nothing but our country's flourishing insularity; it is customarily explained by pretexts thought up after the event. One cannot imagine why people who are not in the least concerned with my art should take such an interest in, and be so well-informed about my private affairs!

My dear boy, or better, my brother, I am very sorry to read that you prefer to explain away these undeniable facts by expressing doubt as to my peace of mind. I would like to assure you that matters are not so. Ask my wife, my sons, my housekeeper if you wish; you would be informed that my mood is invariably good and cheerful, thank Heaven; due to my clear conscience, the outcome of satisfaction with my work, good health, an adorable family and sufficient material comfort. God forbid that I should boast! I am humbly grateful for all this. But as for me and Italy, as for my love and hope for that country, which should represent the crowning of all my powers, you cannot deny the facts, which emanate not *from me* but from the other side, on the contrary, you should be more closely and fully acquainted with them. For these reasons I was obliged, unwillingly and for the first time, to turn down the invitation of the Società del Quartetto.

Now you write that my Violin concerto has been requested, which makes me heartily glad; thank you for your readiness to perform it, of course I shall try to come and conduct. However, at the moment, to conclude, *I do not know* where I shall be, or in what capacity, in the coming season!!

In Italy, as everywhere, there have been *millions of patriots*, but shamefully few who were able to maintain their opinions in the face of the dreadful fluctuations; as for the great artists, they can be counted on the fingers of one hand. Hence: it is easy (as these statistics prove) to be a patriot, it is worth making a show of the fact, but it is most rare to find an oak tree which does not bow to the storm; the artist who resists and unfalteringly follows his path is exceptional. If one so wished, one could see in me the mark of a hero; or, if otherwise inclined, it would be possible, with little effort, to depict me as a reprehensible character.

Thus it is a question of good will.

Similar rumours about me are circulating everywhere; but in England, just as in France, my art and my *demeanour* have stilled them at once. My countenance does not strike me as being any worse than that of those hundreds of patriots who rendered the 'Galleria' impassable (I am speaking of Milan).

Hence you can imagine the amazement with which I read and re-read the phrase underlined on the second page of your letter!

'The greatest enthusiasm, coupled with fullest co-operation', this, according to you, would be awaiting me in Italy 'wherever I should decide to settle'. But how and where should one begin?

It has always been my dream finally, as an act of homage, to present my country with the fruits of my labours; during the war, in seclusion, I was working towards perfecting myself, like some holy man. Today, wherever music and *honesty* are valued, I enjoy the privilege of being considered one of the most outstanding and respected characters amongst musicians.

At the end of the war, having earned a little money in England, I immediately made my way to Milan. Such was my reception that I fell ill, not out of wounded pride but profoundest grief. Then in Paris, where I was received with the honours due to a prince (even if, at that time, I did not deserve them), the difference impressed me most strikingly. Here in London, yesterday as well, the demonstrations of sympathy have been overwhelming. In Paris, as well as London, I have conducted and performed my orchestral works: in both cases the opportunity was offered me *spontaneously and without charge*. In both cases I have been asked to return with such concerts . . .

I have not yet mentioned the question of Germany, but nevertheless I must speak of this. Until now, for various reasons, I have been disregarding, indeed avoiding the country. I shall not bore you by enumerating the many forms of sympathy, impatience, reproach and confidence with which they have been begging me to return. And they have not stopped at words; they have offered me the choice of whatever position or enterprise I should suggest or desire. First and foremost a post at the State Academy with the leading composition class: a position of highest authority, free of all superintendence or restriction.

Had something of the sort been offered me in Rome, I would not for a moment have hesitated to accept it.

And you, on the other hand, my dear friend, you have been able to find your modus vivendi: I am overjoyed, from the love and admiration I bear for you. So you will be living in Bologna? Will you remain in isolation? Will you come to Berlin? (It is still, I believe, a city with many possibilities. I am certain you would be received there with an enthusiasm proportionate to the distance and expense [of the journey].)

Finally, I thank you from the bottom of my heart for your words, your sentiments and deeds; and I shall wait, shall always be waiting for the 'Bonne nouvelle' which I had in my heart of hearts already abandoned, but for which your letter gives me cause, at the age of 54, to hope once again . . .

Soon it will be too late.

293 TO PHILIPP JARNACH
in German

London 2.7.1920

You can scarcely imagine how seductively beautiful London is in the spring, in peacetime, in freedom; for, since the war, there is a sense of release here, human desires and instincts call for respect; the hyprocrisy of the Victorian era seems to have been overcome. On top of this comes the inexhaustibility of events and appearances, enticing to every form of taste and fancy, the wonderful solitude in the midst of the turmoil: – and wherever one is, one is always at the centre, the end is equidistant from every point. – Looked at in this light, London is incomparable and boundless. – If it were also an 'artistic' city it would be unbearable! – But:

'ora incomincian le dolenti note'[1]

as my Matteo says.

One ceases to be and to feel as an artist: one is like a sighted person amongst the blind, and finally – as in a parable by Wells – one becomes convinced that the blind look down on the sighted; however paradoxical that might seem.

The principal and generally confirmed phenomenon here is that one has no new ideas: the influence of the atmosphere is so predominant. Goethe – had he come to England – would have left no complete works. Here everything must constantly be started anew; as if the foundations which one lays slip away under one's feet the moment one tries to build on them. How can an *individual* keep pace? And how can one pair of hands maintain control of the countless problems? – One soon gives up – as does anybody who settles here.[2] This is why, although I adore and am enraptured by London, I do not live here. On several occasions in my life I have considered the question – (once I had already begun looking for a house) – but have always ended up by dismissing it.

– The Russian Ballet has become, second to Wagner, the most perfect organization. Just as certain infusions (what do I understand of biology!!) secrete parts of their organism, which then live on independently, the original Ballet Russe has given birth to a multifarious organization which works everywhere simultaneously and draws on the services of thousands of people; so that everyone one meets plays some part or other in it. Musicians, painters, poets, financiers; luxury, lasciviousness, careerism – all united in this: – pseudo-artistic manifestation, which has in the end become the pretext for ambition of quite another kind. – A respectable critic wrote apropos of my orchestral concert, in the name of his colleagues: he begs Mr Busoni not to consider it impolite that they were obliged to leave the hall in order to visit the Russian Ballet!

Incidentally, the concert was a very great success. But all-absorbing London has already gobbled half of it away – just like Giotto with his food. Nevertheless, I was satisfied. The orchestra was willing, respectful (eventually friendly) and extraordinarily skilful. –

I hope to see you again soon, to tell you more and to hear your news. I expect to be back in Zurich around next Sunday.

[1]'Now begin the tones of woe' Dante, *Inferno*, Canto V, l.25. Busoni quotes the line in the second 'movement' of *Arlecchino*.
[2]In his typewritten transcript of this letter, Benvenuto Busoni has added a footnote of his own: 'And yet, at the same time, B. demanded that I should settle there as an artist! . . .'

294 TO EDWARD J. DENT
in Italian

London 9.7.1920[1]

I have read your study of Chopin[2] with intense interest, and am very grateful for your brilliant defence of my interpretation (masterpiece of advocacy). Many thanks for both. As to the question of whether Mendelssohn has been neglected in favour of Chopin, you are – morally – in the right. But, as late as 1914, I had the opportunity of putting the following question to the 'boss' of Breitkopf und Härtel: which piece of sheet-music – for piano – was most in demand. Even I thought: Chopin. But Dr von Hase replied: the *Lieder ohne Worte*.

I believe this revelation would not displease the historians. But, as for Chopin, it is true that he struggles successfully against growing old, yet the choice of his works is becoming ever more restricted. His dances and most of his Nocturnes have vanished. For me, his 'prophetic' work is the 24 Preludes, which contains the seed of everything following, more or less progressively.

[1]Dent's typewritten transcript of this letter is dated 9 June. However, as the article on Chopin discussed here was not published until 9 July, this is clearly an error.
[2]Edward J. Dent, 'An interpretation of Chopin', in the *Athenaeum*, London, 9 July 1920. The arguments brought forward by Dent can be summarized in the following quotations:
> We English people are Latin by education, by sentiment Teutonic . . . When we form a consciously intellectual judgement, we are for the moment Latin; when we allow ourselves to be guided by sentiment alone, we relapse into our native

Teutonism . . . Busoni is in a certain way the exact opposite of an Englishman. He is Italian by blood, and to some extent German by education. As he grows older he reverts temperamentally more and more to the influences of his father's country. Therefore, in so far as he approaches Chopin instinctively and emotionally, he approaches him from the Italian side . . . Chopin's nocturnes will teach one more about Bellini than Bellini, taken in that form, can teach one about Chopin . . .

What Busoni does in every case is to bring us closer to the mind of the composer than we had ever been before. He shows us, as it were, the music as it existed before the notes were written down.

295 TO ALICJA SIMON
in German

Zurich 16.7.1920

I was unable to write to you until today, two days after returning from London (where I had a very good time): I miss your presence in Zurich. [. . .]

In London there was a production of Puccini's 'Trittico', of which I only liked the last (buffo) piece.[1] This is, in my opinion, typical. For, in the first of the three one-acters – the verismo tragedy[2] – Puccini has achieved (in my opinion) perfection in that for which he had striven in his earlier works.

But, the moment he has found the key to mastery, the public gets tired of this genre and considers the work weaker. In contrast, the 'buffo' is a *novelty* and therefore more striking; even though Puccini makes a sort of début with it. – Hence one can clearly perceive that there is no constant norm in the theatre for that which counts as 'dramatic'. [. . .]

[1] *Gianni Schicchi.*
[2] *Il Tabarro.*

296 TO EDITH ANDREAE [fragment]
in German

[Zurich] 25.7.1920

I was very glad that you wrote. After your last letter, it was difficult for me to decide to write again. You had, very reasonably but not exactly graciously, turned down my request; and it was the first time I had approached you in matters of my own interest. Although you saw things in their true light, the effect on me, in my frame of mind at that time, was truly dispiriting. The situation is too complicated to be clarified adequately in a brief letter: our respective situations were too diverse for us to be able to understand each other.

Certainly, you have yourself experienced and witnessed many things; but these principally for Germany, for your own national, private and human interests; and you remained at home, within your own four walls. I have suffered for the whole world and become – homeless. This is no worse, but totally different. –

Any day now I am expecting K[esten]berg the 'powerful', and hope through him finally to make an end to six years of vacillation and indecision. – Will the Berlin of today be a haven of peace? – Shall I find the necessary tolerance? – And yet I live in hope and belief: otherwise I would refrain from inflicting this experiment upon myself.

'Where are you?' you write. Still in Zurich, or rather: here once again. For until two weeks ago I had been in London, where I also spent the autumn. I spent the whole of March in Paris, February in Italy. – Everywhere I experienced my own renaissance, more so indeed, compared with previous occasions. – It is said that my playing has improved, and I have established a new reputation for myself as composer and conductor. [. . .]¹

---

¹After one further paragraph (which contains repetition of news contained in other letters), this letter breaks off.

297 TO GISELLA SELDEN-GOTH
in German

Zurich [undated]¹

Yesterday I went to 'Fatinitza'.² You know, this man Suppé had *talent*. Of all the musical supplements to 'Anbruch', not one has remotely as much talent. They contradict the loud-mouthed 'manifestos' of the verbal texts. 'Es gibt wohl Unterschiede der Begabung' . . . . .³

I make an exception in the case of a brief fragment by Schreker.⁴ It gives the impression of integrity and of the composer's own naïve emotional involvement in his ideas: in this it reminds one of Tchaikovsky. –

This man Suppé has more theatre blood: he belongs to the same school as Victor Hugo and Verdi. Everything 'works'. – Sadly enough: there are deficiencies all round and he mixes up all kinds of styles. The libretto is unbearably Viennese. – I knew Suppé in my childhood. He was kind-hearted and entirely unaffected. A realist.⁵ He did not overestimate himself. Proudly told me that he had also composed masses. At that time, at the age of twelve, I was already a counterpoint hunter: Suppé wrote a short fugato for my album, just to prove that he could manage that as well. Of course he could! Do you know the canon-quartet in Donna Juanita?⁶ – This and the quartet in Fatinitza are masterpieces. –

I urge you to write your essay against nationalism . . . one cannot say it often enough. – When you have the chance, you should also write: there is no such thing as 'expressionism' in music; it would be nonsense to misuse this word so consciously.

In painting, Expr. signifies:

schematically alluding

to the object to be reproduced,

rather than slavishly imitating it. – As music is *unable* slavishly to imitate an object, it is by nature 'expressionist', in the sense that the word is used today: therefore one cannot speak of expressionist music as being a specific genre. – Is that clear? –

[1]A letter to Jarnach dated 5.8.1920 tells us that the performance of *Fatinitza* mentioned here took place in Zurich on 3 August. Hence this letter can be dated 4.8.1920.
[2]*Fatinitza*, opera by Suppé, first performed in Vienna on 5 January 1876.
[3]'There are indeed various grades of talent.'
[4]The Schreker number of *Musikblätter des Anbruch* (January 1920) included the closing song of Alte Liese from his opera *Das Spielwerk*.
[5]Orig. Real-Politiker.
[6]*Donna Juanita*, opera by Suppé, first performed in Vienna on 21 February 1880.

298 TO EDWARD J. DENT
in Italian

Zurich 5.8.1920

Do you think that – if one rearranged things a little – it would be possible to revive one of Alessandro Scarlatti's theatrical works – and which one?★ – and where could one dig it out? –

I have taken the idea to heart with a mind on Italy, for a certain enterprise which is being born and on which I am collaborating.[1] Unfortunately I am without your book on A.S.[2] I have it in Berlin and it shall be restored to me (let us hope) in a few weeks, when I hope to be restored to myself.

And you, are you restored?

★I am thinking of a *buffo* opera.

[1]Probably a reference to Busoni's plan to bring the Teatro dei piccoli from Rome for a tour of Germany.
[2]Edward J. Dent, *Alessandro Scarlatti: his Life and Works*, London, 1905.

299 TO MARCHESE DI CASANOVA
in Italian

Zurich 7.8.1920

[. . .] In Berlin I shall find discord and deprivation, but also satisfaction and a diversity of interests. The irony of the situation is that I shall be occupying a post parallel to that of Pfitzner as head of a composition class at the State Academy. My operas are to be performed at the Staatsoper.[1] The thought of being reunited with my library fills me with joy. I am somewhat excited but thoroughly determined.

I have attempted to make my peace with the Italians but have been unsuccessful. Alas, you are right. But even so, my time will come, and there have already been some signs of an approach. I have been invited to Rome and shall probably go. Paris and London (where I was given a magnificent welcome) shall be a permanent feature of my annual tours. This is the outline of my 'vita nuova'.

I would in any case have departed from Zurich, which has returned to a state of stupor; the people of Switzerland will have to find their miracles in their own ranks.

It looks as if *Petri* will probably become director of the piano class in Basle. What a pity that he is arriving just as I take my leave!

Please excuse my silence; believe me, I am ashamed of it. I have no right to be forgiven; but the fact that I have evidently written about 5,000 letters during my time in Zurich will perhaps make you more lenient towards my apparent negligence. –

Thus I am at present one five-thousandth ahead of Rilke.

[1]*Turandot* and *Arlecchino* were staged in Berlin; the first night was 19 May 1921 (see letter no. 309).

300 TO GISELLA SELDEN-GOTH
in German

Zurich 8.8.1920

'Le chromatique procède par plusieurs semi-tons consécutifs, ce qui produit une Musique efféminée, très convenable à l'amour.' (Note de Voltaire pour 'La Pucelle', 1762.)[1]

From the postcript of your critical letter one could infer that you consider it high time I had myself 'Steinached'![2] – Would it not be better for us to wait a little longer? – In the meantime you can write your essay and I, my endocrine glands unaffected, could perhaps complete my Doktor Faust. Then I could cry, with the poet of the great Faust (or write in a registered letter): gib meine Jugend mir zurück.[3] And thereupon I would see 'Helena in every woman'.[4] –

Have you noticed that, from the moment of his rejuvenation, Faust does nothing except travel around chasing after women? Only 'in his dotage' and 'blinded' does a thought enter his head again! You are quite right in objecting to 'A-tonality' (one always gives the A when tuning up), and the word itself concedes the existence of war. – 'Expressionism' in music, as you explain it according to its apostles, is to be found *on occasion* in every great composer: it is a sporadically applicable measure. The error lies in making it into a universal rule: every movement and party (social, too) contains a grain of truth, but this is never the supreme fulfilment. Therefore I reject *every* party.

I can and will not write any more.

[1]'Chromaticism is a succession of several consecutive semitones which produce an effeminate music most suited to love.' (Voltaire's note to *La Pucelle*.) The quotation is dated 4.8.1920, the rest of the letter 8.8.

[2]Allusion to Prof. Eugen Steinach, 1861–1944, a celebrated Viennese experimental surgeon, whose chief areas of research were sexuality and rejuvenation. His most celebrated patient was Sigmund Freud, who succumbed to his knife in November 1923 for a *Steinachsche Verjüngungsoperation* (ligature of the sperm ducts). In 1940 Faber and Faber published Steinach's book *Sex and Life; forty years of biological and medical experiment*.

[3]'Give me back my youth'. These words do not appear in Goethe's *Faust*.

[4]Goethe, *Faust*, Part I, 2604–5.

301 TO PHILIPP JARNACH
in German

[Zurich] 13.8.1920

[. . .] What you wrote about Berlioz gave me great pleasure. Apart from their innate genius, these men of the 1830s lived in a propitious age. Where the reaction against the baroque fancies of the *rococo* period had resulted in magnificence but also earnest chill (Empire), the reaction against *this* particular rigidity – the triumph of temperament – came in the wake of the magnificence which *Empire* had bred. Temperament and subjectivity on the grandest scale, never quite renounced in the art of antiquity, were the hallmarks of Berlioz, Delacroix and Victor Hugo. I believe that these three – (together with Balzac?) – illustrate my argument exhaustively and that together they present a unified picture. To their ranks belong – (as offshoot) – Meyerbeer – still – and even Wagner; however, in his case decadence and conventionality are substituted for unruliness, and German-Jewish attitudes detract still further. The decline leads to Gustav Mahler. – How pure and utterly isolated was the figure of Franz Liszt, that cosmopolitan Catholic idealist!! –

Now we are moving towards a reaction, and we have to play a Puritan role once more. A truly beautiful art will evolve, which you will still consciously experience, and to which you will contribute. It is a question of *perfecting* all the experiments for which the 20th century has paved the way. I have chosen the word [Vollendung] for perfection intentionally. It means: to bring to a conclusion, to consolidate, to say the last word.

This turn in the road leads to a distant – but also limited – turning point. – I would so much like to have you in Berlin, where you could play a part in everything and also develop further! This coming winter, Egon Petri will be living in Basle. What a pity that Zurich and Basle are so independent of each other that this proximity, Philipp and Egon, is almost meaningless to both of you. – The Bavarians will long continue to consider Bayreuth their capital city. Names like Weil-Heim appear to be intended to pay homage to the 'master':

> Hier wo mein Weilen heimisch ward,
> Weil-Heim sei das Wort gepaart.[1]

On Saturday 21st I shall be giving a modest farewell party: an orchestral rehearsal of the flute piece.[2]

(NB) Chantavoine[3] has supplied me with a vocal score of Arlecchino into which he has written the complete French translation. – (Very fine) . . . .

I have nearly completed the composition of a Toccata for piano (in three movements).

[1] Here, where my sojourn a home became,
    Let Weil-Heim be my dwelling's name.
[2] Divertimento for flute and orchestra, op. 52.
[3] Jean Chantavoine, 1877–1952, French musicologist. He also translated Beethoven's letters and several other opera texts into French.

IX

1920 – 1922
Return to Berlin

Berlin 2–3.10.1920

I am gradually beginning to write to my friends. As long as Gerda was not
here I had sealed myself off hermetically, both from a social and moral point
of view, enjoyed the isolation, wandered through my apartment discovering
forgotten things, greeting familiar ones and keeping myself fully occupied. I
am by no means finished with this manner of behaviour: – only yesterday I
came upon an edition of Don Quixote 'unknown' to me, Madrid MDCCL,
with curious old woodcuts; I had had this book bound in parchment (shortly
before my fateful farewell), with black lettering on the spine. At that time I
was going through a bind rage[1] and I am very glad that I did so. Today a
folio volume in full leather costs: 1,000 Marks; in the old days I used to pay
50 for it!

– I was able to set to work straight away in my 'Cité des Livres'. Today, an
hour ago, I finished a 'Tanzwalzer' for orchestra (43 pages of score) and the
Toccata, too, arising as it did from anguish and unstable emotions, has been
brought to its conclusion here. (It is not actually 'encore deux pages de la
même façon', as you predicted, but offers the opponent no unexpected
manoeuvres.)[2]

My morale would hence appear to have returned to normal. But it is a
different matter with my emotions, which strike me as being strange and not
entirely comprehensible. I am becoming altogether isolated and am surprised
that others do not notice my remoteness from them. The people and the
whole city. – Most of the former have remained as I left them. But it is
precisely the ones taking pains to keep up with the times who strike me as
being debilitated – these are the ones with whom I get on worst of all, because
there have been changes both in them and in myself; while I am familiar from
previous times with the manner of the more unpretentious people and – with
an effort – I can attune myself to them. – In the evenings Berlin is dark.
Nobody goes out into the streets for his pleasure. At ten o'clock in the
evening, when things used to 'get going', everything is now dead. But the
people have a kind and modest way about them. Their clothes are all
rehashed. *Here* a man still wearing his military jacket, *there* a woman with a
re-tailored pre-war outfit. The young girls are serious and good-mannered.

They all have some post or profession and go pensively about their business.

Prices – judging by the figures – are out of this world. But in actual fact I am still living off the 500 Francs I brought with me and which I would have spent in Zurich long ago. – Enough for today, and thank you for your kind letter. Greetings!

Sunday morning

Yesterday's letter was not posted, so I opened it and read it through. Meanwhile I have added six pages of 'introduction' to the 'Tanzwalzer'[3] and this has become the best part of the piece. That cheers me up; – a beautiful autumn morning; my windows overlook the big square and the garden[4] where, in the afternoons, children play and nannies knit. Four different tram lines pass by. There is an abundance of motor cars. – But I am unable to rid myself of my melancholia. I am having to fight once more to preserve my standards, my steady course and my humour. These are the exertions which remain unnoticed by the outside world. This personal discipline is consuming most of my strength. – For the first two days Gerda was cheerful and almost happy. – Now she is silent. – It seems to me quite impossible that one single person can restore all that has been submerged: and I am profoundly reluctant to acknowledge the fact. How shall I be feeling and thinking by the end of the season? – In the meantime the furniture van has arrived and its contents, now they have been brought into my apartment, bind me all the more firmly to Berlin.

[1]Orig. Binde-Wut.
[2]Orig. Er macht keine für den Gegenspieler verblüffende Rösselsprünge. Busoni here uses the language of chess.
[3]*Tanzwalzer*, op. 53. Dedicated to the memory of Johann Strauss.
[4]Viktoria-Luise-Platz.

303 TO PHILIPP JARNACH
in German

Berlin 30.10.1920

[. . .] Today I read an article by P. Bekker attacking Berlin's Dr Krebs,[1] who depicts me as the eyesore of the city's musical life. This is the kind of welcome I am enjoying here. – Yesterday I attended a rehearsal of my 'Concerto', played by a certain Erdmann[2] and conducted by someone called Meyrowitz.[3] Both are well-intentioned and thus make a kind of contrast with the abovementioned vexations.

The festivities in the Ducal park at Parma[4] have come into being. There will be about 30 large pages of score before I arrive at the first words of the text; 16 of them have been written. This is already the third project I have accomplished in Berlin. As always with me, they are all interrelated and I am making reciprocal use of them for the main work. – Two days ago I accepted an invitation to watch a new film based on Calderón's 'El Alcalde de Zalamea'. Even in this form the genius of the Spaniard wins through: it is astonishing and moving to see how he dominates life and stage alike. And de la Barca wrote no fewer than two hundred such plays! Unfortunately I do not know the 'Judge of Salamea' and, to my horror, I see that my library has a complete dearth of Spanish literature. You have an edition, 'Biblioteca de autores españolas', which is always cited as the best. It must be a splendid publication. Does your father perhaps possess it?—You see that there is no lack of occasion for me to enjoy my seclusion. – Now I am preparing for my piano recitals.[5] – It is difficult to live fully. I am still trying to learn how to do so.

(NB) Best wishes to Biolleys[6] – Andreae – Benni.

To have a few books bound, I had to use an old leather handkerchief case belonging to our dressmaker.

[1]Dr Carl Krebs, 1857–1937, Berlin music critic and secretary of the Akademie der Künste.
[2]Eduard Erdmann, 1896–1958, Latvian-born pianist and composer. Pupil of Ansorge and Tiessen in Berlin.
[3]Selmar Meyrowitz, 1875–1941, German conductor. He worked at the Metropolitan Opera, New York, from 1900 to 1903.
[4]i.e. First Tableau of *Doktor Faust*.
[5]Busoni was to give two recitals at the Philharmonie, Berlin on 18 and 28 November 1920.
[6]Albert Biolley and his wife Elisabeth. Biolley, 1857–1932, a Swiss banker and amateur flautist, had helped the Busoni family financially when they settled in Zurich.

304 TO HUGO LEICHTENTRITT
in German

Berlin 16.12.1920

Today just to confirm with thanks that the copy of the Formenlehre has arrived. For the honour of the repeated references to my name – my special thanks. On first thumbing through, everything I read seemed clear and convincing to me; some of it is new. I shall carefully study the chapter on *monodic* forms. – What place would you allocate to monodic phrases beneath a pedal note? –

(Gounod)

(very popular in opera, with 'tremolo'.)
But whole pedal-chords could also imply monody:

The harmony of *our* (European) music is toujours sous entendue; even if it can intentionally be varied, as in the harmonization of certain folk-songs. –

Gregorian chant is our finest example, it fascinates me; especially when heard in the Catholic church under certain conditions. – Once, at sunset, I entered Strasburg Cathedral. Invisible men's voices rang out:

Boys answered from the opposite direction:

You will find both in the slow movement of my [Piano] Concerto.

Monodic ideas like the two opening phrases of Parsifal are quite clearly harmonically conceived. Just as the fanfares of natural instruments. (Also the English horn in Tristan.)

I think: in comparison, Gregorian chant is 'absolute'.

But: I burble on. – Fate is knocking at the door to demand that I practise the 'Emperor' concerto:

Like that. (I beg your pardon!)

305 TO HUGO LEICHTENTRITT [postcard]
in German

Berlin 17.12.1920

Yesterday, only after I had posted my hasty letter, did yours arrive. [. . .] Another Beethovenian combination of themes has since occurred to me. I send it to you as a curiosity:

Adagio
Pathétique

Adagio of
the IXth

It is not so much a 'combination' as an equation. (The last period always resembles the first more closely.)

Incidentally, the construction of Beethoven's Adagio-themes is almost systematic. – Including that of the 'Emperor' concerto. – Which I successfully performed yesterday in a pleasant ambience.[1] This, too, 'fits' with the two above. Thus every light-source is held captive at the centre of its own corona. How much more so in the case of a lesser light. As for example

Yours truly,
F. Busoni.

[1]cf. letter no. 306.

306 TO VOLKMAR ANDREAE
in German

Berlin 28.12.1920

I envy you being able to rehearse the Beethoven Mass; I myself have played nothing more than the 'Emperor' concerto at the Staatstheater (with [Karl] Muck) and have turned down several offers from leading newspapers to write about B, as I have not yet overcome the crisis which has been troubling me for some years. My every word would have been bound to give rise to misunderstandings, and these would only have served to brand me. Indeed, my gratuitous remarks in Zurich provoked a certain outrage! – Thank you for your kind interest in my Berlin concerts.[1] I have also not been idle in other fields and have recently completed (apart from the piano Toccata, a Waltz for orchestra and cadenzas for Mozart's F major piano concerto)[2] over 50 double pages of 'Doktor Faust' score. – More than this has not been possible in the past three months, but I have no bad conscience. – As yet I am insufficiently informed about Schreker. Paul Bekker seems to bear a good deal of the responsibility for this. His first steps in Berlin were not propitious. He himself, now that I have got to know him, is evidently an inoffensive, ingenuous practical musician – (there is also such a thing as an 'honest-to-goodness'[3] careerist, qui sait) – and he utilizes his 'divine inspiration' fairly aimlessly but enthusiastically and with good grace. It is said that he spends whole nights playing and singing his operas to his pupils – and having them played and sung – with his wife lending a helping hand. – What an idealized, cosy domestic scene. – Well, if one changes a few of the details, here Austrian, there Swiss, there is also such a man in Zurich. – They both are, all things considered, agreeable fellows and know how to radiate an awkward charm – and to take advantage of it . . . Where, before the war, it was difficult for the young and up-and-coming to make themselves felt, indeed even to make themselves heard, now it is impossible to silence them. Music jumbled up out of Strauss and Schoenberg, quite *without talent*, is coming to the fore and meeting with approval. I think of your early works (and of mine as well) and am ashamed of the present generation. [. . .]

With *Weiss*[4] it is another story, for which – (I must stress) – I am not to blame, as I did not recommend him and have never heard him play the Brahms concerto. – Meanwhile he has fallen in love and become engaged – which may have impeded him. 'Allein, das Glück, wenn's wirklich kommt, ertragen – ist keines Menschen, wäre Gottes Sache'[5] (sings Platen). – I have not heard Reznicek's symphony,[6] but have, on the other hand, seen his opera 'Ritter Blaubart'.[7] The wonderful story has been ruined here by the text and the music! The librettist adheres to the generally accepted story of locked-up women and a murder cabinet. – But the infamous *Gil de Rais* was Marshal of France, an alchemist and exorcist. He made a pact to sacrifice children to the Devil and himself had a perverse predilection for the sexual abuse of his victims. It is a Faust story turned macabre, and a colossal theme. – The book I have been reading on recent evenings is connected with it, a little-known work of Walter Scott: 'On Demonology and Witchcraft'. It is 'all of a piece'. The ideas are, for me at least, fascinating. – Further to Gil de Rais, I would draw your attention to *Huysman's* masterly novel 'Là-bas', which also makes use of the legend. [. . .]

[1]On 7, 13 and 27 January were scheduled the so-called *Anbruch* concerts in the Philharmonie, Berlin: three concerts devoted entirely to Busoni's orchestral works, the first two conducted by the composer.

[2]These cadenzas were Busoni's Christmas 'offering' for 1920.

[3]Orig. olle ehrliche Arrivist (part Berlin dialect).

[4]Edward Weiss, born 1892, American pianist and longest surviving Busoni pupil. On 29 and 30 November 1920 he had played the Brahms Concerto no. 1 in d with Andreae at the Tonhalle, Zurich.

[5]'But fortune, when it really comes, can be endured by no man – 'twould be God's affair.' August von Platen, Sonnett LX.

[6]Presumably Reznicek's Symphony no. 4 in f, composed in 1919.

[7]*Ritter Blaubart*, with a libretto by Herbert Eulenburg, was first performed in Darmstadt on 29 January 1920.

307 TO PHILIPP JARNACH
in German

London 10.2.1921

[. . .] The work in Berlin[1] was actually more strenuous than I had realized in the midst of my exertions. Having remained on my feet for altogether forty hours, from leaving Berlin to sleeping in a real bed in London, I promptly had the pleasure of travelling to Bradford and back, and taking part in a rehearsal and concert between the two journeys. – The physical outcome was subsequently disquieting; but after only four days' vegetating and four nights' good sleep I am back in the saddle, as behoves a *Chevalier*, and one indeed who is no longer the youngest. [. . .]

I was glad you thought well of my conducting; if I had more frequent opportunities, I would be better at it! The last concert[2] was packed and I played particularly well. The effect was immediate. Despite (or because of?) which, the critics are trying to pass it over with a mere gesture. An old hag once brought me a rose and – while making her presentation – drove the thorns firmly into my hand! Dr L. Schmidt's behaviour, when he comes up with a critical bouquet, is not much different.

Flaubert's St Antoine and Mendelssohn's symphonies are treasure trove from the great chest of the 19th century. Unfortunately I am not familiar with Beyle's Italian novellas. – Just imagine: so significant a novelist as Wassermann is only now (at my behest and with my copy) getting to know 'Les Misérables'! – Only yesterday I wrote to enlighten a celebrated English novelist[3] who asserted that short stories were only being written in England, France and Russia, and who did not even mention Pirandello amongst the great writers in this genre! So much for the professionals. It is excusable, by comparison, for a musician not to have read Stendahl [sic]. Why does he write his name Stendhal? Probably on account of the same French orthographic blindness that changed Liszt to Listz (or Litz). This fellow Beyle, namely, cherished fond memories of being garrisoned in Stendahl (the first outpost to the west of Berlin) and used his *Souvenir de Garnison* as a *Nom de guerre*. – 'Les Amis' of M. Barbey d'Aurevilly have managed to elevate the latter to a state of literary inseparability from Villiers de l'Isle-Adam: I have never fallen for this, and B.d'A. figures just as little in my library as, for example, C. F. Meyer as counterpart to G. Keller. Admittedly, this is not entirely unbiased; but in art I have never had time for half measures; hence my harsh and intentionally derisive comments, which depict the situation 'net'. Thus I am fully aware what might be of value in Braunfels,[4] but I have to 'isolate' it. [. . .]

A new French musical journal[5] has made its début with an issue *à la mémoire de C. Debussy*. Musical wreaths are laid on his tomb by Fl. Schmitt, Malipiero and Stravinsky. You should see them! The Tartar cuts a pretty figure:

and so on for two pages, in this style or similar. Do you now understand *que nous sommes de la vieille feraille?*[7] (And they are the new clay, the Neutöner.)[8]

This is not so much a letter as a causerie; it lacks vis-à-vis and the accompanying bottle of wine. There is prohibition here until 6 o'clock in the evening, and my first glass must be not so much adjourned as ad-soir-ed.[9]

But once again you write nothing of yourself. Why?

Shall I try a new libretto for you in the summer? What sort of atmosphere would you care for this time? Maybe the first deed of Don Juan's grandson? (He discovers that he has seduced his own sister – and that she had already made love with Grandpa) . . . . . .

Assez!

[1]i.e. the *Anbruch* concerts.

[2]On 27 January Busoni had played the *Konzertstück*, op. 31a, the Indian Fantasy, op. 44, and the Piano Concerto (!). The conductor was Gustav Brecher.

[3]Identity uncertain; possibly Arnold Bennett.

[4]Walter Braunfels, 1882–1954, German composer.

[5]*La Revue Musicale.*

[6]Busoni misquotes this passage from Stravinsky's *Tombeau de Debussy* completely. The text is in fact:

[7]Literally 'that we are the old iron'.

[8]Orig. Und sie sind der neue Ton, Neutöner. Play on the double meaning of Ton = note *or* clay. Neutöner was a description often given to modern composers. Busoni complicates the issue still further by writing the old-style *Thon.*

[9]Orig. ver-abenden (invented word, play on vertagen = adjourn).

308 TO EDWARD J. DENT
in Italian

[Berlin] 5.4.1921

The first page – <u>Chapter the first</u> – of your lovely book on Mozart as opera composer[1] gave me food for thought.

You quote a distinguished living composer who proclaims the music-drama Trinity of *Mozart, Wagner* and *Verdi*.[2] From the quotation it is not clear whether the opinion of this distinguished composer is shared by the author of the book. But you continue from this point of departure, developing it as the foundation of your arguments and tacitly admitting that you approve of the idea. To me it seems audacious to place Mozart and Wagner on the same plane – Boito on that of Gluck – Charpentier in the same class as Meyerbeer, and Rossini in the shade.

You know, better than I, that the approval won by Meyerbeer and the influence he exercised were – at least – as great as Wagner's, also that Wagner himself is successor rather to Meyerbeer than to Mozart – and truly, that Wagner bears the same relationship to Meyerbeer as Zola to Balzac. Meyerbeer (like Balzac) was the more theatrical, the more original; Wagner (like Zola) was heavier, more systematic and *conscious*. – But where does one find the *uniqueness* of a piece like *The Barber of Seville*?! Neither in Verdi nor in Wagner, perhaps not even in Mozart himself! If you mention Boito and Charpentier, why do you omit the likes of Puccini?

Please excuse this outburst, but my artistic integrity will justify it. I await your reply (providing you consider one worth writing) with suspense.

From 16 April until 1 May: at the Augusteum, Rome.

[1] E. J. Dent, *Mozart's Operas*, London, 1913.
[2] Dent issued a revised edition of his book in 1947, in which this entire discussion is omitted. 'If any reader takes the trouble to compare this edition with the first, he will find that I have cut out large quantities of dead wood,' he remarked in his new preface.

309 TO VOLKMAR ANDREAE
in German

Berlin 14.5.1921

[. . .] I come from Rome, where I fared well and was appointed *Commendatore*. The return journey was hampered by interruptions and delays caused by a strike in Tyrol. In a hut on the 'Brenner', amidst the snow, arose an unexpected opportunity to give a counterpoint lesson. My young fellow traveller and sufferer, Heimann,[1] a very talented composer, solicited the situation – through his questions. Manuscript paper and pencils were produced and I initiated the young man into the mysteries of symmetrical inversion; a doctrine of Bernhard Ziehn's, to which I would draw your particular attention – for your composition classes. (In case I am not already too late!) (*B.Z. Canonische Studien.* Published by Kaun, Milwaukee and Berlin.)

Six days later I arrived here, just in time to watch over the final preparations for my operas. The productions promise very well. The orchestra is quite perfect, as is the conductor [Leo] Blech, and Artôt-Padilla[2] as Turandot. – This score has never sounded so satisfying. The rest is not quite on the same level; though the buffo tenor (Henke[3] as Truffaldino and Leandro) is reported to be remarkably reliable and adroit; due to his present complete hoarseness I have not yet heard him, and the first night has been postponed from the 13th to the 19th. – That will afford greater security and gain an extra rehearsal. –

– It was a fortunate coincidence for me that the latest novelty preceding my pieces was a most effective and successful production of '*Così fan Tutte*'. By fortunate, I mean that the public was able to cross a light, airy and pleasurable bridge from Schreker and Reznicek – to me.[4] It 'preached' the advantages of transparency of texture and conciseness of form to the public, and gave them – pleasure. – A comparison with my one-act operas would, of course, be less to my favour: but at the heart of the matter remains the fact that the people learnt once more to appreciate clarity and amiability as something valuable. When I came here six months ago, people were turning up their noses at such things. – I have found this particular state of affairs to a certain extent everywhere; in particular – where I least expected it – in England! – Incidentally, this was the first chance in my life to see Così fan Tutte. – Although I already knew the score well, it gave me several surprises (especially in its sonorities), which delighted me.

From a distance, the rumours about la gloire et la décadence du Docteur Reucker[5] afford no clear picture of the state of affairs in Switzerland's leading theatre. Denzler[6] signed his letter to me as 'Directeur'; on the other hand, I was told of the sudden closure of this temple of the Muses. (NB Denzler was writing for particularly personal reasons: this fact does not contradict my opening words.) – All the more radiant, then, should be the reopening of the opera house with the international festival.[7] – I would, however, have imagined something other than 'Parsifal' for this purpose, but the work makes a fine gateway, even if not exactly leading towards international domains, but rather into a German stateroom. – I believe I have become 'durch Mitleid wissend';[8] but, as yet, only very few people believe in my wisdom. However, the reaction is slowly setting in, eating away at the foundations of this palace in the style of the 70's. The younger generation (particularly those who are not professional musicians) is apathetically allowing the building to dilapidate. This is happening without hatred or demonstration: with tragic indifference. – Therefore, unfortunately, nobody is taking the trouble to replace the edifice with a new one: and this is where we – who have become 'durch Mitleid wissend' – have to take action, have to teach. –

It was a good omen that you once again paid a substantial tribute to Berlioz.[9] One should serve up 'The Trojans' as well, before they get completely cold.

Once again, the marionette theatre in Rome gave me great joy, this time with Rossini's 'La Gazza ladra'. – I hope to bring this group, which now has 60 works in its repertoire and possesses about 1,000 puppets, to Germany.

[1]Identity uncertain. Possibly a relative of Busoni's friend, the writer Moritz Heimann, 1868–1925.
[2]Lola Artôt de Padilla, 1886–1933, celebrated mezzo-soprano, daughter of the famous singers Mariano Padilla and Desirée Artôt; Strauss conceived the role of the Composer in *Ariadne auf Naxos* for her.
[3]Waldemar Henke, 1876–1945, German tenor. Joined the ensemble of the Staatsoper, Berlin, in 1911.
[4]The repertoire at the Staatsoper, Berlin, in the spring of 1921 included Reznicek's *Ritter Blaubart*, d'Albert's *Tiefland* and *Die toten Augen*, Schreker's *Die Gezeichneten* and Schillings's *Mona Lisa*. Busoni's *Turandot* and *Arlecchino*, in a production by Franz Ludwig Hörth, were performed five times in May and June 1921.
[5]Alfred Reucker, the Intendant of the Stadt-Theater, Zurich, terminated his contract at the end of the 1920–1 season to take up a similar position at the Sächsisches Staatstheater, Dresden.
[6]Robert F. Denzler, 1892–1972, Swiss conductor and composer. In 1921 he became Director of the Stadt-Theater in Zurich.
[7]The Zurich International Festival opened on 24 June 1921 with a performance of *Parsifal* conducted by Bruno Walter and with Karl Erb in the title role.
[8]'Wise through compassion', Wagner, *Parsifal*.
[9]Andreae conducted *La Damnation de Faust* in Zurich on 6 and 8 February 1921. The previous year he had performed the Grande Messe des Morts; in 1922 he conducted *Roméo et Juliette*.

310 TO EDWARD J. DENT
in Italian

Berlin 30.5.1921

[. . .] This evening the operas are receiving their fourth performance at the Staatstheater. They are being repeated next Saturday and probably also during June. They had a wonderful success and provoked much discussion. The third performance of Arlecchino was wellnigh perfect. – I don't know whether you have read Bekker's review of the Wellesz in the Frankfurter Zeitung.[1] I have no idea what kind of opinion you have of B. as a music critic. To me it seems that he says some most significant things in this article (17 May): particularly in a certain passage about *the fear of not being 'up to date'* in modern art. I endorse his comment. For the rest, his judgement of Wellesz's opera is one of harsh censure. Bekker denies any qualities in the work whatsoever. I am sorry for the composer and his librettist: but I am delighted

at some *general* ideas of great lucidity which the occasion has brought
forth. [. . .]

Manuel de Falla, Claude le Ville – what beautiful, sonorous names, how
aristocratic and chivalrous! One is led to imagine some new romantic era.
And they harmonize completely with the historical traditions which you
imply with regard to English *choral societies*. I must confess that my Concerto
was not conceived for British choirs: and, since I have never taken the liberty
of soliciting a performance of this work from a choral society, it would seem
out of place for me to modify it according to the demands of these respectable
institutions.

Anyway, the chorus in the Concerto should remain *invisible* and add a new
register to the sonorities which precede it. I cannot clearly understand your
prudent advice, which reproaches me with having failed to follow Beethoven,
and with having imitated Liszt; especially as I am conscious of having copied
neither of them, and as you yourself speak of Beethoven's Choral Fantasy as a
work which is *not* exemplary. God forbid that I should compare my piece to a
mass of Bach's or Beethoven's; but I see no need to transform the Concerto
into an oratorio. – It may well be that the chorus would find it entertaining to
perform complicated vocal works, but – on the other hand – I am not sure
whether the audience would derive the same pleasure from listening to them.
– To conclude: on this occasion your aesthetic criteria are unconvincing. I say
this with all respect for that erudition, honesty and friendship of yours which
has inspired and continues to inspire me. – In the archives of Breitkopf &
Härtel there exists an unpublished version of the Concerto *without chorus*. I
do not readily like to admit this: for the ethical reasons which determined the
form of the Concerto, over which I pondered for *three years*, and which I shall
expound to you on some other occasion – perhaps verbally – are against it.

[1]Egon Wellesz's opera *Die Prinzessin Girnara*, op. 27, with a libretto by Jakob
Wassermann, had received its world première on 15 May 1921 in Hanover. Paul
Bekker's review had the effect of an anathema; however, Wellesz revised the work
and it received a second production at Mannheim in 1928.

311 TO HUGO LEICHTENTRITT
in German

Berlin 10.6.1921

You showered me with such rich and delightful gifts yesterday that I have to
thank you once again, in writing! – And now this morning some Monteverdi
madrigals,[1] as I read them through, cast their light and warmth upon me: so
beautiful and ingenious, with such intensity of feeling – literally breathing it
– that I find it ever harder to understand how, after scaling such heights,
things like the address to the swan[2] or 'am stillen Herd'[3] could have been
considered models of expressiveness!

Although I scarcely knew this old Italian music, I identify myself very closely with it: there must be a tinge of atavism lying dormant in me, that links me with it. – You will come upon a few phrases in Faust that betray a heredity for which I can find no other explanation.

I have taken much upon myself for the summer (and will be glad if I manage to achieve half of it):[4] but now the task of reading Ambros-Leichtentritt[5] must be added to the rest.

My personal acquaintance with the original author and his editor spans 45 years of my life!

[1]Leichtentritt had just published a volume of Monteverdi madrigals (see letter no. 313).
[2]From *Lohengrin*, Act III.
[3]From *Die Meistersinger von Nürnberg*, Act I.
[4]cf. 'Plan der Sommer Arbeit 1921 (p. 338–9).
[5]A. W. Ambros *Geschichte der Musik*. This fourth edition, published in Berlin, 1909, was edited and extended up to 1650 by Leichtentritt.

312 TO EDITH ANDREAE
in German

[Berlin] 13.6.1921

[. . .] Would that you could see the programme I have planned for my work this summer.[1] You would gain the impression that I had burdened myself with more than I shall probably achieve. This state of affairs is causing me much trouble, and I am economizing on all sides; sometimes – I must admit – without accomplishing very much here or there but, generally speaking, making fruitful progress!

Thus time seems to be constantly rushing by, while my work crawls along; and this results in a form of nervousness which I would describe as moral possessiveness. – But one's external activities also swallow up time and energy. On 1 July I 'officially' open my class at the Academy. That means appearing in armour before a dozen critical youngsters, withstanding each cut and thrust, parrying objections and contradictions, playing the 'Master'. – A periodical, 'Faust', will occupy me as editor responsible for musical questions. – New orchestral concerts, planned in a wide-ranging style, will occasion my return to the rostrum. I shall also play the piano. – My life is shrivelling up. That's how it is with me, and I feel obliged to explain this to you. Thank you for your continued sympathy and loyal devotion.

I am altogether of the opinion that the thread which binds us has not yet been spun to its end; I depend upon and hope for the possibility of our mutually spinning it further. Be patient and considerate. – I am in good form and more impressionable than usual: less impetuous, but more deeply (often painfully) impressionable. – I can and may only do what I am able to do most proficiently: and, I think, this is a rule which would be well applied to each individual and to society as a whole; if it were generally observed. –

I embrace you.

[1]Here is Busoni's'Plan der Sommer Arbeit 1921' (p. 339).

Summer work-plan 1921[1]
[facsimile on facing page]

New catalogue
Liszt–Busoni edition
Mozart–Busoni edition
Revision of piano works and new impression
Orchestration examples from my own works★

‒‒‒‒

Libretto volume[2]
Foreword to Faust
x Fantasia Contrapp. for 2 pianos
   (integration of the two preludes)
[Arrange Tanz]Walzer for piano, or 2 pfte.
complete Paganini–Liszt
Critical edition of Mozart's C minor concerto

‒‒‒‒

Proof reading
Sort books
– Shadow-play in Turandot
Doktor Faust, continue and complete
– Das Wandbild as Faust-scene
– Mozart cycle in the autumn

★eg. 1 flute, 2 flutes, 3 fl., as solo, as group, as middle voice, as doubling, in relationship to other instruments – The major groups – linear orchestration – construct missing examples.

[1]By courtesy of the Rowe Music Library, Cambridge
[2]From a letter to Hans Heinz Ewers dated 28.6.1922 it transpires that Busoni was planning to publish ten of his libretti in book form. These would have been: *Der mächtige Zauberer, Die Brautwahl, Frau Potiphar, Das Geheimnis, Die Götterbraut, Arlecchino, Turandot, Arlecchino* Part II, *Das Wandbild* and *Doktor Faust*.

Plan der Sommer Arbeit 1921

Neues Verzeichnis

Liszt - Busoni - Ausgabe

Mozart - Busoni - Ausg.

Revision der Klav. Werkes u. Neu Auflage   *

Instrumentations beispiele aus eigenen Wke.

Textbücher - Band.

Vorwort zu Faust

X Fantasia Contrapp. zu 2 Klav.
(Zusammenfassung der beiden Vorspiele.)

Walzer für Klav., od. 2 Kl.

Paganini = Liszt vervollständigen

Kritische Ausgabe von Mozarts Cmoll Konz.

Korrekturen

Bücher ordnen

— Schattenspiel in Turandot

Doktor Faust weiter u. zu Ende.

— Das Wandbild, als Faust-Szene

——— Mozart Zyklus im Herbst

* 3.B. 1 Flöte, 2 Flöten, 3 Fl., als Solo, als Gruppe, als
Füllstimme, als Verdoppelung, im Verhältnis zu
anderen Instrumenten. — Die grossen Gruppen. —
die lineare Orchestration. — Fehlende Beispiele konstruieren.

16 The composition class in the music-room, Berlin 1922 (from l. to r.) Kurt Weill, Walther Geiser, Busoni, Luc Balmer, Vladimir Vogel. One of Busoni's Buddhas is clearly to be seen behind Weill.

313 TO VOLKMAR ANDREAE
in German

Berlin 15.6.1921

Your insights about Italy being the land of beauty and the 'Camorra'[1] are quite correct. – 'Nach England möchte ich gern, wenn nicht die Engländer wären' was already Heine's song;[2] and this is how it is – cum grano salis – with every country: (excepting Switzerland, of course). Meanwhile my last visit to my home country was more satisfying and my standing has 'risen'. – As a foreigner, you have an easier time of it in Italy than a native. It is no coincidence that the phrase 'Nemo propheta in patria' comes from *Rome*.

I congratulate you on your string quartet and the progress of *Casanova*.[3] The author of your libretto recently sent me another of his works for inspection: I have not got round to reading it: firstly due to lack of time; but also because I sense that I – as a composer – can find no use for the words, phrases, metaphors, feelings, omissions and prolixities of someone else. – I recently read a notable essay on this problem by an older music critic, *Riehl*.[4]

– I had to laugh about Wanda Landowska, the Mono-Pole. – But it is a wretched custom in her country, this agreement by which the poor girl is being boycotted in every town. Therein lies a (defensive) strength which I have not yet been able to categorize as instinctive or systematic. – In the last few days I have been reading through the madrigals of Monteverdi (Leichtentritt's edition, published by Peters) and they have made an overwhelming impression on me. This intensity of expression which breathes and speaks, and this freedom and beauty of form stand beside Bach and Mozart at the summit. What this man could signify for Italy – today! – has become so forcibly clear to me, that I wrote a special letter about it to the Ministry of Fine Arts in Rome. –

– Petri brought an interesting youngster with him from Basle, – Balmer,[5] who showed me a remarkable quartet. – He and Laquai[6] have been recommended for Donaueschingen, where a festival of contemporary chamber music is to take place in August under the auspices of Prince Fürstenberg. – I am working hard, and not a week goes by (scarcely a single day) without bringing forth new offers and plans. – Concerts, newspapers, theatres, foreign countries. – On 1 July my class at the Academy begins.

A few days ago Paul Bekker wrote a fine review of my Bach Edition.[7] – Do you see anything of Benni? . . . .

---

[1]Neapolitan criminal organization.

[2]Heine, *Romanzero*, Book Two: Lamentationen, 'Jetzt wohin?':

Gern würd ich nach England gehn,
Wären dort nicht Kohlendämpfe
Und Engländer –

To England would I gladly roam
Were the place not full of fogs
And Englishmen –

[3]Andreae's String Quartet in e, op. 33, and his opera *Die Abenteuer des Casanova*, op. 34, with a libretto by F. Lion.

[4]Wilhelm Heinrich Riehl, 1823–1897, German musicologist.

[5]Luc Balmer, born 1898, Swiss composer and conductor. He had studied with Hans Huber at Basle and came to join Busoni's class in Berlin.

[6]Reinhold Laquai, 1884–1957, Swiss composer.

[7]Paul Bekker's lengthy review in the *Frankfurter Zeitung* on 11 June 1921 includes the following observation:

Busoni's new edition of the 'Well-tempered Clavier', in its technical, formal and stylistic stimuli, is not merely an enrichment of the didactic literature which can scarcely be passed over. It is more: the first far-reaching approach to contemporary pianism, the one and only 'highest school' of modern virtuosity. Apart from its significance for this one instrument, it is a revelatory investigation of the spiritual and technical basis of music as a whole.

314 TO RAFFAELLO BUSONI
in German

Berlin 18.6.1921

Already more than two years ago, as you know, I brought the term 'Young Classicality' into the world and prophesied popularity for it, even then. My experiences in this respect have been curious; for today the phrase is in general circulation, but nobody remembers who coined it. Hence it is sometimes said that even Busoni adheres to Young Classicality . . .! To arrive at its formulation, one need be no prophet. After an unconscionable series of experiments, starting with the 'Secessionists', who were then subdivided into counter-secessions and finally into bevies of independent sub-groups, the need for a comprehensive certainty of style inevitably arose. But – as with everything else – here, too, I have been misunderstood, in that the multitude construed Classicality as something retrospective. This is confirmed in painting – e.g. in the rehabilitation of Ingres who – master in his own right – presents a horrifying example of ossified forms. (My opinion here is intentionally harsh.) My idea (or rather perception, personal necessity rather than fabricated principle) is that *Young Classicality* should signify completion[1] in two senses: as *perfection* and as ending, as the *conclusion* to all preceding experiments.[2] I lay stress on the importance of the word 'Young' in order to distinguish Classicality from conventional classicism. Every recent or new means, should it be capable of expressing something which cannot be expressed in any other way, ought to be adopted and employed; intentional disdain of effective new achievements strikes me as unreasonable and im-poverished. Just as unreasonable and impoverished as the system of devising and proclaiming one particular new means of expression – and thereby denying every other. But the artist of integrity will realize all this without deliberation. He attempts to attain what he imagines to be perfection – the ambience of the period makes its influence automatically felt – according to his own conception, his own nature – and he believes – should he possess a degree of individuality – that what he has created is perfectly normal, while others remain perplexed and astonished. In my youth one was indeed *warned* against following the vogue. 'That sounds too "Wagnerian" – "Brahmsian" – "Scandinavian"' – was the reprimand. Be true to yourself to the best of your ability and with genuine forms. Today I can fortify you only with these words and in no other way, least of all for the technical intricacies and fundaments of your art. But these lines are universally valid. Finally, let me cite a relevant example. When Cazotte published his 'Diable amoureux'[3] he laid himself open to the most fiendish scorn on account of the book's illustrations. It featured (anonymous) satires on the Expressionists of the time, in the form of etchings by the accomplished master, Moreau le jeune.[4] The difference between the unsurpassable, serious drawings of Moreau and this counterfeit bungling is stupendous – and yet – the artist's soul is not disavowed, refuses to be suppressed, indeed the caricatures are altogether meaningful and well-formed! The Bibliothèque des Bibliophyles [sic] incorporated the old engravings in a reprint[5] but also felt obliged (as the publishers stated) to include new ones (Eaux fortes by Buhot),[6] which are serious in intention and terribly shoddy. – This happened in the year of grace 1878. – I find the clumsy, poorly drawn satires valuable, while Buhot's accurate and serious contributions are altogether insignificant.

'Das gibt zu denken'.[7] Be of good heart.

[1]Orig. *Vollendung*.
[2]The opening of this letter (up to this point) was published in the 2nd Edition of Busoni's *Wesen und Einheit der Musik*, 1956.
[3]Jacques Cazotte, *Le Diable amoureux*, Naples and Paris, 1772.
[4]Louis Gabriel Moreau, 1739–1805, actually called l'Aîné, not le jeune.
[5]The book was published in a series entitled 'Petite bibliothèque de luxe'. Busoni bought his copy in 1909 (see letter to Gerda, 12.8.1909) and briefly considered adapting the work as an opera or mime.
[6]Félix-Hilaire Buhot, 1847–1898, French book-illustrator.
[7]'Food for thought'. Quotation from the libretto of *Arlecchino*, fourth movement.

315 TO EGON PETRI
in German

Berlin 22.6.1921

[. . .] I am busy: have finished a new piece for piano + orchestra,[1] 2 new albumleaves,[2] have reworked the Fantasia Contrappuntistica for 2 pianos and come as far as the 1st fugue. – Today I completed a new musical number for Turandot which was previously spoken dialogue and, to my mind, always poorly spoken.[3] – Have written 54 pages of the score of Faust. – As you see, I am letting no grass grow under my feet.

Scarcely a day passes without news of some venture or offer. For you, too, there are several prospects. I confidently hope that you will develop and rise to prominence. Look forward more than I can express to your being here.

[1]*Romanza e Scherzoso*, op. 54, conceived as an extension to the *Konzertstück*, op. 31a. It was completed on 21 June 1921.
[2]Nos. 2 and 3 of the Drei Albumblätter. No. 2 was composed in Rome, i.e. in April 1921; no. 3 is dated 25 May 1921.
[3]This 'Nachtrag zu *Turandot*' is not incorporated in the published vocal score and today exists only in one copy of the orchestral score with Breitkopf und Härtel in Wiesbaden. The sketch for these 90 bars is indeed dated 22 June 1921.

316 TO RAFFAELLO BUSONI
in German

[Berlin] 15.7.1921

It is good of you to write so often and so cheerfully; we read your letters at the breakfast table and are delighted with their form and content. – Of late you are thinking some things over and entering the inevitable 'period of reflection' which every talented person has to go through. Naturally this takes the form apt to each individual – according to time – place – profession. – As a musician in the 19th century and in Leipzig, I had other headaches than a painter in the 20th century and in Paris. I am experiencing the difference with my pupils, with whom I opened a course of study in this month of July. So far there are four: a headstrong Russian, who always likes to be in the right and accomplishes little;[1] a somewhat perfumed Croatian who is already 'professor' in Zagreb;[2] a very fine little Jew (who will certainly make his way and is already something of a factotum around the house);[3] and finally a small podgy youth who looks like an inflated tyre, wears enormous glasses perched on his nose and is undoubtedly talented.[4] The two latter are a source of pleasure. But *where* does one begin to teach? At the moment this is quite a problem. They have great ability and are yet incapable of the simplest things, their forms are complex and yet not diversified, and they exercise the general right of today's youth to proclaim every crooked line as individuality and freedom. Where does one start? I can only bring them to reason gradually and patiently. Were I to 'drive my point home', I would become ridiculous in their eyes and fail to convince them. Am I not one of the 'leaders of modern trends'? Are they not fulfilling – this is what they feel – my boldest dreams? – Oh, what misunderstanding!

– Since the operas were over, I myself have been working harder than almost ever. I only took a break from 4 to 7 July. In these few weeks I have completed two entire major works and sketched out much more. Now it is again – and finally – time for Faust. It has already been accepted for performance in the Staatstheater here. – You once wrote, in jest, that all my *titles* no longer fit on an envelope. Just for fun, I want to enumerate them for you.

I am: (but for this one needs a whole new page) –

Honorary member of the Royal Academy in Bologna,
    twice: as pianist and as composer
    since 1883, when I was 17 years old.
Laureate of the Rubinstein Prize (1890).
    a) Imperial Professor in Russia[5]
    b) K.& K. Professor in Austria
    c) State Professor in Berlin.
Court Pianist to the Grand-Duke of Weimar.
Doctor at the University of Zurich.

Chevalier de la Légion d'honneur.
Commendatore della Corona d'Italia.
Senator of the [Prussian] State Academy.
Ex-director of the Liceo musicale, Bologna.
One should also mention several appointments and honours, for example:
Member of the Royal Academy in Stockholm, committee member of the
Neue Bach-Gesellschaft, of the Liszt-Stiftung – etc. etc. – shortly to become
[music] editor of a journal, 'Faust'.
   – Are you satisfied with your father? – [. . .]

[1]Vladimir Vogel, 1896–1982. Busoni seems later to have revised his opinion of him.
[2]Identity uncertain; probably Božidar Sirola, 1889–1956, who had studied in Zagreb
and Vienna.
[3]Kurt Weill, 1900–1950.
[4]Robert Blum, born 1900. He fell ill after three months in Berlin and had to return to
Zurich.
[5]Busoni makes no mention of his professorships at Helsinki or Boston.

317 TO PHILIPP JARNACH
in German

Berlin 22.8.1921

[. . .] I had to smile a little at the 'effervescent talent' and wild immoderation
of our mythical Hindu.[1] He has committed an error of taste from which I
must first recover; has namely 'set' to music one of those unqualifiable pieces
of amateurism (a so-called drama) by the painter Kokoschka, as an . . .
opera.[2] – I have been following your progress in Donaueschingen with
satisfaction. 'Der Vogel der heut' sang'[3] – you seem to have shot him down.
Suffering as he does from pathological arrogance, Weissmann[4] writes: 'We
can be proud of him' – what a cheek! – (But a brilliant introduction . . . . . .)
For he speaks in the name of all the Germans and has taken it upon himself
to invade Spain on their behalf; having judged it worthy of invasion. – I have
gladly taken the 'Kaminski'[5] business ad notam. Such a case cannot be
supported for less than 25,000 Marks and I shall have to think this over.
   I am fairly tired, having worked *uninterruptedly* for 3 months.

[1]i.e. Paul Hindemith.
[2]*Mörder, Hoffnung der Frauen*, composed in 1919. The world première was at
Stuttgart on 4 June 1921. In 1924 this work shared the stage with Busoni's *Arlecchino*
and Stravinsky's *Petrushka* at Weimar.
[3]'The bird that sang today' from Sachs's monologue in Act II of *Die Meistersinger von
Nürnberg*, i.e. Vladimir Vogel.
[4]Adolf Weissmann, 1873–1929, the most influential Berlin critic of his time.
[5]Heinrich Kaminski, 1886–1946, German composer.

318 TO EDITH ANDREAE
in German

Berlin 12.9.1921

[. . .] I have been in 'Parma' and 'Wittenberg'[1] where, for a few weeks, I visited the tavern first thing every morning. Indeed, I worked continuously from June until the end of August and produced several things. – (My wife has recently taken to calling me 'le père Gustave'; an allusion to Flaubert, who was interested in nothing except a well-constructed sentence.) – Now I am preparing myself for what is to come. – Firstly, the operas wish to put in a new appearance, with 'Turandot' in a new edition. On 1 October appears a new journal, 'Faust' (monthly, at 25 Marks per issue), in whose 1st number a major essay of mine is to be published.[2] (G. Hauptmann is also involved in it.) – In November I shall be giving a 2-piano recital with *Petri*,[3] who is now engaged as a professor at the Hochschule. – The Staatsoper is planning a Mozart cycle, for which I am to play six piano concertos. – In January I am off to England. – These are my active obligations. I have planned at least as much for my contemplative moments. All in all these make my life calm and productive, meanwhile I am creating a new home for my books. (I hope to be able to show you round it before Christmas.) But also to see you anyway and converse with the old rapport.

I find that Berlin – in which I have *today* been resident for exactly *one year* – has improved noticeably in the intervening time. I find it stimulating, even if I get to see no more of it than from here to the Nollendorfplatz.[4] – But it pulses with life. –

[1]i.e. working at the First and Second Tableaux of the *Hauptspiel* of *Doktor Faust*.
[2]The 'Outline of a foreword to the score of *Doktor Faust*', republished in *Von der Einheit der Musik*.
[3]The recital, on 16 November 1921 in the Beethovensaal, Berlin, in which Petri played *first* piano, consisted of Mozart's Sonata in D, K. 448, and three works by Busoni: Improvisation on 'Wie wohl ist mir', Duettino Concertante after Mozart and *Fantasia Contrappuntistica*.
[4]From Busoni's house to the Nollendorfplatz was a distance of some 200 yards!

319 TO VOLKMAR ANDREAE
in German

Berlin 16.1.1922

Very nice of you to write! (Did Allegra spur you to it?) Even nicer that your enthusiasm waxed in the process and that one card soon became four. For this card-trick I would gratefully say, with Goethe's Kaiser: 'Ich wünsche mir dergleichen Scherze viel.'[1] You say that the second act of 'Casanova' has been absorbing you but do not mention whether it is finished. I hope so. (Has our friend, the Marchese of the same name, also sent you his book of poetry? He writes exceptionally good German! But what infecundity and lifelessness . . . Which one could certainly not say of his lead-chambered namesake.[2] –

– Sadly I have taken all too little notice of the death of my dear friend Hans Huber;[3] although deeply moved by the news, I mean that I have written neither to Switzerland nor anywhere else about it. This was due to the time at which the news reached me. I myself was unhappy and, besides, over-strained; moreover I had written an obituary of Saint-Saëns only a few days previously:[4] a dismal state of affairs, in which one also did not quite comprehend one's own grief. I valued Hans Huber highly and loved him even more. Was the event passed over in silence in Switzerland, or has there been a public manifestation? —— Thank you for continuing to think of me so kindly. The article in 'Faust'[5] has not, as yet, been widely circulated; but those who have read it have done so with undivided attention. Vol. III of 'Faust' will include my outline for a scenic production of the St Matthew Passion, the first inspiration for which came to me in Zurich. –

The Mozart cult is gradually on the increase here and Wagner's domain is slowly being reduced. There was a fine performance here of
Così fan Tutte
And I played six piano concertos in two evenings,[6] a few days ago we had the first night of a new Zauberflöte production[7] and Edwin Fischer has given a —— Bach–Mozart recital!

Also the trashy bogus daubings of the expressionists are gradually being jettisoned. When I came here, only le dernier cri was valid – no matter what it sounded like – (or looked like). This pestilence is now moving abroad, it would seem. Thus Jarnach's quintet is said to have been rejected in Amsterdam as being outmoded. For my taste, Jarnach writes too many 'Deutsche Lieder', of the meaningful sort, moreover . . . Nevertheless, we are very fond of each other, he is an intelligent and true friend. I only see him when he calls on me, as I myself go *nowhere*. But if I do set off somewhere, then it is to London; as will once again be the case next week . . . .

– But to return to Mozart. I recently astonished Herr von Schillings[8] (I fear) with a conjecture that Mozart had a pretty poor time of it, whereas Beethoven lived in relatively splendid circumstances. Thus it was that Mozart had enough opportunity in real life to give vent to his ill-feelings, leaving nothing but his own serenity for his art (implicitly overshadowed here and there by an accent of pain); while it was the evil streak in the more fortunate Beethoven that drove him to express his bad temper in music. The latter idea is phrased a little superficially, I have not yet found the formulation which would psychologically explain what I feel to be the truth of the situation.

– The case of Schopenhauer is almost identical: he lived very comfortably in Frankfurt, free to do as he wished; and in theory he found the whole world evil – in which he was not unjustified, but for which he had, on the other hand, no justification.

– Your news of Benni's engagement has taken me *completely* unawares.[9] For a long time he has sent me no news at all, and I am quite uninformed about this turn of events. You will soon be receiving a printed copy of the Sarabande und Cortège, as well as other pieces.

[1]Goethe, *Faust*, Part II, 5988: 'I wish more entertainments of the sort.'
[2]From 1755–6 Giacomo Casanova was imprisoned in the Venetian 'lead-chambers'.
[3]Hans Huber died on 25 December 1921.
[4]Saint-Saëns died on 16 December 1921. Busoni's obituary notice, 'Erinnerungen an Saint-Saëns', was published in the *Vossische Zeitung* (also later incorporated in *Von der Einheit der Musik*).
[5]See footnote no. 2 to previous letter.
[6]Busoni played K.491 in c, K.453 in G, K.482 in Eb; K.466 in d, K.488 in A, K.467 in C. These two programmes were performed in December 1921 at the Philharmonie, Berlin, conductor Otto Marienhagen, and repeated in January 1922 at the Staatsoper, conductor Leo Blech.
[7]Franz Ludwig Hörth's production of *Die Zauberflöte* opened on 13 January 1922. The conductor was Leo Blech.
[8]Max von Schillings, 1868–1933, composer of the opera *Mona Lisa*. He was appointed Intendant of the Staatsoper, Berlin, in 1919. Busoni referred to him sarcastically as 'penny pieces' and thought little of *Mona Lisa*, whose vocal score he had seen in 1915.
[9]Benvenuto Busoni was engaged to the 21-year-old Henriette Rinderknecht, a seamstress from Zurich. It is said that he chose her as his bride because she was the only person he met in Zurich who had never heard of his father. They married on 28 January 1922.

320 TO EGON PETRI
in German

London 10.2.1922

Today I received two letters forwarded from Berlin, the first to arrive since I got to London (i.e. for two weeks), which were to me what the dove was to Noah.

– Therefore I have refrained from writing even to you, as I had only 'stipulated limits', which we would not have exceeded.

All the same, I sent off a group of letters into the blue because I enjoy writing, and in this comfortable smoking-room I can sit, write and imbibe to my heart's content all morning, as if in a sanatorium.[1]

I just wanted to remind you to bring the five pieces for the 2-piano recital, which has already been advertised;[2] furthermore to ask you to pack up the orchestral parts of the Romanza and Scherzoso. Gerda suggests the Indian Fantasy as well, in case anything unforeseen should happen. Not enough. It would be desirable for you to bring several copies of the Toccata, the Albumleaves, the Carmen Fantasy, indeed of all my more recent pieces. They are unobtainable in London or Paris! (This, amongst other things, is part of my fate as a composer, that Br. + H. seem practically to withhold my pieces!) – And, finally, my leather slippers! I miss them greatly. – The higher my reputation rises as a pianist (and it seems still to be on the increase), the more unjust is the opinion of me as a composer. By trying to help myself, I am working against my own interests. I should have been born a hermaphrodite, in the sense of that heroic-fantastic being in Voltaire's 'La Pucelle'; a man by day and a woman by night, and both with equal impetus . . . I am indeed something of the sort, except that this other side of me is not accredited.

If standards were so high that I were obliged to admit my own deficiency, I would understand this. But recently, in Glasgow, I heard two works by Sir [Edward] Elgar[3] which are rated here as the acme of the art of composition: an Andante for strings, which falls somewhere between the 'Preislied' and Mascagni's Intermezzo, and the orchestration of a Bach fugue with *incessant* accompaniment of cymbals, tambourine and bass drum. It was appalling. Quite apart from the Turkish music, the scoring lacked organization, the interpretation was terre à terre. – Thus the foreshortening of my works is being seen not from the aspect of a bird on the wing, but rather from a frog's-eye view!

London is beautiful, yesterday evening at dusk it was bewitching, early in the morning five days ago (when I arrived back from Glasgow) it was full of secret promise for the dawning day. [. . .]

[1]Busoni was staying at the Langham Hotel.
[2]Petri and Busoni played at the Wigmore Hall on 18 February 1922. The programme was: Mozart–Busoni, Fantasie für eine Orgelwalze (completed on 23 January 1922), Busoni, Improvisation on 'Wie wohl ist mir', Duettino concertante after Mozart and *Fantasia Contrappuntistica*. The programme was repeated in Paris on 8 March.
[3]This was a concert at St Andrew's Hall, Glasgow, on 7 February 1922. Busoni played the Liszt Concerto no. 2 in A, then his *Carmen* Fantasy and Weber's *Perpetuum Mobile*. These latter were preceded by the Andante from Elgar's Serenade for Strings and the Bach–Elgar Organ Fugue in c, op. 86. Busoni presumably did not stay for the 'Enigma' Variations, which concluded the concert.

321 TO LEO KESTENBERG
in German

Paris 3.3.1922

Today I received a registered letter from the Berlin Ministry in which I was requested *for the 3rd time* to inform them of my name and profession, as well as other details concerning my dubious person. Via this tortuous route my thoughts turn to you, hence this letter.

Here in Paris (the city in which I am least at home and where I know nobody), I am being treated *very* well. So well that I have to perform 5 different programmes in 10 days, of which three alone call for six piano concertos.[1] Moreover, each of these programmes includes a number of my own works. And these wonderful orchestras play them magnificently.

From Haydn's horse-drawn carriage via Wagner's locomotive-art, music has arrived at the aeroplane stage, here as everywhere. Mozart's fine, upright gait is not appreciated: an attempt to perform Don Giovanni at the Opéra comique has failed . . . My style takes everyone aback: too young for the old, insufficiently mindless for the young, it constitutes a clear-cut chapter in the disorder of our times. – Inasmuch, it will hold its own better with subsequently fluctuating later generations.

Incidentally (I would like to record this observation here too) I have reflected that the fame of a virtuoso is *more durable* than that of a creative artist! This seems to contradict every conventional dictum, but I would justify the idea as follows: a virtuoso's fame cannot be tested by later generations, who adopt and recognize it on trust. The creative artist's claim to fame is tested afresh by every new generation and often disavowed, frequently reduced, at any rate greeted with scepticism and rarely fully confirmed. [. . .]

Unfortunately, the gramophone companies are now seeing to it that later generations can also criticize the virtuoso: I recently exposed myself to this situation by playing for a phonograph recording![2] A devilish invention which *lacks the demonic nuance.* [. . .]

---

[1]Busoni's Paris schedule: 4 March 1922, Concert Colonne, with Mozart's Concerto in c, K. 491, and Busoni's Concertino, op. 54 (first performance in France), conductor Gabriel Pierné; 5 March, Concert Colonne, with Mozart's Concerto in C, K. 467, Busoni's *Berceuse élégiaque* and *Rondò arlecchinesco*, Liszt's Concerto No. 2 in A, conductor Gabriel Pierné; 8 March two-piano recital with Egon Petri (for programme see footnote no. 2 to previous letter); 12 March, Société des concerts du Conservatoire with Mozart's Concerto in G, K. 453, Busoni's *Sarabande und Cortège*, op. 51, and Saint-Saëns' Concerto No. 5 in F, conductor Philippe Gaubert; 15 March recital at Salle Erard, programme of Bach, Beethoven, Busoni and Chopin.

[2]On 27 February Busoni recorded the following works in London for Columbia Records:
  Bach: Prelude and Fugue no. 1 in C (Well-tempered Clavier, Book I)
  Bach–Busoni: Chorale prelude 'Nun freut euch, lieben Christen'
  Beethoven–Busoni: Ecossaises
  Chopin: Prelude in A major, op. 28 no. 7
          Etude no. 5 in Gb, op. 10 no. 5
          Nocturne no. 5 in F#, op. 15 no. 2
          Etude no. 17 in e, op. 25 no. 5
  Liszt: Hungarian Rhapsody no. 13

322 TO GISELLA SELDEN-GOTH
in German

Paris 13.3.1922

Did I ever tell you the story of how my Barber-Fantasy came into being?[1] It is just as humorous and 'Baghdad' as the work of Cornelius . . . was meant to be.[2] Here is a man who lived with the reassuring certainty of being 'the greatest' (happy fellow); and was in fact – to put it mildly – just a better sort of littérateur. – For an entirely accurate appraisal you must refer back to 'Entführung', to 'Beatrice and Benedict' and 'Oberon'. Here everything is achieved which you, in your fine enthusiasm, ascribe to the 'Barber' and which is consciously, if somewhat feebly proclaimed in the work. However, I admit that it should be judged as a serious attempt by an intelligent (and, above all, cultivated) mind, to whom *internationalism* remained completely inaccessible. – His intentions were well-meant. He too was swallowed up by Fafner; indeed, altogether, that monster's method of remaining in the lead was to strike down any of those around him who might have overshadowed him even so slightly.

The contrast serves to throw the Barber into relief against this weighty background. Incidentally, Cornelius wrote easy pieces with great difficulty, which confirms the intentions. And therefore, in the course of a very long life he wrote very little. – This is my *present* opinion of the season's 'great operatic success' (whereby you should not overlook today's nationalist significance) and by which you have been somewhat overwhelmed. [. . .]

[1]See letter no. 17.
[2]A new production of Cornelius's *Der Barbier von Bagdad* had opened at the Staatsoper, Berlin, on 27 February 1922. Selden-Goth had written an enthusiastic review of the production.

323 TO EGON PETRI
in German

Berlin 4.4.1922

This very morning – as if in answer to your question of the previous day – I received this review about you, you and me, and me. I am sending it to you with a friendly but wistful eye to the resultant 60 thorns in your flesh. But [Isidor] Philipp (who sent me the cutting) had just returned from Versailles, where he had had to tolerate over 100 thorns. One says of contagious diseases that what they gain in propagation, they lose in malignity: do you find a similar phenomenon with our beloved piano-playing?

Incidentally, I have never been to Versailles – because I could never decide to leave Paris – but, until Philipp's report, the mention of this town had made an entirely different impression; whereby piano-playing (and even then only in small doses) had nothing to do with it. – How did you get on with the *Bechstein* in Zurich after the Paris *Erard*? –

I imagine a more monumental cadenza for the (25th) concerto [K. 503] of Mozart, into which I would like to weave the fugato from the *Jupiter* symphony.[1] One will say of it: quod licet Jovi . . . . . (I know!) –

[1]Busoni wrote this cadenza in June 1922. His first-movement cadenza to the Concerto in c, K. 491, similarly incorporates music from the Symphony in g, K. 550.

324 TO HUGO LEICHTENTRITT
in German

Berlin 20.4.1922

Yesterday I received a book catalogue which listed *Descartes*'s '*Compendium Musicae*'. I ordered it, but it had already been sold. However, with the aid of available books I occupied myself (for six hours) with Descartes. *Riemann* maintains that this publication of the 21-year-old author is one of the most penetrating discourses on music.

Hawkins summarizes its contents (which amount to geometrical formulae): but he quotes remarkable sentences from it. The whole thing is said to amount to 58 pages of folio.

I am sure you know the book.

Would it be apt to prepare a new, German edition of it: with footnotes and the like?

I pass the idea on to you.

325 TO VOLKMAR ANDREAE
in German

[Berlin] 26.5.1922

Don't be surprised if you should one day find an article of mine about Einstein's Theory in the Z[ürcher] Z[eitung]: here in the B[erliner] T[age-blatt] we have had reports on your International Festival, in which the rays emitted by the music have been so curved that the relativity of the reporter to the object of his report remained only vaguely perceptible. Nevertheless, one could (or should) gather from the correspondents that it was a great success, on which I congratulate you. [. . .]

– I have managed to introduce Laquai at *Donaueschingen* this year. The modest programme seems to have been successful and may well gain and retain significance for a while, so long as the Prince remains in charge. A curious friend of mine – Bernard van Dieren – is being heard there this time, with a string quartet. – The Berlin press is preparing itself for the pilgrimage to Dusseldorf, which follows soon after Donaueschingen; the hospitality of our noble Lord and an '*Extra-Bräu*' beer put the critics in an agreeable frame of mind, thus ensuring that the composers are well served.

Here too, an extension to the Easter holiday is being planned, out of consideration for the hordes of citizens of the Untidy States[1] arriving from Oberammergau. – Monarchical state of affairs! –

Well, you yourself will no doubt be refraining from all these 'attractions' and driving 'Casanova' home (as I expect and hope). Soon the vocal score will be appearing. Oder . . . . .? (As they say in Switzerland.) –

One is beginning to become 'familiar' with Mozart, which I find galling. But it is a great shame that you did not have the superb Berlin production of 'Così fan Tutte' transported to Z. (Particularly with Leo Blech.)

Now I have my whole family with me in B., supplemented indeed by a new union which connects me intimately with Switzerland.[2] (I mean: thanks to my 'Schwyzer'-Tochter.)[3] – I spend my days surrounded by books, an imposing collection which fills two large rooms. They afford me undistilled pleasure. – And also with my work, which continues to absorb me.

More news of the latter when something more important occurs.

[1]Orig. Verunreinigte Staaten = polluted states, wordplay on Vereinigte Staaten = United States.
[2]See footnote no. 9 to letter no. 319.
[3]Wordplay on Schwiegertochter = daughter-in-law and Schwyzer = Swiss, in Zurich dialect.

326 TO VOLKMAR ANDREAE
in German

[Berlin] 28.5.1922

[. . .] I have just been looking at 'Roméo au tombeau des Capulets',[1] which strikes me as uneven. But in the case of Berlioz, the sound of the orchestra is the deciding factor. I would consider it a *most worthy* cause to assail the public with it!

I was truly delighted at your request that I should visit you. Permit me a little time to consider. I would be happy to play the Mozart G major concerto [K. 453] (of which I gave the Berlin 'first performance' last winter) and my own Romanza e Scherzoso (with orchestra). – To perform Bach *en masse* would make me somewhat apprehensive. All line, no colour, little contrast. –[2]

Schoeck has completely abandoned me.

I have not entirely given him up.

He lacks (or *lacked*) certain ingredients, which are not available at the chemists'. Which should however be manufactured in his own laboratory.

[1]Orig. Romeo's Grabgewölbe.
[2]The day after writing this letter, Busoni was to make his last public appearance as a pianist.

X

1922 – 1924
Final Illness

in German

[Berlin] 15.6.1922

Today I am approaching you about a specific matter. Please listen to me patiently; and, if possible, be so good as to comply with my request. A certain Herr Jörg Mager[1] is planning to construct an electrical instrument which would produce pitches of any desired frequency. – (Inspired by my little book: – you know what I mean.) It is a matter of investigating new possibilities in the division of the octave. – (Thirds of tones, quarter-tones and every intermediate gradation.) Herr Mager has succeeded in interesting *Graf Arco*[2] (Director of the State Electrical Laboratory) in his scheme. He is making many facilities available to Mager. The Ministry of Culture has promised a subsidy. – 50,000 Marks are still required for the experiment!

Dear Doctor, should you be successful in making these 'paltry' 1,000 Francs available for the experiment, then – I believe – Switzerland would be playing an honourable part in a not insignificant, perhaps highly *significant* step in the development of music. – I find the matter really important and deserving of support. – To what extent does it interest you; and would you be prepared to take it upon yourself to win a few people over to the idea? – The money would not have to be donated. It would be possible to pay it back with interest in the not too distant future. But it would be necessary to raise it quickly.

– Just think. Old dreams – similar to those which prompted man's desire to fly – could now come true: *da cosa nasce cosa,*[3] who knows to what it could lead!

– Please send me a reply.

[1]Jörg Mager, 1880–1939, German organist and experimental instrument builder. Encouraged by Alois Hába he introduced his *Sphärophon* in 1926, an electronic instrument which could play microtones, following it in 1927 with the *Kaleidosphon*, on which chords could be made to 'glide'. In 1931 he developed the first electronic bells for *Parsifal* at Bayreuth.
[2]Georg Wilhelm Alexander Hans, Graf von Arco, 1869–1940, physicist. Director of

AEG-Telefunken from 1903 to 1930. Not to be confused with Anton Graf von Arco auf Valley, who murdered the Prime Minister of Bavaria in 1919.

[3]'One thing leads to another.' The following extracts from the autobiography of Alois Hába, *Mein Weg zur Viertel- und Sechsteltonmusik*, Dusseldorf, 1971, throw an interesting light on the question of Busoni and microtone music (which he proclaimed as early as 1906 in the *Outline of a New Aesthetic of Music*):

> Once a week – I believe it was between 3 and 4 o'clock in the afternoon – musicians were welcome to look in and talk with him or the other guests . . . In his genial way he called me 'Ali Baba' instead of Alois Hába . . . Once he took me, his favourite pupil Jarnach . . . and some other guests to one side and questioned me apropos our previous conversations about quarter-tone music in a mildly provocative manner: 'Tell me, dear Ali Baba, why do you compose with quarter-tones? The system of thirds and sixths of tones, which I advance, is more interesting than the quarter-tone system . . .' I replied: 'I only compose the way I can . . . But – why have *you* not shown us how to compose with thirds and sixths of tones?' He, musingly: 'Well – dear Ali Baba, so far I have had too much to say with semitones. Besides which the circumstances were unfavourable. For instance, I have so far found no firm either in America or Europe which was interested in constructing a sixth-tone harmonium according to my specifications.'

As a result of this conversation, Hába did indeed compose a string quartet using sixths of tones, but it has never been performed.

328 TO EDITH ANDREAE
in German

Berlin 24.6.1922

There can be but few irrational people who do not deeply regret the tragic fate of your brother, who would not unconditionally condemn the deed.[1]

It is my duty respectfully to acknowledge my support for the rationally minded, and to assure you at this unprecedentedly trying moment of my heart-felt sympathy, of my faithful devotion.

[1]On the morning of the same day, Saturday 24 June 1922, Edith Andreae's brother, Walter Rathenau, Foreign Minister to the Weimar Republic, was assassinated in Berlin.

329 TO EGON PETRI
in German

Berlin 19.7.1922

Yesterday, the 18th, the *first half* of the score of 'Doktor Faust' was completed. – Perhaps it would be a good idea if you were to take a look at it; from the standpoint of the difficulties it would present the 'vocal scorer'. – But I shall also need to know if you can come before or after I have sent it to the binders. – When you have looked through it – (bound or in paper covers) – you can tell me 'unbindingly' if you are going to take the job on; as it would require effort and time, and these would have to be found with little delay.

'So stehn die Dinge, wähle!'[1] says Mephistopheles. – And please answer, by telephone, by letter or in person, as you wish: – but one of these must be done!

Sincerely regretting that I have to point the pistol of assiduity at the breast of accruing duty (how lovely), I greet you with all old affection.

[1]From Vorspiel II of Busoni's *Doktor Faust*: 'That's how matters stand, choose!'

330 TO EGON PETRI [postcard]
in German

Berlin 22.9.1922

I need the *harmonization* of a few bars in Vol. 1 of Faust. They occur in the Intermezzo; unless I am mistaken, following the words: 'den Mann, den Mann, den ich suche! Erbarmen!' – The melody is:

Would you write it down and send it to me?[1] And thank you! – With kindest greetings from Schöneberg[2] to Schoenberg.

[1]Busoni required this harmonization for the reappearance of the quoted theme in the Final Tableau of *Doktor Faust*, bars 473–480. The fragmentary closing monologue breaks off only twelve bars later, hence one can see that here there was no cliché of 'death preventing the Master . . .'. Although Busoni composed two scenes for the Second Tableau of the opera in 1923, he wrote no more of the closing scene after 1922.
[2]The area of Berlin in which Busoni lived.

331 TO VOLKMAR ANDREAE
in German

[Berlin] 22.12.1922

[. . .] Thank heaven, you have virtually everything you need, spiritually and otherwise. May you retain all these things – indeed, may you, if possible, increase them – this is my fondest wish and prophecy. —— Good health, above all. – It has been a shock to me in the past six months to realize what it means to be without it. – I am gradually reconstituting myself; . . . but the anguish! The lost time! However: spiro, spero. – Instead of a *gift* for Christmas, the result has been – sadly – a *loss* at Easter.

After most careful consideration, I am unable to decide to perform the Faust fragment in concert form in Zurich. – An initial presentation of this kind leaves its definitive and influential stamp on a work. – 'Faust' in concert form, should it be convincing, would be a disavowal of the theatre; should it *not* be convincing, it would cast a shadow on any later scenic performance. – And I am not sufficiently accredited to let myself in for games of chance.

332 TO EDWARD J. DENT
in Italian

[Berlin] 14.2.1923

In response to my official nomination,[1] I answered (in Italian), asking to be informed of the nature of my duties, but
                              also of my rights
as member of the honorary committee in this new Society. I fear that my rights will also be purely 'honorary', which is to say *that I have to hold my tongue*.

Strange rumours are penetrating to the hermit (which I have been for some time), rumours which would sometimes give me ground *to let my tongue loose*. Therefore I am today returning to the source to seek authentic information. A meeting was held in Berlin two days ago, at which there seems to have been considerable disagreement between Bekker and Scherchen. It also seems that the programme would be brought into balance by a further concert, devoted chiefly to the tastes of the younger generation . . . .[2]

I do not possess a copy of the constitution and hence I have not yet grasped the spirit and intention of the Society. Meanwhile Wolffheim[3] has handed in his resignation . . .

Thank you for your kind words, which do me honour.

I am very pleased at the good news about Walton;[4] I once warned him that music need not be so complicated, but calls rather for a warm heart and lively imagination. This humble but undeniable truth brings me to my little book,[3] which I hope you have received. Let me assure you that I am very much relying on your translation and on Chatto & Windus . . .!

My warmest thanks once again for everything!

[1]Busoni had been nominated for the committee of the International Society for Contemporary music which had just been inaugurated. Dent was president of the society until 1938.
[2]Orig. minorenne (suggests: minors, adolescents).
[3]Dr Werner Wolffheim, 1877–1930, music critic and lawyer. Owner of a valuable library that was auctioned in 1929.
[4]William Walton was introduced to Busoni in July 1920.
[5]i.e. *Von der Einheit der Musik*, published in 1922.

333 TO ISIDOR PHILIPP
in French

[Berlin] 14.3.1923

[. . .] – I was relieved to read that you had received the *Prélude*. It was good of you to let me know. You were in haste to leave for Brussels (from where I trust you have now returned) and had the kindness to 'survey' the manuscript and reply to my questions. All this is proof of your friendship. – The same goes for your project with Heugel.[1] – Last Friday I had another mild *crisis*; having only just recovered from a chill which had forced me back to bed. Hence a new interruption to my work which had been promising so well during February (the weather and the circumstances[2] are dreadful). I hope to be able to resume it anew but am so intimidated that I dare make no further promises. – The Seigneur de Roubaix has written twice; the Jules Verne books have arrived; writing to thank him for them, I bragged about your 'extraordinary voyage' by which I was most touched.

I have looked through all Nodier's[3] stories and also thumbed through the pages on Senancour;[4] I thank you with a 'Handkuss' for the information on Mérimée's L'Inconnue[5] with which I have become most intimately acquainted. I found it impeccable and perfect. (I have never had the same success with Th. Gautier whom I find tiresome and difficult to read.) –

Now I am most interested to hear of the fate of my two little pieces. Is your School of Arpeggio finished? When? – I know you are so overburdened with work and occupied with countless projects and I have no right to divert your attention from them to my trifling affairs; but this time I shall be so bold as to ask you not to delay the decision. – Consider that I am sick, captive in more than one sense in a country on the verge of disaster, ignored by my publisher – I do not believe I deserve all this – you are sure to understand and pardon my insistence.

---

[1]The Prélude et Etude en Arpèges, originally intended for an *Ecole des Arpeggios* by Isidor Philipp, were published in 1923 by Heugel; Busoni, who had earned no concert fees for almost a year, was thus able to earn a modest sum in a 'hard' currency.
[2]Orig. le temps et les temps.
[3]Charles Nodier, 1780–1844, French writer.
[4]Etienne Pivert de Senacour, 1770–1846, French writer. His most celebrated book is the novel *Obermann* (1804).
[5]Prosper Mérimée, *Lettres à une Inconnue*, Paris, 1873.

334 TO EMIL HERTZKA
in German

[Berlin] 21.4.1923

I received the most kindly heralded package with Křenek's piano piece[1] only three days ago, and I thank you! I have read it through carefully. It is a pleasing demonstration of energy, built on diversified foundations. The composer's character is not yet fully established: I am not saying this because I know how young he is;[2] but because it represents an uneasy compromise between tradition and the urge to conceal it. As with all the young composers who have emerged from the revolution, the concealment lies chiefly in the choice of intervals and harmonies. He takes the edge off the latter by his avoidance of contrasts; by renouncing the consonances which would set the free harmonies in relief, as does a cushion for a polygonal stone. Křenek works to this end with contrasts of *tempo*, slower and faster. If played well (I have not heard it), the work should make an impression, while not affecting the nerves. A proficient demonstration of mental energy (I repeat), which is to be valued as such. – Is it his ascendance or his zenith? – A definitive evaluation depends on this question: I myself believe that Křenek will develop further, and sincerely hope so. Thank you once again for your making me acquainted with him.——

If you received my last letter, one should still consider whether you might be able to incorporate at least my complete operatic works in the U.E. Did you also receive my little book? I ask, because I would like to draw your attention to the catalogue of works at the end of the volume. –

[1]Reference either to Křenek's *Toccata und Chaconne*, op. 13, or *Kleine Suite*, op. 13a, both of which were published by Universal Edition in 1922.
[2]Křenek was 22.

335 TO VOLKMAR ANDREAE
in German

[Berlin] 25.4.1923

I have heard, through a third party, that you have been ill, and this has caused me great concern. I myself, confined to my home and often bed-ridden, am all the more disposed to sympathize with your condition. [. . .]

– I have experienced a long, uneventful winter. But some items of news penetrated my four walls. I was touched, inwardly and outwardly, by the 'new youth' and the activities of the new International Society for [Contemporary] Music. I wrote an article about the former in the 'Börsen Courier' (on 1 April), giving my blessing to the older and the youngest. I have an official relationship to the latter; in particular thanks to my friendly relations with Edward Dent, one of their founders. I would be interested to know to what extent and in what form *Switzerland* is involved in this alliance. – I had three pupils from your country in my class at the Academy. – The most prominent of these is Luc Balmer from Berne; – without thereby wishing to decry Geiser[1] and Blum. I was stunned that Balmer himself has been rejected by your Tonkünstler Verein. Having recovered from my disappointment, however, I found that this was just: for the more inoffensive composers have a free ticket – while the more significant ones have to pay a high price for their admission. – *You* should be delighted at such fine young talent! – There are indeed a good half-dozen composers of note in Switzerland, who should be heard abroad through an exchange scheme. A stipulation to this effect would be that the Swiss should make a welcoming gesture to the English: this, at least, would appear to me the appropriate course of action.

I am writing to you because I would not wish to see our friendly relations waning: I have nothing but good memories of you, for which I am grateful. – We got on well with each other, I believe, and did after all spend five years in spiritual wedlock, a fact that cannot be struck out of our biographies! – So let me have news of yourself from time to time.

– My health seems to be improving, if only very gradually. The uphill road is harder than the downhill. My doctor and I have set our hopes on better weather, but this cannot yet be predicted with any accuracy.

[1]Walter Geiser, born 1897, Swiss composer.

336 TO HANS REINHART
in German

Berlin 25.5.1923

Following your welcome greetings card, 'Der Schatten'[1] arrived today, as announced, and also your kind accompanying letter. Both of these delighted me and deserve my thanks, of which I assure you.

Firstly, I was delighted at the appearance of the publication and at the handsome quantity of other works [by the same author] enumerated. – This week I shall also occupy myself with attentively reading 'Der Schatten'. –

One could well assume that your new life will become a dreamworld in *another form*, that it could have a counteractive effect on 'life' altogether. – Since my childhood, I have found it distressing that South-German art flirts so much with death and uses it as an ever-recurring theme. My Latin temperament rebels against this. Our inability to approach the subject of death is most clearly reflected in Verdi's 'Requiem' or Rossini's 'Stabat mater', in which the persistence of life overshadows that which has perished. – Even Dante's 'Hell' is retrospective and concerns itself with the deeds for which the damned came to be accused during their lifetimes. In Orcagna's

'Dance of death' living persons walk past coffins, holding their noses. . . .!

I have never heard so much talk of death as in Switzerland, where the people (let us be honest) take immense care and the most elaborate and prudent precautions to guarantee their earthly existence; indeed base their whole lives on caution and security, more so than anywhere else. People of Latin origin, on the other hand, will give their lives for an idea, without the least wish for death but rather because of their desire to enrich life.

I was genuinely shocked to read in Thomas Mann: 'What attracts me to Pfitzner is the death-wish common to both of us.'[2] – All this is more (my own) *confession than a criticism* and has no direct bearing on yourself. I am using the occasion to express what is on my mind, and ask you to forgive me if it should cause offence. – [. . .]

[1]Hans Reinhart, *Der Schatten. Ein Nachtstück aus Andersen in 4 Akten*, Zurich, 1923.
[2]Thomas Mann, *Betrachtungen eines Unpolitischen*, Berlin, 1918. In the essay entitled 'Von der Tugend' is a lengthy discussion of Pfitzner's 'Futuristengefahr' and the opera *Palestrina*, in which Mann declares his sympathy for both works. Pfitzner is quoted as having said to Mann, 'In *Palestrina* everything looks to the past, it is dominated by partiality to death.'

337 TO EGON PETRI
in German

Berlin 29.5.1923

I have written, as fruit of my convalescence, a series of shorter piano pieces, of which I would like you to give the '*first performance*'. They form a single programme item:

1. Prélude
2. Etude[1]
3. Three short pieces for the cultivation of part-playing
   – a) Andante
   – b) Molto tranquillo
   – c) Allegro[2]

I would add the
   Perpetuum mobile[3]
to these as conclusion, making *six* altogether.

(There is no question of the Armed Men.)[4]

Let me know as soon as possible if you have the time and inclination to do this in the autumn; because I would then attempt to withhold the pieces from any other contender.

Hope for a *verbal* reply.

[1]Prélude et Etude en Arpèges (see letter no. 333).

[2]Nos. 1, 2 and 3 of the Fünf kurze Stücke zur Pflege des polyphonen Spiels auf dem Klavier, composed between March and May 1923. (The tempo marking of no. 1 was later altered to *Sostenuto*.)

[3]*Perpetuum mobile*, based on the second movement of the Concertino, op. 54, for piano solo. Composed in 1922.

[4]Reference to no. 5 of the Fünf kurze Stücke, which is a free transcription of the chorale of the Armed Men from *Die Zauberflöte*.

338 TO PHILIPP JARNACH
in German

[Berlin] 17.6.1923

The mountain would have to come to Mohammed, affording unerring proof that his faith can move mountains. The mountain – no iceberg – found it a little cool, but the mountain – also no volcano – was able to control itself. It rolled – like a tank – all the way from Berlin to Weilheim[1] and found the prophet scribbling manuscript paper full with magic signs that looked like Hebrew characters. The mountain was thrown into confusion; for a few days previously it had received a letter from Munich, in which it had been accused of blatant anti-Semitism.[2]

Having for decades been undeservedly suspected of Zionism – 'welche Wendung nach Gottes Fügung'![3] But he is able to defend himself. Inasmuch as he was visited the day before writing this letter by Prof. Weissmann, Prof. Kestenberg and Generalmusikdirektor O. Klemperer. This Zionistic triumvirate (which proved itself to be triumvi-ratifying) reconstituted my earlier reputation. Added to which comes my predilection for Wagner, who was also kosher. This rehabilita-Zion is placatory, for the Jewish correspondent from Munich as well. – Herr Gutmann [sic] has achieved all this with his singing! –

I have had another slight relapse, and the summer has a diffidence about it which is altogether Aryan in character. A blond summer, it lacks the confidence to make its entrance, although it would indeed be welcome – even without knocking.

The indubitably Christian adventure story of Frau Gisella[4] has been brought to its conclusion after 65 episodes. She is having an illegitimate child and going on a honeymoon with her husband. So there is a happy ending.

I wish (enviously) that you are enjoying better weather than we are. I am sitting in my library with a paraffin-stove to keep me warm. I wish (ditto) that you have your supply of inspiration pills, which my doctor is unable to prescribe for me. The chemists say they would have to be imported from abroad, that there is a surfeit of them in America, but that one has to pay for them in dollars. (But I believe inspiration has been confused with inanity.)[5] A tangled letter. A mangled letter. (But at least a letter) –

[1]cf. letter no. 301. This letter is adorned by a drawing which wittily illustrates Busoni's idea but is unfortunately not available for publication.
[2]Busoni had composed a new version of the 'Grausige Geschichte vom Münzjuden Lippold' from *Die Brautwahl*. The baritone who was to perform the work, Wilhelm Guttmann, refused to do so on grounds (which were not altogether unjustified) that the text was anti-Semitic.
[3]'What a providential turn of events.' Busoni was indeed of partly Jewish origin, from his mother's side.
[4]Gisella Selden-Goth was in fact Jewish!
[5]Wordplay on Einfall = idea and Abfall = garbage.

339 TO EDWARD J. DENT [postcard]
in Italian

[Berlin] 17.6.1923

The Italians are complaining that they have been neglected in the choice of the programme for Salzburg. Today Gatti[1] wrote to me (from Zurich) that a group of *six* have withdrawn their works. Nobody has had the courtesy to inform me of this event; and hence mine is the sole remaining Italian name on the programme. If I also withdraw, they will accuse me of interfering in their affairs; if I remain, it will look as if I were setting myself against my own country. What should be done? Stupid situation! Please suggest something.

[1]Guido M. Gatti, 1892–1973, Italian music critic. Later editor of *La Rassegna Musicale* and director of the Teatro Regio, Turin.

340 TO EDWARD J. DENT
in Italian

Berlin 24.6.1923 [postmark]

I should like to know why, on what grounds, a group of *Italians* should come to write a letter in *German* to an *English* society.

As a matter of fact, Casella sent me the letter, which – conceived in Italian – could at least have passed for a modest work of *literature*; instead of which it merely bears witness to defective education. I am sorry to say: I am not aware of the facts behind this precious document, nor of the titles or composers of the works which have been collected or rejected. I don't know if I am right; but it seems to me that, in an international society, the Italians should have as much justification in rejecting the Germans from a programme as these reserve for themselves 'pro motu contrario'.[1]

I wrote to Gatti and said that, before pointing an accusing finger at the foreigners, one should consider if there may be a certain element of 'mea culpa'. If we are never agreed amongst ourselves, we shall never gain enough strength to cross the frontiers. The Russians, who managed to transform Berlin into a Russian township in two years, have a mutual admiration society; Valishev extols the praises of Karmanzov, Karmanzov eulogizes Valishev, and both weep tears of admiration for somebody else. Here they have theatres, libraries, newspapers, restaurants in Russian style, in the Russian language. The Italians call down the wrath of God on each other. – I also wrote to Gatti that another hindrance to international interest is the fact that a purely *Italian* school of composition, today, *does not exist*. Some take a bit of Strauss, others some Debussy, others a little Stravinsky, while Wagner remains the Dalai Lama. It is only natural that foreign countries would rather hear the *originals* than these pale imitations.[2]

Gatti replied, he was sorry to read that I thought so little of my countrymen. I answered that I was thus actually showing more concern for Italy, and the wrongness of the situation grieved me out of a legitimate sense of self-respect.

– Thus my arguments are impartial, but all this does not conceal the fact that the Italians have rather been left in the lurch; condemned as they seem to be to a passive role.

Thus, for example, I am somewhat astonished that the members of the German section have

'*taken it upon themselves to hold the responsibility*' for *my* co-operation at Salzburg. It would be fairer if I took the decision myself. But, as I said, the dispute arises out of the fact that the Italians themselves have excluded me from their section. Were I to shelter under the protection of the Germans, to act against the Italians, this would scarcely strike me as being 'international' demeanour . . . (while recognizing that the German attitude is agreeable to me). –

It is less than agreeable for me to be dragged against my convictions into such a controversy.

You will have had enough of this preaching. Permit me therefore to come to an end.

[On the back of envelope:] I have not yet received a reply from Chatto and Windus.

---

[1]The situation is clarified in a letter from Hermann Scherchen to his wife, Augusta Maria Jansen-Scherchen, dated 'Friday evening after the brutalities' (which can hence be dated 22.6.1923):

> I have . . . written to Dent: as Busoni recounted to me, the Italians, who have withdrawn all their compositions from Salzburg in a huff, because they were allegedly selected by the jury in a totally unsatisfactory way, are asserting that the German representative – i.e. myself – had forced this through. And the situation is exactly the opposite. I have demanded that Dent rectify the situation, otherwise I would contact Pizzetti and Casella myself.

From Hermann Scherchen . . . *alles hörbar machen, Briefe eines Dirigenten 1920 bis 1939*, Berlin, 1976, ed. Eberhardt Klemm.

[2]On 21 June 1923 Busoni wrote to the same effect to Alfredo Casella, the dedicatee of his *Romanza e Scherzoso* (1922):

> Would I have dedicated one of my works to you if I thought nothing of you? If I were not your friend? (Or do you not believe me? Even so, I have never told a lie.) [. . .]
>
> I fully appreciate the talent, the aspirations and also, in good part, the results of the contemporary Italian school but I cannot perceive anything specifically Italian in it. And this worries me. Here I am more nationalistic and more Italian . . . than any of you.
>
> I live in Germany, where I do nothing but *fight for Italianism* in music; and you, the Italians in Italy, rejoice in Strauss, Stravinsky, Debussy! You revile Puccini, repudiate Verdi and prostrate yourselves – in Rome – before German mediocrities. [. . .]

The original letter is published in its entirety in Sergio Sablich, *Busoni*, Turin, 1982, p. 70.

341 TO EGON PETRI [postcard]
in German

[Berlin] 24.7.1923

At Scherchen's request, I have today written to *Gropius* in Weimar; have passed on your assent, together with your name and the programme.[1]

At the same time written to Dent, *cancelling* Salzburg.[2]

Shall let you have the pieces.

Thank you for your kindness and patience.

Programme: 1. Toccata
2. Prélude + Etude
3. Three short pieces
4. Perpetuum mobile.

[1]Petri was to play in the Nationaltheater, Weimar, on 18 August 1923 in a concert organized by Hermann Scherchen for a 'Bauhaus week'. He shared the programme with a performance of Hindemith's *Marienleben*.

[2]Dent must have exercised some remarkable diplomacy, for the first festival of the ISCM at Salzburg did eventually include a performance of Busoni's two-piano version of the *Fantasia Contrappuntistica*.

342 TO EGON PETRI
in German

Berlin 30.7.1923

I received your letter today, and would ask you for your terms, which I shall pass on.

I hope that the affair with your apartment is making progress – I intend to write an article discussing *how often* an *artist* is actually able to function as an artist. (Scarcely ever.)

It would be nice if my little pieces could help you to take your mind off it all.

343 TO ISIDOR PHILIPP
in French

[Berlin] 5.8.1923

[. . .] Here we are in a state of almost extreme recession. I can see no end to it. Confined to the country on account of almost insurmountable legal restrictions, our movements are limited and we are obliged to subject ourselves to the general fate. My dear wife has a daily struggle to find butter at *300,000* Marks a pound! (Everything else in proportion.) Often enough there is none to be had. – Even if one did leave: where would one go? Where would one find a new domicile? How could one begin again? Anyway I shall be in no position to burden myself with new troubles and emotions. –

In Paris I would have harmed nobody! I would have merely requested that I should be well treated! – At present we are suffering no hardship, we lack none of the necessities of life. But one must be prepared for everything . . .! A violent crisis is approaching, is all but upon us.

Then one loses all sense of values, one becomes insensitive without realizing it. One is in danger of becoming selfish.

How unpleasant this all is! Wicked! Inhuman! The masks are falling. They reveal nothing but the deformities which had been so shamefacedly concealed . . . How that resounds into contemporary art! The oxen on the roof and the swine in the cellar.[1]

Yet another explosion.

Have patience.

---

[1]Orig. Les boeufs sur le toit et le[s] cochons dans la cave. The world première of Jean Cocteau's ballet *Le boeuf sur le toit*, with music by Darius Milhaud, had been given in the Théâtre des Champs-Elysées, Paris, on 21 February 1920. Hence it is not unlikely that Busoni, who arrived in Paris on 3 March 1920, would have attended a performance of it.

17 Busoni in Paris, November 1923. One of the last photographs of Busoni, taken by Man Ray

344 TO ROBERT FREUND
in German

Berlin 27.8.1923

[. . .] I am still convalescing after nearly a whole year's illness. It was the first time in my life that I had been stricken by anything of the sort, just as we were stricken by war after a lifetime of peace.

Both now seem improbable to me; but it is in the ineradicable traces that we consciously sense the dreadful events. Germany, in particular, has to bear this more than any other nation, and my illness is partly connected with aggravation caused by the war.

Nevertheless, but for an interruption of six months, which was a humiliation and mental torment for me, I have remained continuously active.

Now I am in the process of bringing *Faust* to its conclusion and making the final revisions to a 'Klavierübung' which will occupy about 250 pages of print.[1]

This is a short chronicle of long sufferings; it embraces the most diverse of details.

Do write from time to time! I was always glad to receive your letters.

¹*Klavierübung in zehn Büchern*. This was the second edition, which Busoni revised and expanded. It was published posthumously in a very small edition, in 1925.

345 TO EDWARD J. DENT
in Italian

Berlin 30.8.1923

I have sorted everything out with Chatto & Windus and, commercially speaking, all obstacles to an English translation of my book have been removed.¹

You have not yet replied to my suggestion of including the Outline of a new aesthetic in the volume. The rights of the Aesthetic are free (this is not a verdict). –

Messrs Chatto & W. have had the exquisite kindness of sending me an edition of [Wilkie] Collins. I was truly happy and grateful!

Two Ballads with orchestra,² works of mine, were included in the last concert of the N.M.G.³ and were 'encored', hence very well received. Unfortunately I was only able to attend the rehearsal. A third piece (grausige Historie [sic]), taken from 'Die Brautwahl', with reduced orchestration and extended for concert use, was *rejected* because of . . . the anti-Semitism of the text. (One gets a glimpse of furtive discretion!) – Strange world, astonishing mentality. Let us pray.

¹This project never in fact materialized. *The Essence of Music and other papers*, translated by Rosamond Ley, was published by Rockliff, London, in 1957. There has been no new English-language edition of the *Outline of a New Aesthetic of Music* since 1911, only reprints.
²'Lied des Mephistopheles', op. 49 no. 2, and 'Zigeunerlied', op. 55 no. 2, were performed on 27 April 1923 at the Philharmonie, Berlin.
³Neue Musikgesellschaft.

346 TO EGON PETRI
in German

Paris 24.9.1923

I have before me a copy of Fétis's Biographie et Bibliographie des Musiciens, a dictionary in eight volumes. A collector has had about 600 engravings and lithographs bound into *this* copy; it is thus unique and extremely valuable. To try to put such a thing together for a second time would be a hopeless task. (Maybe with energy and patience or – as the Americans would say – <u>with money</u>.) – Once again one sees just what fame really is. Although most of the pictures naturally do not depict the *most celebrated* artists, there is a horrifying number of forgotten names amongst them, particularly of virtuosos. From my mother's recollections I happen to know some of them, of whom you have perhaps not heard. But ask my pupils. They don't even know some of the names that were on people's lips just before the war.

Gloire, que me veux-tu? – On the other hand, it is quite astounding how some names obstinately persist, though less significant than the forgotten ones, and seem truly predestined for 'eternity'. Just think of the German, Körner, who is known to every bookbinder. It's the same story with the works. Master-scores have vanished, but the 'Entr'acte to Rosamunde' lives (unhappily) ever after. Now and then, some speculator or idealist manages to raise the dead. – Thanks to my lively encouragement (as I read), Mozart's Idomeneo is being considered for Dresden this year. – What would we know of Bach today, were it not for Mendelssohn's exertions? In such cases, only the ambitiousness of the young can help, and one should always count on them. – One should also learn from them. Their vigour and challenge guide them towards ideas and open up new vistas to which they lead us. (Even here one could reveal weaknesses: this we are at liberty to test.) – I have just come in from the street, where I saw a hoarding (they have a special name for them here)[1] with the programme of the Opéra comique for this week, the real comedy of which is its 'pot-bellied' pertinacity. Carmen, Mignon, Cavalleria, Contes d'Hoffmann – so it has gone on for decades, and that's what it is this week as well. And I think the next will be no different. Here I must stand up for Berlin, which makes steady progress with (not always successful) experiments – or at least aspires to progress. –

My (physical) progress is hampered by unpleasant autumn weather. But altogether I feel 'satisfactory' rather than satisfied. The latter state comes but seldom. – (Don't make consoling noises, I beg you!)

---

[1]Busoni means the *colonnes Morris*.

347 TO PHILIPP JARNACH
in German

Paris 7.10.1923

[. . .] My health had been improving noticeably from day to day, until I caught a cold due to a sudden change in the weather two days ago. – I am beginning to get a thick head and running nose; like the fountain gushing out of the stone.[1] – I shall have to do without my stroll through the streets today: one's enjoyment of these walks is impaired because one constantly has to watch out for automobiles. There are about 300,000 of them and all are on the move.

I have received several pessimistic reports from Berlin, and some of the grievances are matters with which I am personally acquainted. – You admit all these, with the exception of the 'Hindemiths', whom you honourably defend. – I am well aware that my opinion 'throws out the baby with the bath-water'; but – as has been my experience – an assertion carries less weight when one makes concessions. Only if stated brusquely is there an impact, as in your case. But I must protest against your speaking of an *attitude* from which I view the matter. An attitude would imply partisanship, special pleading or obstinacy. But even these would not be able to '*reduce the world around us to a heap of rubble*', because I find this already to be the case. There is no single perfect work of music in existence. Therefore one can *only* accept that which supersedes already extant work or betrays a desire to follow one of these two goals. – I readily admit that your protégé has talent; but this is only a basic requirement for becoming an artist. Once again I cite the case of Mozart, who, as you know, took the greatest of pains to find the solution to every problem, and who was truly no less talented than our musically enthusiastic colleague; composing comes just as naturally to him as barking to a dog or crowing to a cock. And that you call an 'attitude'! What I deplore is that one has made such a *celebrity* of our composing viola-player, and that this has strengthened his own belief in his attainment of mastery; whereby I mean better for him than his admirers do. –

I don't know Weill's Frauentanz.[2] Considering his reserved vein and painstaking efforts, this youngster's productivity is surprising. He has any amount of 'ideas' – as you say – but they are concealed or inferred, so that only 'the likes of us' can discover and admire them. He – Weill – does not seem to be conscious of when he has arrived at the right place; instead, he passes over it as if over sand and rocks between which beautiful, individual flowers grow, which he neither tramples on nor plucks, and over which he does not linger. His wealth is great, his selectivity at present inactive. One envies him and would like to help. – But he will come to the right thing of his own accord! – The eternal question: is he still developing, or has he already reached his peak? –

The greatest are 'in the making' until their death, and leave behind unfulfilled expectations. The '*arrivés*' are to be pitied, and one asks oneself despairingly if one numbers amongst them . . . .

Thus this letter ends, inconclusively.

---

[1] Allusion to Moses' miracle with the rod and the stone.

[2] Kurt Weill composed his *Frauentanz*, op. 10, for soprano and five instruments, in July 1923. In May 1924, Busoni arranged the third song, 'Ach wär' mein Lieb ein Brünnlein', for voice and the piano. This was the last piece of work he lived to complete.

348 TO EGON PETRI
in German

Paris 23.10.1923

Our 'intelligent' friend Guttmann (who, being of the opinion that the 'Münzjude' was an anti-Semitic demonstration, cancelled it – at the wish of his orthodox Mamma – thus bringing it into disrepute) – has conversely misunderstood Pfitzner, who most certainly is an anti-Semite, and takes him for a dedicated friend of Israel. – According to Weissmann, his [Pfitzner's] lieder are 'masterly in form but seldom strong.' How *often* are lieder supposed to be strong? – and *what* is 'strong'? He (A.W.) has a way of asserting things without substantiating them, proof of extreme insolence. It is as much as saying: what *I* say needs no justification: because I am *A.W.* (Evidently A.W. stands for: All Waffle.)[1]

But he writes, brilliantly:

'The *Grotrian Hall*. This place too has been thoroughly inoculated with modern music.'

If only it were at least a hospital! And does he mean that modern music is a disease, like smallpox; or is this just some sort of innuendo? . . . But an inoculation is supposed to *protect* the patient against the disease! – In short: a masterly statement. –

As you may know, I am in Paris. – Everything here is French. (Andersen writes so finely: in China all the people are Chinamen; even the Emperor is a Chinaman.) Everything was invented *here*. I have been informed that the automobile, the cinematograph and wireless telegraphy are all French inventions. It is well known that books are written in French the world over. The *elegy* was invented by Andreas Chénier, the *ode* by Victor Hugo. Inoculation (see above) is likewise the speciality of Pasteur; although a monument to *Jenner* can clearly be espied behind the cathedral in Bologna.

All this increases the sense of national awareness; is officially recorded and heaps tradition upon tradition. They spare their 'blague' only for Wagner: for his sake they have sold and betrayed their own music. (Wagner, namely, still parades under the banner of 'music', because the real thing has vanished here.)

What a pity that your letters vanish too. [. . .]

[1]Orig. au weia! (colloquial).

349 TO HUGO LEICHTENTRITT
in German

Paris 13.11.1923

Would that I had Heine's quill (and what else?), to portray Paris as vividly to you as he describes London in the first scene of Ratcliff. He would say: one still plays chess in the Café de la Régence, late arrivers at the Opéra can see the grisettes with dissatisfied looks on their faces, mincing to the bus-stop around closing time. But truly, there is little ground for dissatisfaction here. The abundance and quality of comestibles, cloth and other articles of handwork bear witness to wellnigh sumptuous prosperity. The fact that the older people complain 'de souffrir beaucoup' is the sign of a changing generation and faulty memory. – Also to a certain extent of a bad conscience which would like to show that hardship exists not only elsewhere and that the consequences of 1914 are disastrous and ineradicable. Yes, soon it will be ten years since I asserted, in the Viktoria-Luise-Platz, that I would never again see Berlin as it is (in 1914), or was! Whereupon a few bystanders barked at me, without however demonstrating any of the other good habits of dogs. –

A few days before I return home, I would like to ensure that you receive a souvenir of myself addressed from here.

I have heard no music and am in no position to make a statement about it. If you visit this city in the course of the following decades, you will certainly be able to hear 'Le Faust' at the Grand Opéra, 'Carmen' at the Opéra comique and, with a bit of luck, 'Cavalleria' as well. Even now (to continue in the style of Heine) 'la classe de solfège' occupies the most important place in the Conservatoire, and there are no conductors to hand. The longevity of the institutions runs parallel to that of the 'Maîtres', who generally take their leave at the age of 90 or so. 'C'est dommage que Massenet soit mort si jeune; il n'avait que soixante-dix ans',[1] an old friend said to me recently. – It is with this dignified reserve that the country approaches its traditions, towards which every Monsieur décoré is ushered, his little key in his pocket; which he scarcely needs, incidentally, to open his door.

Overwhelmingly beautiful autumn days are shining wistfully down on me. Later you will be able to add to my biography: in 1923 F.B. spent two months in Paris. Which is all there is to say of the matter.

I look forward to my return, even if the . . . difference in temperature may have an unhealthy effect. [. . .]

---

[1] 'It's a pity that Massenet died so young; he was only seventy.'

350 TO JELLA OPPENHEIMER
in German

Berlin 5.3.1924

I came upon your letter as I awoke – and outside the sun was shining. I have been deprived of both for a long time and greeted them with joy and gratitude. We have had a stubborn winter, and for two months I was again unable to enjoy the fresh air. I also yearn for Italy; I want to make every effort to see the country again. Your plan would indeed be the direct way: let us hope that I would be capable of fulfilling it.

I am not pleased that you have been reading 'Ulrike'.[1] There is nothing more deplorable than looking back; even to pleasant recollections, to say nothing of the disagreeable ones. In art, the principle of remaining uninvolved in the events which one narrates (or describes) is right and proper; but there is a reciprocal requirement that the reader, too, should only 'assimilate' and not 'experience'.

But when our Jella – even in fiction – comes into contact with the likes of Ulrike, the experience assumes a greater significance than description: the moment of artistic enjoyment recedes perforce in favour of painful compassion.

I would ask for the Dr Max Mell,[2] with which I am still unacquainted and which you kindly offered to send me. When it comes to accepting books, I know no shame; I could even beg for them, occasionally even steal a few. Of course we must 'see' each other. Should 'Dr Faust' be performed in Dresden this autumn, I would lay no slight value on your being present.

At the moment a remainder of the work is still 'within the soul of the creator', assuming that he possesses a soul at all. In this case, pills and drops and massages are not to the slightest avail; just as little as baths or sport. Leonardo (as d'Annunzio once said to me) was a skeleton that carried a blazing torch in place of a skull. I think (in a different sense from d'Annunzio) that the head of even a dead body can still glow.

I warmly wish you a beautiful spring on earth and in your feelings (in your heart it is always so).

[1] In a previous letter to Jella Oppenheimer Busoni identifies this lady more precisely as *Ulrike Woytich*, but the author and full title are untraceable.
[2] Max Mell, *Das Apostelspiel*, a verse-play in one act, Munich, 1923. The first performance was in Graz on 1 January 1924; in 1925 Max Reinhardt produced it in Berlin.

351 TO PHILIPP JARNACH
in German

Berlin 25.3.1924

Have read the quartet[1] from beginning to end with sustained interest. Not one note is written unintentionally, and that *counts*. Thus it is a perfect work of art. Even if I cannot always grasp the 'intention'. I was glad to see that you occasionally make concessions to the Italian language. What you are thereby aiming at is international communication. Once, years ago, I studied a piece by Balakirev[2] (ça valait la peine), but I stalled at the Russian terminology. So much so that I had to have it translated. – In your quartet a consistent use of language has not yet been established; on page 31 you write: Tempo,

Zeitmass, nach und nach verhallend, poco a poco smorzando. Despite your perfectly justified admiration for German music, surely it is not your aim to put an *un*-European art on the map? And I personally find that military command (Dämpfer weg)[3] aesthetically unpleasing. I wanted to give you some concrete examples of what I meant, because l have often made insufficiently serious allusions to the problem. Irony is the most wretched educational weapon; I came to realize that, too late, in the case of my son Benni. –

I fear I shall be unable to attend the performance of the Rondò arlecchinesco (dubbed by Breitkopfs in wartime *Harlekins Reigen*).[4] It is very important to me that the style and spirit of the work (for which there exist no true antecedents) should be correctly portrayed. Couldn't you watch over it a little? – Can I see you beforehand?

I have been confined to my bed for over three days on a low diet and am now weaker than ever. [. . .]

[1]Jarnach's String Quartet, op. 16, composed in 1923 and first performed at the ISCM Festival, Salzburg, in August of that year.
[2]Busoni performed Balakirev's *Islamey* at a Helsinki recital in 1890. There is no mention of this in the repertoire list appended to Edward J. Dent's *Ferruccio Busoni: a Biography*.
[3]Mutes off.
[4]Likewise the *Berceuse élégiaque* was performed in wartime Germany under the title 'Elegisches Wiegenlied'.

352 TO EDITH ANDREAE
in German

[Berlin] 26.4.1924

Once again I have been a prisoner in my own house for over three months. The last I saw of Berlin was the temple of the arts built by our local *Palladio* on the Bülow-Platz.[1] An imaginary fairground piece was performed there with music by Stravinsky;[2] very successful and exciting, a miniature 'Gesamtkunstwerk'. The result of this outing was that I got a touch of pneumonia, from which I recovered, but without daring to venture out again. At present I am not only fairly weak but also out of practice in all pursuits. Even the act of putting this letter to paper required determination, if only physical.

How kind of you it was to drop by once again. Better days alternate with less good ones: on one of the former, I would gladly like you to call; but would always fear you might not come at an opportune moment . . .

And so I hope to see you again soon; not quite as in old times, but no less affectionately.

[1]Reference to the Theater am Bülowplatz, built between 1913 and 1914; the architect was the Berliner Oskar Kaufmann. The building still stands in the Rosa-Luxemburg-Platz – as it is now called – and operates as the Volksbühne.

[2]This was a performance of *L'Histoire du soldat* on 13 January 1924, with Carl Ebert (narrator) and Lina Carstens (princess). The conductor was Hermann Scherchen.

The most substantial documents to have survived from the last weeks of Busoni's life are his jovial letters (some originally attached to specimen jars and in verse) to Dr Müller, the physician who treated his fatal kidney and heart inflammation. In early July Busoni dictated his visionary essay 'The Essence of Music'. He died on 27 July 1924 in his Berlin apartment; the officially recorded cause of death was 'heart failure'.

18 The funeral procession leaving Viktoria-Luise-Platz 11 on 30 July 1924. The cost of the funeral was met by the Akademie der Künste, whose members are here to be seen amongst the mourners

Appendix

The Schoenberg – Busoni Correspondence
1903 – 1919

These letters are published by courtesy of Verlag Neue Musik,
Berlin, and Mr Lawrence Schoenberg, Pacific Palisades, California.
The German original text appeared in *Beiträge zur
Musikwissenschaft*, 1977, Vol. 19 No. 3, edited by Jutta Theurich.
Annotations to this translation not by Dr Theurich are identified
by the marking (AB). The letters to Emil Hertzka (Director of
Universal Edition) did not appear in the German edition and are
published here for the first time.

1 BUSONI TO SCHOENBERG

Berlin 14.9.1903

Thank you for your interesting letter, which has made me very curious about your score.[1] I would therefore be grateful if you would send me the manuscript. Maybe I, some later Siegfried, shall succeed in penetrating the fiery barrier which makes your work inaccessible, and in awakening it from its slumber of unperformedness.[2]

[1]*Pelleas und Melisande* op. 5, which Shoenberg had evidently suggested for Busoni's Berlin concerts of contemporary music.
[2]The first performance of *Pelleas und Melisande* took place on 26 January 1905 in Vienna, under Schoenberg's direction. (AB)

2 BUSONI TO SCHOENBERG

Berlin 15.10.1903

I have received your Pelleas und Melisande – and read it right through. You are a master of orchestration; from first impressions this seems to me undeniable. I have not yet been able to form an opinion about the contents; – (consider that I am simultaneously occupied as pianist, composer and conductor, and that I have no opportunity for quiet contemplation) therefore this is – at present – my fault. The dances by Schenker[1] have also arrived, and I am glad that I can place your name on the programme[2] at least in this form.

[1]Heinrich Schenker's Syrian Dances, for piano, orchestrated by Schoenberg.
[2]Busoni conducted the Syrian Dances in a concert with the Berlin Philharmonic Orchestra on 9 November 1903.

3 SCHOENBERG TO BUSONI

Steinakirchen am Forst 13.7.1909

I have often had the pleasure of hearing of favourable comments you had made about my compositions. Therefore, in asking you if you felt inclined to perform something of mine, I hope I am not approaching you in vain. I do not know if you are still continuing your orchestra series. I do have several orchestral works, which could only rely upon a suitable public in such concerts. But I have this less in mind than something considerably easier to bring about. I have two piano pieces[1] (several others have been started, but their completion was interrupted by another work)[2] which could only be played by someone who, like yourself, takes the side of all those who seek. Only a person, then, whose imagination is able to perceive fulfilment where sluggards cannot even find signs of promise. Somebody who can indeed imbue the works of another with so much of his own imagination that a perfection emerges which can result only from visualization, from imagination, but never from factuality or outward appearance. – It seems I have thus actually outlined the nature of the performer, the public and the artist as epicures. The motive seems slight – two piano pieces – but it happened unintentionally, so let it stand, at the risk of briefly offending a feeling of sympathy. You will, I hope, not take it amiss.

Now to the two pieces: technically they scarcely present any particular difficulties. But their interpretation demands belief and conviction. Therefore it is to you that I am writing – anyone could do it otherwise – and I ask you kindly to inform me if I may send you the music.

You will surely not object to being bothered by such a small matter. I myself am venturing it only in consideration of your good opinion of my works and in the hope that the pieces, when you have examined them, may perhaps be worth the trouble.

[1]Piano Pieces, op. 11 nos. 1 and 2.
[2]Reference to the composition of the Five Pieces for Orchestra, op. 16.

4   BUSONI TO SCHOENBERG

Berlin 16.7.1909

I was truly delighted at the trust to be sensed in your letter, and will be glad to justify it, so far as is within my powers.

In the coming season my orchestra series will *not* be taking place[1] – (I had already been considering your chamber symphony) – ; the piano pieces interest me intensely and I would ask you to carry out your good intention and send them to me.

In your just appraisal of the reproductive artist, you seem to have forgotten the duties of the 'co-operative' public. Good art can be (and should *only* be) accordingly presented to a circle of sympathetic friends. Do you have a publisher who has interest and confidence in you?

[1]The last of Busoni's concerts of contemporary orchestral works with the Berlin Philharmonic Orchestra was on 2 January 1909 with music by Franck, Mozart,

Schubert, Bartók and Liszt. There were some later concerts in the same style with the Blüthner Orchestra. (AB)

5   SCHOENBERG TO BUSONI

Steinakirchen am Forst 20.7.1909

Many thanks for your kind letter. I have just made new copies of the piano pieces and am sending them to you today.

I can counter your objection that I may have forgotten the 'co-operative' public: I do not think about the public, but I do not overlook them. This same process applies to all productive and reproductive art, provided it is done with intuition; not calculatedly, but in full consciousness of our human conditions and relationships. This is the source of our creativity, we believe we are merely depicting ourselves, but are simultaneously fulfilling those duties which our fellow men assign to us. Instinctively! But then all the more unerringly. And it is only this unconscious creative strength that has persuasive power. There are no errors of judgement here, because there is no calculation. It has an impact; the receptive circles may be limited; but it has an impact; on those who are like-minded. On those who possess a receiving organ which corresponds to our transmitting organ. As with wireless telegraphy. Therefore, I think, every art created without 'calculation of optimum effect' must eventually and finally find those for whom it is valid. And the more intensive the artist's relationship to a state of universality – whether of the present or the future – the greater will be the circle of those for whom it is valid.

In this sense, I think, one does not necessarily have to consider the public when analysing the productive or reproductive artist. The public merely co-operates when it is induced, when it is, so to speak, invoked. *Whether* it is induced, however, is a question quite beyond the calculations and efforts of the creative artist.——

Unfortunately I can give no affirmative answer to your question as to whether I have a publisher who trusts me. For a time I was connected with the firm of 'Dreililien'. At first things went quite tolerably. But actually, for a long time now, my relationship with them has been strained, so that I was recently obliged to publish my quartet privately, its publication having been so important to me on account of the scandal staged against me.[1] Thereby I have severed all connections with this firm, except perhaps for a debt of thanks which I still owe them for their initial interest. But I think that my thanks would be rather cold comfort to them.

I look forward to hearing your opinion of my piano pieces and cherish the fond hope that they mean something to you.

[1]String Quartet no. 2, op. 10. Schoenberg refers to the scandal provoked by the first performance of his String Quartet no. 1 in Vienna on 5 February 1907.

6   BUSONI TO SCHOENBERG

[Berlin] 26.7.1909

I have received your pieces and the accompanying letter. Both point to the thinking and feeling person I had already believed to have discovered in you. I know a quartet of yours, some lieder, and at one time a score of Pelleas und Melisande passed through my hands. Your instrumentation of Schenker's dances (which I performed in Berlin) bore witness to your astounding orchestral virtuosity. From these established points of reference, your piano pieces came as no surprise to me – that is: I happened to know what I could expect. It was therefore self-evident that I should find a subjective, individual art based on emotion – and that you would make me acquainted with refined artistic entities.

All this has come to pass, and I rejoice heartily over such a phenomenon.

My impression as a pianist, which I cannot overlook – be it due to upbringing or professional considerations – is otherwise. – My first qualification of your music '*as a piano piece*' is the limited range of the textures in time and space.

The piano is a short-breathed instrument, and one cannot do enough to assist it.

It is now five days since I received your pieces, and I have occupied myself with them every day. I believe I have grasped your intentions and feel confident, after some preparation, to produce sonorities and atmospheres according to your expectations. But the task is hindered by their excessive *conciseness* (that is the word).

As I fear I might be misunderstood, I am taking the liberty – in my own defence – of appending a small illustration to what I have written. You write:

Translating this from *orchestral* into *piano* writing:

But perhaps this does not represent your intentions at all.

I shall work the pieces through until they are completely absorbed into my blood. Then perhaps I shall think differently.

This is neither intended as judgement nor as criticism – to neither of which I would presume (in the face of so unique a person as yourself), but simply a record of the impression made and of my opinion as a pianist. –

Meanwhile my thanks and kindest greetings. I would be happy to retain your confidence, and tell me if there is anything else I can do [for you].

7   SCHOENBERG TO BUSONI

Steinakirchen am Forst [undated]

I have considered your reservations about my piano style at length and come to the conclusion that, from a certain standpoint, you are absolutely right. The ingenious way in which your example illustrates what you mean has also made clear to me what it is that you are concerned with. None the less, I think I may say that it does not seem that this is a deficiency which is not rooted in the nature of the music. Clearly, whenever a new technique is established, older virtues must fall. I also think that a wide range of textures must be as exceptional in music that cultivates so rapid a harmonic rhythm as it can be frequent when chords are more widely dispersed. To make ornaments and decorations by splitting up the chords is really only easily possible if a chord has sufficient duration. But, as I think that the piano texture is governed more by the sequence of chord-making elements than by their simultaneity, it is self-evident that the texture must have a relative lack of brilliance and richness. But apart from this, it seems to me that particularly these two pieces, whose sombre, compressed colours are a constituent feature, would not stand a texture whose effect on one's tonal palate – in the customary sense – was all too flattering. I think I can best prove this to you with some other piano pieces[1] which – I don't know when – will be ready.

I hope to have news from you again soon. I am particularly anxious to hear if you like the pieces, and what they mean to you. Maybe you will be able to write to me during the course of your journey.[2]

[1]Evidently a reference to three fragments dating from around 1909, of which one can be considered the original version of op. 11 no. 3 (Fragments 5, 6 and 7 in the Schoenberg Complete Edition, Series II, vol. 4).
[2]Busoni was about to take a brief holiday in Italy (cf. letter to Egon Petri, 16.8.1909, no. 73).

8   BUSONI TO SCHOENBERG

[Berlin] 2.8.1909

I received your letter in time to be able to answer it.

I must do so, because I have a good conscience about you – and a bad one, and I felt the need to make them both known to you.

I have occupied myself further with your pieces, and the one in 12/8 time[1] appealed to me more and more. I believe I have grasped it completely, all the more in that it coincides with some of my own ideas about the immediate mission of music. – Although I have become completely at one with the content, the form of expressing it on the piano has remained inadequate to me. Even now. Whether you hold my frankness for a virtue or me for limited – no matter. Where you write the marking < > over 4-note held chords – in an unsuitable register – this signifies an intention which is not fulfilled in the writing. This is not pianist's prejudice but irrefutable fact. – So I have studied your beautiful work from every angle and in great detail, which should prove to you – considering the extent of my activities – how seriously I have approached it and how much it has commanded my attention. (Were you here to interject that the piece deserves as much, you would be right.) At any rate – and this is where my *bad* conscience comes in – I have penetrated so deeply and closely into your thoughts that I myself was irresistibly urged to translate your evident intentions into *sound*. – When you speak of a 'tonal palate in the customary sense', you have in mind – in me – the so-called virtuoso pianist. Here *I* must again defend myself, for I am very conscious of having particularly devised pure, unspecified, refined ideas for the piano, *sound without technique*.

To complete my confession, let me tell you that I have (with total lack of modesty) 'rescored' your piece. Although this remains my *own business*, I should not fail to inform you, even at the risk of your being annoyed with me.

I am of course anxious to see the subsequent pieces, and look forward to them eagerly.

Let us hope that you will honour me further – despite this or that – with your confidence: should it be otherwise, I would be most disappointed.

I am going away for just 10 days, after which I shall be at your disposal again.

[1]op. 11 no. 2.

9 SCHOENBERG TO BUSONI

Steinakirchen am Forst [undated][1]

Above all, you are certainly doing me an injustice. But it seems that one has mutually to perpetrate injustice in one way or another if one is also prepared to recognize other mutual qualities. The regions of two individuals seem to be disposed like eccentric circles which partially intersect. Sectors of greater or lesser magnitude coincide – but there are the alternate segments, which confront each other. I take this to be something natural, which must be so, and hold it therefore for a good thing. And, of course, my trust absolutely cannot be shaken by this divergence. On the contrary, it has increased since I personally came in contact with you. The intuition I already had about the nature of your personality has been confirmed. And now I have formed a fairly clear picture. I can perceive a facet of your personality that is infinitely valuable to me: the endeavour to be just! And I value this endeavour higher than justice itself, just as I would rate the *struggle* for truth *higher* than the truth itself.

Therefore, even if you are in fact doing me an injustice, nothing in the world could give me greater pleasure than the *way* in which you do so.

But, as I said: I believe in actual fact that you are wrong.

I hope you will come to acknowledge this. However, I am no pianist. But none the less, I had imagined that I had laid the foundations for a modern piano style in these pieces and in some of my lieder. This may sound presumptuous but, as I believed it, nothing could stop me from also speaking it out. And truly, I tackled this problem in all consciousness, thought a lot about earlier piano styles and the requirements of expressing what I am striving for, and some of this has become clear. Of course: this kind of thing cannot succeed completely at the first go. And: even if the virtues of my piano style lie perhaps more in what I do *not* do than in having introduced anything novel, I still think I have clearly achieved one thing: I believe I have clearly moved away from what I call '*vocal score* style'.

There can be no doubt that the piano style of a period bears a certain resemblance to its orchestral style. I find that one can even see this in Mozart and Beethoven. All those for whom expression was the principal concern *composed for the piano* in that they *composed* according to the instrument's needs and demands. Composition is the dominant factor; one takes the instrument into account. Not the contrary.

In this way, I think one could find a relationship between modern orchestral technique and modern piano writing. But otherwise not at all, I hope. This, at least, was on my agenda, so to speak: away with vocal-score style; away with piano writing which overstretches the expressive possibilities and mobility of the piano yet is nothing more than a good, or less good, transcription of orchestral music.

The objection which you raise against the marking $<$ $>$ over static chords, on the other hand, does not seem justified.

I actually added this marking later and have since made continual use of it with specific meaning. Naturally, I never imagined that one could make these chords grow louder and softer. Just as I never believed in the possibility of playing

which I wrote on another occasion (although this is a different case).

I borrowed this former marking from Brahms. Apparently he does not use it in the same way as I. In such cases, I always mean a very expressive but soft *marcato* sforzato. Roughly comparable with the portamento marking

or the like. Recently I have always used it in this sense. Sometimes also (for strings or wind instruments) in a place of 'espress'.

And the latter marking is of course also not to be taken literally. It should simply be an indication of the direction of the line. Or of the degree of intensity. More an aid to comprehension of the line than a marking for performance. And then, there is also an ulterior motive in using these markings: it will surely not be long before the piano will be in a position to execute everything which we now find lacking in it. Amazing that this is not already possible. And only piety, or rather: conservatism, more precisely: musicians' indolence has had the consequence that, for more than one hundred years, no improvements worth mentioning have been made to the piano. Were the piano an instrument important to the cotton industry, say, it would have long been perfected. But I think that this will come to pass.

And so, markings which may today appear to be merely hopeless wishes should be employed to indicate how it really should sound.

To close, I must add that I was overjoyed to hear that you already like the one piece. And I really hope that you will later come to like the other one. Earlier I also preferred the 12/8 one (which I composed second) to the first. But recently I looked at the first one again: I almost believe that what I had conceived in terms of freedom and variegation of expression, of unshackled flexibility of form uninhibited by 'logic', is much more evident in the first than the second.

What I had visualized has been attained in neither. Perhaps, indeed definitely also not in the third, which will soon be finished. In a few orchestral pieces which I wrote very recently,[2] I have in certain respects come closer, but again in others have turned far from what I considered already achieved.

Perhaps this is not yet graspable. It will perhaps take a long time before I can write the music I feel urged to, of which I have had an inkling for several years, but which, for the time being, I cannot express.

I am writing in such detail because I want to declare my intentions (encouraged by your comment: my music affects you because you envisage something of the kind as the goal of our immediate developments).

I strive for: complete liberation from all forms
from all symbols
of cohesion and
of logic.
    Thus:
away with 'motivic working out'.
Away with harmony as
cement or bricks of a building.
Harmony is *expression*
and nothing else.
    Then:
Away with Pathos!
Away with protracted ten-ton scores, from erected or constructed
towers, rocks and other massive claptrap.
My music must be
brief.
Concise! In two notes: not built, but *'expressed'*!!
And the results I wish for:
no stylized and sterile protracted emotion.
People are not like that:
it is *impossible* for a person to have only *one* sensation at a time.

One has *thousands* simultaneously. And these thousands can no more readily be added together than an apple and a pear. They go their own ways.

And this variegation, this multifariousness, this *illogicality* which our senses demonstrate, the illogicality presented by their interactions, set forth by some mounting rush of blood, by some reaction of the senses or the nerves, this I should like to have in my music.

It should be an expression of feeling,[3] as our feelings, which bring us in contact with our subconscious, really are, and no false child of feelings and 'conscious logic'.

Now I have made my confession and they can burn me. You will not number amongst those who burn me: that I know.

=====

I inadvertently forgot to post this letter for a few days. Meanwhile I have managed to complete the 3rd piano piece[4] (before which I wrote an orchestral piece),[5] and I shall immediately take the opportunity of sending it to you: I am very interested to hear how it appeals to you. At present I myself have no opinion about it. As is often the case, I wrote it very swiftly and hence I myself generally need to grow accustomed to my music.

I would like to mention one other thing. You once asked me if I had a publisher and, on another occasion, if you could do anything for me. Yes, that would suit me very well; I am in great need, for there are no further prospects with my present publisher. And then, the pile of unpublished and unperformed works is growing tremendously. Although I do not write as much as I could, I have no fewer than 9 unpublished works ready,[6] most of them extensive. Apart from those I do not wish to publish, and several which are at present incomplete, but which will probably be finished sooner or later, there are, as I said, 9 works extending to more than 400 pages. It seems to me that I really should publish something again. Especially as some of them, compared to my present stage of development, are downright out of date.

I would therefore be most grateful if you could bring your influence to bear on a publisher.

But first I am anxious to hear your opinion of the new piece and how you will react to the question of my piano style.

[1]The postmark on the envelope of this letter is almost illegible but can be construed as 13 or 18.8.1909.
[2]Three of the Five Pieces for Orchestra, op. 16, nos. 3, 4 and 5, completed respectively on 1 July, 18 July and 11 August 1909.
[3]Orig. Sie soll Ausdruck der Empfindung sein. Allusion to Beethoven's comment about his 'Pastoral' Symphony, 'Mehr Ausdruck der Empfindung als Malerei' = more an expression of feeling than painting.
[4]The third piece of op. 11 was completed on 7 August 1909.
[5]i.e. no. 4 of the Five Pieces for Orchestra, op. 16.
[6]These included *Pelleas und Melisande*, op. 5, Six Songs for voice and orchestra, op. 8, the Chamber Symphony, op. 9, Two Ballads for voice and piano, op. 12, 'Friede auf Erden', op. 13, Two (Three) Songs, op. 14, *Das Buch der hängenden Gärten*, op. 15, Three Piano Pieces, op. 11, and Five Pieces for orchestra, op. 16.

10   BUSONI TO SCHOENBERG

[Berlin] 20.8.1909

Your last letter is an interesting document, which I value very highly – (also in that it is addressed to *me*) –. I have divined your intentions and, as you will see from some passages in my little book[1] – which I am sending to you 'for your information' – they are not unfamiliar to me.

Happily we have struck an attitude of frankness to one another, and I would ask:

to what extent do you realize these intentions?

And how much is *instinctive*, how much is *'deliberate'*?

The third piece, which you sent me in such good faith, supplements the two preceding ones without presenting any new facet; so it seems to me.

Particularly from a harmonic standpoint, it does not overstep the established boundaries. Chord-figures built on major 7ths and minor 9ths recur again and again – (the latter frequently and self-deceptively written as an augmented octave).

Laconicism becomes a mannerism. (A brilliant mind like yours turns criticism to advantage, even when misdirected.)

The 'asceticism' (let us so describe it) of the piano writing seems to me a pointless avoidance of foregone achievements. You are proposing a new value in place of an earlier one, instead of adding the new one to the old. You will become *different* and not *richer*.

If I felt unprepared for your art, I would bow out and bide my time. But I have prepared myself thoroughly.

So – for the present – we shall each remain at the centre of our respective circles, whose circumferences – as you rightly say – are tangential.

===

You will probably have difficulties with publishers in the immediate future. But times are changing more rapidly now. What I am now going to suggest is a modest proposal: the publisher Zimmermann is starting to issue a series of volumes under my editorship, with the title 'An die Jugend'. The first three volumes, already at the press, consist of my own compositions and arrangements.[2] 'An die Jugend' is intended to signify that the publications are conceived for the new generation. Would you be able to reconcile yourself to the idea that e.g. a fourth volume should contain the *original version* of your $\frac{12}{8}$ piece *and my paraphrase*? If so, I would suggest it to the publisher and assign the fee (which is very modest and would perhaps amount to 300 Marks) to you.

As you pass over my paraphrase in silence, it was with some effort on my part that I arrived at this proposal, but it was the first point of contact that occurred to me.

[1]Busoni sent Schoenberg a copy of his *Outline of a New Aesthetic of Music*, with a dedication: 'Dem Komponisten Arnold Schoenberg zur Verständigung' = to the composer Arnold Schoenberg, for his information.
[2]These were: 1 'Preludietto, Fughetta ed Esercizio' (original), 2 'Preludio, Fuga e Fuga figurata' (after Bach) and 3 'Giga, Bolero e Variazione' (after Mozart). (AB)

11   SCHOENBERG TO BUSONI

Steinakirchen am Forst 24.8.1909

Above all, I must apologize for something which is only partly my fault and only my fault in a way that allows forgiveness. While I was writing the first half of my previous letter, I had intended to ask you for your transcription, but then forgot. Then I was going to do so in the postscript and forgot again.

Finally I wanted to follow this long letter with a postcard – but I forgot for a third time. Can you forgive forgetfulness? I am banking on it, for it continually brings me into conflict. I trust that you will look upon the matter more from this angle, and that your ill-feeling on this account will evaporate.

But now I beg you to send me your transcription as soon as possible; I am truly anxious to get acquainted with the 'motivic report' of your proposals for improvement.

Further, I must thank you kindly for your suggestion of printing the one piece together with its paraphrase, which, considering your entirely justified ill-feeling, is truly magnanimous. But here new dificulties arise, and I really do not know if we would be able to come to an agreement over the new problems. Firstly a purely material consideration, the publication would have to be so arranged that my rights to republish the piece would not be encroached on, otherwise my 'opus' would be split up. I would also require authorization from my publisher, but this would in fact be easy to obtain. Then it would prey on my mind if I accepted the entire fee, when your transcription should also have a right to it.

But for me the most important and decisive factor is the artistic question. And will we find a solution here . . . ? . . . ?

You must consider the following: it is impossible for me to publish my piece together with a transcription which shows how I could have done it *better*. Which thus indicates that my piece is *imperfect*. And it is impossible to try to make the public believe that my piece is *good*, if I simultaneously indicate that it is *not good*.

I could not do this – out of my instinct for self-preservation – even if I believed it. In this case I would either have to destroy my piece or *rework it myself*.

But now – please forgive my unrestrained frankness, just as I do not take yours amiss – *I simply don't believe it*. I firmly believe you are making the same mistake as every *imaginative critic*: you do not wish to put yourself in the writer's place but seek rather, in the work of another, yourself, *only yourself*. And that just isn't possible. An art which is at one and the same time its creator's and its appraiser's cannot exist. One of these has to give way, and I believe this must be the appraiser.

And your reasoning seems to me quite unsound, when you say that I shall become different but no richer by pointlessly doing without what is already established.

I do not believe in putting *new wine* into old bottles. In the history of art I have made the following antipodal observations:

Bach's contrapuntal art vanishes when Beethoven's melodic homophony begins.

Beethoven's formal art is abandoned when Wagner introduces his express-ive art.

Unity of design, richness of colouring, working out of minutest details, painstaking formation, priming and varnishing, use of perspective and all the other constituents of older painting simply die out when the Impressionists begin to paint things as they *appear* and not as they *are*.

Yes indeed, when a new art seeks and finds new means of expression, almost all earlier techniques go hang: seemingly, at any rate; for actually they are retained; but in a different way. (To discuss this would lead me too far.)

And now: I must say that I actually dispensed with more than just piano sound when I began to follow my instincts and compose *such* music. I find that, when renouncing an *art of form*, the architecture of the leading voice, the polyphonic art that Brahms, Wagner and others brought to a high degree of perfection in the past decades – the little bit of piano sound seems a mere trifle. And I maintain: one must have grasped, admired and marvelled at the mysterious wonders of our tonal harmony, the unbelievably delicate balance of its architectural values and its cabbalistic mathematics as *I* have, in order to feel, when one no longer has need of them, that one requires new means. Questions of sonority, whose attraction ranks scarcely so high amongst the eternal values, are by comparison trivial.

Nevertheless, I take a standpoint in this question from which it is absolutely unnecessary to consider me a renouncer, a loser. Were you to see my new orchestral pieces, you would be able to observe how clearly I turn away from the full 'God and Superman' sound of the Wagner orchestra. How everything becomes sweeter, finer. How refracted shades of colour replace the former brilliant hues. How my entire orchestral technique takes a path which seems to be leading in quite the opposite direction to anything previously taken. I find this to be the natural reaction. We have had enough of Wagner's full, lush sonorities, to the point of satiation: 'Nun laßt uns andere Töne anstimmen . . .'[1]

And now I must add that I feel myself justified in believing (I must repeat this) that my piano writing is *novel*. Not only do my feelings tell me so. Friends and pupils express the opinion that the sonorities of my piano writing are completely novel.

For me the matter is as follows:

I do not consider my piano texture the result of any sort of incompetence, but rather the expression of *firm resolve, distinct preferences and palpably clear feelings*.

What it *does not* do is not what it *cannot*, rather what it *will* not.

What it does is not something which could have turned out differently, rather what it *had* to do.

Therefore it is distinctive, stylish and organic.

=====

I fear that a transcription, on the other hand, would either

introduce what I avoid, either fundamentally or according to my preferences;

add what I myself – within the limits of my personality – would never have devised, thus what is foreign or unattainable to me;

omit what I would find necessary, or

improve where I am, and must remain, imperfect.

Thus a transcription would be bound to do me violence: whether it helps or hinders my work.

In your pamphlet, which gives me uncommon pleasure and truly proves how the same thoughts can occur to different people at once, you write about transcription. I particularly agree with your thesis that all notation is transcription. I argued similarly some years ago when Mahler was publicly attacked for changing Beethoven's orchestration. But again: whether one improves upon Beethoven's undoubtedly *old-fashioned* treatment of instruments and orchestration on account of undoubtedly superior *newer* instrumental techniques, or whether one improves upon my piano style with older techniques or, at any rate, techniques whose greater appropriateness has today not yet been established, there is no doubt at all that these are two different matters.

I can at present say this without your having to take it as any harsh criticism, because I have not yet seen your transcription. After all, your arrangement could always prove that I am mistaken. But also, apart from that, I am sure you will not take my vehemence amiss, I am certain, because your opinion of my work was otherwise neither harsh nor unfavourable.

Another point occurs to me which seems a suitable argument against you.

Do you really set such infinite store by perfection? Do you really consider it attainable? Do you really think that works of art are, or should be, perfect?

I do not think so. I find even God's works of art, those of nature, highly imperfect.

But I find perfection only in the work of carpenters, gardeners, pastry-cooks and hairdressers. Only they produce that smoothness and symmetry which I have so often wished to the Devil. Only they fulfil every requirement one can expect of them, but otherwise nothing human or god-like in the world.

And if

Notation = Transcription = *Imperfection*

then also

Transcription = Notation = *Imperfection*.

For if a = b and b = c, then also

a = c.

Why then replace one imperfection with another?

Why eliminate that which perhaps contributes to the appeal of a work and substitute something added by a foreign hand?

Don't the characteristics of a man's personality also include his defects? Do these not have an effect, even if unbeautiful, then at least as contrast, like the basic colour upon which the other shades are superimposed?

I have often thought that one should give Schumann's symphonies (which I believe you have greatly underestimated[2] and which I rate *far above* those of Brahms) a helping hand by improving the orchestration. The theoretical aspects were quite clear to me. This summer I spent a little time on this and – lost courage. For I can see exactly that wherever things misfire, something highly original was intended, and I lack the courage to replace an *interesting idea*, which has not been quite successfully carried out, with a *'reliable'* sonority. And with a true work of art, the imagination of an outsider can achieve no more than this! –

From a purely technical angle, I would like to ask you if you have perhaps taken too slow a tempo. That could make a great difference. Or too *little* rubato. I never stay in time! Never in tempo! –

Your 'Outline of a New Aesthetic of Music' gave me uncommon pleasure, above all on account of its audacity. Particularly at the beginning, there are a few powerful sentences, of compulsive logic and superlative acuteness of observation. I have also thought a lot about your idea of thirds of tones, though in a different way. But I had been thinking of quarter-tones, am however now of the opinion that it will depend less on the construction than on other things. Moreover, one of my pupils[3] calculated, at my suggestion, that the next division of the octave with similar properties to our twelve semitone division would have to introduce 53 notes. If you adopt 18 thirds of tones, that would be approximately equal, for $3 \times 18 = 54$. But then the semitones would disappear completely.

Earlier I thought out the following method of notating quarter-tones:

< and > are
mathematical symbols.

However, I scarcely think that such attempts at notation will catch on; for I confidently hope that the notation of the future will be – how can I say: 'wirelesser'.

I also think differently about tonality – my music shows that. I believe: everything one can do with 113 keys[4] can also be done with 2 or 3 or 4: major-minor, whole-tone and chromatic. Anyway, I have long been occupied with the removal of all shackles of tonality. And my harmony allows no chords or melodies with tonal implications any more.

Now to your questions.

To what extent I realize my intentions? Not as far as I would like to. Not one piece has yet satisfied me entirely. I would like to achieve even greater variegation of motifs and figures without melodic character; I would like to be freer and less constrained in rhythm and time-signature; freer from repetition of motifs and spinning out of thoughts in the manner of a melody. This is my vision: this is how I imagine music before I notate=transcribe it. And I am unable to force this upon myself; I must wait until a piece comes out of its own accord in the way I have envisaged.

And thus I come to answer your other question: how much is intentional and how much instinctive.

My only intention is

to have *no* intentions!

No formal, architectural or other artistic intentions (except perhaps of capturing the mood of a poem), no aesthetic intentions – none of any kind; at most this:

to place nothing inhibiting in the stream of my unconscious sensations. But to allow anything to infiltrate which may be invoked either by intelligence or consciousness.

If you knew how I have developed, you would have no doubts. But I have prepared myself for this question and am thus able to answer it. I knew one would question the naturalness of my intentions, precisely because they are natural. That one would find them formalized for the very reason that I avoid anything formal.

But when one sees how I have developed in stages, how I was long ago approaching a form of expression to which I now adhere freely and un-reservedly, one would understand that nothing unorganic, no 'schmock aestheticism,'[5] is involved, but that *compulsion* has produced these results.

As I am now fairly clear about the theoretical side, only those can scoff who imagine the unconsciously creating artist to be a sort of half-cretin; and who cannot grasp that after unconscious creativity follows a period of *quiet clearsightedness*, in which one renders account of one's situation.

As for the third piece, which you do not care for at present, as can be inferred from your caustic criticism, I find it goes a considerable way beyond what was successful in the other two. At any rate, as far as the above-mentioned variegation is concerned. But also in the 'harmony' – if one can speak so architecturally here – there seems to be something novel in it. In particular: something more slender, more linear.[6] But I also consider it unjust to expect that one can revolutionize music in three *different* ways in 3 little piano pieces. Does it not seem permissible, having departed so far from convention, to pause for a moment's breath, to gather new strength, before one rushes on? And is it not unjust to describe laconicism as a mannerism? Is formalism just as much a manner as pointillism or impressionism? Must one build? Is music then a savings-bank? Does one get more when it is longer?

If I was wrong *there* to be brief, I have *amply* compensated for it in this *letter*! But there were indeed several things I wanted to say – that I could not express them more concisely can be blamed upon my technical shortcomings.

And finally: I hope my frankness does not annoy you, and that you maintain your interest in me.

Maybe you will find a formula, an explanation, through which I shall be able to publish my piece in your series.

Or perhaps you could publish all three and your paraphrase, with an explanation some other time??

In any case, I hope not to lose your goodwill if I now ask you to tell me whether you wish to play the pieces. For, clearly this would mean an enormous amount to me.

One other curious thing, to close: before composing these piano pieces, I had wanted to contact you – knowing of your predilection for transcriptions – to ask if you would take one of my chamber or orchestral works into your repertoire, transcribed for piano solo.

Curious: now we come into contact again through a transcription! Was I misunderstanding a message from my subconscious, which made me think of you in the context of a transcription?

This has just occurred to me!

[1]Intended as a quotation from Beethoven's Symphony No. 9. The actual words are: 'O Freunde, nicht diese Töne! Sondern laßt uns angenehmere anstimmen . . .'. Schoenberg's words mean: now let us strike up other sounds.

[2]In the *Outline of a New Aesthetic of Music* Busoni writes: 'All composers have drawn nearest the true nature of music in preparatory and intermediary passages . . . where they felt at liberty to disregard symmetrical proportions, and unconsciously drew free breath. Even a Schumann (of so much lower stature [than Beethoven]) is seized, in such passages, by some feeling of the boundlessness of this pan-art (recall the transition to the last movement of the D Minor Symphony); and the same may be asserted of Brahms in the introduction to the Finale of his First Symphony.' (Trans. Theodore Baker.) (AB)

[3]This was the philosopher Dr Robert Neumann, who studied with Schoenberg from 1907 to 1909.

[4]In the *Outline of a New Aesthetic* Busoni writes: 'I have made an attempt to exhaust the possibilities of the arrangement of degrees within the scale; and succeeded, by raising and lowering the intervals, in establishing *one hundred and thirteen different scales.*' (Trans. ibid.) (AB)

[5]Orig. nichts 'Verschmockt-Ästhetisches'.

[6]Orig. manches dünnere, zweistimmigere.

12 BUSONI TO SCHOENBERG

[Berlin] 26.8.1909

I am afraid I cannot answer your letter in detail today, although so interesting – even if also sometimes self-contradictory – and, on the other hand, I feel compelled to endorse it.

I thank you, and believe I have *understood all*, both the artistic and ethical sides.

Today (amongst other things) I took the liberty of writing the following letter behind your back to Breitkopf und Härtel: in these words:

'During the past few months I have come into correspondence with a certain Arnold Schoenberg, who is otherwise unknown to me. – The motive was his sending me three original piano pieces. – In these, Schoenberg shows himself to have a highly individual, even strange mind, yet – as his letters prove – also a sense of purpose. The pieces interested me so much that I "transcribed" one of them for my concert use. The few lines – which I am enclosing here by way of explanation – are intended to preface this transcription [sic] (as an aid to comprehension). *Without his knowing of this*, I would like to ask whether you would be interested in helping this aspiring person by publishing his 3 pieces – admittedly quite "unpopular" but significant as they are (each is about 4 pages long) – under your auspices. –'

I mention the transcription 'for my concert use' in the letter to Br. & H. simply to make it clear to these people how strong an interest I am taking in the pieces. – I myself am omitting the transcription but sending the little preface to Br. & H., which adds certain things, so as to arouse their interest as publishers. – The preface runs as follows:

'In a short paper which was intended to pave the way to wider perceptions, one finds the sentence:

Kaleidoscopic swirling of the 12 semitones in a chamber lined with the triple mirrors of feeling, taste and intuition: the essence of today's harmony.

The idea expressed in this sentence seems to have been realized – perhaps for the first time – in Schoenberg's piano piece; the concept of major and minor scales with their 12 transpositions is eradicated. The editor sees in this work a starting point for a music of the future. Its performance demands of the player the greatest refinement of touch and pedalling; intimate, improvised, 'gliding', perspicacious interpretation; affectionate immersion in its content. The editor considers it an artistic honour to be its interpreter – in the mere function of piano transcriber. F.B.'[1]

I hope you will construe this free manner of handling things in the same spirit in which it was conceived. – In no way does it compromise you. – I shall send the reply on to you, and I have sent you an exact copy of my letter, so that you need suspect no further intervention on my part in the reaction from Br. & H. (No matter how it turns out.)

[1]When Busoni's *konzertmäßige Interpretation* was published by Universal Edition in 1910, only the last sentence appeared – slightly altered – by way of introduction.

13 SCHOENBERG TO BUSONI

Steinakirchen am Forst [undated][1]

My warmest thanks for your kind exertions. I certainly hope that they will be successful. But even if they are not: my success in winning the interest of someone like you is worth more to me.

For today I shall but briefly mention the following, which will perhaps be of interest to you, and is the cause of my brevity: I have started on a new composition;[2] something for the theatre; something quite new. The librettist (a lady),[3] acting on my suggestions, has conceived and formulated everything just as I envisaged it. More news shortly; for at present I am head over heels in work and hope to be finished in 14 days.

[1]According to the sequence of the correspondence and bearing in mind that work on *Erwartung* began on 27 August 1909, this letter dates from 27 or 28.8.1909.
[2]*Erwartung*, op. 17. The composition was completed on 12 September 1909.
[3]The doctor Marie Pappenheim, 1882–1966, also active in the field of literature.

14 BUSONI TO SCHOENBERG

[Berlin] 29.8.1909

Assuming you received my last letter, I am now glad that I passed the exact wording of my appeal to Br. & H. on to you. As you see, a misunderstanding has arisen – as if I hadn't expected it – due apparently to a mere cursory inspection (in Leipzig).——

– What would you like me to do?
– Please return the Leipzig letter with your instructions.

15 SCHOENBERG TO BUSONI

Vienna 6.10.1909

I have received no news from you for a long time and am racking my brains to 'find the reason'[1] for your sudden silence. I cannot think of any, and have to assume that some kind of misunderstanding has arisen, because I have not the faintest notion of having done anything intentionally to offend you. Or have I forgotten something? That is more probably the case. My energy only suffices for relevant matters and always flags at the prospect of mere formalities. I have never been able to make a '*cordial*' polite remark to anyone, and I also never try. My sympathy and respect manifest themselves less directly: by demonstrating to someone that I wish to associate with him, to speak with him. Therefore, as any conscious intention on my part must have been lacking and as your ill feeling would grieve me, I beg you to tell me what has happened. I am sure I can find an explanation.

Until two days ago I myself was working very intensively, first on the composition and then on the scoring of my latest work. It is a monodrama (for the stage) and I believe it has come out extraordinary well. The rest of the time was occupied with negotiations which I had with my old publishers, Dreililien Verlag, and my future ones, Universal Edition. The latter made me an offer at the beginning of September which, according to the decision we made yesterday, will be binding for the next 10 years. And so I must also thank you sincerely and inform you that I shall be unable to be published by Breitkopf und Härtel. I did not wish to write to you any sooner about this, as it looked for a long time as if nothing would come of the Univ. Ed. and I did not want to fall between two stools. Apart from that, I was unaware that U.E. would have an effect on my entire output. As this now turns out to be the case, please be so kind as to inform Br. & H.

I read that you will be in Vienna in December.[2] The Tonkünstler-Verein and the Verein für Kunst und Kultur want to organize a concert with my new pieces.[3] Would it not be possible, if we scheduled it close to your concert, that you could perhaps play the 3 piano pieces? I am actually very eager to hear you play them, and that would be a good opportunity. However, I should prefer it if you were to programme them in your own concert, because I far prefer contact with the general public to that with a specialized one.

One more request: Universal Edition, who want to publish these three piano pieces as well, would first like to have an undertaking that you will play the pieces in public. I too would like to have this certainty, which would give me great pleasure. Could I beg you to make me a promise to this effect?

[1]Orig. 'den Grund mir aufzufinden': quotation from Sachs's 'Wahn' monologue in Act III of *Die Meistersinger von Nürnberg*.
[2]Busoni was due to give a recital in Vienna on 1 December 1909 as part of a brief tour (with further concerts in Budapest and Lvov).
[3]Schoenberg's concert did not take place until 14 January 1910, in the Ehrbar-Saal, Vienna. The pianist Etta Werndorf performed the op. 11 pieces in this concert.

16   BUSONI TO SCHOENBERG

Berlin 7.10.1909

My apparent silence is explained by the simple fact that my last letter to you has been mislaid. Pity. It enclosed the information that Br. & H. were interested in your pieces (the letter from the firm was enclosed) but that some misunderstanding had arisen and Br. & H. thought the pieces were transcriptions of mine. I then wrote to you that I was now glad to have passed on the exact wording of my previous letter to Br. & H. to you, and that I would await your instructions: whether I should now send the three original pieces (with *or* without my transcription) to Br. & H.
                    Is that clear?
As I am going away on the 11th, I would ask you to reply immediately. (The remainder of your letter does just that.)

I am so glad that your monodrama has been a success! *I* for my part interpreted *your* silence as meaning that you were hard at work!

Amongst the 871 (!) piano pieces entered for the *Signale Prize Competition*, I thought I 'recognized' you in a Praeludium & Fugue (?).[1] At any rate, the piece has come into the final round.

Now I read in your letter of the agreement with U.E. and am heartily glad to hear it.

For various, unfortunately conventional reasons, I am unable to give my formal assent to play your pieces, but I shall always be on your side whenever there is talk of you, or whenever the opportunity arises to raise the subject. –

NB. Your pieces have inspired me to the idea of a new 'Piano Notation' which – I believe – is a real 'discovery'.[2]

---

[1]Entries for a competition to further the cause of good new works for the piano were invited in *Signale für die musikalische Welt*, no. 22, 31.5.1909. The composer of the Praeludium and Fuge was, as later transpired, Karol Szymanowski. Schoenberg, however, seems to have thought it was Busoni's pupil Louis T. Gruenberg. In Schoenberg's 'Berliner Tagebuch', there is the following comment on Gruenberg dated 23.1.1912:

> And Busoni wanted to confuse me with this person: who entered the piano pieces (for a competition) which Busoni believed he recognized as being by me. He does not seem to have understood me in any depth. For one should really be able to sense that my music has something about it which rules out any similarity to that of Herr Gruenberg. (AB additions.)

[2]*Attempt at an Organic Piano Notation*. See footnote 1 to letter no. 80.

BUSONI TO EMIL HERTZKA

Berlin, 6.12.1909

Thank you for so kindly sending me the beautiful edition of Bach! Thank you also for being so obliging. Despite certain reservations, I have decided to send you my concert interpretation (how should I entitle it?) of Schoenberg's unnamed, atmospheric piece, which I – by way of mediation between him and the listener – have entitled Notturno.

I have taken great care over his interpretation. It arose from a feeling – the justification for which, however, Schoenberg *denies* me – that Schoenberg himself has not adequately entrusted his intimate thoughts and feelings to the *piano*; that they hence remain imperfectly expressed. I have *not* – as Schoenberg seems to fear – created a virtuoso piece out of it, but on the contrary it was my endeavour to preserve the subtlety of Schoenberg's original. He himself will probably not agree, as I have expanded the excessively laconic moments, to enable the listener *to assimilate them* and to make the instrument sound well. – I myself attach importance to it, because this transcription *points in the direction which piano composers should henceforth follow.* I myself am ambitious enough to wish therewith to make my contribution to this trend.

At any rate – you will see that the piece will be more *readily* accepted and played in my edition than in the original. It would be worth making my version known, if only to lend the composer's remarkable spirit a more pliant representative in the indifferent world.

Let me have some definite news before my departure for America (about the 20th). I leave the terms to your discretion.

P.S. In Vienna[1] I hope to see you and also Schoenberg. Unfortunately I have not yet met him in person. Send him my regards.

[1]Having given a recital in Vienna on 1 December, Busoni returned (via Budapest and Lvov) to Berlin, only to set out anew for a further concert in Vienna a few days later. He did not, however, make Schoenberg's personal acquaintance on either of these occasions: a meeting of the two composers seems not to have been possible until autumn 1910 (cf. letter from Busoni to Emil Hertzka, dated 7.11.1910).

BUSONI TO EMIL HERTZKA

Berlin 16.12.1909

I cannot hold it against Schoenberg that he summons up no enthusiasm for my encroaching on his independence as a composer, and indeed finds it indelicate. But – on the other hand – when I am deeply engrossed in a matter, it is my nature to *have* to play an active role – and I *have* devoted much time and attention to Schoenberg!

This season I shall scarcely be able to perform the piece publicly in America but I have in principle nothing against doing so.

But S.'s manner of handling his affairs is also not exactly delicate and, in this respect, neither of us is beyond reproach. This is what happens when hard-headed people come together. Except that Schoenberg has done nothing for *me*. Thus it is characteristic of our correspondence that S. only speaks of *himself*, while I have spoken only of *him* and about him.

But I respect his pride and am delighted with his sum and substance.

BUSONI TO EMIL HERTZKA

Berlin 17.6.1910

Your letter of the 16th was most welcome.

You have indeed achieved everything possible with Schoenberg.

I profess myself to be satisfied with the 'tolerant' attitude, but I must however have some idea of what Schoenberg wishes to write, as you yourself have suggested.[1]

As for the work – I shall play it in public.[2] I can make neither head nor tail of your proposed terms; for this piece (taking into consideration the 'complicated circumstances') I would like to settle for the *lowest* figure I have ever requested or received: 300 Crowns. –

It is a constant pleasure to correspond with Schoenberg.

[1]Hertzka had suggested that Busoni's transcription of op. 11 no. 2 should be published as an appendix to op. 11, with an introductory note by Busoni and a rejoinder by Schoenberg.
[2]There is no record of Busoni ever having played any work of Schoenberg's in public.

I7 SCHOENBERG TO BUSONI

Vienna 3.7.1910

My publishers' intention of issuing my piano pieces and your transcription of the one, together with your foreword and my rejoinder to it, gives me the opportunity of resuming our correspondence, which has remained dormant for some time. Enclosed is my rejoinder,[1] which I ask you to regard as a *draft*. I myself believe it has turned out somewhat caustic, but I would not know how to make it any less caustic if it is also to remain accurate. But I shall of course [do so] if you are not in agreement with it. You could also *amend your 'foreword' accordingly* if necessary; I would then, however, have to see it. But I hope we shall reach an agreement. I hope you will understand that I cannot condone alterations to the form without damning that aspect of my work. It seems to me rather like correcting the crooked lines in a picture of van Gogh's and replacing them with correct, straight ones. With just one difference: van Gogh paints crooked lines where straight ones would have seemed just as satisfactory to him, if not more so (anyway: who knows?!?); but in my work there is not a line which I could imagine any other way. I feel that: for my sense of form, your arrangement represents no improvement because it cannot signify any such. But I consider it possible that some people might understand it better in that form. Just as it often happens that one looks at the vocal line of a song on its own and thus understands it better. Whether one should on that account publish the vocal line alone is a question which I should not like to have to decide.

I would urge you to revise your transcription. Perhaps you could at least decide to remove the additions (which as repeats, *unvaried*!! repeats, scarcely correspond with the style of the piece as a whole). I am sure: he who knows how I write will realize that this is not in the spirit of my work. And there are people who really understand me so well. Also the harmonic additions! I find these particularly dubious. According to my sense of form, it is not the same if a chord has 3 or 4 notes. This causes a shifting of the balance. Also some of the rhythmical alterations. I could never sanction these. Nor the following: you take the first bar twice; that is too long. Apart from which you anticipate the effect of the subsequent entrance of the low F. In my version this does not enter until several bars later. In your arrangement this effect is lost. To explain this with an illustration, it strikes me as follows:

To begin like this

is as if one were completely immersed in a certain mood.

If one begins thus  , it is as if one were returning

(gradually) to the opening idea after a disturbance. This is not intended to be programmatic. But just an ad hoc attempt at an interpretation. You lose this effect in your arrangement.

Another thing: the figure   does not correspond in the least

to the expression I had intended in the   passage. It should

not be 'dolce tranquillo' but rather very expressive, strident, expansive; oboes with cello portamento. But apart from that: if the semiquaver figure represents the further developed form of this idea, then surely the original form from which it is derived should not be missing?!?

Otherwise your transcription contains any number of ingenious details which prove how deeply you have penetrated this piece and how sensitively. Some things are wonderful, highly interesting and very precisely thought out. And I must admit: 'were I not Diogenes, then . . .',[2] i.e. had I not wished (and been *able*) to write *this* piece, then I would have wanted to write yours, your transcription. But I have written mine, and your arrangement has not convinced me that mine is not good. On the contrary, a good but by no means brilliant pianist has made it sound very well. Maybe you have been playing it at a tempo other than that intended. I prescribe: 'moderate quavers'; yes, moderate quavers. But a moderate quaver is of course faster than a moderate crotchet; because it is, of course, a *quaver*, and otherwise there would be no reason to write quavers. Perhaps this has misled you. Perhaps I should have written: moving quavers[3] (circa MM ♪ = 80–90). That is moderate for quavers, because the value would thus become ♩. = 26–30!

At the time you wrote to me approximately as follows: 'I hope that such a (*fine?*) head as yours does not take criticism as (*abuse?*)'. I have not done so, nor do I expect you to do so. I therefore hope you will have nothing against the wording of my foreword. But, as I said, should you have any objections, then I shall be prepared to make alterations. For, you surely understand, I am grateful to you above all for your kind interest and I feel positively *honoured* by the well-meant intentions of your transcription. I have indeed written this and herewith assure you of it once again. But I cannot therefore bring myself to consider my piece imperfect and in need of improvement. Certainly no less imperfect than anything else I have written. I almost believe it is better. And if it seems imperfect to me in certain ways, then these are quite other matters, in which I am now more adept than at the time.

I must thank you kindly for sending me your 'Organic Piano Notation'. I shall write in detail about it soon.

Unfortunately I have much to do, therefore I cannot write about it just now. I am writing a Harmonielehre, am scoring part 3 of my Gurrelieder (an earlier work of mine), have written a libretto,[4] am painting etc. So: another time please.

I hope I shall hear from you soon, because the pieces must go to print and should be there before the 15th; otherwise it would be too late for the autumn.

[1]Schoenberg's rejoinder has not been preserved.
[2]Adapted from a saying of Alexander the Great: 'If I were not Alexander, I would like to be Diogenes.'
[3]Orig. gehende Achtel.
[4]The text for *Die glückliche Hand*, op. 18.

18 SCHOENBERG TO BUSONI

Vienna 16.7.1910

You are annoyed with me, but without justification. I would not have dreamed of wishing to insult you in my rejoinder. Nor can I find that anything in the 4th paragraph could be construed as insulting. It is somewhat nonchalantly worded; rather racy in style. But whatever: it was certainly not intended as an insult. On no account should you construe it that way. I beg you.

But: I wished to express my attitude clearly towards the alterations to my work. Please consider it a virtue in me that I tend to equate 'clear' with 'caustic'. I hope you prefer someone whose reaction is caustic to one who doesn't react at all. One gains nothing, generally speaking, from such people. Their mildness may have a temporarily pleasing effect but, because they *lack* stimulus, they become tedious in the long run.

For the same reason I ask you not to take the comments amiss which I have written on the score of your arrangement.[1] I believe they are *factually* caustic; but not personally. And that could scarcely be otherwise. Because the causticity lies *in the* very *controversy* I am fighting out with you here. Not in the personalities. Do I have to add that, after all I have heard about you, I admire you greatly. But one can still have a difference of opinion (at least in the form of an art-work).

So I ask you not to look askance at the metaphors I have used. Consider that one makes such comparisons in order to magnify something that is too small – or to diminish something that is too large. A comparison is thus bound to change (distort) the dimensions and thus occasionally to exaggerate them –. One wishes to express oneself clearly and to present an argument in such a way that one's opponent understands what one means.——

One more thing: I have discussed another form for the publication of your arrangement with director Hertzka.

Namely this:

Your arrangement should not appear in the same volume as my pieces, but independently.

In which case my rejoinder would be omitted.

I hope you agree to this.

I am posting the arrangement to you today and ask you to return the finally edited version of the piece to me or Univ. Edition as soon as possible.

I have asked my pupil Kapellmeister Dr Jalowetz[2] to send you the original. But please: there could be some errors in this copy. I have not yet checked it myself.

I could not answer your letter until today because I had to speak with director Hertzka first.

I hope to have news from you soon and will be particularly pleased if you could reassure me that you are not annoyed.

---

[1]Busoni's manuscript, with Schoenberg's pencilled comments, is preserved in the Deutsche Staatsbibliothek, Berlin.
[2]Dr Heinrich Jalowetz, 1882–1946, conductor. He studied with Schoenberg from 1904 to 1908.

19 BUSONI TO SCHOENBERG

Berlin 18.7.1910

I shall work your 2nd piece through again and comply with your wishes. Of course I respect you.

No, I am not annoyed; your marginal jottings made me laugh until I had to suppress a tear and then blow my nose as well![1] The original has not yet arrived. Let us wait awhile. The idea of a special (separate) publication is more fitting. – In paragraph 4 of your foreword you write: I have no objection *if a passage is unclear to somebody* . . . Please note that I understand your piece just as you wrote it and that it was my concern – *because* I am fond of it – to make it comprehensible to others.

Your means of expression are new, but not your piano textures, which are simply poorer. I believe you have a far greater command of, say, the orchestra.

It looks like this: 'the arranger did not understand several passages' . . . In the *public* eye that would be impossible. As far as I am concerned, you can write it in a letter, although I believe – as I said – that I do not deserve it. I enclose my latest composition.[2]

[1]Over bars 61–2 of Busoni's version Schoenberg had written: 'The entry of the chord

in my version is roughly as if someone were suppressing a tear. Here he also blows his nose.' (AB)
[2]The *Edizione definitiva* of the *Fantasia Contrappuntistica* for piano had not yet been printed, although Busoni was putting the finishing touches to it at this time. Hence he will have sent Schoenberg one of the 100 copies of the limited edition of the 'Grosse Fuge', the original version of the same work. (AB)

BUSONI TO EMIL HERTZKA

[Berlin] 25.8.1910

I must ask you kindly but firmly to make a decision about the Schoenberg affair. If negative (which I would now find entirely *desirable*), then I would ask you to return my manuscript.

I *cannot* accept Schoenberg's version of the foreword. In the long run I am getting tired of playing the role of the accused (which I do not deserve).

My respect and sympathy for S. remain unimpaired, but it is intolerable to find oneself being treated in quite the opposite way.

20   SCHOENBERG TO BUSONI

Vienna 4.9.1910

I beg you not to be angry with me for not having written for so long. I have been working very very hard; have finished a Harmonielehre, orchestrated the second part of my Gurrelieder, written the text for a drama with music (actually very brief) and done many other things. Hence I have had no peace and was simply too busy to look through your very complicated piano work with the care which so serious a composition demands. And I would really not wish to say anything superficial about it. If I am obliged to do so after all, then as an indication of my goodwill. I would rather run the risk of saying something conventional or superficial than of appearing impolite. What I most admire is that you have so completely succeeded in penetrating the style and idea of Bach's theme that the harmony, which in places comes close to the most recent developments, never diverges from the tone of the whole. For me this is proof of an opinion which I have held for quite some time: that style, when it really is a *true* attribute of a work of art (and not just an imaginary or insignificant one), is by no means linked to the technically orientated findings of the theoreticians, but that it lies in a completely different region. That of overall personality!

But I shall examine your work much more closely and discuss other aspects of it with you.

And now something which I have long been meaning to ask you: I would like to know some other works of yours. Those which actually put into practice what you have promised in your pamphlet.

Would you be so kind?

If you are interested in getting to know my quartet op. 10 (with voice), I can send you the score.

Please forgive me, I must finish now. Today I have to answer some letters which are over four weeks old, because tomorrow I shall probably have to work again.

BUSONI TO EMIL HERTZKA

Schloss Bottmingen, near Basle 15.9.1910

Thank you for your letter and your mediation – I am delighted at the positive outcome and at the publication.

Unfortunately, due to my absence, the proofs have not yet reached me – as soon as I have them, I shall check them through and return them at once.

When you have the opportunity, please pass on my thanks to Schoenberg for his last kind letter.

BUSONI TO EMIL HERTZKA

Berlin 7.11.1910

[. . .] I would like to ask for a dozen copies [of the Schoenberg–Busoni]. I was very pleased to see you and talk to you again and to make the acquaintance of Schoenberg, who is most congenial.

I am particularly interested in the complete edition of my Bach transcriptions.

Not long afterwards I would like to organize a similar collection of my original piano works.

Have you considered publishing the Etudes of *Ch. V. Alkan* in the U.E.? They are the most significant after Chopin and Liszt.

I look forward to receiving Schenker's study of the Chrom. Fantasia.[1]

[1]Heinrich Schenker, *Erläuterungsausgabe der 'Chromatischen Phantasie und Fuge'*, Vienna, 1910.

BUSONI TO EMIL HERTZKA

Berlin 14.11.1910

Thank you for so kindly letting me have the copies of the *'Schoenberg'*. –

I also received the *Reger–Stradal*[1] and *Bach–Schenker*. – I do have a certain respect for the former, but his world is entirely remote from mine!

I scarcely understand Schenker any more. We used to be good musical friends. This manner of gaping open-mouthed at a master's earthly achievements is, to my mind – too uncritical.

What would such a 'researcher' (who has written 30 pages of close print about a 15-page keyboard work) have to do if he were to work through Bach's *complete* compositions?

However – music and music-research are two different matters. Let us allow Schenker his contribution.

Many thanks for all your good intentions with regard to my works. – I would like to have a copy of Schoenberg's 3 piano pieces – send him my kindest regards.

[1]Reger's Fantasia and Fugue on B-A-C-H, for organ, op. 46, transcribed for piano by August Stradal, which had recently been published by Universal Edition. Strange coincidence that it might be, a letter from Reger to Stradal, dated 31.12.1910, discusses Schoenberg's op. 11 Piano Pieces and represents the reaction of the majority of his contemporaries: 'Even I cannot make head or tail of this; I don't know if this kind of thing can be given the name of "music": my mind is really too old-fashioned for that! Now the misunderstood Strauss and all that is coming out! It's enough to make you turn conservative.'

21   SCHOENBERG TO BUSONI

Berg am Starnberger-See 29.8.1911

I have heard that you are interested in the move to Berlin which is being planned for me. I am turning to you because, due to an unfortunate event, an element of haste has entered into the matter, giving rise to a situation which only a strong hand can disentangle.

I cannot tell you the whole story; it is too long and too unlikely. Tomorrow I shall tell [Oskar] Fried everything and he will pass it on to you. The main point is the following: some brute who lives in the same house as I and is doubtlessly mad (but who cannot at present be medically certified) has got it into his head that he *has to kill me*. The reason he gives for his fury is a lie, but, even as such, so insignificant that it is unqualified as justification for this insane desire to take my life. On 4 August, after several unsuccessful attempts via the authorities and even with a revolver to restore peace and order, I and my family were obliged temporarily to avoid the danger either of my being murdered or imprisoned, due to an infringement of the laws of self-defence, with all the fuss that would be bound to arise, by taking flight. That is why I have come here. I had, however, hoped to clear the matter up in the meantime through my solicitor but, after sending off any number of letters, I see that I have no prospect of ridding myself of this undoubted lunatic, who *is meanwhile still raving!!!*

So I am unable to return to Vienna!! So the question of my moving house is no longer a matter of free will but, due to these unfortunate circumstances, which are 'force majeur', I am compelled to.

Nevertheless, I could not readily embark on so hazardous a venture as this move with my family without the assurance that I could play a passive role in Berlin for a season at least, until I have established myself.

Dear Mr Busoni, please do not misunderstand me: this is no 'clever' trick, no attempt to sponge on strangers or to shirk one's duties, etc. On the contrary: I am indeed one of the most industrious people alive! Thus, if I must demand the dues that the public should actually accord me without my having to demand them, on account of my achievements, then I do so with the greatest reluctance! Although I should have a right to them!!

But this is how matters stand: my money is running out. I have obtained from my friends a sum to cover the high costs, which would otherwise have ruined me, and only thus has it been possible to live here from 4 August until now.

At the beginning of September I *ought* to be in Vienna; but I cannot. And in 14 days I shall no longer have the money for the return journey.

Please do not misunderstand me: I am not touching you for a loan; on the contrary, it is my wish that *you should only use your influence* to help me raise money, and nothing further!!!

But I beg you this: I haven't a week to spare and am terribly anxious about the future. We are, after all, four people; that isn't so easy! And why should I, a creator of values, have to live in squalor! I therefore beg you one thing: do your *utmost* for me through your friends and acquaintances, but above *all*:
do it quickly!!

I am terribly sorry to have to come to you with such matters. But I think: one can come to an artist, that is someone who is a true human being, with anything. And surely I shall not have to turn to my enemies.

22 BUSONI TO SCHOENBERG

Berlin 16.9.1911

I have just returned from a brief holiday of 14 days, the first I have allowed myself in 2 years.[1] At the bottom of a large pile of outstanding correspondence I find your letter.

Your story is most remarkable – at the moment, when I have to catch up with all overdue and urgent matters – I can scarcely do much. Yesterday our appeal was published in Pan.[2] I am not very happy about the wording (which I did not see until it was in print). It is not you who should have to wait for 'pupils' but the pupils (and the whole of musical Berlin) who should wait for you. I fear the appeal will thus not be effective.

But you see, we are taking steps.

As soon as there is more to report, I shall do so.

Please forgive my brevity and haste. I really don't know how to cope with all my obligations.

[1]Busoni spent about two weeks in Varese (cf. letters no. 108 and 109 to Egon Petri).

[2]The appeal was published in *Pan*, vol. 1, 1910–11, p. 741. It ran as follows:

> The composer Arnold Schoenberg is living in Vienna. He cannot remain there any longer. (The days when musicians fled to Vienna are evidently no more.)
>
> Vienna, itself a magic music, old, resounding, blissfully resplendent, has something against those who are so rash as to open new gates to this music.
>
> At all events, Arnold Schoenberg wishes (and his friends wish for him) to come to Berlin.
>
> If enough pupils present themselves, he will come here. The object of these words is to announce this. Young people studying music should read them. (Mature men, who promote music by their actions, as well . . .)
>
> We therefore ask prospective Schoenberg pupils to inform this journal of their name and address.
>
> *Ferruccio Busoni   Oskar Fried   Arthur Schnabel*
> *T. E. Clark   Alfred Kerr*

23   SCHOENBERG TO BUSONI

Berg am Starnberger-See 19.9.1911

Many thanks for your very kind letter. I was becoming very uneasy at not receiving a reply. I could not explain it at all and presumed that, without intending it, I had somehow offended you. Now, happily, the situation turns out otherwise.

To come to the point: you are certainly right that the appeal, although well meant, is rather ineffective. It lacks above all the necessary factual clarity. Such things should not be expressed with uncommon words and euphonious phrases, but in the plainest of terms. I don't know Kerr[1] and I am very grateful to him for his goodwill. But I am sure it would have been advantageous if you had read it beforehand.

I think the whole scheme should be handled rather more energetically. For example, I have sent Mr Clark[2] a draft for his announcement of my course. I would have thought it a good idea to have it published in a few papers.

It would be a good thing if I could be in Berlin, and therefore I would like to tell you more about this later. Above all, because I have taken further steps towards securing an income and would like to do even more. Thus I have given Max Reinhardt my two stage works for production (two short pieces: 'Monodrama' and 'Die glückliche Hand') and have arranged with him that I should conduct them myself. At the same time offered him my services as conductor for other musical works he wishes to perform this season. He was *very interested*, and I think that if I could speak to him again, the matter would be settled. I was also hoping that he would do a work of yours. That would be a great pleasure for me and most interesting to conduct. Could you not use your influence here? So far, Reinhardt has been greatly in favour! And I certainly hope that, if he also receives your encouragement, he will engage me. – You need have no fear that I am a bad conductor. In fact I am most certainly an excellent one! How could I not be, for I am able to *rehearse* my own pieces!!! There is nothing more difficult than that, and rehearsing is the most important part of it all! I certainly have the manual ability! Thus, the mistrust that mediocre people always have is more unjustified than ever!

I believe counterpoint is even harder than conducting!

As to my further possibilities for moving, I am counting very much on the co-operation of prospective benefactors. And here I am founding my highest hopes on you. A word from a man like you, who, as I could myself see, is so justifiably respected, must certainly suffice.

But, as I wrote in my first letter, the matter is very urgent. And now more so than ever, for I shall soon be vis-à-vis du rien! Therefore the gentlemen with money will have to put their hands into their pockets in the next few days, if they are going to enable me to get into action again.

However, my dearest wish is that you should enable me as quickly as possible to receive the amount of money necessary for moving house. I am sure that things will then develop in Berlin. Unfortunately this is quite a considerable sum, as I must pay the rent in Vienna so as to gain access to my furniture, must cover the removal costs and have something to live on for the start. I believe this cannot be done for less than 2,000 Marks. But 3,000 would be better.

If you could manage this, above all quickly enough for me to come to Berlin at the end of this week or the beginning of the next, then I would be well off! I think I must come. I have so many plans that I really must have my way with everything I wish for.

As well as teaching, I want to be active as a conductor and have already made a contact in that direction which should be very useful to me.

In short: if the benefactors could for the meantime at least cover the cost of the move and agree to help me out later on a little if things don't sort themselves out straight away, then I have little doubt that all will go well.

But I think: *it must be done extremely quickly*!

If only you could intervene in the matter!

Please don't take it amiss that I am troubling you. But I feel that a generous person like you will be no stranger to such things.

[1]Alfred Kerr, 1867–1948 (real name A. Kempner), influential Berlin theatre critic and editor of *Pan*.
[2]Edward Clark, 1888–1962, English music journalist. He was Berlin correspondent of *The Musical Times* and later enrolled as Schoenberg's first pupil in Berlin.

24 SCHOENBERG TO BUSONI

Berlin-Zehlendorf[1] 24.10.1911

I have now finished setting my apartment in order and would very much like to call on you soon (until now I have had no time). When can I find you alone? Would you be so kind as to drop me a line?

[1]Schoenberg had settled in Berlin on 1 October 1910.

25 SCHOENBERG TO BUSONI

Berlin 11.11.1911

On 24 October I wrote to ask you when I could talk to you. You have not answered. But this is surely not intentional: rather perhaps the contrary! Therefore I am writing to you once again. In the meantime I was at the performance of the Turandot music,[1] of which I would prefer to see the score before discussing it with you. The same goes for the piano piece which I heard in Vienna.[2] I have been meaning to ask you for this for quite some time. Then I would like to come to at least one of your recitals[3] (could I have 2 tickets?). But apart from that, I wanted to tell you that on 20 November at the Stern Conservatoire I shall be giving the first of a series of circa 8–10 lectures on the subject of 'Aesthetics and the teaching of composition'. I wanted to invite you to this and ask you to send along as many intelligent people as possible (if necessary with complimentary tickets, which I shall be glad to provide). What I have in mind is of course neither talking shop nor going over the rudiments, but rather a serious investigation, which must for once be carried out. Not just for musicians therefore. On the contrary: I should like to have artists and patrons of the arts in attendance.

Perhaps you will therefore write me a card. I hope you do not intend to do me the dishonour of not replying.

[1]Busoni's incidental music to Gozzi's *Turandot* was performed at the Deutsches Theater, Berlin, for the first time on 27 October 1911 in a production of the play adapted and translated by Karl Vollmoeller and directed by Max Reinhardt.
[2]i.e. the Piano Concerto.
[3]Between 31 October and 12 December 1911 Busoni gave six recitals devoted entirely to Liszt, to mark the 100th anniversary of the composer's birth.

26 SCHOENBERG TO BUSONI

Berlin 22.1.1912

The question of who is to perform the 8-handed arrangement of my orchestral work[1] is now settled. And now that I could no longer be suspected of using flattery to persuade you to play in it – for this eventuality had in fact been deterring me – I can with all due warmth say everything I feel urged to say about your compositions.[2]

I felt most drawn to the Berceuse, which is a very beautiful, deeply arresting piece. It made a strong impression on me from beginning to end and, as I say, really moved me. And then the Piano Concerto, which I didn't like at all when I heard it in Vienna[3] (I say this quite openly), pleased me enormously this time. I don't understand why, and it seems that we, who consider ourselves to belong to the élite, make bad mistakes often enough. I had a really excellent impression. The piece is a movement of fabulous architecture from A to Z, flows uninterruptedly, full of ideas and wonderful moods. It is astonishing how you maintain constant control over a piece of such proportions, so that it always comes across as an unbroken whole. But: I couldn't really enjoy the fugue because of the poor performance and the unbelievably inappropriate instrumentation. During the concert I said to Webern: 'One never hears the leading voices at all, but only the themes.' The performance and the orchestration had an equal share of the blame for that. For it is naturally the subsidiary voices in a fugue that produce the unifying contrasts. But giving exclusive prominence to the main theme creates an impression of great erudition yet never produces a sense of a piece of music. I almost think that the theme should appear mostly as an accompaniment to the subsidiary voices. The theme, so to speak, as basic colour, as neutral background upon which the design, its form and colours, should stand out. But when the background obtrudes (!!!), then everything else is overshadowed. All atmosphere, all flow, all contrast is destroyed. – None the less, I could sense the broad outline and expressive powers of this work too – which I already knew through reading the piano version. And, above all, the contrapuntal art!

It is a great pleasure for me to be able to say all this to you, for until now I had perhaps failed to find the right attitude towards you, because I had viewed your compositions in the wrong light. Now, however, that I have also, to my very great joy, come to value this aspect of yourself, I hope that this will certainly change. Naturally, I had valued you as a reproductive artist, as a personality and human being. But for me the creative artist is the important thing, and for that reason I had not done you justice until now.

NB. Would you like to listen to a rehearsal of my orchestral pieces? The first is at Ibach's (Steglitzer Strasse) on Tuesday at 3 o'clock![4]

[1]Schoenberg had planned a concert of his own works for 4 February 1912, including the first performances of *Das Buch der hängenden Gärten*, op. 15, and the Six Little Piano Pieces, op. 19. Erwin Stein, a pupil of Schoenberg's, had allegedly made an arrangement for two pianos, eight hands, of the Five Pieces for Orchestra, op. 16, (although the arrangement was published in 1913 as the work of *Webern*) of which nos. 1, 2 and 4 were to be played by three Busoni pupils, Louis T. Gruenberg, Eduard Steuermann and Louis Closson, and Anton Webern. Busoni attended the concert and reviewed it for *Pan*.

[2]Schoenberg had attended a concert of Busoni's works given on 19 January 1912 by the Berlin Gesellschaft der Musikfreunde. The programme consisted of the *Sinfonia Contrappuntistica* (Stock's orchestration of the *Fantasia Contrappuntistica*), the *Berceuse élégiaque* and the Piano Concerto. On 20 January 1912, Schoenberg made the following entry in his diary:

> . . . Was at Fried's concert yesterday. Until now I had not liked Busoni's works. But yesterday I liked the 'Berceuse'. Downright moving piece. Deeply felt. I have been most unjust to him. Yet another! – . . . Then got to know van Düren [sic]. Said to be very interesting. Am curious. Wanted to visit me and show his compositions. (AB additions.)

[3]Schoenberg would have heard the performance with Leo Sirota in December 1910 (cf. letter no. 90 to Egon Petri). (AB)

[4]Extract from Schoenberg's Berlin diary for 23 January 1912:

> . . . By the way: Busoni! Yesterday I sent him a very cordial letter about his compositions. I felt an urge to compensate for my injustice. Today he tells me through van Düren that he is very grateful; was delighted; but cannot write to me because he is too busy. – In such a case, I would have found time to write! He isn't coming to my rehearsal. Evidently because I was not at his. Only he forgets that I invited him, but he did not invite me. How should I know whether he objects or not? (from Schoenberg, *Berliner Tagebuch*, ed. Josef Rufer, Berlin, 1972.)

27 SCHOENBERG TO BUSONI

Carlshagen auf Usedom 9.7.1912

Mr Clark told me that you are intending to set up a conservatoire for me and your friend Petri, in which you yourself would hold master-classes, while I should have the post of general director. I was delighted at this idea and would gladly have come to you to discuss it in detail. But, on the one hand, I was so busy (with packing and with the visit of a house guest), on the other hand you did not tell me when I could be certain of finding you home. This should, however, be no obstacle for me to pursue the matter further; for, as soon as you find it necessary, I shall interrupt my work here in order to call on you. However, I would ask you to settle as much as possible verbally or in writing. Perhaps you could pass on everything which may be concerned with the preliminary questions to Mr Clark (who is a very pleasant and intelligent person), and he would then write to me; I would then answer directly – unless you yourself may wish to drop me a few lines (why, by the way – you certainly used to write to me!)

I must ask one thing of you: please let me know *as soon as possible* whether you wish to support the idea and whether *one can be certain that something will come of it*!

For my position is as follows:

I have turned down the Academy in Vienna (nothing to do with this project, simply because I consider it inopportune to go to Vienna just now), so I shall be remaining in Berlin!

Therefore I really must undertake something for the coming season, and I am primarily thinking of announcing the courses again. Thus, if your idea could not be carried out, I would have to know as soon as possible, so as to announce the courses straight away.

That is why I ask you to make haste!

I very much regret that we have met so seldom. I had envisaged this otherwise. But believe me: the fault is not *mine* but yours.

---

28   BUSONI TO SCHOENBERG

Berlin 27.7.1912

In the course of a conversation, I – not Clark – threw out an idea which had arisen spontaneously. With characteristic impulsiveness, you have taken up this forgotten idea and embroidered upon it with your ever-active imaginative powers – unless of course you received a distorted report of the matter. In my remarks I made no mention either of my master-classes or of your general directorship. What I actually said (if not precisely verbatim) was, it would be desirable to set up a sort of music school on a purely artistic basis. The first person to consider would be Schoenberg; I would undertake that Petri and Kindler – in their respective departments – should assist him. Furthermore, that sufficient funds would be required to make the enterprise independent of financial speculation and to found an artistically appropriate 'home'. (I must confess that, however assured and profound my respect for and my belief in yourself may be, they do not extend to appointing you my superior: this has nothing to do with yourself, whom I salute as friend and master – but rather with the independence I have so slowly and painstakingly won for myself.) This only in parenthesis.

Thus my idea was to unite true artists in a pedagogic act, whereby the freedom and broadmindedness, lacking in the Conservatoires, should be maintained. It would consist entirely of master-classes held in informal exchange with the pupils, within tasteful surroundings. I considered the general directorship unimportant, the founders would consult mutually. Once again:

one would need a good deal of money; but then the matter could at once become significant.

It is regrettable that we see each other so seldom and that you consider me to hold the blame for this.

I do not believe that I ever took more genuine and active an interest in anybody than I have in you: on the other hand, I have requested, but also received, nothing in return.

For 8 months of the year I am on the move and, as you know, exceptionally busy. Please consider the situation at least *quantitatively*.

29 SCHOENBERG TO BUSONI

Carlshagen auf Usedom 28.7.1912

You are unjust to me and my imaginative powers. I will not dispute the fact that they have sometimes taken fire for an object whose actual value they themselves had created. Perhaps this is what has happened, as in the case of the works of art in whose creation I allowed them to play their part, perhaps they have always reacted in this way, because they were always accustomed to do so: creating the object, its value and the fire themselves. But here the matter is rather more down to earth.

Namely: what I wrote to you was reported to me by Clark as being your intention. Nothing more than that. I have added absolutely nothing! Really nothing! For matters on which I act (or to which I add something, in which case they must already have some substance) are matters already developed! Please forgive me: but I simply cannot allow my imagination to be wronged. For my imagination is myself, for I myself am only a creature of this imagination. And nobody allows his parents to be insulted.

My dear Mr Busoni, do you really presume that my imagination, in its relationship to you at a place of learning in which you held master-classes while I was general director, would only be able to think in terms of who was senior to whom? Isn't someone who gives master-classes independent of such a general directorship from the outset? But isn't someone who lives in Berlin for 10 months of the year more suited to the directorship than someone who is 'out of Berlin for 8 months of the year and anyway exceptionally busy'?

I have no desire to continue with this polemic. Perhaps one should lay the blame on the fact that something you said uncategorically has been passed on to me as being categorical. You have written some other categorical things in your letter which carefully envelope the incivility you actually wanted to impart to me. You will have to permit me to consider these, too, as being uncategorical. I always wish for clarity, and such wrappings disturb me. Allow me to preserve the categorical wrappings in which you have enveloped your incivility in the place where I always store up wrapping materials (I am, as can be confirmed, a passionate [collector of wrapping paper]),[2] but the actual contents, the enveloped incivility, in the place I set aside for such things. And please permit me briefly to summarize the contents of your letter: you repudiate my impudence in suggesting that I would like to be your superior by describing it as an emanation of my over-active imagination!

[1]This letter was first published in Arnold Schoenberg, *Ausgewählte Briefe*, ed. Erwin
Stein, Mainz, 1958.
[2]Sentence left unfinished by Schoenberg; the completion is by Erwin Stein.

30   BUSONI TO SCHOENBERG

[Berlin undated]

What a pity, now you have taken offence at my innocuous letter.

How can men, who really are fairly compatible, come to such misunderstandings?

If you read my letter through calmly, you will find your own objections are
already included in it. Why get involved in polemic with *me*, when I have
nothing against you and think *so much* of you? Dedicate this aspect of your
talent to Dr L. Schmidt[1] – although I, too, found it regrettable at the time. –

[1]Leopold Schmidt's review of Schoenberg's concert on 4 February 1912 in the
Choralionsaal had sparked off a substantial controversy with him in the pages of *Pan*.

31   SCHOENBERG TO BUSONI

Berlin-Südende 18.11.1914

I would like to call on you once again. When will you be at home *for me*? I
have no specific object – I would just like to have a chat with you again.

Perhaps you would be so kind as to let me know, if necessary by telephone,
on which morning or afternoon I could come to you.

32   BUSONI TO SCHOENBERG

Berlin 19.11.1914

I was delighted at your news. Come any afternoon (I work in the mornings);
at present I rarely have visitors and, if so, then mostly on Thursdays.

Wherever possible I have asked after you. Steuermann reported the
completion of the vocal score of your stage work.[1] I would dearly love to get
to know it.

This Sunday, exceptionally, I shall not be at home.

Looking forward to seeing you.

[1]Evidently the vocal score of *Erwartung*, which is the work of Eduard Steuermann. It
was published in 1916.

33 SCHOENBERG TO BUSONI

Berlin-Südende 3.2.1915

I have found a more direct way to your address than via the address which others are sending you.[1] While I would gladly put my name to any suitable contents intended to bring you joy and respect, I would not wish to hide behind the names that are unavoidable in a crowd, even if the contents should be more – appropriate to me. Therefore permit me to find my own way to you and to say that I, too, would be glad to know that you were in Berlin once again; simply for the egoistic reason: that I hope – should *you* find your way back – that we would come into more frequent contact again. I – who take everything as a symbol – *cannot silence* my birthday greetings and, at the risk of your looking upon them as an empty formula, would like to send: warmest congratulations!

[1]Several Berlin friends had sent a joint letter of goodwill to mark Busoni's 49th birthday, which he celebrated in New York (cf. letter no. 171, dated 12.4.1915, to Egon Petri). (AB)

34 SCHOENBERG TO BUSONI

Vienna 14.11.1916

I hear that you are in Zurich, that you have written an article about peace,[1] that the war is thus afflicting you – hence I must write to you immediately.

I am suffering terribly from this war. How many close relationships with the finest people it has severed: how it has corroded half my mind away and shown me that I can no better survive with the remainder than with the corroded portion.

Please send me your article about peace and let me have other news of yourself. If only we *two* and the *likes of us in every country* could sit down and deliberate on a peace settlement. Within a week we could pass it on to the world and with it a thousand ideas which would suffice for half eternity, for a half-eternal peace.

Yes, men are evil. But not so evil that one could not mediate between them. They are terribly evil – only the war has shown that. At least, in peacetime it did not seem so – one could almost believe: they were not yet like that. A mediator would certainly need a rod to smite those who are to blame. You see, evil and misfortune are identical in the material sense. In the spiritual sense one speaks differently: unfortunate, hence good.

I was a soldier for ten months; now I have been exempted, because in the end I was unfit for service at the front. Of course, I have been through a good deal! Consider: an apprentice soldier at 42 years of age; when one has, after all, made the greatest sacrifices all one's life to maintain one's independence, suddenly to become a trainee and to have to take orders from idiots![2]

[1]Reference to Busoni's article 'Der Kriegsfall Boccioni', published in the *Neue Zürcher Zeitung* on 31 August 1916.
[2]The last two words are crossed out by Schoenberg; the letter was opened by the censors.

35 BUSONI TO SCHOENBERG

[Zurich] 24.11.1916

Your letter came as a most pleasant surprise and I value most highly the fact that you have chosen *me* to give vent to your feelings.

Your 'Pelleas und Melisande' was on the programme for the 3rd symphony concert in Zurich and the right-minded were already looking forward to these sounds when the work vanished from the list – because the music had failed to arrive.[1]

Only yesterday – with an intelligent Herr Bülau[2] – we were singing the praises of your harmony book.

From this you will gather that one still finds some time for good things. Therefore I would have wished to receive more detailed information about your current creative work. The enforced 10-month interruption must have weighed heavily upon it, but then it should burst forth again all the more impetuously.

I wrote a short feuilleton about the death in action of an outstanding painter; not a pacifist publication but one in which art – in a brief innuendo – was weighed up against war. It has provoked a gentle resonance, as one can already conclude from the fact that something of it has reached your ears.

What have you heard of Frau Mahler?

What company is she keeping?

Now we must remain optimistic and work towards peace in the sense that it should not take us unawares before we have achieved something in the field given to us. That will be our proudest victory, when we can hold up the products of our creativity against the destruction of the other! Durability versus decay.

Let each of us do what he does best; let the fullest exploitation of one's own resources remain life's truest fulfilment.

I send you the friendliest greetings.

[1]*Pelleas und Melisande* was scheduled for performance on 30 and 31 October 1916 in the Tonhalle, Zurich. The music did indeed fail to arrive from Vienna and the work was replaced by Bartók's *Deux Images* for orchestra. (AB)
[2]Dr Franz Wolfgang Bülau, 1883– ?, a qualified lawyer, who was *Konzertmeister* of the Tonhalle Orchestra for the 1916–17 season. (AB)

36 SCHOENBERG TO BUSONI

Vienna 30.1.1917

Buffeted as I was by hopes of peace and by disappointments, I found no repose to thank you for your kind letter.

One motive causes me to write to you again. At last I have succeeded in committing to paper an idea which I have been harbouring for a long time. Inspired by President Wilson,[1] who had recently raised some hopes for peace, I would like to publish it. But if possible in a neutral paper so that it could be read everywhere, should it make any impression. I enclose the short article[2] but, as it is not very good (evidently I am not so good at writing about things which have no connection with my profession), I would not wish to publish it under my name but with a pen name: A. Börnscheg. Now I would like to ask you: can you find a publisher for the article somewhere, if possible of course one of the major German-language newspapers in *Switzerland*? I would prefer to see it printed *without any alterations*. But on no account should it become known that I am the author. I hope that much will come of this idea. If one carries it to its logical conclusion, one realizes that a truly *durable peace* would be guaranteed. Tell me what you think of it; please!

My work in progress; you ask after it; it is scarcely worth mentioning. During the war, before I was called up, I started work on a major project. A symphony. In 4 movements.[3] The first two on poems by Dehmel, the other two on my own texts. The 1st movement: 'Freudenruf', the 2nd 'Der bürgerliche Gott', the 3rd 'Totentanz der Prinzipien', the 4th 'Der Himmelsleiter'. I have finished the text of the 3rd, that of the 4th is two-thirds completed. As long as there was any prospect of peace, I was able to work. Then my courage left me. In the army it was, of course, impossible to work. And now: it isn't much. First I want to finish a 2nd chamber symphony that I began almost 10 years ago,[4] then continue work on my symphony. Meanwhile a partly revised version of my Harmonielehre for the 2nd Edition and proof-reading ('Glückliche Hand' and the 'Monodrama' have been engraved and should be appearing soon; also 4 songs with orchestra).[5] That is all.[6]

Could you not send me your article on the death of an outstanding painter? I beg you. Can I send you anything of mine?

Frau Mahler has married. Her husband, the architect Gropius,[7] has been in the field as a lieutenant since the beginning of the war. He is a very pleasant fellow. There was a nasty disagreement between Frau Mahler (Gropius) and myself (for nearly a year), which has now been patched up, that is why I have so little news of her. But tomorrow I shall call on her and send her your best wishes.

You write: 'Let each of us do what he does best; let the fullest exploitation of one's own resources remain life's truest fulfilment.' That is very fine and true. – But unfortunately at the moment I cannot apply it to myself. I am scarcely able to find my peace of mind. And as my nerves are under constant strain, I can find no repose. And without peace of mind I can do nothing well.

Have you heard that I am supposed to conduct the 'Gurrelieder' in New York? But I simply cannot get there, because the English are letting nobody through.

Isn't that terrible: 'the English'. 30 months ago I spoke with pride of my English, French and Russian friends and now these are my enemies? Do you believe that? I must say that, for me, no international value has ceased to exist, not even in the first few weeks. But it is terrible that most people have long since abandoned them!

I hope to hear from you *soon*.

Please also send me news of your dear wife and give her my warmest greetings.

[1]President Thomas Woodrow Wilson, who had declared war on Germany on 6 April 1917, sent a note to the warring countries in Europe, dated 18.12.1916, which contained suggestions and conditions for an end to hostilities.
[2]Schoenberg's article 'Friedenssicherung' (Safeguarding of peace), a 15-point plan for the establishment of a large-scale international peace-keeping force whose chief object would be to prevent the manufacture of arms and training of troops. The article was first published in 1977 in the German edition of this correspondence. (AB)
[3]Schoenberg worked between 1912 and 1914 at a major vocal symphony which he never completed. Passages from it were incorporated in *Die Jakobsleiter*, which he began on 19 July 1917.
[4]Chamber Symphony No. 2, op. 38. The work was begun in 1906, taken up again in 1911 and 1916, but not finished until 1939.
[5]Four Orchestral Songs, op. 22.
[6]Schoenberg completed the new version of his *Harmonielehre* in 1921 and it was published in 1922 by Universal Edition, Vienna. The vocal scores of *Erwartung* and *Die glückliche Hand* were published in 1916 and 1917 respectively.
[7]Walter Gropius, 1883–1969, later a founder member of the Bauhaus. He married Alma Mahler in 1915.

37 SCHOENBERG TO BUSONI

[Vienna April 1917]

Could you please let me know whether you have received a manuscript which I despatched more than 10 weeks ago?

38 SCHOENBERG TO BUSONI

Mödling 26.2.1919

Although I have received no reply to letters which I sent you recently, I feel urged to write to you again today, and in the face of such pressure no personality cult or prestige politics can keep pace with me, I take no heed of myself or of others but simply write. The motive: Steuermann is playing your 6 Elegies in the Verein für mus[ikalische] Priv[at]aufführungen[1] and I like them so very much that I have to tell you so. I do not know if this will interest you. But perhaps you will be interested in the society I have founded. I have had a complete success with it. We already have over 300 members and during the year this should increase to 500. This is the first step towards far-reaching reforms in concert life. The first step – nobody knows where it could lead. It would be my wish to see such societies being founded everywhere. That could have a beneficial effect. However: the chief prerequisite is impeccable preparation of the performances. To give you some idea of what I mean, I would like to remind you of the rehearsals for my Pierrot. I can say that we have on average maintained this level, although I have by no means had such good players available for everything. Sometimes however we have also surpassed it. For example in the piano four-hand performance of Mahler's VIIth[2] and Strauss's Don Quixote. Steuermann plays your Elegies *very beautifully*!

Could you not tell me which work of yours we should perform in the near future?[3] I would prefer to have something from your more recent period.

I send you the warmest greetings and would like to think that you will do me the honour of a few lines once again.

After all: I am not the worst of men.

[1]The Society for private musical performances, founded in Vienna on 23 November 1918. It survived until 1922, was then continued in Prague until 1924. Eduard Steuermann performed the Elegies for the Society on 2 March 1919; there were altogether six repeat performances, the last of which was on 2 May 1921. (AB)
[2]Schoenberg writes 'Mahler's VIIIth', but there is no record of a Society performance of this work. Mahler's Symphony No. 7, arranged for piano duet by Alfredo Casella, featured in the Society's opening concert on 29 December 1918 and was later scheduled for five further performances. (AB additions)
[3]On 26 September and 12 October 1919 Eduard Steuermann played Busoni's Sonatina [no. 1]. Later Society concerts included Busoni's Violin Sonata no. 2 (11 April and 5 October 1921) and the *Toccata* for piano, played by Hilde Merinsky on 30 May and 6 June 1921. (AB)

Biographical Notes on Recipients

Detailed information on IRMA BEKH (Letters 100, 122, 134, 209), a piano pupil of Busoni in Vienna and Berlin, HARRIET LANIER (Letters 172–4, 178, 181, 184, 203), president of the Society of the Friends of Music in Philadelphia, and CURT SOBERNHEIM (Letter 160), Berlin banker and close personal friend of the Busonis, has unfortunately not been forthcoming; it seems unnecessary to provide biographical notes on VERDI (Letter 32), SCHOENBERG or OTTO KLEMPERER (Letter 255).

EDITH ANDREAE, 1883–1945, was the daughter of Emil Rathenau, the founder of the German AEG concern. She met Busoni in Berlin through their mutual friendship with Max Reinhardt. Volkmar Andreae was only distantly related to her (through marriage). Letters 130, 148–9, 165, 177, 194, 197, 211, 216, 270, 296, 312, 318, 328, 335, 352.

VOLKMAR ANDREAE, 1879–1962, Swiss composer and conductor. He studied in Berne and Cologne and was subsequently engaged as assistant conductor at the Munich Opera. From 1906 to 1949 he was chief conductor of the Tonhalle Orchestra, Zurich, and from 1914 to 1939 director of the Zurich Conservatoire. Letters 245, 249, 257, 260, 263, 268, 271, 273–5, 278, 291, 306, 309, 313, 319, 325–7, 331.

EMILIO ANZOLETTI, 1874–1950, studied engineering in Bologna and in Berlin. An amateur cellist of mixed Viennese and Italian parentage, he and his brother, Augusto, were close friends of Busoni. In 1918 Emilio Anzoletti settled in Bergamo, working for the firm of Italcementi, remaining there with his wife and two children for the rest of his life. Letters 46, 52, 70, 81, 161.

EMILE-ROBERT BLANCHET, 1877–1942, Swiss pianist and composer. He studied with Busoni at Weimar and Berlin. From 1904 to 1917 he taught at the Lausanne Conservatoire, then moved to Paris, where he became established as soloist and composer. He also wrote books on mountaineering. Letters 169, 234.

LUDWIG VON BÖSENDORFER, 1835–1919, succeeded his father Ignaz as director of the famous Viennese piano manufacturers in 1859. The Bösendorfer Saal, which he opened in 1872, became one of the most popular venues in Vienna for chamber music and piano recitals. Letters 33, 55, 67.

ANNA BUSONI née Weiss, 1833–1909, was the daughter of a Bavarian-born merchant seaman, Josef Weiss. She was brought up in Trieste, where she was known as a talented pianist and composer. She married Ferdinando Busoni in 1865. Letters 3–4, 12–15, 31, 39, 50.

FERDINANDO BUSONI, 1834–1909, virtuoso clarinettist, was the father of Ferruccio Busoni. Born in Empoli, near Florence, he was of Corsican origin. For many years he led the life of a travelling virtuoso; he was responsible for his son's earliest musical tuition. Letters 1–2, 8–9, 21, 28, 34, 43.

RAFFAELLO BUSONI, 1900–1962, was the younger son of Ferruccio and Gerda Busoni. He studied art in Paris and, having emigrated to the USA in the thirties, made a successful career as a book illustrator. Letters 314, 316.

MARCHESE SILVIO DIONIGIO CAMILLO DELLA VALLE DI CASANOVA, 1861–1929, studied the piano with Liszt at Weimar and read German and philosophy at the university of Stuttgart. As amateur poet and Germanophile he held open house at his villa on Lake Maggiore, San Remigio (near Pallanza) for artists and writers. Letters 256, 299.

EDWARD JOSEPH DENT, 1876–1957, celebrated English musicologist, teacher, critic and composer. A Fellow of King's College, Cambridge, from 1902, he was appointed Professor of Music to the university in 1926. In 1922 he founded the International Society for Contemporary Music whose president he remained until 1938. Letters 82, 98, 121, 182, 294, 298, 308, 310, 332, 339–40, 345.

HERMANN W. DRABER, 1878–1942, Silesian-born flautist, musicologist and critic. He studied the piano with Busoni at Weimar and was later active for a time as his assistant. His wife GERTRUD DRABER is also recipient of one letter included in this book. Letters 74, 80, 95, 135–6, 139, 156, 251 (Gertrud), 253, 262.

ROBERT FREUND, 1852–1936, Hungarian-born pianist and composer. He studied with Moscheles and Coccius at Leipzig, later also with Tausig and Liszt. From 1875 to 1921 he lived in Zurich, after which he returned to Budapest. Letters 40, 48, 57, 63, 89, 116, 120, 228, 344.

EMIL HERTZKA, 1869–1932, was director of Universal Edition, Vienna, from 1907 until his death. Born in Hungary, he was largely responsible for the promotion of Schoenberg and his school but also of Janáček, Bartók, Szymanowski and other distinguished composers. Letters 279, 283, 334.

HANS HUBER, 1852–1921, Swiss composer. He studied at Leipzig, returning to Switzerland in 1877. From 1896 to 1918 he was director of the Basle Conservatoire. He was a prolific composer but his works are today scarcely performed, even in Switzerland. Letters 87–8, 217, 220, 226, 236, 250, 252, 259, 264–6.

PHILIPP JARNACH, 1892–1982, French-born composer of Spanish origin. He studied in Paris with Risler and Lavignac, then settled in Zurich where he met Busoni and became his assistant and pupil. From 1918 to 1921 he taught counterpoint at the Zurich Conservatoire, then followed Busoni to Berlin. From 1949 until his retirement in 1959 he was director of the Hamburg Conservatoire. Letters 238–9, 241, 272, 281–2, 284–6, 288, 290, 293, 301–3, 307, 317, 338, 347, 351.

OTTO VON KAPFF, c.1856–c.1920, German journalist and poet. He was born in Königsberg and settled in Vienna, where he was for some years active as a critic. He befriended Busoni in 1878. According to Dent he was 'by temperament a romantic sentimentalist who modelled his appearance on King Ludwig II of Bavaria'. For eight years he was married to the Jewish feminist writer Franziska von Kapff-Essenther. He died in poverty. Letters 6–7.

LEO KESTENBERG, 1882–1962, Hungarian-born pianist and pedagogue. He studied with Kullak, Busoni and Draeseke. In 1918 he was appointed musical adviser to the Prussian Ministry of Science, Culture and Education. In 1938 he emigrated to Tel Aviv where he became general manager of the Palestine Orchestra (later Israel Philharmonic). Letter 321.

HUGO LEICHTENTRITT, 1874–1951, Polish-born musicologist, critic and composer. He studied at Harvard, Paris and Berlin, establishing himself as an authority on early music. In 1933 he was appointed lecturer in music at Harvard University, a post which he retained until his retirement in 1940. Letters 123, 126–7, 154, 183, 190, 196, 198, 205, 208, 210, 212, 248, 254, 258, 261, 289, 304–5, 311, 324, 349.

GIOVANNINA LUCCA née Strazza, 1810–1894, became director of the influential Milan music publishers Lucca in 1872 as successor to her husband Francesco. In 1888 she sold the firm to Ricordi. Letter 10.

SIR ALEXANDER CAMPBELL MACKENZIE, 1847–1935, Scottish composer and conductor. He was permanent conductor of the Philharmonic Society, London, from 1892 to 1899 and general president of the International Musical Society from 1908 to 1912. Letter 137.

MELANIE MAYER, ? – ?, was the daughter of Busoni's composition teacher in Graz, Wilhelm Mayer-Rémy. She married the Austrian music critic Dr Fritz Prelinger. Letters 16–20.

JOSÉ VIANNA DA MOTTA, 1868–1948, Portuguese pianist and composer. A pupil of Liszt and von Bülow, he became well known as a soloist in Germany, having been appointed Prussian court pianist in 1902. From 1915 to 1917 he was professor of piano at Geneva; he then returned to Lisbon where he was active as director of the Conservatoire and conductor of the symphony orchestra. Letters 202, 215, 221–3, 227, 229–31, 235, 237.

BARONESS JELLA OPPENHEIMER née Todesco, 1854–1943, was a lifelong friend of Busoni. Through her husband, Felix Freiherr von Oppenheimer, she became a close friend of Hugo von Hofmannsthal and Jakob Wassermann. The Oppenheimer estate, near Alt Aussee, was open house to many celebrated writers and musicians. Letters 159, 186, 188, 219, 243, 350.

EGON PETRI, 1881–1962, German pianist. He initially studied the violin and indeed occasionally played in his father's celebrated string quartet. He also studied the organ, horn and piano, taking lessons in the latter with Carreño at Leipzig. After a period of study with Busoni in Berlin he held a teaching post at the Royal Manchester College of Music from 1905 to 1911. He then returned to Berlin but eventually settled in Zakopane, making a career as a soloist. After a brief period teaching at the Basle Conservatoire he settled in Berlin in 1921, where he taught at the Hochschule für Musik. In 1926 he returned to Zakopane, remaining there until 1938. By this time he had earned a considerable reputation and was looked upon as the true inheritor of Busoni's pianistic legacy. In the USA he taught at Cornell University and later at Mills College, Oakland. Letters 44–5, 47, 49, 51, 53–4, 56, 59–62, 65–6, 69, 71–3, 75, 78–9, 83–6, 90–4, 96–7, 99, 101–15, 117–19, 124–5, 128–9, 131–3, 138, 140–7, 150–3, 155, 157, 163, 166–8, 170–1, 176, 189, 191–3, 195, 199, 200, 204, 213–14, 218, 224–5, 240–2, 244, 246–7, 269, 315, 320, 323, 329, 330, 337, 341–2, 346, 348.

HENRI PETRI, 1856–1914, Dutch virtuoso violinist and composer, was Egon Petri's father. A pupil of Joachim, he held posts as concert-master in Sondershausen, Hanover and Leipzig. In 1884 he moved to Dresden where he founded the Petri Quartet. His wife KATHI PETRI is also the recipient of several letters in this book. Letters 22–7, 35–8, 42, 76–7.

ISIDOR PHILIPP, 1863–1953, Hungarian-born pianist. He studied at the Paris Conservatoire, where he himself was piano professor from 1893 to 1934. After the outbreak of World War II he emigrated to the USA. Letters 185, 333, 343.

HANS REINHART, 1880–1963, Swiss industrialist and writer. He was a co-director of Volkart Brothers in Winterthur, where he and his three brothers, Werner, Georg and Oskar, were generous patrons of the arts. Hans Reinhart wrote plays and opera libretti and also made German translations of several important contemporary stage works. Letters 232–3, 336.

CARLO SCHMIDL, 1859–1943, Italian music publisher and writer on music. In 1872 he joined the Trieste firm Vicentini which he himself took over in 1880. He wrote an important Italian dictionary of music and collected manuscripts and early printed editions of Italian music. Letters 58, 64, 68.

GISELLA SELDEN-GOTH, 1884–1971, German composer and writer on music. She was best known as a collector of important musical manuscripts, which she bequeathed to the Library of Congress, Washington. Her publications include biographies of Busoni and Toscanini. Letters 287, 297, 300, 322.

ARRIGO SERATO, 1875–1948, Italian virtuoso violinist. He was a pupil of

Joachim. From 1895 to 1914 he lived in Berlin, where he became well known as a soloist. In 1914 he returned to Rome, where he was professor of violin at the Accademia Santa Cecilia until his death. Letters 187, 201, 206–7, 292.

ALICJA SIMON, 1879– ?, Polish musicologist. She emigrated to Zurich in 1913 where she wrote a dissertation on Polish elements in German music. In 1921 she returned to Warsaw. Letters 267, 276–7, 280, 295.

FREDERICK STOCK, 1872–1942, German violinist, conductor and composer. He studied composition at Cologne with Humperdinck, emigrating to Chicago in 1895 where he was engaged as a violinist in the Theodore Thomas Orchestra. Upon Thomas's death in 1905 he succeeded him as the orchestra's chief conductor. Letter 175.

THEODORE THOMAS, 1833–1905, German conductor. His family emigrated to the USA in 1845 and there he soon established a reputation as violinist and concert conductor. He formed his own orchestra in New York in 1864; in 1891 he then founded the Chicago Orchestra (later Theodore Thomas Orchestra and since 1912 the Chicago Symphony). Letters 29–30.

ANTONIO ZAMPIERI, *c*.1850–1919, Italian conductor, composer and music-ologist. One of a large family of musicians; his wife, Caterina Fröhlich, was a pupil of Liszt. Zampieri studied in Trieste (his home town) and Leipzig. He founded the Trieste Municipal Orchestra and was professor of music at the city's Giuseppe Verdi Conservatoire until his death. Letter 11.

Sources

Autograph material

Letters to
Irma Bekh: property of Dietrich Fischer-Dieskau;
Hermann and Gertrud Draber: Stiftung Rychenberg, Winterthur;
Emil Hertzka: Universal Edition, AG, Vienna;
Otto Klemperer: property of Dietrich Fischer-Dieskau;
Hugo Leichtentritt: Library of Congress, Washington DC;
Isidor Philipp (Nos. 333 and 343): Bibliothèque Nationale, Paris;
Carlo Schmidl: Civici Musei di Storia ed Arte, Trieste;
Frederick Stock: Newberry Library, Chicago;
Theodore Thomas: Newberry Library, Chicago.

Newspapers and journals

Letters to
Raffaello Busoni (No. 314): 'Zwei unbekannte Briefe Busonis', ed. Willi Reich, in *Der Auftakt*, vol. 16, Prague, 1936, pp. 180–2.
Leo Kestenberg: unidentified news-cutting, Rowe Music Library, Cambridge.
Melanie Mayer: Melanie Prelinger, 'Erinnerungen und Briefe aus Ferruccio Busonis Jugendzeit' in *Neue Musik-Zeitung*, 1927, No. 1–2, pp. 6–10, 37–40, 57–61.
Jella Oppenheimer: *Neue Zürcher Zeitung*, 21–22.6.1931.
Hans Reinhart: *Individualität*, Autumn 1926, vol. 1 No. 3, pp. 49–53.
Giuseppe Verdi: 'Brief an Giuseppe Verdi', trans. and ed. Friedrich Schnapp, in *Zeitschrift für Musik*, Dec. 1932, No. 12, p. 1057.
Antonio Zampieri: Claudio Sartori, 'Adolescenza ardente di Ferruccio Busoni e un suo primo ignorato progetto di opera lirica' in *La Rassegna musicale*, 1940, pp. 183–95.

Books and monographs

Briefe Busonis an Edith Andreae, ed. Andres Briner, Zurich, 1976.
Briefe Busonis an Hans Huber, ed. Edgar Refardt, Zurich, 1939. Also in: Edgar Refardt, *Hans Huber*, Zurich, 1939.
Letters to Gisella Selden-Goth in: *Fünfundzwanzig Busonibriefe*, ed. Gisella Selden-Goth, Vienna-Leipzig-Zurich, 1937.
Letters to Arrigo Serato in: Andrea della Corte, *Arrigo Serato*, Siena, 1950.

A selection of letters to Marchese Silvio della Valle di Casanova was published in *Musica Università*, Rome, No. 23, Dec. 1966, pp. 16–25.

An abridged selection of letters to Henri and Kathi Petri, ed. Friedrich Schnapp, was published in *Neue Rundschau*, 1934, pp. 71–84.

All other letters published in this selection are translated or transcribed from typescripts preserved in the Rowe Music Library, Cambridge.

Index of Busoni's
Works and Writings

III. PIANO WORKS

An die Jugend, 92n, 95, 96, 97n, 98–9,
  100, 112, 113, 154, 391
Berceuse, 95, 96n, 99, 100
Drei Albumblätter, 267, 343, 348
Chopin Variations, 27n
Concert transcription on motifs from
  Goldmark's opera *Merlin,* 25n
Elegies, xvii, 80n, 87–9, 97, 99, 113, 124,
  126, 145, 196, 266n, 423
Six Etudes op. 16 (1883), 14, 15n, 223
Etude en forme de variations op. 17
  (*c.* 1883), 223
Etude en forme d'Adagio d'une Sonate
  (unpubl. *c.* 1894), 188n
Fantasia nach J. S. Bach, 95, 97, 99, 100,
  156n
Fantasia Contrappuntistica, xvii, 112,
  113, 118, 131, 132, 135, 136, 159–60,
  266n, 407n, 414, 415n; *Edizione
  minore,* 111, 150, 154
Fantasy on motifs from Peter Cornelius's
  The Barber of Baghdad, 24, 351
Una Festa di Villaggio op. 9 (1881), 11,
  17, 18n
Fünf kurze Stücke zur Pflege des
  polyphonen Spiels, 364, 365n, 368
Gavotta op. 25 (1878), 14n
Grosse Fuge, 109, 110n, 111, 113, 116,
  407–8
Indianisches Tagebuch, 203n, 233, 266n
Klavierübung, 267, 272, 273n, 282, 287,
  370, 371n
Macchiette medioevali op. 33 (1882-3),
  12, 13n
Marcia di Paesani e Contadine op. 32
  (1883), 11, 12, 13n
Minuetto op. 14 (1878), 14n
Perpetuum mobile, 364, 365n, 368
Prélude et Etude en Arpèges, 361, 364, 368
24 Préludes op. 37 (1881), 14, 223, 242,
  243n
Scherzo op. 17 (1879), 7n
Sonata in C op. 7 (1877), 8
Sonata in D op. 8 (1877), 8
Sonata in E op. 9 (1877), 8
Sonata in F minor (1880), 10, 11n
Sonatina (no. 1), 112, 114, 156n, 176,
  266n, 423n

Sonatina ad usum infantis (no. 3), 203n,
  222, 227, 230, 266n
Sonatina brevis (no. 5), 282
Sonatina in diem nativitatis Christi
  MCMXVII (no. 4), 272, 273n
Sonatina seconda, xvii, 150, 151, 162n,
  165, 176, 196, 241
Sonatina super Carmen (no. 6) (*Carmen
  Fantasy*), 305, 306, 309, 310, 348,
  349n
Studio contrappuntato (1875), 4n
Toccata, 321, 325, 329, 348, 368, 423n
Variationen und Fuge in freier Form
  über Fr. Chopins Praeludium C–moll
  (op. 28 no. 20) op. 22 (1884), 26, 27n,
  154, 223
Vierte Ballett-Szene op. 33a, 97, 266n
Zwei Tanzstücke, 266n

IV. ORGAN WORKS

Praeludium und Fuge op. 7 (1880), 10,
  11n

V. CHAMBER MUSIC

Albumblatt for flute and piano, 267n,
  274
Andante and Allegro vivace for string
  quartet op. 13 (1878), 8n
Andantino for clarinet and piano op. 18
  (1879), 7n
Bagatelles for violin and piano op. 28
  (1888), 39, 41n
Capriccio for two pianos op. 36 (1879), 7
Concerto in D minor for piano and string
  quartet op. 17 (1878), 8
Fantasia Contrappuntistica for two
  pianos, 338, 343, 346n, 349n, 368n
Improvisation on 'Wie wohl ist mir' for
  two pianos, 239, 243, 244, 247, 255,
  300, 346n, 349n
Kleine Suite for cello and piano op. 23
  (1886), 24, 47n
Menuetto for string quartet op. 15
  (1879), 8n
Minuett in F for string quartet (1877), 8n
Serenade no. 2 for clarinet and piano
  op. 19 (1879), 7n

General Index

Page numbers in **bold** type indicate the recipient of a letter; page numbers in *italics* refer to plates.